D1478764

JEFFERSON,
MADISON,
AND THE
MAKING OF THE CONSTITUTION

We the People

of the United States, in order to form a more perfect Union, establish Justice, insure domestic Tranquility, provide for the common Defence, promote the general Welfare, and secure the Blessings of Liberty to ourselves and our Posterity, do ordain and establish this Constitution for the United States of America.

Article. I.

Section. 1. All legislative Powers herein granted shall be vested in a Congress of the United States, which shall consist of a Senate and House of Representatives.

Section. 2. The House of Representatives shall be composed of Members chosen every second Year by the People of the several States, and the Electors in each State shall have the Qualifications requisite for Electors of the most numerous Branch of the State Legislature.

No Person shall be a Representative who shall not have attained to the Age of twenty five Years, and been seven Years a Citizen of the United States, and who shall not, when elected, be an Inhabitant of that State in which he shall be chosen.

Representatives and direct Taxes shall be apportioned among the several States which may be included within this Union, according to their respective Numbers, which shall be determined by adding to the whole Number of free Persons, including those bound to Service for a Term of Years, and excluding Indians not taxed, three fifths of all other Persons. The actual Enumeration shall be made within three Years after the first Meeting of the Congress of the United States, and within every subsequent Term of ten Years, in such Manner as they shall by Law direct. The Number of Representatives shall not exceed one for every thirty Thousand, but each State shall have at Least one Representative; and until such enumeration shall be made, the State of New Hampshire shall be entitled to chuse three, Massachusetts eight, Rhode-Island and Providence Plantations one, Connecticut five, New-York six, New Jersey four, Pennsylvania eight, Delaware one, Maryland six, Virginia ten, North Carolina five, South Carolina five, and Georgia three.

When vacancies happen in the Representation from any State, the Executive Authority thereof shall issue Writs of Election to fill such Vacancies.

The House of Representatives shall chuse their Speaker and other Officers; and shall have the sole Power of Impeachment.

Section. 3. The Senate of the United States shall be composed of two Senators from each State, chosen by the Legislature thereof, for six Years; and each Senator shall have one Vote.

Immediately after they shall be assembled in Consequence of the first Election, they shall be divided as equally as may be into three Classes. The Seats of the Senators of the first Class shall be vacated at the Expiration of the second Year, of the second Class at the Expiration of the fourth Year, and of the third Class at the Expiration of the sixth Year, so that one third may be chosen every second Year; and if Vacancies happen by Resignation, or otherwise, during the Recess of the Legislature of any State, the Executive thereof may make temporary Appointments until the next Meeting of the Legislature, which shall then fill such Vacancies.

No Person shall be a Senator who shall not have attained to the Age of thirty Years, and been nine Years a Citizen of the United States, and who shall not, when elected, be an Inhabitant of that State for which he shall be chosen.

The Vice President of the United States shall be President of the Senate, but shall have no Vote, unless they be equally divided.

The Senate shall chuse their other Officers, and also a President pro tempore, in the Absence of the Vice President, or when he shall exercise the Office of President of the United States.

The Senate shall have the sole Power to try all Impeachments. When sitting for that Purpose, they shall be on Oath or Affirmation. When the President of the United States is tried, the Chief Justice shall preside: And no Person shall be convicted without the Concurrence of two thirds of the Members present.

Judgment in Cases of Impeachment shall not extend further than to removal from Office, and disqualification to hold and enjoy any Office of honor, Trust or Profit under the United States: but the Party convicted shall nevertheless be liable and subject to Indictment, Trial, Judgment and Punishment, according to Law.

Section. 4. The Times, Places and Manner of holding Elections for Senators and Representatives, shall be prescribed in each State by the Legislature thereof; but the Congress may at any time by Law make or alter such Regulations, except as to the Places of chusing Senators.

The Congress shall assemble at least once in every Year, and such Meeting shall be on the first Monday in December, unless they shall by Law appoint a different Day.

Section. 5. Each House shall be the Judge of the Elections, Returns and Qualifications of its own Members, and a Majority of each shall constitute a Quorum to do Business; but a smaller Number may adjourn from day to day, and may be authorized to compel the Attendance of absent Members, in such Manner, and under such Penalties as each House may provide.

Each House may determine the Rules of its Proceedings, punish its Members for disorderly Behaviour, and, with the Concurrence of two thirds, expel a Member.

Each House shall keep a Journal of its Proceedings, and from time to time publish the same, excepting such Parts as may in their Judgment require Secrecy; and the Yeas and Nays of the Members of either House on any question shall, at the Desire of one fifth of those Present, be entered on the Journal.

Neither House, during the Session of Congress, shall, without the Consent of the other, adjourn for more than three days, nor to any other Place than that in which the two Houses shall be sitting.

Section. 6. The Senators and Representatives shall receive a Compensation for their Services, to be ascertained by Law, and paid out of the Treasury of the United States. They shall in all Cases, except Treason, Felony and Breach of the Peace, be privileged from Arrest during their Attendance at the Session of their respective Houses, and in going to and returning from the same; and for any Speech or Debate in either House, they shall not be questioned in any other Place.

No Senator or Representative shall, during the Time for which he was elected, be appointed to any civil Office under the Authority of the United States, which shall have been created, or the Emoluments whereof shall have been encreased during such time; and no Person holding any Office under the United States, shall be a Member of either House during his Continuance in Office.

Section. 7. All Bills for raising Revenue shall originate in the House of Representatives; but the Senate may propose or concur with Amendments as on other Bills.

Every Bill which shall have passed the House of Representatives and the Senate, shall, before it become a Law, be presented to the President of the

United States; if he approve he shall sign it, but if not he shall return it, with his Objections, to that House in which it shall have originated, who shall enter the Objections at large on their Journal, and proceed to reconsider it. If after such Reconsideration two thirds of that House shall agree to pass the Bill, it shall be sent, together with the Objections, to the other House, by which it shall likewise be reconsidered, and if approved by two thirds of that House, it shall become a Law. But in all such Cases the Votes of both Houses shall be determined by yeas and Nays, and the Names of the Persons voting for and against the Bill shall be entered on the Journal of each House respectively. If any Bill shall not be returned by the President within ten Days (Sundays excepted) after it shall have been presented to him, the Same shall be a Law, in like Manner as if he had signed it, unless the Congress by their Adjournment prevent its Return, in which Case it shall not be a Law.

Every Order, Resolution, or Vote to which the Concurrence of the Senate and House of Representatives may be necessary (except on a question of Adjournment) shall be presented to the President of the United States; and before the Same shall take Effect, shall be approved by him, or being disapproved by him, shall be repassed by two thirds of the Senate and House of Representatives, according to the Rules and Limitations prescribed in the Case of a Bill.

Section 8. The Congress shall have Power To lay and collect Taxes, Duties, Imposts and Excises, to pay the Debts and provide for the common Defence and general Welfare of the United States; but all Duties, Imposts and Excises shall be uniform throughout the United States;

To borrow Money on the credit of the United States;

To regulate Commerce with foreign Nations, and among the several States, and with the Indian Tribes;

To establish an uniform Rule of Naturalization, and uniform Laws on the subject of Bankruptcies throughout the United States;

To coin Money, regulate the Value thereof, and of foreign Coin, and fix the Standard of Weights and Measures;

To provide for the Punishment of counterfeiting the Securities and current Coin of the United States;

To establish Post Offices and post Roads;

To promote the Progress of Science and useful Arts, by securing for limited Times to Authors and Inventors the exclusive Right to their respective Writings and Discoveries;

To constitute Tribunals inferior to the supreme Court;

To define and punish Piracies and Felonies committed on the high Seas, and Offences against the Law of Nations;

To declare War, grant Letters of Marque and Reprisal, and make Rules concerning Captures on Land and Water;

To raise and support Armies, but no Appropriation of Money to that Use shall be for a longer Term than two Years;

To provide and maintain a Navy;

To make Rules for the Government and Regulation of the land and naval Forces;

To provide for calling forth the Militia to execute the Laws of the Union, suppress Insurrections and repel Invasions;

To provide for organizing, arming, and disciplining the Militia, and for governing such Part of them as may be employed in the Service of the United States, reserving to the States respectively, the Appointment of the Officers, and the Authority of training the Militia according to the discipline prescribed by Congress;

To exercise exclusive Legislation in all Cases whatsoever, over such District (not exceeding ten Miles square) as may, by Cession of particular States, and the Acceptance of Congress, become the Seat of the Government of the United States, and to exercise like Authority over all Places purchased by the Consent of the Legislature of the State in which the Same shall be, for the Erection of Forts, Magazines, Arsenals, dock-Yards, and other needful Buildings; And

To make all Laws which shall be necessary and proper for carrying into Execution the foregoing Powers, and all other Powers vested by this Constitution in the Government of the United States, or in any Department or Officer thereof.

Section 9. The Migration or Importation of such Persons as any of the States now existing shall think proper to admit, shall not be prohibited by the Congress prior to the Year one thousand eight hundred and eight, but a Tax or duty may be imposed on such Importation, not exceeding ten dollars for each Person.

The Privilege of the Writ of Habeas Corpus shall not be suspended, unless when in Cases of Rebellion or Invasion the public Safety may require it.

No Bill of Attainder or ex post facto Law shall be passed.

No Capitation, or other direct, Tax shall be laid, unless in Proportion to the Census or Enumeration herein before directed to be taken.

No Tax or Duty shall be laid on Articles exported from any State.

No Preference shall be given by any Regulation of Commerce or Revenue to the Ports of one State over those of another; nor shall Vessels bound to, or from, one State, be obliged to enter, clear, or pay Duties in another.

No Money shall be drawn from the Treasury, but in Consequence of Appropriations made by Law; and a regular Statement and Account of the Receipts and Expenditures of all public Money shall be published from time to time.

No Title of Nobility shall be granted by the United States: And no Person holding any Office of Profit or Trust under them, shall, without the Consent of the Congress, accept of any present, Emolument, Office, or Title, of any kind whatever, from any King, Prince, or foreign State.

Section 10. No State shall enter into any Treaty, Alliance, or Confederation; grant Letters of Marque and Reprisal; coin Money; emit Bills of Credit; make any Thing but gold and silver Coin a Tender in Payment of Debts; pass any Bill of Attainder, ex post facto Law, or Law impairing the Obligation of Contracts, or grant any Title of Nobility.

No State shall, without the Consent of the Congress, lay any Imposts or Duties on Imports or Exports, except what may be absolutely necessary for executing its inspection Laws: and the net Produce of all Duties and Imposts, laid by any State on Imports or Exports, shall be for the Use of the Treasury of the United States; and all such Laws shall be subject to the Revision and Controul of the Congress.

No State shall, without the Consent of Congress, lay any Duty of Tonnage, keep Troops, or Ships of War in time of Peace, enter into any Agreement or Compact with another State, or with a foreign Power, or engage in War, unless actually invaded, or in such imminent Danger as will not admit of delay.

Article II.

Section 1. The executive Power shall be vested in a President of the United States of America. He shall hold his Office during the Term of four Years, and, together with the Vice President, chosen for the same Term, be elected, as follows:

Each State shall appoint, in such Manner as the Legislature thereof may direct, a Number of Electors, equal to the whole Number of Senators and Representatives to which the State may be entitled in the Congress: but no Senator or Representative, or Person holding an Office of Trust or Profit under the United States, shall be appointed an Elector.

The Electors shall meet in their respective States, and vote by Ballot for two Persons, of whom one at least shall not be an Inhabitant of the same State with themselves. And they shall make a List of all the Persons voted for, and of the Number of Votes for each; which List they shall sign and certify, and transmit sealed to the Seat of the Government of the United States, directed to the President of the Senate. The President of the Senate shall, in the Presence of the Senate and House of Representatives, open all the Certificates, and the Votes shall then be counted. The Person having the greatest Number of Votes shall be the President, if such Number be a Majority of the whole Number of Electors appointed; and if there be more than one who have such Majority, and have an equal Number of Votes, then the House of Representatives shall immediately chuse by Ballot one of them for President; and if no Person have a Majority, then from the five highest on the List the said House shall in like Manner chuse the President. But in chusing the President, the Votes shall be taken by States, the Representation from each State having one Vote; A quorum for this Purpose shall consist of a Member or Members from two thirds of the States, and a Majority of all the States shall be necessary to a Choice. In every Case, after the Choice of the President, the Person having the greatest Number of Votes of the Electors shall be the Vice President. But if there should remain two or more who have equal Votes, the Senate shall chuse from them by Ballot the Vice President.

The Congress may determine the Time of chusing the Electors, and the Day on which they shall give their Votes; which Day shall be the same throughout the United States.

No Person except a natural born Citizen, or a Citizen of the United States, at the time of the Adoption of this Constitution, shall be eligible to the Office of President; neither shall any Person be eligible to that Office who shall not have attained to the Age of thirty five Years, and been fourteen Years a Resident within the United States.

In Case of the Removal of the President from Office, or of his Death, Resignation, or Inability to discharge the Powers and Duties of the said Office, the Same shall devolve on the Vice President, and the Congress may by Law provide for the Case of Removal, Death, Resignation or Inability, both of the President and Vice President, declaring what Officer shall then act as President, and such Officer shall act accordingly, until the Disability be removed, or a President shall be elected.

The President shall, at stated Times, receive for his Services, a Compensation, which shall neither be encreased nor diminished during the Period for which he shall have been elected, and he shall not receive within that Period any other Emolument from the United States, or any of them.

Before he enter on the Execution of his Office, he shall take the following Oath or Affirmation:—"I do solemnly swear (or affirm) that I will faithfully execute the Office of President of the United States, and will to the best of my Ability, preserve, protect and defend the Constitution of the United States."

Section. 2. The President shall be Commander in Chief of the Army and Navy of the United States, and of the Militia of the several States, when called into the actual Service of the United States; he may require the Opinion, in writing, of the principal Officer in each of the executive Departments, upon any Subject relating to the Duties of their respective Offices, and he shall have Power to grant Reprieves and Pardons for Offences against the United States, except in Cases of Impeachment.

He shall have Power, by and with the Advice and Consent of the Senate, to make Treaties, provided two thirds of the Senators present concur; and he shall nominate, and by and with the Advice and Consent of the Senate, shall appoint Ambassadors, other public Ministers and Consuls, Judges of the supreme Court, and all other Officers of the United States, whose Appointments are not herein otherwise provided for, and which shall be established by Law: but the Congress may by Law vest the Appointment of such inferior Officers, as they think proper, in the President alone, in the Courts of Law, or in the Heads of Departments.

The President shall have Power to fill up all Vacancies that may happen during the Recess of the Senate, by granting Commissions which shall expire at the End of their next Session.

Section. 3. He shall from time to time give to the Congress Information of the State of the Union, and recommend to their Consideration such Measures as he shall judge necessary and expedient; he may, on extraordinary Occasions, convene both Houses, or either of them, and in Case of Disagreement between them, with Respect to the Time of Adjournment, he may adjourn them to such Time as he shall think proper; he shall receive Ambassadors and other public Ministers; he shall take Care that the Laws be faithfully executed, and shall Commission all the Officers of the United States.

Section. 4. The President, Vice President and all civil Officers of the United States, shall be removed from Office on Impeachment for, and Conviction of, Treason, Bribery, or other high Crimes and Misdemeanors.

Article. III.

Section. 1. The judicial Power of the United States, shall be vested in one supreme Court, and in such inferior Courts as the Congress may from time to time ordain and establish. The Judges, both of the supreme and inferior Courts, shall hold their Offices during good Behaviour, and shall, at stated Times, receive for their Services, a Compensation, which shall not be diminished during their Continuance in Office.

Section. 2. The judicial Power shall extend to all Cases, in Law and Equity, arising under this Constitution, the Laws of the United States, and Treaties made, or which shall be made, under their Authority;—to all Cases affecting Ambassadors, other public Ministers and Consuls;—to all Cases of admiralty and maritime Jurisdiction;—to Controversies to which the United States shall be a Party;—to Controversies between two or more States;—between a State and Citizens of another State;—between Citizens of different States;—between Citizens of the same State claiming Lands under Grants of different States, and between a State, or the Citizens thereof, and foreign States, Citizens or Subjects.

In all Cases affecting Ambassadors, other public Ministers and Consuls, and those in which a State shall be Party, the supreme Court shall have original Jurisdiction. In all the other Cases before mentioned, the supreme Court shall have appellate Jurisdiction, both as to Law and Fact, with such Exceptions, and under such Regulations as the Congress shall make.

The Trial of all Crimes, except in Cases of Impeachment, shall be by Jury; and such Trial shall be held in the State where the said Crimes shall have been committed; but when not committed within any State, the Trial shall be at such Place or Places as the Congress may by Law have directed.

Section. 3. Treason against the United States, shall consist only in levying War against them, or in adhering to their Enemies, giving them Aid and Comfort. No Person shall be convicted of Treason unless on the Testimony of two Witnesses to the same overt Act, or on Confession in open Court.

The Congress shall have Power to declare the Punishment of Treason, but no Attainder of Treason shall work Corruption of Blood, or Forfeiture except during the Life of the Person attainted.

Article. IV.

Section. 1. Full Faith and Credit shall be given in each State to the public Acts, Records, and judicial Proceedings of every other State. And

Congress may by general Laws prescribe the Manner in which such Acts, Records and Proceedings shall be proved, and the Effect thereof.

Sect. 2. The Citizens of each State shall be entitled to all Privileges and Immunities of Citizens in the several States.

A Person charged in any State with Treason, Felony, or other Crime, who shall flee from Justice, and be found in another State, shall on Demand of the executive Authority of the State from which he fled, be delivered up, to be removed to the State having Jurisdiction of the Crime.

No Person held to Service or Labour in one State, under the Laws thereof, escaping into another, shall, in Consequence of any Law or Regulation therein, be discharged from such Service or Labour, but shall be delivered up on Claim of the Party to whom such Service or Labour may be due.

Sect. 3. New States may be admitted by the Congress into this Union; but no new State shall be formed or erected within the Jurisdiction of any other State; nor any State be formed by the Junction of two or more States, or Parts of States, without the Consent of the Legislatures of the States concerned as well as of the Congress.

The Congress shall have Power to dispose of and make all needful Rules and Regulations respecting the Territory or other Property belonging to the United States; and nothing in this Constitution shall be so construed as to Prejudice any Claims of the United States, or of any particular State.

Sect. 4. The United States shall guarantee to every State in this Union a Republican Form of Government, and shall protect each of them against Invasion; and on Application of the Legislature, or of the Executive (when the Legislature cannot be convened) against domestic Violence.

Article. V.

The Congress, whenever two thirds of both Houses shall deem it necessary, shall propose Amendments to this Constitution, or, on the Application of the Legislatures of two thirds of the several States, shall call a Convention for proposing Amendments, which, in either Case, shall be valid to all Intents and Purposes, as Part of this Constitution, when ratified by the Legislatures of three fourths of the several States, or by Conventions in three fourths thereof, as the one or the other Mode of Ratification may be proposed by the Congress; Provided that no Amendment which may be made prior to the Year One thousand eight hundred and eight shall in any Manner affect the first and fourth Clauses in the Ninth Section of the first Article; and that no State, without its Consent, shall be deprived of its equal Suffrage in the Senate.

Article. VI.

All Debts contracted and Engagements entered into, before the Adoption of this Constitution, shall be as valid against the United States under this Constitution, as under the Confederation.

This Constitution, and the Laws of the United States which shall be made in Pursuance thereof; and all Treaties made, or which shall be made, under the Authority of the United States, shall be the supreme Law of the Land; and the Judges in every State shall be bound thereby, any Thing in the Constitution or Laws of any State to the Contrary notwithstanding.

The Senators and Representatives before mentioned, and the Members of the several State Legislatures, and all executive and judicial Officers, both of the United States and of the several States, shall be bound by Oath or Affirmation, to support this Constitution; but no religious Test shall ever be required as a Qualification to any Office or public Trust under the United States.

Article. VII.

The Ratification of the Conventions of nine States, shall be sufficient for the Establishment of this Constitution between the States so ratifying the Same.

done in Convention by the Unanimous Consent of the States present the Seventeenth Day of September in the Year of our Lord one thousand seven hundred and Eighty seven and of the Independance of the United States of America the Twelfth. In witness whereof We have hereunto subscribed our Names,

Go. Washington—Presidt. and deputy from Virginia

Attest William Jackson Secretary

Delaware
Geo: Read
Gunning Bedford jun
John Dickinson
Richard Bassett
Jaco: Broom

Maryland
James McHenry
Dan of St Thos Jenifer
Danl Carroll

Virginia
John Blair—
James Madison Jr.

North Carolina
Wm Blount
Richd Dobbs Spaight
Hu Williamson

South Carolina
J. Rutledge
Charles Cotesworth Pinckney
Charles Pinckney
Pierce Butler

Georgia
William Few
Abr Baldwin

New Hampshire
John Langdon
Nicholas Gilman

Massachusetts
Nathaniel Gorham
Rufus King

Connecticut
Wm Saml Johnson
Roger Sherman

New York
Alexander Hamilton

New Jersey
Wil: Livingston
David Brearley
Wm Paterson
Jona: Dayton

Pennsylvania
B Franklin
Thomas Mifflin
Robt Morris
Geo. Clymer
Thos FitzSimons
Jared Ingersoll
James Wilson
Gouv Morris

JEFFERSON, MADISON,

AND THE

MAKING OF THE CONSTITUTION

Jeff Broadwater

THE UNIVERSITY OF NORTH CAROLINA PRESS

Chapel Hill

This book was published with the assistance of the
Thornton H. Brooks Fund of the University of North Carolina Press.

Designed by Jamison Cockerham
Set in Arno, Cutright, Dear Sarah, and Telmoss
by codeMantra, Inc.

Manufactured in the United States of America

The University of North Carolina Press has been a member
of the Green Press Initiative since 2003.

Jacket and pp. ii–vi illustrations: portrait of Thomas Jefferson by Rembrandt Peale (1800),
portrait of James Madison by Gilbert Stuart (ca. 1805–1807),
and the Constitution of the United States from Wikimedia Commons.

LIBRARY OF CONGRESS CATALOGING-IN-PUBLICATION DATA
Names: Broadwater, Jeff, author.
Title: Jefferson, Madison, and the making of the Constitution / Jeff Broadwater.
Description: Chapel Hill : The University of North Carolina Press, [2019] |
    Includes bibliographical references and index.
Identifiers: LCCN 2018049278| ISBN 9781469651019 (cloth : alk. paper) |
    ISBN 9781469651026 (ebook)
Subjects: LCSH: United States. Constitution. | Constitutional history—United States. |
    Jefferson, Thomas, 1743–1826—Political and social views. |
    Madison, James, 1751–1836—Political and social views.
Classification: LCC KF4520 .B76 2019 | DDC 342.7302/9—dc23
LC record available at https://lccn.loc.gov/2018049278

To

JACK,

ANDREW,

GEORGIA,

MALLORY,

and

LIZA BENNETT.

Mentors of a sort.

CONTENTS

PREFACE

SINCE THE PUBLICATION OF Charles A. Beard's *An Economic Interpretation of the Constitution of the United States* in 1913, historians have debated the extent to which the Constitution should be seen as a conservative retreat from the supposedly egalitarian ideals of the American Revolution. Some historians have seen a conflict between the idealistic rhetoric of the Declaration of Independence, with its affirmation, for example, of human equality, and the more pedestrian language of the Constitution, which, by way of contrast, includes provisions countenancing chattel slavery. To complicate the possible paradox, Thomas Jefferson, the primary author of the Declaration, and James Madison, remembered by history as "the Father of the Constitution," enjoyed a lifelong friendship and an unshakable political alliance despite the ostensible tension between the two documents with which they are most closely associated.[1]

We can go a long way toward unraveling that paradox by considering together the evolution of Jefferson's and Madison's constitutional thought from roughly the adoption of the Declaration of Independence to the ratification of the Constitution and the passage of the Bill of Rights. Admittedly, Jefferson and Madison were only two among the many people who played a part in the American founding, but no other two had larger roles in the events that unfolded between 1776 and 1789. As John Quincy Adams, who knew both men, once observed, "The mutual influence of these mighty minds upon each other is a phenomenon, like the invisible and mysterious movements of the magnet." In their relationship, Adams predicted, "the future historian may discover the solution of much of our national history not otherwise accountable."[2]

Viewed from the perspective of the Jefferson and Madison partnership, the conflicts between the Declaration of Independence and the Constitution seem more apparent than real, in part because the two documents served different purposes. The Declaration articulated broad principles; unlike the Constitution, it did not create a framework for a new government.

Jefferson and Madison, moreover, had much in common. Both Virginians favored a central government vigorous enough to promote American trade overseas, to support westward expansion, and to preserve the union. Both believed an agrarian society fostered most naturally the civic virtue necessary to sustain a republican government. Both men sought to reconcile majority rule with individual liberty. Jefferson's and Madison's constitutional views were the product of similar and extensive reading in history, law, and political philosophy, along with years of experience in politics and government, where they often worked in tandem.

They had their differences. They disagreed in their assessment of human nature, more markedly in their reaction to social unrest and most fundamentally in their faith in the capacity of a national government to protect minority interests. Although Madison recognized that in a republic, the people must ultimately rule, he viewed them with considerable skepticism and mistrusted their representatives in the state legislatures. Jefferson's and Madison's experiences in the 1780s help explain their differing perspectives. On a diplomatic assignment in France, Jefferson saw how well-off most white Americans were compared with the average European. Sweeping constitutional reform at home seemed less urgent to him. Madison, meanwhile, divided his time between service in a parochial state assembly and in an ineffectual national legislature; for him, reform seemed essential to the survival of the republic. Madison came to believe that a properly constructed national government could better maintain law and order and protect individual liberties from oppressive majorities than could the states. Less fearful of the masses and less disillusioned with state governments, Jefferson saw centralized political power as almost inevitably dangerous and wanted as many decisions as possible to be made at the local level.[3]

Yet in at least one case, Jefferson's optimism helped preserve their friendship. Although Jefferson had serious reservations about the Constitution that Madison had helped to write, Jefferson's faith in the people and in the future would not allow him to become an Anti-Federalist. If the people supported the Constitution, as Jefferson thought they did, he felt confident they could make it work and repair its defects once they became apparent.

Constitution-making did not come easily. The federal Constitution of 1787 and the Bill of Rights of 1789 reflected years of study and practical legal and political experience. The new government was not a product of mere self-interest or psychological anxieties or ideology. Although the political theories of their day offered Jefferson and Madison tools with which to understand events and to attempt to manage them, historians should be wary of ideological explanations that neglect political realities.[4] Jefferson's and Madison's constitutional thought evolved in response to changing circumstances. As Madison explained to Noah Webster years later, "The change in our Govt. like most other important improvements ought to be ascribed rather to a series of causes, than to any particular & sudden one."[5] Neither Jefferson nor Madison got the Constitution he really wanted. By 1789, however, they had found a viable middle ground between the High Federalism of Alexander Hamilton and the locally oriented Anti-Federalism of Patrick Henry. It might be called small-government nationalism.

Their relationship, it should be noted, united political equals. Madison was not Jefferson's disciple or protégé. If, as Jeremy Bailey has cogently argued, Madison began during the ratification debate to move closer to Jefferson philosophically, Madison, along with Hamilton, still dominated the debate.[6] Jefferson was the more charismatic personality, the more popular politician, the more facile writer, and the more versatile intellect, but Madison had thicker skin, thought about the problems of governance more deeply and more systematically, and produced more substantive state papers. Jefferson left a more profound imprint on the American psyche. Madison made a greater mark on American law.

———

This book began as the 2014 Anne T. Moore Humanities Lecture at Campbell University, and I must thank Lloyd Johnson of the Department of History, Criminal Justice, and Political Science and the department's indomitable chair, James I. Martin, for the opportunity to speak at Buies Creek. Closer to home, Barton College provost and vice president for academic affairs Gary Daynes and James A. Clark, Elizabeth H. Jordan Chair of Southern Literature and dean of the School of Humanities, provided invaluable support, in particular through the award of an Edna Earle Boykin Fellowship in the Humanities. I also want to thank the staffs of Barton's Hackney Library and the Davis Library at the University of North Carolina at Chapel Hill for their assistance. My editor at the University of North Carolina Press, Charles Grench, has been a constant source of encouragement. Copy editor Julie Bush saved me from innumerable embarrassing mistakes. James Read and Todd Estes provided useful and supportive comments on the initial drafts of the manuscript. Cyndi and the rest of my family, as they always do, contributed everything from moral support to office supplies. I hope I have justified their confidence.

JEFFERSON,
MADISON,
AND THE
MAKING OF THE CONSTITUTION

ONE

The Coarse and Dry Study of the Law

1743–1774

THE EARLIEST SURVIVING LETTER in Thomas Jefferson's hand was written to John Harvie, one of the executors of his father's estate, in January 1760. The sixteen-year-old Jefferson proposed he enter the College of William and Mary in Williamsburg, Virginia. Another executor, Peter Randolph, had suggested the idea, and Jefferson heartily concurred. He complained that he was losing a quarter of his study time at the family's Shadwell plantation to company. Not only would William and Mary be more conducive to his studies, but his absence from Shadwell would mean fewer guests, which would "lessen the Expences of the Estate in Housekeeping." Jefferson conceded he could read Greek and Latin at home as well as he could in Williamsburg, but he hoped William and Mary could teach him "something of the Mathematics." In hindsight, another argument proved most prophetic and compelling: "By going to the College I shall get a more universal Acquaintance, which may hereafter be serviceable to me."[1]

—

JEFFERSON had been born at Shadwell, in the foothills of Virginia's Blue Ridge Mountains, in April 1743 to a prosperous planter of Welsh descent, Peter Jefferson. "My father's education," Jefferson wrote years later, "had been quite neglected; but being of strong mind, sound judgment and eager after information, he read much and improved himself." Peter Jefferson is best remembered for drawing, with Joshua Fry, a onetime mathematics professor at William and Mary, the first real map of Virginia. Jefferson seems to have revered his father. He never said much about his mother, Jane Randolph, who came from one of the colony's most prominent families. "They trace their pedigree far back in England & Scotland," he wrote in his autobiography, "to which let every one ascribe the faith & merit he chooses."[2]

Jane Randolph's cousin William Randolph died in 1745, and Peter Jefferson and his family moved to the Randolphs' Tuckahoe plantation north of Richmond to manage the estate and raise William's three children. Thomas Jefferson reportedly learned to read before he started school at the age of five in a one-room schoolhouse on the Randolph plantation. As a small boy, he read all the books in his father's modest library. When he was nine, the Jeffersons returned to Shadwell, where Jefferson entered a "Latin school" run by the Reverend William Douglas. The mature Jefferson described Douglas as "a superficial Latinist, less instructed in Greek, but with the rudiments of these languages he taught me French." He also exposed the boy to the most substantial library he had ever seen.[3]

Jefferson suffered a devastating blow in 1757 when his father died at the age of forty-nine. Peter's death, however, did not disrupt Jefferson's education. The following year he entered Reverend James Maury's boarding school in Fredericksburg. Jefferson later adjudged Maury "a correct classical scholar," and the Anglican clergyman soon had his pupil reading the classical authors in the original Greek and Latin. In roughly two years in Fredericksburg, Jefferson developed a lifelong love of the classics, and he added to his native intellectual gifts a remarkable industriousness. "A mind always employed is always happy," he would one day write one of his own children. "This is the true secret, the grand recipe for felicity."[4]

By 1760, Jefferson's intellect, work ethic, and social status had made the College of William and Mary a logical next step, and he found there a favorite professor. "It was my great good fortune, and what probably fixed the destinies of my life that Dr. Wm. Small of Scotland was then professor of Mathematics." In six years at William and Mary, Small, the only member of the faculty who was not a clergyman, taught a variety of courses, including moral philosophy. He had, in Jefferson's words, "a happy talent of communication, correct and gentlemanly manners, & an enlarged and liberal mind." For his part, Jefferson seems to have been a model student. His friend John Page thought Jefferson studied fifteen hours a day and went nowhere without his Greek grammar book. Williamsburg's young women distracted Jefferson a good bit—he developed a crush on Rebecca Burwell, the sister of a fellow student—but Small must have appreciated Jefferson's ability, love of books, and an emerging affability that would prove to be an incalculable political asset.[5]

Jefferson and Small became good friends, and Small introduced his student to Francis Fauquier, Virginia's popular and urbane royal governor. Fauquier impressed Jefferson as "the ablest man who had ever held that office." By his late teens, Jefferson was a fixture in the capital's most elite social circles. Before Small returned to Europe in 1762, he arranged for Jefferson to study law with one of colonial America's most distinguished attorneys, George Wythe. "He might truly be called the Cato of his country, without the avarice of the Roman," Jefferson would write in 1820, "for a more disinterested person never lived."[6]

Jefferson turned to the law because of a lack of suitable alternatives, not an uncommon phenomenon among law students. He had no interest in the ministry, the military, or business, and colonial Virginia offered few opportunities for a gentleman to make a living in the arts or sciences, which did appeal to him. At the same time, the status of the legal profession was on the rise. A legal education, Jefferson advised a young relative after the Revolution, "qualifies a man to be useful to himself, to his neighbors, and to the public." Jefferson may or may not have been interested in a political career as a young man, but he came to regard the law as "the most certain stepping stone to preferment in the political line."[7]

His relationship with Wythe proved to be among the most fortuitous of Jefferson's life. Colonial legal education was hit-or-miss at best. A student would often pay a fee to be an apprentice to a lawyer who might simply use him—they were all men in those days—as a source of cheap clerical labor. Wythe, by contrast, took his duties as a mentor seriously. Wythe had studied law with his uncle Stephen Dewey in Elizabeth City County; Dewey had put his nephew to work tediously copying documents. Wythe's students would fare better.[8]

Wythe had moved to Williamsburg about 1748. He worked for a time as a clerk in the House of Burgesses, was elected alderman for the town, and served briefly as mayor. Wythe lost two races for an assembly seat from Elizabeth City County, perhaps because he refused to "treat" the voters with alcohol on Election Day, as was the custom. He was finally elected in 1761, the year before he took Jefferson on as a law student. As relations with Great Britain worsened, he served on Virginia's Committee of Correspondence, and in 1765 he led opposition in the assembly to the hated Stamp Act. Less outspoken than the fiery Patrick Henry, he was nevertheless, in the words of one biographer, "so radically democratic by the end of the Revolution that he objected to the aristocratic styles of powdered wigs and the capitalizing of nouns."[9]

Revered for his integrity and the breadth of his intellectual interests, Wythe maintained a successful practice before the general court, Virginia's highest tribunal, although Henry's oratorical skills made him the more effective trial lawyer. Wythe believed a sound legal education combined practical experience, reading in the law, and study in the liberal arts. When the general court was in session in Williamsburg, Wythe required Jefferson to observe its proceedings. Otherwise, he suggested Jefferson spend his mornings, when the mind was its sharpest, reading law. Afternoons could be devoted to political philosophy and political economy; Wythe recommended Jefferson read John Locke, Algernon Sidney, Thomas Malthus, Francis Hutcheson, and Lord Kames, among others. In the evenings, Jefferson could relax with fiction and poetry.[10]

Jefferson spent five years under Wythe's tutelage, although for much of that time he was reading on his own at Shadwell; he turned twenty-one in 1764, which allowed him to take title to his father's estate. His legal studies began with Lord Coke's ponderous *Institutes*, the staple of colonial legal education. William Blackstone's famous *Commentaries* did not appear until two years after Jefferson began his law practice. Stylistically, Coke suffered by comparison; Blackstone's work was better written and better organized. Infamous for dull prose and a confusing structure, Coke's *Institutes* started with a commentary on Thomas Littleton's treatise on English land law. A second volume discussed the Magna Carta and other landmarks in English legal history. Volume 3 treated the criminal law, and a final volume tried to explain the English court system.[11]

Jefferson struggled to wade through it all. Writing his friend John Page on his way from Williamsburg to Shadwell in December 1762, Jefferson committed himself "to get through Old Cooke [*sic*] this winter; for God knows I have not seen him since I packed him up in my trunk in Williamsburgh.... I do wish the Devil had old Cooke, for I am sure I never was so tired of an old dull scoundrel in my life." Yet he came to appreciate the old scoundrel. In retirement, when they were trying to recruit a law professor for the new University of Virginia, Jefferson wrote James Madison that "a sounder whig never wrote, nor of profounder learning in the orthodox doctrines of the British constitution, or in what were called English liberties. You remember also that our lawyers were then all Whigs." Jefferson bemoaned Coke's replacement by Blackstone, a conservative and a champion of parliamentary supremacy. His "honied" prose had seduced a younger generation of lawyers. When Blackstone "became the Student's Hornbook," Jefferson lamented, the legal "profession . . . began to slide into toryism."[12]

Coke provided Jefferson with a method of legal analysis as well as a substantive knowledge of the law. Sixteenth- and seventeenth-century legal commentators, among whom Coke was the most influential, tended to conflate history and law. Coke believed in the antiquity of the common law and presumed, in the words of John Pocock, "that any legal judgment declaring a right immemorial is perfectly valid as a statement of history." The antiquity of English case law, combined with the idea it embodied a "reasonableness" that had been discovered, not made, by trained and impartial judges, led fairly easily to a view of the common law as a constitution, or in other words, a fundamental law that could limit the prerogatives of the king or the discretion of Parliament.[13]

We often think of the British constitution as an unwritten collection of laws and traditions; we could more accurately say simply it is not written in one place. It was written in statutes and judicial decisions, and especially, Coke argued, in the Magna Carta. Coke, a judge himself, observed in the celebrated *Dr. Bonham's Case* (1610) that "it appears in our books, that in many cases, the common law will control acts of parliament, and sometimes adjudge them to be utterly void." By the 1650s, Coke's dictum was being challenged by the new doctrine of parliamentary supremacy, but it reappeared occasionally in other legal opinions and treatises.[14]

Coke had sowed the seed for the practice of judicial review in American law, the process by which courts can set aside legislative or executive acts they deem to violate the federal or state constitutions. As a practicing politician, Jefferson would waffle on the propriety of judicial review, but, more important at this stage of his life, his legal education introduced him to the contested concept of "unconstitutionality." It would be central to the developing crisis in Anglo-American relations. In 1761, only a year before Jefferson began his study with Wythe, the Boston lawyer James Otis argued that writs of assistance, or general search warrants, even if authorized by Parliament, were unconstitutional and therefore void. A Virginia county court would later declare the Stamp Act invalid on similar grounds.[15]

William Wirt, a younger lawyer who rose to political prominence himself, knew both Wythe and Jefferson, and he thought Jefferson learned from Wythe an "unrivaled neatness, system and method in business" that he carried "through all his life." Studying law also allowed Jefferson to hone his writing style. He kept a commonplace book in which he copied, word for word, poetry and other literary works that impressed him. He had a separate commonplace book for his legal reading, and there he summarized legal cases as concisely as possible with the goal, he said, of "never using two words where one will do." The effort paid off. As one biographer has written, "Jefferson's greatest works are masterpieces of concision." Presumably, Jefferson also completed his studies with an idea of the law as a way to organize a proper republican society. In less than a decade he would be Virginia's most prominent advocate of legal and constitutional reform.[16]

Some confusion exists as to the date Jefferson passed the bar. He recalled in his autobiography being admitted to practice before the general court in 1767, but lawyers had to be admitted to the colony's inferior courts for a year before they could practice in the higher court, which heard appeals and more important cases, and Jefferson apparently never practiced in the lower courts.[17] A fellow lawyer, Edmund Randolph, remembered Jefferson as "indefatigable and methodical in whatever he undertook" and as an adequate speaker but a more impressive writer. Comparisons with Patrick Henry seemed inevitable: "Mr. Jefferson drew copiously from the depths of the law, Mr. Henry from the recesses of the human heart." Jefferson, Randolph later wrote, quickly established "advantageous connections among those classes of men who were daily rising in weight."[18]

Despite his success as a lawyer, Jefferson saw himself first as a gentleman planter, and he retained a certain ambivalence about the law and about lawyers. He once joked that the job of the lawyer was "to question everything, yield nothing, & talk by the hour." When Thomas Turpin asked him to take on his son as a law student, Jefferson declined his request. "I was always of the opinion that the placing of a youth to study with an attorney was rather a prejudice than a help. . . . The only help a youth wants is to be directed what books to read and in what order to read them," he explained. It was not a fair description of his experience with Wythe; perhaps he simply did not want to assume the responsibility for a protégé. He did encourage Turpin to buy law books for his son—"a lawyer without books would be like a workman without tools"—and he sent Turpin a reading list, as he would do for others who asked his advice. One list included readings for morning, noon, and night and probably resembled the routine Jefferson had followed with Wythe. He recommended the aspiring lawyer begin the day with Coke but devote his evenings to reading history. The "other branches of science," he wrote a nephew, "and especially history, are necessary to form a lawyer."[19]

Of course, the law was only one part of his life. In 1769 he began construction of his Monticello mansion. The following year a fire destroyed

The Coarse and Dry Study of the Law

Shadwell and all his law books, except one he had loaned out. He soon began rebuilding his library. In 1772, Jefferson married a wealthy young widow, Martha Wayles Skelton. It was a happy marriage, and Jefferson found his father-in-law, the planter and lawyer John Wayles, to be "a most agreeable companion, full of pleasantry & good humor." Wayles died shortly after Jefferson and Martha married, leaving Jefferson with 11,000 acres and responsibility for his substantial debts, a mixed blessing from which Jefferson never fully recovered.[20]

And then there was politics, especially the deteriorating relationship between Great Britain and its American colonies. Americans had learned to live with, and sometimes evade, the Navigation Acts that were intended to keep most American trade within the British Empire. But victory in the French and Indian War had left Britain with a hefty war debt and an expensive empire to maintain in Canada. Britain's financial woes led to unprecedented taxes on the colonies. As a law student, Jefferson stood in the door of the House of Burgesses and heard an impassioned Patrick Henry denounce the stamp tax: "He appeared to me to speak as Homer wrote." In the face of such protests, Parliament repealed the Stamp Act, without, however, conceding its right to tax the colonies.[21]

Albemarle County voters elected Jefferson to the House of Burgesses in 1769. At about the same time he ordered a short list of books on political philosophy from London; they included John Locke's *Two Treatises of Civil Government* and Montesquieu's *The Spirit of the Laws*. The imperial crisis prompted Jefferson and many of his contemporaries to read deeply in English and continental history and political theory, but they approached their task more often as lawyers than as systematic political philosophers. Jefferson wanted concrete, if sometimes debatable, historical and legal precedents that would limit the jurisdiction of Parliament over the colonies.[22]

In May, the Virginia house passed a series of resolutions denouncing the 1767 Townshend Duties, which taxed imported lead, paint, paper, glass, and tea. The royal governor, Norborne Berkeley, Baron de Botetourt, immediately dissolved the assembly. Jefferson and most of the burgesses reconvened to the Apollo Room at the Raleigh Tavern and signed an "association," or agreement, to boycott British imports to protest "the late unconstitutional Act, imposing Duties . . . for the sole Purpose of raising a Revenue in America." The association, which was part of a larger boycott movement throughout the colonies, proved difficult to enforce in Virginia, where large planters bought goods directly from British factors. In the northern and middle colonies, pressure on a relatively small number of American merchants could achieve more obvious results. On balance the Townshend Duties produced little revenue, and the boycott inflicted substantial losses on British exporters. In 1770, Parliament repealed them, except for the duty on tea; it remained as a largely symbolic assertion of Britain's authority to tax the Americans.[23]

A modest tax on tea could not sustain a protest movement. "Nothing of particular excitement occurring for a time," as Jefferson put it, "our countrymen seemed to fall into a state of insensibility to our situation." Far better read and somewhat better traveled than the average Virginian—Jefferson had gone as far north as New York City on a sightseeing trip in 1766—he was also less parochial and more attentive to constitutional strictures. Edmund Randolph thought Jefferson's "fund of knowledge" made him "ripe for stronger measures than the public voice was conceived to demand." The presence of British regulars in Boston, a hotbed of American resistance, may have offended him; republican theory routinely condemned standing armies as a threat to liberty. He may also have been radicalized by the *Gaspee* Affair, which involved a British customs schooner that had been burned by a mob after running aground in Narragansett Bay in June 1772. A royal proclamation threatened to take the culprits, if captured, to England for trial, a procedure Jefferson would have seen as a violation of the common-law right to a trial by a jury of peers in a defendant's vicinage.[24]

Jefferson had by now become identified with a militant faction in the House of Burgesses that included Patrick Henry, Richard Henry Lee, Francis Lightfoot Lee, and Jefferson's boyhood friend Dabney Carr. Jefferson doubted "our old & leading members" were "up to the point of forwardness & zeal which the times required." The militants hatched a plan to organize a committee of correspondence, as Massachusetts had done, to coordinate resistance to Britain's imperial polices. The House of Burgesses adopted the proposal and named Jefferson to the committee.[25]

A new governor, Lord Dunmore, dissolved the assembly, which preserved a modicum of royal authority until events began to spiral out of control with the passage of the Tea Act in the spring of 1773. Intended to rescue the financially troubled East India Company, the act maintained the threepenny-per-pound tax on imported tea but gave the company other tax breaks and a right to bypass, and underprice, American merchants and sell tea directly to American consumers. Seen in the colonies as a threat to local retailers and as a scheme to induce Americans to buy taxed tea, the act provoked the Boston Tea Party. Destruction of East India Company tea in Boston harbor in December 1773 prompted Parliament to pass the Coercive Acts, punitive measures that included a provision closing the harbor.[26]

The Boston port bill, Jefferson recalled later, "excited our sympathies for Massachusetts." Convinced by the spring 1774 legislative session that the lead on the issue could "no longer be left to the old members," Jefferson and his allies among the more outspoken burgesses decided that "we must boldly take an unequivocal stand in line with Massachusetts." Bold, but not foolhardy. They drafted a seemingly innocuous call for a day of prayer and fasting in support of their New England brethren and persuaded a pious conservative, Robert Carter Nicholas, to introduce it. The measure passed easily. After Dunmore issued another order dissolving the assembly, Jefferson and most of the delegates reconvened at the Raleigh Tavern to organize a new boycott and issue a call for a continental congress to meet in Philadelphia. A few days later, the burgesses still in Williamsburg—Jefferson may have been among them—proposed Virginians elect representatives to a convention to meet in August. It would consider an embargo of the colony's exports to Great Britain, and it would assemble entirely outside the sanction of royal authority.[27]

———

How did Thomas Jefferson justify resistance to British policies in America and ultimately a rebellion against British rule, and where would he turn for materials to construct a new government to replace the one he would be instrumental in overthrowing? At this point, we can only consider some partial answers. He did not have an overly systematic political philosophy, and as Drew McCoy has written, in most cases, "it simply makes no sense to approach Jefferson in terms of specific lines of intellectual influence." The problems of government competed with Jefferson's many other interests for his attention.[28] Yet he was very much a product of the Enlightenment. He considered Francis Bacon, Isaac Newton, and John Locke to have been the three greatest men who ever lived. Fundamentally, but not unreservedly, optimistic about human nature, he believed in progress and in the ability of human reason to understand the natural laws that governed the universe.[29]

Good governments left their subjects free to pursue intellectual inquiry, but if he instinctively valued liberty, Jefferson was not a radical egalitarian. His tolerance of slavery suggests the limits of his liberalism. He deplored any "artificial aristocracy" based on "wealth and birth," but he believed in a "natural aristocracy" of "virtue and talents," and he thought its members should govern. "May we not even say," he wrote John Adams, "that that form of government is the best which provides the most effectually for a pure selection of these natural aristoi into the offices of government."[30]

The imperial crisis and his entry into politics stimulated his intellectual curiosity. In addition to the works of Locke and Montesquieu, when he entered the House of Burgesses in 1769 he ordered from his London factors several volumes of parliamentary history and books on natural law and the law of nations. Sensing an analogy between Ireland's place in the British Empire and America's, Jefferson also ordered William Petty's *Political Survey of Ireland* and Ferdinando Warner's *The History of Ireland* and *The History of the Rebellion and Civil War in Ireland*. He eventually acquired all the basic works of natural law and the law of nations by Jean-Jacques Burlamaqui, Hugo Grotius, Samuel von Pufendorf, and others. It was an amorphous field, as much a matter of tradition and opinion as of statutes and judicial decisions; Jefferson looked for areas where the commentators had reached consensus.[31]

Jefferson synthesized his considerable readings, picking and choosing the ideas that seemed most relevant to the American experience, and he did some of his own research. His commonplace book on politics contains extensive notes on European constitutions; they conclude by crediting "the Northern nations" of Europe for "introducing or restoring" ancient democratic institutions that had been lost almost everywhere else.[32] In the years leading up to the American Revolution, the idea of recovering ancient liberties would be one of the two or three most important concepts in Jefferson's intellectual repertoire.

Locke had theorized that societies created governments by compacts among individuals who surrendered to their rulers only those prerogatives necessary to maintain law and order. Citizens retained the rights to life, liberty, and property, along with a right to rebel if the government infringed upon those rights. Jefferson agreed, but Locke mistrusted Catholics and atheists while Jefferson had a broader view of religious freedom. To him, progress depended on untrammelled intellectual inquiry, which demanded the broadest tolerance in matters of religion.[33]

Likewise, Jefferson could find any number of congenial themes in Montesquieu's *Spirit of the Laws*: a fear of political corruption as a threat to democracy; a call for more humane criminal laws; a concern for civil liberties, including freedom of religion; and the conviction that constitutions and laws must be adopted to "climate, local conditions, and new circumstances" and must change with the times. The Frenchman obviously impressed the young Jefferson; his commonplace book on government contains more entries from Montesquieu than from any other author. Over the years, however, Jefferson's admiration for Montesquieu waned. Concluding Montesquieu was much too enamored of the British system, Jefferson could not share his veneration of a "mixed government" of king, lords, and commons. Montesquieu's claim that republics could flourish only in small states could never be accepted in America. "I suspect that the doctrine that small states alone are fitted to be republics, will be exploded by experience," Jefferson wrote in 1795. A republic "must be so extensive . . . that on any particular question, a majority may be found in it's [sic] councils free from particular interests, and giving, therefore, an uniform prevalence to the principles of justice."[34]

At the same time, Jefferson drew inspiration, or at least arguments, from Obadiah Hulme's *Historical Essay on the English Constitution*, which praised the Saxons for engaging their people in politics by concentrating power at the local level. He especially admired the republican theorist Algernon Sidney, a favorite among American Whigs. Sidney believed citizens should give up as little freedom as possible to the state. As did Locke, he also argued that revolution could be justified only when necessary to restore a lawful government. Modern historians have often attempted to distinguish Locke's liberalism, with its emphasis on individual rights, from Sidney's republicanism, which supposedly put more stress on civic virtue and the public good. Jefferson did not worry about the difference.[35]

Another republican with perhaps an even greater impact on Jefferson was Lord Bolingbroke, a controversial English politician; an outspoken critic of Robert Walpole, often considered Britain's first modern prime minister; and a foe of Britain's ruling court party and its developing party system. Bolingbroke's attacks on organized religion made him notorious in some quarters, but not with Jefferson. Quotes from the British polemicist take up almost half of Jefferson's surviving literary commonplace book. In addition to his skepticism about the historical reliability of the Bible, Bolingbroke expressed hostility toward Plato's idealistic epistemology and all forms of metaphysical speculation, embracing instead materialism and, as he saw it, reason.[36]

Bolingbroke probably helped Jefferson clarify his thinking about the nature of a constitution by distinguishing it from a mere "government." A government referred to what rulers actually did—in essence, public administration. A constitution, by contrast, should embody fixed principles, aimed at the public good, under which the people were to be governed. A "constitution is the rule by which our princes ought to govern at all times," and it should be "founded on the eternal rules of right reason, and directed to promote the happiness of the whole, and of every individual."[37]

Jefferson rejected Bernard de Mandeville's argument in his *Fable of the Bees* "that private vices produced public benefits." He preferred the "moral sense" philosophy of Lord Shaftesbury, Francis Hutcheson, and Lord Kames. Shaftesbury believed humans possessed "social affections" that allowed them to achieve happiness by pursuing virtue and setting aside short-term self-interest. Hutcheson took Shaftesbury's theories a step further. The pursuit of virtue, or "benevolence," was an act of will; only those who could act independently, therefore, could truly be happy, thus making freedom an essential element of contentment. In that vein, Jefferson's assertion in the Declaration of Independence of a right to "the pursuit of happiness" meant something more than simply a quest for personal pleasure.[38]

Hutcheson conceded people did not always act virtuously. Governments sometimes had to regulate the human will by law, but the moral sense philosophy was democratic to the extent it assumed most adults had the capacity to discern right from wrong: "The Author of Nature has much better furnish'd us for a virtuous conduct, than our Moralists seem to imagine." In a frequently quoted letter to his nephew Peter Carr, Jefferson echoed Hutcheson: "He who made us would have been a pitiful bungler if he had made the rules of conduct a matter of science." Because "man was destined for society," he had to have an inherent sense of right and wrong that allowed him to live with others. Jefferson acknowledged reason could be helpful in matters of ethics, but it was less useful than common sense: "State a moral case to a ploughman & a professor. The former will decide it as well, & often better than the latter, because he has not been led astray by artificial rules."[39]

The prolific legal scholar Lord Kames reduced the moral sense philosophy to a system of jurisprudence. He put more emphasis on the desire of people to protect their property; they organized governments, he believed, largely to safeguard property rights. He distinguished "duty" from "benevolence." Duty required us to honor our commitments and refrain from harming others; benevolence meant charity toward them. Law could enforce duties, but it generally would not compel generosity. Kames also provided Jefferson with a theory of moral progress. Civilizations passed through four stages of development, from hunters and gatherers to pastoral nomads to agricultural and finally commercial societies. Scarcity forced people to compete for resources and coarsened human hearts, but as economies developed and goods became more plentiful, societies and laws became more humane. Jefferson took extensive notes on Kames and owned at least ten of his books, including his most important, *Principles of Equity*.[40]

Jefferson was, it should be noted, hardly a passive receptacle for the ideas of others. Some writers he disliked or conveniently ignored. He had no use for Plato's idealism, much preferring Aristotle's granularity. He hated the historian David Hume and Thomas Hobbes, author of *The Leviathan*, as apologists for royal absolutism. The great Irish parliamentarian Edmund Burke, with his belief in gradual, organic change, was too conservative for Jefferson, despite his sympathy for the American cause. Notwithstanding the appreciation Jefferson eventually developed for France, the greatest French thinkers of his era made little impression on him. He appears to have read Voltaire only sporadically, and "the influence of Rousseau," Gilbert Chinard has written, "was absolutely negative."[41]

The classical writers of antiquity occupy a more ambiguous place in the shaping of Jefferson's political thought. Passages from the classics fill almost half his literary commonplace book. They likely influenced his writing style; classical rhetoric valued the simplicity, brevity, and rationality that appear repeatedly in Jefferson's work. His favorite philosopher was the Athenian Epicurus, who, much like Shaftesbury, Hutcheson, and Kames, taught that happiness came through virtue and reason. Jefferson rejected the fatalism of the Stoics, but he accepted their belief in "intuition" or, in other words, a moral sense. Classical motifs shaped his taste in architecture at Monticello and in the new state capitol he designed in Richmond in the 1780s, a copy of the Maison Carrée, a first-century Roman temple at Nîmes. When it was proposed that a statue of George Washington be commissioned, Jefferson lobbied to have the work done by Jean-Antoine Houdon in the Roman style.[42]

A passage he excerpted from the Roman historian Tacitus, "The more corrupt the commonwealth the more numerous its laws," foreshadowed his preference for limited government. Jefferson and Wythe admired Roman law, although it would disappear from American courts in the 1800s. Jefferson took from the Romans the idea that cities bred corruption and that independent yeoman farmers made the best citizens. Classical pastoralism became a critical feature of Jefferson's rhetoric. Romanticizing farmers was shrewd politics in an overwhelmingly agricultural nation, but the classical tradition had its limits. Jefferson criticized Greek and Roman imperialism. He accepted territorial expansion and even conquest, but he believed people in newly acquired territories should be represented in the governments that ruled over them. Intrigued by classical examples in the 1780s, he would eventually conclude that the advent of representative democracy had made the old forms obsolete. An Athenian-style direct democracy, he ultimately determined, would be impractical in a large republic like the United States, and he doubted the general public could manage the day-to-day affairs of government efficiently.[43]

If, in short, Jefferson was a student of many schools, he was a captive of none. Perhaps the most salient broad idea he took from his reading was a conviction that most people possessed sufficient virtue—in his case, "sociability" might be the better word—to select their own rulers and to enjoy a considerable degree of personal freedom. He was also in 1774 a lawyer trained in the common law and in the English constitution, one with specific grievances against a British administration, and he would, as we shall see, draw on England's constitutional history to make his case.[44]

IN MAY 1774, James Madison visited his former college classmate William Bradford in Philadelphia. He probably watched as a mob burned effigies of Thomas Hutchinson, the royal governor of Massachusetts, and Alexander Wedderburn, the British solicitor general who had recently harangued Benjamin Franklin before the Privy Council. News of the passage of the Coercive Acts arrived during Madison's visit, and before he left for home, a meeting at Philadelphia's City Tavern had endorsed a call for a continental congress.[45]

Madison and Jefferson had not yet met, although as an adolescent Madison may have seen Jefferson argue a case in court. Jefferson was seven years older and at least half a foot taller, but they had much in common: birth into the Virginia gentry, comparable educations, a shared intellectual world, and similar political opinions. Madison's father, James Madison Sr., was the wealthiest planter in Orange County. James Jr. was the oldest of seven children who survived to adulthood; his mother, Nelly, was pregnant twelve times yet lived to be ninety-seven. The house where Madison spent his early years disappeared long ago, but he remembered moving into a new structure, Montpelier, as a small boy. About thirty miles from Monticello and within sight of the Blue Ridge Mountains on a clear day, it would be home for the rest of his life.[46]

Nelly suffered from a variety of ailments, so Madison's grandmother Frances Taylor Madison, a devout Anglican, became his first teacher. He also studied under two local tutors, John Bricky and Kelly Jennings. When he was about twelve, Madison entered a boarding school taught by a Scottish Presbyterian, Donald Robertson, in King and Queen County. Madison spent five years with Robertson, studying Latin, Greek, mathematics, geography, the rudiments of French, and what Madison later called "miscellaneous literature." Robertson introduced Madison to the classics, Montesquieu, Locke's *Essay Concerning Human Understanding*, and his *Letter Concerning Toleration*. Madison's commonplace book, which is far less extensive than the ones

The Coarse and Dry Study of the Law

Jefferson compiled, also shows references to Machiavelli and Hobbes. Robertson must have been a demanding and inspiring teacher. "All that I have been in life," Madison said later, "I owe largely to that man."[47]

After leaving Robertson's school, Madison spent two years with a private tutor, Thomas Martin, the rector of the nearby Brick Church, an Anglican parish where James Madison Sr. was a vestryman. Thomas Martin and his brother Alexander were graduates of Princeton University (or the College of New Jersey, as it was then called, or Nassau Hall, the name of its main building). The Martins undoubtedly contributed to Madison's decision to enroll at Princeton in the summer of 1769.[48]

The College of William and Mary would have been a more obvious choice, but Princeton had its advantages. Madison said in his autobiography that the Williamsburg climate "was unhealthy for persons going from a mountainous region," and he had cause for concern about his health. He suffered throughout his life from intestinal complaints. Worse yet, he displayed, in his words, "a constitutional liability to sudden attacks, somewhat resembling Epilepsy, and suspending the intellectual functions." A recent historian has diagnosed his disorder as temporal lobe epilepsy. Irving Brant, Madison's most indefatigable biographer, labeled it "epileptoid hysteria." Madison does not appear to have suffered from epilepsy in its most common form, and his case is complicated by a possible tendency toward hypochondria, sometimes exaggerated by stress and overwork.[49]

In attributing his decision to attend Princeton to his fragile health and Williamsburg's sultry climate, Madison may have been trying to be tactful. At the time, William and Mary seemed to be in decline; Jefferson's mentor, William Small, had left the college, and its current president, James Horrocks, had a reputation as "a High Church Tory." Princeton, by contrast, attracted a more diverse student body than did the other colonial colleges, and it was cheaper than its competitors.[50]

Unashamedly affiliated with American Presbyterianism, Princeton offered twice-daily prayer services while becoming, perhaps incongruously to the modern mind, a citadel of religious freedom. Liberty of conscience apparently appealed to Madison's father, and he in all likelihood steered his son to New Jersey. As a member of the Orange County Court, James Madison Sr. had refused to enforce a Virginia law barring Baptist ministers from preaching without a license. On another occasion, he raised no objection to an evening mass meeting of Baptists near his family's property, despite a law against nighttime assemblies.[51] James Madison's celebrated commitment to religious liberty was, at least in part, inherited.

Much of Princeton's allure derived from its new president, John Wither-spoon, a Presbyterian cleric who had come to America from Scotland in 1768. If Donald Robertson had been Madison's William Small, Witherspoon would become his George Wythe. Described by the historians Stanley Elkins and Eric McKitrick as "the greatest teacher of his day in America," Witherspoon, an imposing figure with a commanding presence, may have been the leading exponent of the Scottish Enlightenment in America. He was not an original thinker; he did, however, earn a reputation for integrity, common sense, and, as the only clergyman to sign the Declaration of Independence, a devotion to the American cause.[52]

In the Scottish church, Witherspoon had been associated with conser-vative critics of a so-called Moderate faction. Inspired by Francis Hutcheson, the Moderates minimized the doctrines of orthodox Calvinism and preached a forerunner of the Social Gospel that emphasized the Christian's duties to society at large. In America, Witherspoon moved toward the theological center and the political left, combining in his lectures and sermons elements of evangelical Christianity, classical republicanism, Lockean liberalism, and Hutcheson's moral sense philosophy. Witherspoon's Princeton course on moral philosophy drew heavily on Hutcheson's writings and attacked by name Mandeville's *Fable of the Bees*. "Luxury and vice only waste and destroy," he told Madison and his classmates; "they add nothing to the common stock of property or of happiness."[53]

Witherspoon also taught his students that individuals enjoyed certain "perfect rights in a state of natural liberty." These included property rights: "Without private property no laws would be sufficient to compel universal industry." They also included "a right to private judgment in matters of opin-ion," and that encompassed religious freedom: "We ought in general to guard against persecution on a religious account as much as possible because such as hold absurd tenets are seldom dangerous. Perhaps they are never danger-ous, but when they are oppressed."[54]

For all his personal dignity, Witherspoon appears to have had a populist streak; he had reportedly been troubled by what he saw as the elitism of the Scottish Moderates, and he could sometimes sound like Thomas Jeffer-son. One speech to the Continental Congress echoes Jefferson's "plough-man and professor" letter to Peter Carr: "A person of integrity will pass as sound a judgment on subjects" of right and wrong "by consulting his own heart, as by turning over books and systems." As did Jefferson, the Prince-ton president also embraced the commonsense philosophy of Thomas Reid and Dugald Stewart. Closely related to Hutcheson's theories of moral sense,

The Coarse and Dry Study of the Law

philosophical common sense repudiated the work of David Hume and idealistic philosophers who questioned what we could know of the world from our own senses. Common sense, their critics countered, made certain truths "self-evident."[55]

Witherspoon wanted to prepare students for public service, and he enjoyed considerable success. Princeton produced more signers of the Constitution than Harvard and Yale combined. A Princeton education included formal, public debates on contemporary issues, and the school's political leanings were not in question. At its annual commencement in 1769, which was the first that James Madison observed, the school awarded honorary degrees to John Hancock and John Dickinson, who had led colonial opposition to the Townshend Duties. The following year, when New York merchants ended their boycott of British imports and wrote a letter urging their Philadelphia counterparts to do the same, Princeton students burned the letter, Madison reported to his father, "in the college yard, all of them appearing in their black Gowns & the bell Tolling." According to one study, of the 335 students John Witherspoon taught between 1769 and 1783, only five were active Loyalists.[56]

Madison liked Princeton from the moment he arrived. He helped organize a social club, the Whig Society, and became close friends with Hugh Henry Brackenridge, William Bradford, and Philip Freneau. Brackenridge went on to serve on the Pennsylvania Supreme Court and to write a popular novel, *Modern Chivalry*. Bradford later became attorney general of Pennsylvania and, shortly before his death in 1795, attorney general of the United States. Madison's relationship with Freneau would prove to be the most politically significant. Amid the partisan battles of the 1790s, Madison and Jefferson helped Freneau establish a friendly newspaper, the *National Gazette*, in Philadelphia.[57]

The young Virginian flourished academically as well as socially. Under Witherspoon's direction, Madison read legal commentators like Grotius and Pufendorf, as well as the Scottish moral philosophers. He set himself an ambitious goal of graduating early, sometimes sleeping fewer than five hours a night. He received a degree in the fall of 1771, but fatigue and overwork seem to have aggravated his physical maladies. Of the twelve members of his class, Madison was the only one who did not speak at their graduation. He shared Jefferson's indifferent oratorical skills, but he may have been excused for illness. As he recounted in his autobiography, his "health being at the time too infirm for the journey home," he stayed in Princeton for the winter, in effect doing graduate work in law, Hebrew, and "miscellaneous studies."[58]

Madison returned to Virginia less provincial than he had left it and more religious. At Princeton, in addition to Witherspoon's influence, Madison had read Reverend Samuel Clarke's *The Being and Attributes of God* (1704), which argued for the existence of God from the nature of the physical world rather than from Scripture. Clarke's brand of rationalism fell from grace in the 1800s, but at the time it impressed Madison.[59] His letters to William Bradford, his only surviving correspondence from this period, illustrate his faith. He wrote Bradford in November 1772, "A watchful eye must be kept on ourselves lest while we are building ideal monuments of Renown and Bliss here we neglect to have our names enrolled in the Annals of Heaven." He commended Bradford's plans to spend the winter studying "History and the Science of Morals," adding that he assumed Bradford would "season them with a little divinity now and then." In another letter, he asked Bradford to send him a published collection of sermons, perhaps Witherspoon's. He complained elsewhere of currently popular books that he thought unfairly attacked religion.[60]

He seemed disappointed when Bradford decided to become a lawyer, not a minister: "I can only condole with the Church on the loss of a fine Genius and persuasive orator." Madison urged him to keep the ministry in mind as a possible second career and called religion "the most sublime of all Sciences." The law, by contrast, presented troublesome ethical challenges. "I greatly commend your determined adherence to probity and Truth in the Character of a lawyer," he wrote Bradford, "but fear it would be impracticable."[61]

Madison sounded like a young man who wanted to enter the ministry himself, but he was a poor public speaker, and as he recalled later, when he first returned to Virginia, "he continued for several years in very feeble health." Any hints about his personal religious beliefs soon disappeared from his letters, and he never talked publicly about them. We can only speculate as to why his zeal waned so quickly. John Witherspoon's absence surely played a role. Organized religion in pre-Revolutionary Virginia offered, to Madison's way of thinking, few attractive options. Madison resented the intolerance and privileged position of the established church, and "the enthusiasm" of the dissenting denominations, he thought, "render[s] them obnoxious to sober opinion." Once the American Revolution erupted, the secular world of politics provided a compelling distraction from religion. Perhaps his declining piety reflected frustration at what he saw as his physical incapacity for the ministry.[62]

Yet as his health began to improve, Madison started to read law, not theology. He labored at it off and on for two or three years, but he did not enjoy "the coarse and dry study of the Law," and he never really wanted to be

The Coarse and Dry Study of the Law

an attorney.[63] Constitutional law, especially the issue of religious freedom, however, did interest him. "The principles & Modes of Government are too important to be disregarded by an Inquisitive mind," he wrote Bradford. Madison asked his former classmate for a summary of Pennsylvania's laws pertaining to freedom of conscience and for Bradford's opinion on whether an established church was necessary "to support civil society."[64]

It must have been a rhetorical question. Madison claimed late in life to have been "under very early & strong impressions in favor of Liberty both Civil & Religious." In what would be one of the fundamental principles of his political philosophy, Madison concluded well before the American Revolution that a state church was a threat not simply to freedom of conscience and public morals but to freedom in general and even to economic prosperity. If the Anglican Church had been the established faith in the North as well as in the South, "it is clear to me that slavery and Subjection might and would have been gradually insinuated among us. Union of Religious Sentiments begets a surprizing confidence and Ecclesiastical Establishments tend to great ignorance and Corruption all of which facilitate the Execution of mischievous Projects." In Virginia, with its established church, "Poverty and Luxury prevail among all sorts: Pride ignorance and Knavery among the Priesthood and Vice and Wickedness among the Laity." In Madison's mind, Pennsylvania's tradition of religious tolerance even explained why Bradford's home colony seemed more prosperous than Virginia: "Religious bondage shackles and debilitates the mind and unfits it for every noble enterprize."[65]

In January 1774, when, in the conventional narrative, taxation without representation had estranged American patriots from Great Britain, Madison complained "that diabolical Hell conceived principle of persecution . . . vexes me the most of any thing whatever." Five or six Baptist ministers had been jailed in an adjacent county, apparently for preaching without a license. Madison had lobbied unsuccessfully for their release, and he doubted any relief would come from the assembly. Virginia's elite were too narrow-minded, he thought, and the Anglican clergy's ties to English bishops and the king gave them too much influence.[66]

Meanwhile, the worsening imperial crisis could not be ignored. William Bradford sent him a newspaper account of the Boston Tea Party. Madison ordered from England a copy of Joseph Priestley's *Essay on the First Principles of Government and on the Nature of Political, Civil, and Religious Liberty*, which argued for natural rights and limited government. He asked Bradford to send him a copy of Adam Ferguson's *Essay on the History of Civil Society*;

it emphasized the need for a system of constitutional checks and balances. After his return from his trip north in the spring of 1774, Madison found Virginians "generally very warm" in their support for Boston's patriots and willing to cooperate with the other colonies "in any expedient measure."[67]

———

THOMAS JEFFERSON wrote his first great public paper, *A Summary View of the Rights of British America*, in the summer of 1774. The title was not his creation, and the work had inauspicious beginnings. Albemarle County had elected him as one of its representatives to the convention scheduled to meet in Williamsburg in August. He began the essay as proposed instructions to the delegates whom the convention would send to the upcoming Continental Congress. Although the term "instructions" is typically used to describe his efforts, it is a misnomer. What became known as *A Summary View* was actually a brief against the authority of Parliament and the conduct of George III. Jefferson's earlier readings had not concentrated on the problems of government, but they had included ample doses of political philosophy and constitutional history; the transition from law to politics came naturally. Jefferson planned to take his draft to Williamsburg, but he was waylaid by dysentery on the road and forced to go back to Monticello. Still hoping to influence the deliberations, Jefferson sent copies of his draft to Patrick Henry and Peyton Randolph, who was to preside over the convention.[68]

As far as we know, Henry never shared his copy with anyone. Jefferson suggested later, perhaps unfairly, that Henry may have been "too lazy to read it (for he was the laziest man in reading I ever knew)." Years later, Jefferson conceded that Henry "probably thought it too bold as a first measure." Whatever motivated Henry, when the other delegates saw Peyton Randolph's copy, they dismissed Jefferson's language as too extreme. They adopted more moderate instructions warning that "his Majesty's faithful subjects of this colony . . . are in Danger of being deprived of their natural, ancient, constitutional, and chartered Rights." The delegates also adopted an "association" in which they agreed not to import British goods, except for medicine, after 1 November and, "unless American Grievances are addressed," to halt exports to Great Britain after 10 August 1775. On his printed copy of the convention's instructions, Jefferson added a short list of the "defects in the association." They included a complaint that illustrated his growing sense of American nationalism: "We are to conform to such resolutions only of the Congress as our deputies assent to: which totally destroys that union of conduct in the several countries which was the very purpose of calling a Congress."[69] Even though Jefferson could still speak of the colonies as separate countries, he hoped they would stand united against the British.

According to Edmund Randolph, Jefferson's draft was read at a large, but informal, meeting at Peyton Randolph's house and received a warm reception. If it was too bold for a state paper at the time—and Jefferson admitted later that it likely was—Jefferson had produced a brilliant political polemic. His allies had it printed in Williamsburg under the title by which we know it, and A Summary View was soon reprinted in Philadelphia and London.[70]

Jefferson's argument rested on the colonial charters and English law and, somewhat more heavily, on natural law and English history. Parliament had infringed upon "those rights which God and the laws have given equally and independently to all." He began by asserting a natural right to emigrate and to establish "new societies" as their founders saw fit. Britain's Saxon ancestors had migrated to ancient England "under this universal law," and their country of origin had never claimed jurisdiction over them. America, moreover, "was conquered, and her settlements made, and firmly established, at the expense of individuals, and not of the British public." American colonists adopted the English law with which they were familiar and submitted to the English king, "who was thereby made the central link connecting the several parts of the empire."[71]

The monarchy would soon begin to abuse its prerogatives. Starting with the grant of Maryland to Lord Baltimore in 1632, a "new family of princes" would parcel out America to court favorites. The natural right of "free trade . . . was the next object of unjust encroachment" as Parliament adopted Navigation Acts requiring major American exports be sent to Great Britain and requiring American trade to be carried in British ships. Jefferson argued that "the true ground on which we declare these acts void is, that the British parliament has no right to exercise authority over us." In a similar vein, Jefferson condemned a recent act suspending the New York legislature. The "principles of common sense" and "the common feelings of human nature" would have to be surrendered before Americans could "be persuaded to believe that they hold their political existence at the will of a British parliament." The Intolerable Acts were "the acts of power, assumed by a body of men, foreign to our constitutions, and unacknowledged by our laws."[72]

Jefferson repeatedly combined arguments from natural and English law. "By the constitution of Great Britain, as well of the several American states," the king could veto legislative acts, but George III had used his power arbitrarily. He had vetoed colonial attempts to end the African slave trade while refusing to overrule oppressive acts of Parliament. He had not dissolved Parliament since the Glorious Revolution, but he had, in violation of the natural rights of mankind, dissolved colonial assemblies. "From the nature of things, every society must at all times possess within itself the sovereign powers of legislation," Jefferson declared. "The feelings of human nature revolt against the supposition of a state so situated as that it may not in any emergency provide against dangers which perhaps threaten immediate ruin."[73]

Jefferson moved next to an argument that seems almost extraneous but that was something of an obsession for him: the claim that William the Conquer and Norman lawyers had introduced feudalism to England. The island's Saxon inhabitants had, he claimed, rightfully held their land without feudal restraints. "Our ancestors, however, who migrated hither, were farmers, not lawyers," and they naively accepted land grants in America from the king. In reality, "from the nature and purpose of civil institutions," the territory of a state can be distributed only by the people or their lawful representatives. Otherwise, "each individual of the society may appropriate to himself such lands as he finds vacant, and occupancy will give him title." Contrary to natural law and the Saxon tradition, however, George III had lately made it more difficult to obtain land in America, and "the population of our country is likely to be checked. It is time, therefore, . . . to declare that he has no right to grant lands himself."[74]

A Summary View closes with the rhetorical flourishes that gave it much of its force. One echoed Scottish moral sense philosophy: "The great principles of right and wrong are legible to every reader; to pursue them requires not the aid of many counsellors. The whole art of government consists in the art of being honest." There was an almost perfunctory denunciation of taxation without representation, and then another ringing phrase near the end: "The God who gave us life gave us liberty at the same time."[75]

Publication of *A Summary View* made Jefferson's reputation as a writer. Harsh in his attacks on the Crown and legalistic in his approach to history and precedent, Jefferson had nevertheless produced a political essay of literary grace and pugnacious clarity. Admittedly, it had flaws. He said later there were gaps and inaccuracies that he thought could be "readily corrected" when he reached Williamsburg, but he never got there. Jefferson exaggerated the Saxon tradition of liberty and alodial land ownership, minimized the security Britain had provided its colonies, and showed no concern about paying the costs of imperial administration. Nor was he entirely original, despite his claim later that when he wrote *A Summary View* only George Wythe agreed with him.[76]

The Coarse and Dry Study of the Law

In essence, Jefferson argued that Parliament had no grounds on which to exercise its jurisdiction over the colonies but conceded that they were part of the British Empire and would recognize the authority of the king, although he had often abused his discretion. James Madison said later that "a denial of these principles by Great Britain, and the assertion of them by Americans, produced the Revolution." In July 1774, after reading a pamphlet by the English cleric and apologist Josiah Tucker, Madison wrote William Bradford that Tucker's "ingenious and plausible defence of Parliamentary Authority, carries in it such defects and misrepresentations as Confirm me in political Orthodoxy." The editors of the most comprehensive edition of Madison's published papers conclude from those comments that by then Madison was apparently prepared, with Jefferson, to deny "any rightful authority of Parliament over the colonies."[77] He probably was. Orthodoxy, however, is not easily defined.

Much of Jefferson's argument could be traced to two pamphlets by the venerable Virginia lawyer and burgess Richard Bland, *The Colonel Dismounted* (1764) and *An Inquiry into the Rights of the British Colonies* (1766). Americans were not a conquered people, Bland had reasoned, and accordingly under English law were "only subject to laws made with their own consent." Exercising their natural law right to emigrate, private "Adventurers" had established new political communities in America at no cost to the British nation and then freely negotiated compacts with the monarch. Those colonial charters left them independent in their internal affairs but subjects of the king. Since Americans were not represented in Parliament, Bland's writings made any exercise of parliamentary authority in the colonies suspect, but not willing to go that far, Bland conceded Parliament could regulate the colonies' external affairs, that is, their trade.[78]

Yet parliamentary authority over colonial commerce remained problematic. As early as 1764, Stephen Hopkins of Rhode Island, trying to limit Parliament's jurisdiction over the colonies to the regulation of trade, could find no justification for trade regulations other than necessity: "Some such general power should exist somewhere." Edmund Randolph thought the Virginia convention had refused to adopt *A Summary View* because the delegates accepted John Dickinson's position in his *Letters of a Pennsylvania Farmer* that Parliament could impose duties for purposes of regulating foreign commerce. Even the more militant George Mason could tolerate trade regulations as a matter of prudence and comity, although they were, he wrote, "in some Degree repugnant to the Principles of the Constitution."[79]

By contrast, Mason's younger brother, the lawyer Thomson Mason, who opposed nonimportation as likely to injure innocent victims, argued that the distinction between taxation and trade regulations "is merely nominal, and not worth contending for." He urged Americans to ignore any act of Parliament passed after 1607 since they would have had no part in its adoption. In 1768, William Hicks of Philadelphia published in New York an essay, *The Nature and Extent of Parliamentary Power Considered*, arguing that no reason existed to distinguish taxation from ordinary legislation.[80] By that same year, if not earlier, Benjamin Franklin had come to question the logic of any partial limits on Parliament's jurisdiction. He wrote his son William in March 1768, "Something might be made of either of the extremes: that Parliament has a power to make all laws for us, or that it has a power to make no laws for us; and I think the arguments for the latter more numerous and weighty than those of the former." By 1770, Franklin had embraced the position Jefferson would take four years later. "We have the same king" as England, he wrote a French correspondent, "but not the same legislatures."[81]

In Massachusetts, Sam and John Adams could defend trade regulations on the grounds of "implied consent" while asserting the colony's autonomy in its internal affairs. In North Carolina, another Whig leader, the prominent lawyer James Iredell, seemed willing to accept some acts of Parliament as a matter of convenience.[82] But the logic of American resistance soon carried other lawyers and politicians to more extreme positions. In Pennsylvania, James Wilson's *Considerations on the Nature and Extent of the Legislative Authority of the British Parliament* (1774) made the case that, consistent with natural law, the British constitution provided certain safeguards limiting the power of Parliament. Members were elected, stood for reelection, and shared common interests with the inhabitants of Great Britain. Those checks on the abuse of parliamentary discretion did not apply beyond the British Isles, and Wilson could cite precedents holding that, in the normal course, acts of Parliament did not apply in Virginia, Jamaica, or Ireland. Noting the colonies' opposition to Parliament's efforts to tax them, Wilson concluded, "A denial of it [Parliament's authority] in those instances is, in effect, a denial of it in all other instances."[83]

Wilson's impact on Jefferson is hard to gauge. The Pennsylvania lawyer apparently wrote his pamphlet in 1770, but it was not published until 1774, probably too late to have influenced *A Summary View*. One of Jefferson's commonplace books contains an abstract of Wilson's essay, but it is unclear when Jefferson made his notes.[84] Yet Wilson's *Considerations on the Nature and Extent of the Legislative Authority*, and other slightly more cautious productions, suggests one reason for *A Summary View*'s appeal. If Jefferson was in the vanguard of Revolutionary thought, he was not too far ahead of public opinion. In two years, if not sooner, the public would catch up.[85]

Ironically, the specter of new taxes produced greater anxiety than did existing trade regulations, which were arguably more burdensome than any taxes the British had tried to levy. As Edmund Randolph put it, the American Revolution began "without an immediate oppression, without a cause depending so much on hasty feeling as theoretic reasoning." Their colonial charters had guaranteed Americans the rights of English subjects. Those rights included freedom from taxation without representation, a maxim that "every generation of lawyers imbibed . . . in their studies." If the Americans could be taxed without their consent, American property was at "the mercy of Parliament," and Parliament could no longer be trusted. "Corruption," Randolph recalled after the Revolution, "was making gigantic strides in England."[86]

Until the adoption of the Sugar Act in 1764, which raised duties on a number of imported items, however, Americans had not given much thought to the proper scope of parliamentary power, and there were few, if any, obvious constitutional limits. Opposition to the hated Stamp Act, which imposed a direct tax on printed goods, forced its almost immediate repeal. At the same time, the Stamp Act controversy left many Americans fearful of what Parliament might do next, and it created a need for a constitutional defense of American interests, not one based simply on equity or practicalities. During the subsequent debate over the Townshend Duties, John Dickinson helped de-escalate the Anglo-American crisis by suggesting Americans could accept "eternal" taxes to regulate foreign trade, but the narrow focus on specific forms of taxation inhibited discussion of the broader issues: the colonies' legal relationship to the British government and their constitutional status within the empire.[87]

However muddled those issues can look in hindsight, American thinking was less confused than it might appear. Constitutional arguments in the eighteenth century resembled common-law litigation, not attempts to discover metaphysical truths. American advocates pressed their case with a lawyer's logic, not a philosopher's, and took positions that were "both narrow enough to defend successfully and broad enough to win the point at bar."[88] Jefferson, by contrast, cannot have believed *A Summary View* would have changed minds in Britain, and his apparent disregard for British opinion may have contributed to the essay's unique allure. We cannot be sure of Jefferson's motives, but he may have been aiming his message at an American audience, not British policy makers, and at posterity.

One fundamental issue lurked behind all the rest: the nature of the British constitution. Was it a higher law that could limit the authority of Parliament, or was it simply the will of Parliament itself? After the Glorious Revolution, Parliament gradually evolved from a check on the discretion of the monarchy to the source of sovereignty within the realm. Modern historians have, as a result, tended to disparage American appeals to a higher law that would condemn acts of Parliament as unconstitutional. In reality, constitutional theory in mid-eighteenth-century Britain remained ambiguous at best. If the ramshackle legal arrangements under which the empire operated did not cause the American Revolution, they at least invited a series of constitutional crises.[89]

Several reasons explain the persisting confusion around the emerging doctrine of parliamentary supremacy. While the principal legacy of the Glorious Revolution was to strengthen the hand of Parliament in its dealings with the monarch, it was also a victory for local autonomy, as the rise of representative assemblies in Ireland and in the American colonies attests. The idea of a higher law that had existed since time immemorial had deep roots in English political culture; from that perspective the events of 1688–89 could be seen as an effort to restore ancient, fundamental law rather than as an attempt to establish the sovereignty of Parliament. No less a parliamentarian than Edmund Burke observed that the British people preferred to think of their rights as an inheritance from their ancestors, not as a product of abstract reason. And if British subjects admitted unequivocally that the ancient constitution under which they claimed their liberties had been superseded by a constitution under which the will of Parliament was supreme, how secure would those freedoms be?[90]

Jefferson readily embraced and apparently exaggerated the legacy of Saxon liberty. He believed Saxons of the fifth and sixth centuries had brought to England an elected king, an annual assembly of tribal chiefs, trial by jury, and freehold landownership. Modern scholars have disagreed; Garrett Ward Sheldon points out that "to the extent native Saxons possessed any organized society and government, it was tribal and chieftain rather than the ideal liberal order of John Locke." British writers in Jefferson's day had a different opinion. They saw English history as a struggle to recover rights, lost in the Norman Conquest, that had culminated in the Glorious Revolution. Jefferson, and most of his American contemporaries, disagreed mainly on one point; they believed the restoration effort was ongoing, a view held in Britain only by the "commonwealth men," as the more radical Whigs were sometimes known.[91]

Publication of *A Summary View* did more than establish Jefferson's renown as the most effective writer among American Whigs. It marked his emergence as a major political figure, and consequently the beginning of the end of his legal career. In November 1774 he recorded his last entry in his legal ledger book—for an opinion on a will—and he turned over his law practice to Edmund Randolph. He would need more time to manage the estate he had inherited from his late father-in-law, John Wayles, and he would need more time for politics.[92]

TWO

A Happy Talent of Composition

1774–1776

IN THE FALL OF 1774, James Madison's political views may have been even more radical than Thomas Jefferson's. Writing his college classmate William Bradford in Philadelphia, Madison seemed ready for war with Great Britain. "Would it not be advisable as soon as possible," he asked, "to begin our defense[?]" In September, the First Continental Congress approved the Suffolk Resolves. Introduced by the Massachusetts delegates, the resolves, among other things, declared the Coercive Acts to be unconstitutional and urged the colonies to prepare for war. In October, Congress approved the Continental Association. Based on a proposal from Virginia, it called for an end of imports from and exports to the British Isles. Madison reported to Bradford that Virginians "universally approved" the measures. In December, Orange County voters elected Madison to the county Committee of Safety that would enforce the economic boycott against Britain. Madison was the committee's youngest member; his father was elected chair.[1]

By January 1775, Virginia was busy preparing for "a sudden invasion," while the younger Madison could boast to Bradford that the colony would soon have thousands of "well trained High Spirited men" ready to come to its defense. As a group, only the Quakers, he said, had refused to support the Continental Association. Madison became a champion of civil liberties later in life, but he was not so broad-minded on the eve of the American Revolution. The Orange County committee passed a resolution proposing that pro-British pamphlets be "publicly burnt." Madison may have written it. In any event, he showed no sympathy for ministers of the established church who seemed hostile or indifferent to the American cause. In Orange County, the Reverend John Wingate abandoned his pulpit in the Brick Church after the Committee of Safety seized and destroyed Loyalist pamphlets in his possession. In Culpeper County, the Reverend James Herdman was expelled for refusing to observe a day of prayer and fasting called by the Continental Congress.[2]

In mid-April, fighting finally erupted between British redcoats and American militiamen at Lexington and Concord, Massachusetts. Virginia, meanwhile, faced its own crisis when a nervous royal governor, Lord Dunmore, transferred gunpowder from the public magazine in Williamsburg to a British warship in the York River. Fourteen militia companies, intending to recover the gunpowder by force, assembled in Fredericksburg. Most of Virginia's leaders wanted to avoid violence, and the militia stood little chance of retrieving the gunpowder from the Royal Navy. Not to be deterred, Patrick Henry led his own march on the capital and persuaded the colonial receiver general to agree to reimburse the militia for the lost powder. Henry's boldness irritated Whig leaders who hoped to avoid war, but Madison was unperturbed. Henry's conduct, Madison thought, "gained him great honor in the most spirited parts of the Country."[3]

One concern tempered Madison's revolutionary zeal: the fear of a slave revolt. Months before the hostilities began, he had predicted that if a "hostile rupture" between America and Britain came, "an Insurrection among the slaves may & will be promoted." In the fall of 1774, he reported rumors from one Virginia county that slaves had met, chosen a leader, and agreed to wait for the supposedly imminent arrival of British troops. After the fighting broke out in Massachusetts, Madison began to suspect Dunmore of "tampering with the Slaves." It is, he wrote Bradford, "the only part in which this Colony is vulnerable." Ironically, however, Dunmore's efforts proved counterproductive. His promise of freedom to slaves who would fight alongside the British attracted some recruits, but it mainly served to unite Virginia's elite behind the patriot cause.[4]

Madison felt confident in the "great unanimity" among white Virginians and in their "Military Ardor." In October, the Virginia Committee of Safety commissioned him a colonel in the Orange County militia, putting him second in command behind James Madison Sr. He bragged to Bradford about the expert marksmanship of the riflemen from the "upland counties" and about his own proficiency with a rifle. Yet his contribution to the

Revolution would be more intellectual than martial. He had, true to form, recently ordered a copy of Joseph Priestley's treatise on government from London; fearing now his order would run afoul of the Continental Association, he asked Bradford to send him a copy from Philadelphia. Despite his commission, Madison would never see combat. He was, as he wrote later, "restrained from entering into the military service by the unsettled state of his health and the discouraging feebleness of his constitution."[5]

While Madison struggled with a host of ailments, Jefferson faced new political responsibilities and a series of personal crises. The bloodshed at Lexington and Concord, he wrote William Small, had "cut off our last hopes of reconciliation" and triggered "a phrenzy of revenge" among "all ranks of people." He saw no hope for peace absent "the effectual interposition of arms."[6]

In February 1775, Lord North had proposed in the House of Commons that if a colony would contribute a specified sum to support the common defense and its civil government, Parliament would impose no additional taxes. When the Virginia burgesses assembled in early June, Jefferson's kinsman Peyton Randolph, the Speaker of the house, asked him to draft a reply to North's "conciliatory proposal." Much of Jefferson's response was predictable. A lump-sum assessment by Parliament "only changes the form of oppression, without lightening its burthen." Consistent with the argument he had made in A Summary View, Jefferson claimed that "Parliament has no right to intermeddle with the support of civil government in the Colonies." Less predictable perhaps was the flash of an American nationalism that would become central to Jefferson's thinking: "We consider ourselves as bound in Honor as well as Interest to share one general Fate with our sister colonies, and should hold ourselves bare Deserters of that Union, to which we have acceded, were we to agree on any Measures distinct and apart from them." Virginia, in short, would make no separate peace with Great Britain. The assembly approved Jefferson's draft virtually intact, albeit, as he complained later, with "a dash of cold water on it here & there."[7]

In March 1775, a second Virginia convention had chosen Jefferson as an alternate to the Second Continental Congress in the event Peyton Randolph was unable to serve. After Dunmore issued a call for a June meeting of the assembly, Randolph had left Philadelphia for Williamsburg. Jefferson, in turn, left the Virginia capital on 11 June and arrived in Philadelphia nine days later. A poor speaker, Jefferson rarely participated in legislative debates, but his reticence served him well. It allowed him to avoid publicly challenging or embarrassing an opponent, and he made fewer enemies than did his more loquacious colleagues. Usually quiet on an assembly floor, Jefferson

A Happy Talent of Composition

worked effectively behind the scenes. John Adams found him "prompt, frank, explicit, and decisive upon committees and in conversation."[8]

Jefferson's first major committee assignment was to draft a statement of the American position that became known as the Declaration of the Causes and Necessity of Taking Up Arms. Hoping to produce a draft on which all the delegates could agree, Jefferson took what was, for him, a relatively moderate tone. He repeated many of the arguments from *A Summary View*, but he did not attempt to ground American rights in an ancient Saxon tradition of liberty. He admitted that "some occasional assumptions of power by the parliament of Great Britain, however unacknowledged by the constitution of our governments, were finally acquiesced in thro' warmth of affection." He conceded all had been well until 1763, when a cabal of mischievous ministers had hatched a plot to enslave America, and he appealed to George III to mediate what he framed as a dispute between the colonies and Parliament.[9]

After Parliament's passage of the Restraining Acts, prohibiting trade with America, the mood in Congress had grown more militant. Jefferson's draft seems not to have completely satisfied the committee. John Dickinson, a highly regarded Pennsylvania moderate, substantially revised his work, cutting parts of it and—surprisingly, given Dickinson's views—adding more forceful language. Congress approved the final result. Jefferson apparently resented Dickinson's assistance—he claimed later that his draft had been "too strong for Mr. Dickinson"—but some of his ideas that did not survive Dickinson's editing would reappear in the Declaration of Independence, including his theory of a legitimate government as a voluntary compact between the people and their rulers, not a hierarchical regime of a king and his subjects.[10]

Another assignment went more smoothly and helped solidify his standing with the other delegates. After having prepared Virginia's response to Lord North's peace proposal, Jefferson was a logical choice to serve on a committee with Richard Henry Lee, John Adams, and Benjamin Franklin to draft a reply for Congress. In preparing the committee's report, Jefferson took a combative tone: "The colonies of America are entitled to the sole and exclusive privilege of giving and granting their own money." He linked taxation without representation and the Navigation Acts, which restricted American trade to British ships and for the most part to British ports; if Americans were to be taxed by Parliament, they ought in all fairness be allowed the benefits of free trade. And he did not limit himself to taxation or even trade. He also attacked the Quebec Act, the Quartering Act, and a host of other imperial policies. Congress adopted the draft with only minor changes and then adjourned in early August for a short recess.[11]

The break allowed Jefferson to go to Richmond for a third Virginia convention, which elected him a delegate to the Continental Congress in his own right. He continued to hope, without much optimism, for a reconciliation with Great Britain. Peace, he claimed, would allow him to retire from public life. He doubted now that Congress would agree to a return to the imperial relationship of 1763, and, as Jefferson told his Loyalist cousin John Randolph, "by the god who made me I will cease to exist before I yield to a connection on such terms as the British parliament propose." The winter of 1775–76 would be one of the most stressful periods of Jefferson's life. In September, shortly before he returned to Congress, his eighteen-month-old daughter, Jane, died. In Philadelphia, Jefferson worried about his wife Patty's health and then grieved over the death in October of his popular fellow delegate Peyton Randolph, who died suddenly of "apoplexy." Jefferson went home in the spring, where his mother suffered a fatal stroke in March. The strain left him temporarily disabled by a round of migraine headaches.[12]

Jefferson produced no great state papers in the fall session of Congress. He did prepare an unpublished rebuttal after George III delivered a speech in Parliament stressing Britain's role in establishing the American colonies. The London Company, not the Crown, had founded Virginia, Jefferson replied, and he went so far as to question the legality of Charles I's assumption of the Virginia charter in 1626. Jefferson could still talk of "our own constitution" not as a single written document but as a composite of precedent and tradition that made Virginia independent of Parliament.[13]

More importantly, however, service in Congress encouraged Jefferson to think more deeply about the idea of America as a nation and not simply a collection of autonomous sovereignties. "The enterprising genius and intrepidity" of the New Englanders he encountered in Philadelphia impressed him. He chafed when Virginia lawmakers claimed they would not obey congressional resolutions their delegates did not support.[14]

He took notes when Benjamin Franklin introduced a draft agreement among the states that would have created "a firm league of friendship" to promote the common defense and the general welfare. Presumably sympathetic, Jefferson proposed an unsuccessful amendment giving Congress an exclusive right to buy western lands. As to Franklin's general welfare clause, Jefferson wrote on his copy, "There should be no vague terms in an instrument of this kind. It's [sic] objects should be precisely and determinately fixed." As we shall see, nothing came of Franklin's plan. Jefferson's subsequent report on the powers of a congressional committee to manage the war effort during a recess met a similar fate. But by the spring of 1776, Jefferson had gained invaluable experience in the problems of republican government.[15]

——

ON 4 DECEMBER 1775, roughly a month after Lord Dunmore had declared martial law, the Continental Congress recommended that Virginia hold new elections and "establish such form of government" as the Virginia convention deemed necessary. The colony's leaders hesitated to act because some saw the creation of a new government as a virtual declaration of independence. Events soon pushed them in that direction. George III had ignored Congress's Olive Branch Petition proposing a cease-fire. Reports reached America that the British intended to use German mercenaries—the notorious Hessians—against them. And in January 1776, Thomas Paine's wildly popular essay *Common Sense*, which made a strong case for independence in language anyone could understand, appeared in Philadelphia. The fighting itself helped radicalize Virginians. In December, Virginia and North Carolina militia defeated Dunmore and a Loyalist force at Great Bridge near Norfolk; on the first day of the new year, Dunmore ordered the shelling of the harbor.[16]

On 10 May 1776, the Continental Congress resolved that all the colonies should consider establishing new governments. Five days later the delegates added a preamble to the resolution proposing that royal authority be "totally suppressed." At this point, Virginia's revolutionaries needed no encouragement. On the same day that Congress amended its 10 May resolution, a fifth Virginia convention authorized its congressional representatives to support independence. The Virginia resolution also suggested Congress take "proper and necessary" measures to form foreign alliances and a confederation of the colonies, providing that "the regulations of the internal concerns of each colony, be left to the respective colonial legislatures." The convention then began work on a constitution for what would soon be the new, independent state of Virginia.[17]

Jefferson, who had just returned to Philadelphia after eight days on horseback, hoped he might be recalled so he could assist the convention. Other states that were writing new constitutions had recalled some of their representatives. He called it "a work of the most interesting nature and such as every individual would wish to have his voice in." Organizing new governments, he wrote Thomas Nelson, "is the whole object of the present controversy; for should a bad government be instituted for us in [the] future it had been as well to have accepted at first the bad one offered to us from beyond the water without the risk and expense of contest." Nothing, apart from winning the Revolutionary War, was more important to Americans in 1776 than establishing their state governments. The Virginia convention elected not to recall Jefferson; Richard Henry Lee and George Wythe went in his place.[18]

Jefferson was not deterred. For the rest of May and into early June, he spent most of his time preparing his own version of a Virginia constitution. Going through three drafts, he probably devoted more effort to the constitution than he would to the Declaration of Independence a few days later. By 1776, a consensus had emerged among Americans that a constitution should be a written document, although other issues remained in flux. The idea a constitution could define the prerogatives of a government, and especially of a legislature, as we have seen, was much debated, but the colonial charters had seemed to work that way. As Bernard Bailyn has written, "It took no wrench of mind, no daring leap, to accept, by then, the concept of a fixed, written constitution limiting the ordinary actions of government." The unwritten British constitution, by contrast, had caused Americans troubles without end. They had found themselves in the tenuous position of arguing that acts of Parliament had violated uncodified legal norms, a distinction that evolved in the colonies into the difference between an ordinary statute and constitutional law. Jefferson wanted to make the difference clear.[19]

John Adams's essay *Thoughts on Government*, which was circulating widely among the political elite, may have influenced Jefferson's thinking. Adams and Jefferson rejected the view of Thomas Hobbes and like-minded conservative philosophers who held that sovereignty was an indivisible authority vested by providence in a monarch. They instead believed sovereignty rested in the people, who could distribute power throughout a political system as they saw fit; the idea gave American constitution writers considerable flexibility and would be essential to the creation of a federal system under the United States Constitution.[20]

Adams's essay presumed that "there is no good government but what is republican," a term he defined as "'an empire of laws and not of men.'" *Thoughts on Government* called for the creation of bicameral legislatures and separate executive officers who would be selected by the legislature. The governor could veto legislation and, with the "advice and consent" of the upper house—in the colonial nomenclature, Adams called it the "council"—appoint judges. Judges should be trained lawyers and, to ensure their independence, serve during good behavior. Citing the republican maxim "'where annual elections end, there slavery begins,'" Adams proposed lawmakers and

A Happy Talent of Composition

the governor serve one-year terms, although he conceded that in time the legislature might choose to extend their terms. Leaving so fundamental an issue to legislative discretion suggests that Adams had not solved a problem that would perplex Jefferson and others: How could a constitution limit the legislature while still permitting needed reforms?[21]

Jefferson completed his draft state constitution sometime before the middle of June 1776. He began with a preamble listing a series of grievances against George III, derelictions of duty by which he "has forfeited the kingly office" and effectively discredited the position. "All experience" has shown that "the public liberty may be more certainly secured" by abolishing the monarchy. Jefferson went on to assert that it was now "necessary to re-establish such ancient principles as are friendly to the rights of the people," a claim that echoed his fixation with the myth of Saxon liberty. He closed the preamble with a simple statement that the legislative, executive, and judicial branches must be separate, or, in other words, no person could hold office in more than one branch of government.[22]

Jefferson's first substantive section dealt with the structure and powers of the legislature. It would consist of two houses. Members of the lower house, or "house of Representatives," would be popularly elected by county for one-year terms. Adult males who owned a quarter acre in town or twenty-five acres in the county and paid taxes could vote. All voters could serve in the lower house. Senators had to be at least thirty-one years old and were elected by the lower house for nine-year terms, with no possibility of reelection. The first class of senators would serve abbreviated, staggered terms so one-third of the senators would leave office every three years. Judges of the general court and the High Court of Chancery could participate in senate debates, but they could not vote. Only the lower house could originate or amend bills for levying taxes.[23]

The composition of the senate proved difficult. Almost everyone except Thomas Paine and the most populist of revolutionaries favored a bicameral assembly as a check on popular passions, but why have two houses unless each had a distinctive character? In England, the House of Lords represented the aristocracy, but America would have no legally sanctioned upper class. In 1776, Jefferson saw the senate not as a representative body but as a council of judicious elders. He explained, in designing his senate, "I had two things in view: to get the wisest men chosen and to make them independent when chosen." He thought a selection by the house, as opposed to a popular vote, would ensure the former: "I have ever observed that a choice by the people themselves is not generally distinguished for it's [sic] wisdom. . . . But give to those so chosen by the people a second choice themselves, and they generally will chuse wise men."[24]

He feared allowing senators to run for reelection would compromise their independence. "My idea was," he wrote Edmund Pendleton, "that if they might be re-elected, they would be casting their eye forward to the period of election . . . & be currying favor with the electors." By serving fixed terms, they would understand "that they were at a certain period to return into the mass of the people & become the governed instead of the governor." Jefferson indicated he might reluctantly accept lifetime appointments, or "any thing rather than a mere creation & dependence on the people." He concurred in the prevailing assumption that the senate, to ensure political stability and implicitly to protect property rights, would be less democratic and probably more conservative than the house, but he would go only so far in making it a bastion of privilege. He rejected the idea that there should be any unusual property requirement for service in the senate; "my observations do not enable me to say I think integrity the characteristic of wealth."[25]

The second section of Jefferson's Virginia constitution, dealing with the executive branch, created an "Administrator," not a governor. The break from conventional terminology suggested the pedestrian role Jefferson envisioned for a republican executive. The administrator would be elected annually by the house and could serve three consecutive terms. Among several limits on executive power, the administrator could not veto legislation, dissolve the assembly, or make war, and the chief executive had to act with the advice and consent of a privy council appointed by the house of representatives. The executive enjoyed only a modest power of appointment. The lower house selected the state treasurer and attorney general. Jefferson proposed letting local voters elect county sheriffs and coroners.[26]

A third section established a new state judicial system while retaining much of the common-law legalese. Jefferson provided for county courts and other courts of inferior jurisdiction and, above the local courts, a general court and a High Court of Chancery. Their members would be appointed by the administrator with the approval of the Privy Council, but judges on the general and chancery courts had to be members of the William and Mary law faculty who had practiced law in Virginia for at least seven years. The courts' jurisdiction was to be defined by the legislature. A court of appeals, appointed by the house of representatives, stood at the apex of Jefferson's judicial system. Jefferson apparently intended for judges to serve lifetime appointments, but the court of appeals could remove lower court judges for "misbehavior," and appeals court judges could be removed by the legislature

A Happy Talent of Composition

on the same grounds. At least with regard to the application of criminal law, Jefferson hoped the judge could "be a mere machine," applying acts of the assembly with a minimum of discretion. In fact, increasingly professional American courts would soon begin to assert their autonomy, and Jefferson and James Madison would not know quite what to do with them.[27]

A fourth and final section Jefferson labeled "Rights, Private and Public." He had included language in the first section of his draft banning torture and outlawing capital punishment except for murder and for crimes committed in military service, and in Section 2 he had recognized the right to trial by jury. Here he went even further in trying to protect civil liberties. Citizenship would be granted to anyone who swore or affirmed intent to reside in Virginia for seven years and to abide by its laws. All citizens would enjoy "full and free liberty of religious opinion," and a free press would be guaranteed. Jefferson's draft prohibited standing armies except in time of war and provided that "no freeman shall be debarred the use of arms within his own lands." The legislature could found colonies west of the Allegheny Mountains, but those colonies "shall be free and independent of this colony and of all the world." Primogeniture and entail would be abolished, and in cases of intestate succession, "females shall have equal rights with males." Indian lands could be acquired only by government purchase, and no more slaves could be brought into Virginia.[28]

Jefferson's decision to embed specific safeguards for individual rights in his draft made it distinctive among the first generation of state constitutions, and his work showed other reformist tendencies. He did not recommend substantially changing Virginia's suffrage requirements, but he complained that fewer than half of the state's taxpayers could vote. As a remedy, he proposed giving away unappropriated or forfeited land to ensure that "every person of full age" owned at least fifty acres "in full and absolute dominion." Privately, he favored "extending the right of suffrage . . . to all who had a permanent intention of living in the country." Any permanent inhabitant "must wish that country well," and he was willing to accept residence, family ties, or property ownership as evidence of a sufficient "attachment." More contentious than suffrage in the years to come would be the allocation of seats in the assembly, where the older eastern counties enjoyed an undue advantage over the burgeoning west. Jefferson's constitution required periodic reapportionment to correct inequities. "Equal representation," he wrote Pendleton, "I consider capital & fundamental."[29]

Finally, how could a constitution be made that would truly represent the will of the people and, as a consequence, claim priority over an act of the legislature? Jefferson's initial draft prohibited amendments "but by the unanimous consent of both legislative houses." Yet he failed to provide a process for the ratification of the new constitution itself, and he may have concluded that his amendment process was both unworkable and insufficiently democratic. By his second draft, he found his solution to the problem of amendments: they should require approval by a majority of voters in two-thirds of Virginia's counties. His final draft did not address ratification, although his notes suggest that he assumed it would require a popular vote. If he had not solved the problem of ratification, he was nevertheless years ahead of most of his contemporaries.[30]

Joseph Ellis has fairly described Jefferson's constitution as "an impressive blend of traditional forms and selective reforms." Contrary to some recent interpretations, it was not a radical document that Jefferson felt forced by popular unrest in Virginia to produce. Working alone in Philadelphia, Jefferson has more the look of a man driven by his own idealism and capacious intellect. His 1776 constitution shows the hand of a skilled eighteenth-century draftsman, one familiar with the common law and Virginia politics. He presented no immediate threat to the dominant landed, slaveholding gentry. At the same time, however, with his proposals to expand the suffrage indirectly, to provide for legislative representation based on population, to allow for the election of some local officials, and to guarantee freedom of religion, Jefferson clearly hoped that Virginia could make a dramatic break with its colonial past.[31]

———

ON 25 APRIL 1776, Orange County voters had elected James Madison and his uncle William Moore to represent them at the fifth Virginia convention that would meet in Williamsburg on the first Monday in May. Madison later described his election as his initiation "into the political career." Immediately after adopting Edmund Pendleton's resolution of 10 May endorsing independence, the convention, while Jefferson toiled away in Philadelphia, appointed its own committee to draft a new state constitution. Madison was one of more than two dozen delegates tapped for the committee. George Mason, a late addition to the group, complained to Richard Henry Lee that "the Committee appointed to prepare a plan is, according to Custom, overcharged with useless Members. . . . We shall, in all probability, have a thousand ridiculous and impracticable proposals." Madison reminisced in his autobiography that "being young . . . he did not enter into its debates."[32]

Mason, a wealthy and cerebral planter from Virginia's Northern Neck and an early leader in the resistance movement, quickly took command of

A Happy Talent of Composition

the situation, although Archibald Cary chaired the committee. Pendleton reported to Jefferson that "the Political Cooks are busy preparing the dish, and as Colonel Mason seems to have the Ascendancy in the great work, I have sanguine hopes it will be framed so as to Answer it's [sic] end, Prosperity to the Community and Security to Individuals." Madison came to admire Mason greatly, and Mason, who did not suffer fools gladly, reciprocated.[33]

Consistent with eighteenth-century practice, Mason began with a separate declaration of rights; Jefferson's decision to insert language protecting civil liberties into the text of his constitution was a modest break from precedent. Sometime in the week of 20–26 May, Mason drafted ten provisions; fellow committee member Thomas Ludwell Lee added two more. Drawing on a variety of sources, including John Locke, the English Bill of Rights, and the congressional Declaration of Rights of October 1774, Mason, a veteran polemicist, did not aim for originality, but his first paragraph proved to be especially memorable. It declared "that all Men are born equally free and independent, and have certain inherent natural Rights, of which they can not by any Compact, deprive or divest their Posterity; among which are the Enjoyment of Life and Liberty, with the Means of acquiring and possessing Property, and pursuing and obtaining Happiness and Safety."[34]

Subsequent paragraphs embraced popular sovereignty and the people's right to reform or abolish an oppressive government, banned the creation of a hereditary aristocracy, and called for the separation of powers and frequent elections. Mason produced an embryonic due process clause: "No part of a Man's Property can be taken from him, or applied to public uses, without the Consent of himself, or his legal Representatives." It did not, however, specially provide for compensation in the event an elected legislature condemned private property for a public purpose. A separate paragraph granted some protections to criminal defendants; they included a right to confront one's accusers, the right to a jury trial, and a ban on self-incrimination. Mason also recognized a right to a jury trial in civil cases.[35]

Mason added one clause that might strike a modern reader as a pious banality, but it expressed ideas that eighteenth-century republicans took seriously: "No free Government, or the Blessings of Liberty can be preserved to any People, but by a firm adherence to Justice, Moderation, Temperance, Frugality, and Virtue and by frequent Recurrence to fundamental Principles." Two provisions, in Thomas Ludwell Lee's handwriting, appear at the end of Mason's draft: one dealt with freedom of the press; the other condemned ex post facto laws.[36]

A few provisions would generate debate within the committee and on the convention floor. None proved more contentious than the section on freedom of conscience. Following Locke's *Letters on Toleration* (1667), Mason, in one of his longer paragraphs, had written, "That as Religion, or the Duty which we owe to our divine and omnipotent Creator, and the Manner of discharging it, can be governed only by Reason and Conviction, not by Force or Violence; and therefore that all Men shou'd enjoy the fullest Toleration in the Exercise of Religion, according to the Dictates of Conscience, unpunished and unrestrained by the Magistrate, unless, under Colour of Religion, any Man disturb the Peace, the Happiness, or Safety of Society, or of Individuals. And that it is the mutual Duty of all, to practice Christian Forbearance, Love and Charity towards Each other."[37]

The committee made several amendments and added six new articles, some of which were apparently drafted by Mason, before it reported a declaration of rights to the full convention on 27 May. It extended the suffrage, in ambiguous language, to "all men, having sufficient evidence of permanent common interest with, and attachment to, the community." Other new sections prohibited the executive from suspending the laws, which was a common complaint against royal authority; prohibited excessive bail and cruel and unusual punishment; and established guidelines for search warrants. Another recognized "a well regulated militia" as "the proper, natural, and safe defence of a free state" and proclaimed "that standing armies, in time of peace, should be avoided as dangerous to liberty." The committee made minor but notable changes to Mason's article on religion. His "divine and omnipotent Creator" became simply "our Creator," and the committee deleted his language that would have permitted restrictions on religious exercises where necessary to preserve the "peace" of an individual.[38]

No surviving evidence suggests that Madison played an important role in the committee's deliberations, although Edmund Randolph thought he had impressed the other delegates. Madison's appointment was an education in constitution-making, and Jefferson was not wholly in the dark. Thomas Ludwell Lee may have sent the first draft of the Declaration of Rights to his brother Richard Henry Lee in Philadelphia around the first of June. Richard Henry could easily have shown it to Jefferson. The committee version became a matter of public record when it appeared in John Dixon and William Hunter's *Virginia Gazette* on 1 June. The *Pennsylvania Evening Post* published it on 6 June; two other Pennsylvania newspapers reprinted it shortly thereafter. Because of the vagaries of eighteenth-century communications, the committee's report would become better known than the final document approved by the full fifth convention and set a precedent for attaching a bill of rights as a preamble to a constitution. Jefferson, it appears certain, had the committee report before him when he began writing the Declaration of Independence.[39]

The Cary committee presented its report on 27 May, and the delegates, sitting as a committee of the whole, debated it intermittently until it was formally approved on 12 June. The press of other business—the convention had a war to manage—and three specific issues explain the delay. Robert Carter Nicholas complained early on that Mason's claim in his first paragraph "that all Men are born equally free and independent, and have certain inherent natural Rights" threatened the legal status of slavery. Thomas Ludwell Lee, suspecting Nicholas represented "a certain set of Aristocrats" who feared reform, privately questioned his good faith, but he had exposed the most painful inconsistency in the American cause. After a few days spent on other matters, the delegates answered Nicholas's objection with an amendment proposed by Edmund Pendleton. The phrase "when they enter into a state of civil society" would be inserted after "certain inherent natural rights." If it did not eliminate the hypocrisy of fighting for white rights while enslaving Africans, Pendleton's amendment probably reflected the thinking of most of the delegates: slaves were simply beyond the political pale.[40]

Patrick Henry raised a second substantive issue. Railing against the ban on ex post facto laws, Henry, in the words of Edmund Randolph, painted "a terrifying picture of some towering public offender, against whom ordinary laws would be impotent." The delegates excised the provision.[41]

A third issue, freedom of religion, would provoke even more debate and finally and perhaps predictably engage James Madison. He bristled at Mason's phrase "the fullest Toleration in the Exercise of Religion." Taken from Locke and the English Toleration Act of 1689, the idea of toleration assumed the existence of an established church and implied freedom of conscience was a gift of the state, not an inalienable right. Madison wrote later that he thought Mason "had inadvertently adopted the word *toleration*." Mason, in fact, strongly supported the separation of church and state. The American Revolution made an attack on Virginia's Anglican establishment almost inevitable. The argument against taxation without representation evolved naturally into an argument against taxing dissenters to support an official church, and the Great Awakening had swelled the ranks of Virginia's dissenters. The church's opposition to Virginia's Two-Penny Act of 1759, in which the House of Burgesses had attempted to prevent a windfall to clergy, whose pay was indexed to tobacco, during a period a high tobacco prices, had further fueled anti-clericalism. In 1772, the assembly's committee on religion had introduced a bill to grant dissenters greater freedom, but it never came to a vote.[42]

Madison would now lead a new challenge to the establishment. On his printed copy of the committee report, he wrote an amendment recognizing a right to the "full and free exercise of . . . the dictates of Conscience"; dropping any idea of mere toleration; and providing that "no man or class of men ought, on account of religion to be invested with peculiar emoluments or privileges." Records of the debate are incomplete, but Madison seems to have persuaded Patrick Henry to introduce his amendment, most likely on 11 June, but when asked whether the measure would end public support for the Anglican clergy, Henry apparently hesitated.[43]

Sensing defeat, Madison quickly drafted a second amendment for the more conservative, and reliable, Edmund Pendleton to introduce. It ended no one's "emoluments or privileges" but guaranteed freedom of religion "unpunished and unrestrained by the magistrate, Unless the preservation of equal liberty and the existence of the State are manifestly endangered." Madison's dexterity and Pendleton's reassuring presence won the day. The convention endorsed the free exercise of religion and gave Madison an additional, and presumably unexpected, victory. Cary's committee had earlier deleted Mason's language permitting restraints on religion to avoid giving offense to an individual. The delegates now eliminated the clause allowing restrictions that might be in the interest of the state.[44]

Madison's quiet efforts won a landmark victory for religious freedom in what would generally be regarded as the first modern bill of rights. Perhaps never before had freedom of conscience been given constitutional sanction as a natural right. At the same time, however, the Anglican Church had not been disestablished. Madison's fight to end public support for a state church would go on for another decade. The practical significance of the Declaration of Rights remained in doubt. The idea a bill of rights could be used to limit the power of a popularly elected legislature was not yet well established, and how could a bill of rights be enforced? Traditionally, such declarations had served to educate vigilant citizens, who would, supposedly, rise up in opposition when a ruler violated their liberties. If much was still unsettled, one point was clear. On the issue of religious freedom, James Madison and Thomas Jefferson, working independently, found themselves in almost perfect harmony.[45]

———

GEORGE MASON submitted a draft constitution to Archibald Cary's committee shortly before the fifth convention approved the Declaration of

A Happy Talent of Composition

Rights. Other proposals were in the works. All called for the separation of the legislative, executive, and judicial functions, but they differed in other respects. Carter Braxton had prepared a conservative alternative; it called for lifetime tenure for the governor and members of the upper house. Braxton's draft enjoyed little support. Richard Henry Lee had helped circulate John Adams's *Thoughts on Government* in Virginia and produced his own seven-point outline of Adams's ideas. Lee may have written "A Government Scheme," which appeared in Alexander Purdie's *Virginia Gazette* on 10 May 1776. Lee's "Scheme," if he was the author, showed Adams's influence and envisioned a powerful, bicameral legislature that would elect a governor who would serve a one-year term and be advised by "a council of state." Jefferson sent his draft constitution to Williamsburg with George Wythe, but Wythe did not complete the trip from Philadelphia until 23 June.[46]

Conservatives feared an excess of democracy in a popular assembly as a threat to property rights and typically favored giving a strong governor the veto power. Reformers preferred a more powerful legislature, but their distrust of politicians led them to support limits on lawmakers in the form of short terms of office and a bicameral assembly. A shared concern for the abuse of legislative prerogatives gave conservatives and reformers a measure of common ground and would expedite work on the new constitution. Virginia's harassment of its religious minorities before the Revolution started Madison on the road to his belief that, in a republic, the greatest threat to individual rights, and good government generally, came from ill-informed and shortsighted popular majorities. But Madison was not there yet, and neither were his reform-minded allies. Nor did he have the stature or seniority to exercise great influence within the Cary committee. The leading role would fall to Mason, one of the committee's most respected members and one who could work closely with the reformers without alienating conservatives. As Edmund Randolph wrote later, the plan "proposed by George Mason swallowed up all the rest."[47]

Mason thought members of the lower house should be at least twenty-four years old and should own estates worth 1,000 pounds. Members of his senate were to be at least twenty-eight and own estates of 2,000 pounds. He favored extending the suffrage to long-term leaseholders and to "every householder" who had lived in a Virginia county for one year and fathered three children. In one of his more novel recommendations, Mason proposed members of the senate be chosen by an electoral college in each of twenty-four senate districts. Members of the electoral college would have to be worth at least 500 pounds. His governor could not dissolve the assembly, but the executive could convene, prorogue, or adjourn it with the approval of an eight-person council selected by the legislature. The assembly would elect the governor, who could serve up to three one-year terms, along with the state's judges and its attorney general. Judicial officers would hold office during good behavior "with fixed and adequate salaries." The governor and council would appoint justices of the peace, who would in turn select county sheriffs, clerks, and coroners. Following Locke, Mason called his government a "commonwealth," a term intended to suggest the legislature was first among the branches of government but still subject to the constitution. Mason's procedure for implementing the new constitution was an improvised affair: the convention would select the first group of senators and then the senate, and the convention, acting as the lower house of the assembly, would jointly select a governor and council.[48]

The Cary committee made a few changes to Mason's draft before reporting to the convention on 24 June. The convention made a few more and formally approved the new constitution on 29 June. Less detailed than Jefferson's draft constitution, Mason's plan did not dramatically alter Virginia's political status quo. The delegates debated and rejected an emotional plea by Patrick Henry to give the governor the veto power, and they reinstated the existing property requirements for voting. Mason's plan for an electoral college was eliminated in favor of the popular election of state senators. The county courts regained control over their membership and over the appointment of sheriffs and coroners. The delegates also added a provision barring members of the clergy from serving in the assembly or on the governor's council. The final draft combined conservative and progressive elements, suggesting it was a product of compromise or, just as likely, a result of the lack of large, ideologically coherent blocs among the delegates.[49] As Edmund Randolph explained the convention's deliberations, with a few exceptions, "it was tacitly understood that every body and individual came into the Revolution with their rights and was to continue to enjoy them as they existed under the former government."[50]

Wythe arrived with Jefferson's draft too late for it to alter the course of the proceedings. The delegates did adopt his long list of grievances against George III. Jefferson's language prohibiting dual officeholding, except for justices of the peace who served in the assembly, was added to Mason's provision declaring the legislative, executive, and judicial departments ought to be separate. A clause providing for the continued existence of the general court in the article on the judiciary apparently came from Jefferson; Mason had oddly omitted it in his draft. As Jefferson had proposed, the final draft approved by the convention on 29 June also reaffirmed Virginia's 1609 borders and prohibited private purchases of Indian lands. At the same time, the convention rejected most of Jefferson's more visionary reforms, among them his proposals for independence for new colonies in the West; expansion of the suffrage; an end to the foreign slave trade; and the popular election, with term limits, for certain county officials.[51]

By the standards of the day, the Virginia Constitution of 1776 was a relatively liberal document that, at least in the short term, satisfied the more reform-minded delegates. The constitution, for example, stripped governors of their traditional power to prorogue or adjourn an assembly. The delegates went beyond both Jefferson and Mason in authorizing the popular election of senators, and they rejected Mason's recommendation to establish special property requirements for serving in the legislature.[52]

The Virginians had not, however, solved the practical and theoretical problem of making a constitution legally superior to ordinary legislation. In 1776, no state had. Jefferson had urged Edmund Randolph to oppose a permanent constitution until the voters could elect delegates to a convention called specifically to write one. Randolph tried, only to have the giants in the assembly—Pendleton, Henry, and Mason—tell him that a convention that could declare independence ought to be able to form a new government. Any hesitancy might also have suggested doubts about the legitimacy of the Revolution. Ultimately, Randolph concluded that attempting to initiate a constitutional convention "was a task too hardy for an inexperienced young man." Jefferson and Madison would soon be complaining bitterly about the lack of greater popular participation in the making of the constitution, but Jefferson's decision to submit a draft to the convention undermined his credibility. As an ex-president forty years later, Jefferson could still criticize the convention. Inexperienced in self-government and oppressed by "the abuses of monarchy . . . we imagined everything republican which was not monarchy." Yet within little more than a decade, lessons learned in the states would be used to write a new national constitution.[53]

—

ON FRIDAY, 7 JUNE 1776, Richard Henry Lee introduced in the Second Continental Congress the Virginia resolution declaring "that these United Colonies are, and of right ought to be, free and independent States." Lee's resolution also called on Congress "to take the most effectual steps for forming foreign Alliances" and to prepare "a plan of confederation" for "the respective Colonies." Congress had been moving toward independence for months.

Its Declaration on Armed Vessels of 23 March 1776, which authorized privateering against British shipping, could easily be described as a de facto declaration of independence. Its May resolutions urging the colonies to form new state governments to supplant royal authority left the imperial legal order in shreds.[54]

Lee, Wythe, John Adams, and their allies made practical arguments. A formal statement of independence from Britain would allow Congress to establish diplomatic and commercial relations with the other European powers. As a matter of constitutional law, congressional radicals claimed the colonies had always been independent of Parliament. Jefferson captured their argument in his notes of the debates: "our connection had been federal only," or in other words, through the British monarchy. Typically, American state papers had blamed Parliament or the king's ministers for unpopular policies. Now the king was becoming a target, further straining the bonds of empire. The Declaration on Armed Vessels began by complaining that the colonies' petitions to the king had been "treated with scorn and contempt." Congress's 15 May resolution challenged George III even more directly: "His Britannic Majesty," in conjunction with the lords and commons, had "excluded the inhabitants of these United Colonies from the protection of his crown." The attack on the king had constitutional significance. As Pauline Maier has written, "It was the way Englishmen announced a revolution."[55]

Most of the delegates from New York, New Jersey, Pennsylvania, Delaware, Maryland, and South Carolina hesitated to embrace independence. Everyone understood the magnitude of the decision. Radicals and moderates disagreed over timing and tactics, over the state of public opinion, and over the advisability of awaiting the outcome of ongoing military operations. Moderates feared, in Jefferson's words, "that the people of the middle colonies . . . were not yet ripe for bidding adieu to [the] British connection." A premature declaration of independence could divide the colonies and invite intervention by foreign powers that might see in the chaos an opportunity to seize American territory. Given the reluctance of the more conservative delegates to support Lee's resolution and the tentative nature of their objections, "it was thought," Jefferson later recalled, "most prudent to wait a while for them." Congress decided to postpone a final decision until 1 July.[56]

Congress did not, however, stand still. Anticipating the eventual passage of Lee's resolution, Congress voted to form committees to draft a model treaty for a foreign alliance and articles of confederation. On 11 June, Jefferson, John Adams, and Benjamin Franklin, along with Roger Sherman of

A Happy Talent of Composition

Connecticut and Robert R. Livingston of New York, were named to a third committee to prepare a tentative declaration of independence. The committee left few records of its deliberations, and Jefferson and Adams produced slightly conflicting accounts in their old age. Jefferson chaired the committee, but Adams took credit for persuading him to write its declaration. The Massachusetts delegate thought having a Virginian take the lead might reassure the more timorous southern states, and Jefferson was the "least objectionable" of the Virginians. More socially adept than Adams, he was better liked and a better writer. Jefferson had come to Congress, Adams recalled, with "a reputation for literature, science, and a happy talent of composition."[57]

Adams's explanation is perfectly plausible, except there may have been no real question that Jefferson would be the committee's principal draftsman. Jefferson was serving on at least three other committees, but his colleagues had weightier assignments. Adams and Franklin had been appointed to the model treaty committee, and to make matters worse, an attack of the gout had largely confined Franklin to home. Sherman and Livingston, meanwhile, were members of the committee on the Articles of Confederation. Busy but less harried than his committee colleagues, Jefferson could also write quickly. After meeting with the other members, Jefferson started work on Wednesday, 12 June, or Thursday, 13 June.[58]

The document he was to produce would be called a "declaration," a term that had a technical meaning in English law. A declaration could be a written complaint initiating a civil lawsuit. It could also be an especially important statement of policy by a representative assembly; it might be explanatory and was expected to command broad support. The English Declaration of Rights (1688), which marked the end of James II's reign and the accession of William and Mary, was a model well known to Americans. The Declaration of Independence would contain elements of both kinds of declarations, and perhaps more significantly of a third: an official statement with implications under international law, such as a declaration of war.[59]

Although John Adams later attacked Jefferson's draft for a lack of originality, Jefferson broke with congressional precedent in several respects. Reflecting the view that Parliament had no jurisdiction over the colonies, he leveled American grievances at George III and virtually ignored Parliament; the word "Parliament" does not appear in the final version approved by Congress. In the Declaration Jefferson addressed the world, not the British, and in order to speak to an international audience, he said less about the British constitution or the colonial charters and laid greater stress on natural law, as he announced in his first paragraph when he appealed to "the laws of nature and of nature's God." Before 1776, references to natural law appeared more frequently in the rhetoric of radical republicans than they did in congressional state papers. In the words of historian Craig Yirush, the "adoption of natural rights was a radical departure from traditional English legal norms."[60]

John Adams, writing in 1822, nonetheless complained that "there was not an idea" in the Declaration of Independence "but what had been hackneyed in Congress for two years before." Madison thought "nothing could be more absurd." The strength of the Declaration, he argued, was as a statement of human rights and of the causes of the Revolution "in a style and tone appropriate to the great occasion, and to the spirit of the American people."[61]

Jefferson's better-known response to his critics elaborated on Madison's rejoinder: his charge was "not to find out new principles, or new arguments . . . but to place before mankind the common sense of the subject, in terms so plain and firm as to command their assent." At the same time, he denied in a letter to Madison that any particular source inspired the Declaration: "I turned to neither book or pamphlet while writing it." Of course, a bibliophile like Jefferson did not live in an intellectual vacuum, and scholars have long tried to trace the ideas in the Declaration to one tradition or another. His debt to John Locke in the Declaration's famous second paragraph, with its assertion of a people's right to rebel against a government that threatens their "inherent and inalienable rights," in the words of Jefferson's draft, is obvious. Garry Wills has emphasized the influence on Jefferson of Francis Hutcheson and the Scottish moral sense philosophers. Yet facing a deadline, meeting with fellow committee members, and saddled with other committee duties, in the middle of June 1776, Jefferson hardly had time to do much systematic reading. His explanation that the Declaration reflected popular opinion and ideas from the basic canon of liberal and republican thought seems convincing. "All its authority rests then on the harmonizing sentiments of the day" and on "the elementary books of public right, as Aristotle, Cicero, Locke, Sidney, &c."[62]

A few sources lay close at hand. Congress's July 1775 Declaration of the Causes and Necessity of Taking Up Arms, depicting "a virtuous, loyal, and affectionate people" forced by a decade of abuse to take radical measures, has been called "the blueprint" for the Declaration of Independence, although Jefferson's subsequent work is far more pungent and concise. Jefferson's second paragraph paraphrased George Mason's first paragraph in the Virginia Declaration of Rights. In the second section of the Declaration, which consisted of a long list of allegations against George III, Jefferson reused, with a little editing, the preamble from his version of a Virginia constitution.[63]

Modern readers pause at the first "self-evident truth" in Jefferson's second paragraph: "that all men are created equal." Coming from a slave owner, it seems the rankest hypocrisy. Yet in republican theory, egalitarianism among members of a political society and the survival of republican government went hand in hand. America, in fact, lacked the extremes of wealth and poverty found in Europe, and Jefferson's assertion of equality can be read as a rejection of hereditary privilege and an aristocracy of birth. Jefferson may also have had in mind the common eighteenth-century notion that men enjoyed a moral equality because they shared a generally comparable ability to tell right from wrong. Even apparent differences in intellectual ability could be seen as an accident of circumstance. Adam Smith suggested that the philosopher's intellectual superiority over "a common street porter" might arise principally from the philosopher's habit of doing more mentally challenging tasks.[64]

Viewed in its context—a statement repudiating Britain's right to rule the American colonies—equality, as Jefferson used the word, might best be understood to mean that neither the British people nor their king could claim any moral superiority over Americans. In the last letter he ever wrote, Jefferson expressed the belief that the Declaration had opened the eyes of the world to "the palpable truth, that the mass of mankind has not been born with saddles on their backs, nor a favored few booted and spurred, ready to ride them legitimately, by the grace of God."[65] National independence rested on the equality of political communities.

Jefferson's enumeration of inalienable rights as "life, liberty, & the pursuit of happiness" also invites questions. George Mason had added to Locke's trinity of life, liberty, and property "pursuing and obtaining Happiness and Safety." Why did Jefferson omit so basic a right as property? It may have struck him as redundant. The belief that human happiness was the end of government was commonplace among Whig leaders, and the acquisition of property and the pursuit of happiness were closely related. It may also have been a matter of style; in borrowing Mason's ideas he generally polished his prose. A reference to property rights would also raise complicated questions apt to distract readers from Jefferson's larger argument. The natural right to property was not identical to the property rights a society might recognize; as a practical manner, property rights were everywhere regulated by local law. American states would, in fact, confiscate Loyalist property. In a declaration aimed at an international audience, Jefferson prudently avoided needless confusion over a term that would carry varying connotations from country to country. Finally, Jefferson may have hoped to appeal to Whigs and potential patriots who did not own real property and to discourage suspicions that a wealthy, landowning elite had orchestrated the Revolution.[66]

Jefferson devoted the longest section of the Declaration—and to his contemporaries, the most relevant—to allegations of misconduct against George III, as would be common in a complaint in a civil action. Most of the charges fell into one of three categories: interference with the separation of powers, violations of individual liberties, and acts of war, if not war crimes. "He has," for example, "dissolved representative houses repeatedly for opposing with manly firmness his invasions on the rights of the people," and "he has made judges dependent on his will alone, for the tenure of their offices, & the amount & paiment of their salaries." In an oblique reference to Parliament, Jefferson accused the king of "giving his assent" to "acts of pretended legislation" for, among a string of abuses, "imposing taxes on us without our consent; for depriving us of the benefits of trial by jury"; and "for transporting us beyond the seas to be tried for pretended offences." Near the end of his "long train of abuses & usurpations," Jefferson reached the conduct of the war itself and began a new set of grievances with a dramatic summary: "He has plundered our seas, ravaged our coasts, burnt our towns, & destroyed the lives of our people." George III had hired foreign mercenaries to make war on America, impressed Americans captured on the high seas into British service, and "endeavored to bring on the inhabitants of our frontiers the merciless Indian savages, whose known rule of warfare is an undistinguished destruction of all ages, sexes & conditions."[67]

The elegance of Jefferson's prose sometimes outran the clarity and logic of his arguments. He exaggerated the power of the king under the British constitution, but American constitutional theory demanded it. Because American Whigs had already dismissed Parliament as "a jurisdiction foreign to our constitutions & unacknowledged by our laws," Jefferson's task in the Declaration was to prove that "a prince whose character is thus marked by every act which may define a tyrant is unfit to be the ruler of a people who mean to be free." He had begun the Declaration with an appeal to natural law, but many of the grievances involved English law and charter rights. As Jefferson summarized them, some of those disputes would have mystified foreign readers. He apparently wanted to avoid distracting details. To give the Declaration broad appeal, he included complaints from all the colonies, which made the roots of a few controversies even more difficult to decipher. His claim, to name one, that George III "has suffered the administration of justice totally to cease in some of these states" presumably referred to the "foreign attachment" imbroglio in North Carolina, where a battle between

A Happy Talent of Composition

the royal governor and the assembly over the local courts' jurisdiction over the North Carolina property of British debtors had led to a collapse of the judicial system.[68]

In the end, Jefferson returned to larger themes. The Declaration had begun as an appeal to the world. Events had made it necessary for the colonies "to assume among the powers of the earth the separate & equal station to which the laws of nature and of nature's God entitle them," and "a decent respect for the opinions of mankind" demanded that they explain their actions. Now, after laying out the American case, Jefferson could "finally . . . assert & declare these colonies to be free & independent states, & that as free & independent states, they have full power to levy war, conclude peace, contract alliances, establish commerce, & do all other acts & things which independent states may of right do." The words "free & independent" had constitutional and legal significance. In the 1700s a "free state" had come to mean a republic, and the great international legal scholar Emer de Vattel had declared that a political entity had to be independent before it could assert the rights of a sovereign nation under international law. It is no accident that all the specific rights Jefferson claimed for the new nation involved the management of foreign affairs.[69]

Jefferson sent his draft first to Adams, then to Livingston and Sherman, and later to Franklin for their comments. The initial drafts have been lost, but no evidence exists that any of the other committee members made major alterations. Jefferson late in life produced what he called the "original Rough draught," but it was actually a later work of the committee. Although Jefferson always chafed at the revisions made in Congress, he did not consider the changes made by the committee to be material. At some point Jefferson produced a "fair copy" for the committee that was sent to Congress with handwritten revisions. The draft submitted to Congress showed two changes in Adams's handwriting, five by Franklin, and sixteen by Jefferson. Jefferson may have recorded some changes suggested by others. While it is not entirely clear who recommended which changes, Franklin has often been credited with substituting "self-evident" truths in the place of "sacred and undeniable" truths.[70]

On Friday, 28 June, the Committee of Five reported a declaration to Congress, which tabled the draft and proceeded to debate Richard Henry Lee's resolution declaring independence. Debate on Lee's resolution continued on Monday, 1 July. In a tentative vote, nine states supported independence, but South Carolina and Pennsylvania voted no; Delaware, with only two delegates present, was divided; and New York abstained. Edward

Rutledge of South Carolina asked that a final vote be delayed until the next day. The Americans' opposition to parliamentary supremacy and the British government's intransigence left congressional moderates in an untenable position. By the time debate resumed on 2 July, South Carolina had changed its position, and a third Delaware delegate, Caesar Rodney, had arrived in Philadelphia and tipped that colony's vote in favor of independence. The Pennsylvania delegates who had opposed independence absented themselves, allowing the rest of the delegation to cast the state's vote for Lee's motion. When a second vote was taken, it passed 12–0. New York's delegates, who felt constrained by earlier instructions, abstained again, but New York endorsed independence within a few days.[71]

Congress moved to consider the Declaration of Independence on 4 July. In the course of the debate, Jefferson's colleagues did some minor editing and, much to his consternation, made three major revisions to the committee draft. They cut a long, emotional, and implausible attack on George III for his role in the slave trade. To be sure, the king had vetoed Virginia's attempt to ban the further importation of slaves, but no one had forced Chesapeake planters to buy Africans. In a more subtle edit, Congress removed one of Jefferson's favorite arguments: "that submission to their Parliament was no part of our constitution" because the colonies were settled "at the expense of our own blood and treasure, unassisted by the wealth or the strength of Great Britain." Also deleted was a fairly gratuitous lament that the British voters had continued to reelect "the disturbers of our harmony."[72]

Jefferson's first paragraph had appealed to "nature's God," and his second paragraph traced men's inalienable rights to "their creator." Congress's final edit gave the document an even more sacramental tone. Jefferson had ended his draft with the words "And for the support of this declaration we mutually pledge to each our lives, our fortunes, & our sacred honor." Congress inserted after "declaration" the words "with a firm reliance on the protection of divine providence." Sometime later that morning, Congress passed the Declaration of Independence in its final form.[73]

Shortly before he died, Jefferson said he hoped the world would see the Declaration of Independence as "the signal of arousing men . . . to assume the blessings and security of self-government." Jefferson had not, however, laid down principles for organizing a new government or for dividing power between the national government and the states, and Americans did not initially show much interest in the text of the document. Jefferson's opening paragraphs simply argued that the traditional rights of English citizens were rooted in natural law and ought to have universal applicability. His emphasis on George III's misdeeds could easily lead a reader to conclude he might have accepted a responsible, constitutional monarchy. James Madison put the Declaration in perspective. Sidney and Locke taught men to love self-government "but afford no aid in guarding our Republican Charters against constructive violation. The Declaration of Independence, tho' rich in fundamental principles, and saying every thing that could be said in the same number of words, falls nearly under a like observation."[74]

Jefferson had been irritated to learn in the summer of 1776 that he had been reelected to the Continental Congress with the fewest votes of any incumbent Virginia delegate. He hoped the Declaration of Independence would vindicate him, and ultimately it did. In the 1790s, Jefferson's Democratic-Republicans latched onto the Declaration and his authorship in an effort to present themselves as defenders of the American republic, in contrast to their allegedly pro-British, Federalist opponents. The Declaration grew in public esteem in the 1800s, and critics of slavery could take inspiration from its second paragraph. In 1776, nevertheless, Jefferson's far more prosaic list of grievances against the king represented the crux of the Declaration to most Americans.[75]

Yet it was a founding document, and it served a constitutional purpose. In making a case for the break from Great Britain, the Declaration established, to sympathetic observers, the legitimacy of a new American government. The allegations aimed at George III, R. B. Bernstein has written, "synthesized more than a decade of American constitutional argument."[76] Jefferson assumed the existence of a union of American states that enjoyed "among the powers of the earth the separate & equal station to which the laws of nature and of nature's God entitle them." Accordingly, while the Committee of Five was at work on the Declaration, other committees were drafting the Articles of Confederation and a template for foreign treaties.[77] Legally, the union was weak, but Jefferson considered the emotional bonds holding a people together to be sturdier than formal alliances, and the states had declared independence as a group through Congress, not individually through their legislatures, as they might have done. Since *A Summary View*, he had seen Americans as a nation forged by their own unique history. The Declaration carried on Jefferson's argument that Americans were a distinct and single people, however their governments might be organized.[78]

THREE

A Friendship Was Formed

1776–1781

MUCH OF THE DEMAND for constitutional reform in the 1780s would be a reaction against the widely maligned Articles of Confederation. They deserve some attention, although they received relatively little when they were written in 1776 and 1777. American leaders, including Thomas Jefferson and James Madison, gave more care to drafting new state constitutions. Most people assumed the Continental Congress would manage the war effort and foreign policy, while the states remained virtually autonomous in their internal affairs. Gordon Wood has described the congressional debate over the Articles as "intellectually insignificant." Yet drafting the Articles forced Congress to consider, however briefly, the proper division of authority between the national and state governments. The leading student of the Articles has called that debate "the first chapter in the constitutional history of the United States."[1]

Congress commanded respect and exercised considerable power in the early years of the war: organizing an army, putting George Washington in command, printing money, and sending diplomats to Europe to borrow more. Many Americans assumed Congress had inherited the prerogatives of the British Crown, and the delegates' assertion of authority seemed a necessary, if ad hoc, response to the Revolutionary crisis. Congress could also claim to represent the American people, or at least the American states.[2]

Most of the delegates eventually came to see the need to put the powers of Congress in writing. As we have seen, in July 1775 Benjamin Franklin presented to Congress a plan for a confederation of the states that he had already shown to Jefferson and a few others. Franklin proposed the costs of the war and representation in Congress be allocated among the states based on population. His plan gave broad authority to the national legislature, including the jurisdiction to regulate trade, and it was flexible. Amendments could be made by a simple majority of the states. Congress debated the plan off the record but took no further action. Some delegates thought Franklin's draft conferred too much power on the central government, and conservatives in particular feared a formal confederation would make reconciliation with Great Britain more difficult.[3]

Meanwhile, Silas Deane prepared a second plan, which, apparently working with fellow Connecticut delegates Roger Sherman and Eliphalet Dyer, he substantially revised over the winter of 1775–76. Published in March 1776, the Connecticut Plan attracted no more support than Franklin's proposal had, but it highlighted the most vexing issue the delegates would face: how to reconcile the interests of small and large states in apportioning voting rights in Congress. Deane and his colleagues proposed basing representation on population, but their plan provided that important decisions would require a majority of the delegates and a majority of the states. If the small states voted as a bloc, a perhaps unlikely prospect, they would enjoy a virtual veto. Otherwise, none of the early drafts went into great detail, perhaps because their authors could not devote much time to them, and very likely because they hoped to avoid unnecessary controversies.[4]

The drive to create a formal confederacy gained momentum on 7 June 1776, when Richard Henry Lee moved that Congress, in addition to declaring independence and seeking foreign alliances, prepare "a plan of confederation." On 12 June, Congress appointed a committee, consisting of one delegate from each state, to produce a draft. Conservatives dominated the committee, and the cautious but influential John Dickinson took charge of its work. He drafted a plan that allocated expenses among the states based on population but gave each state an equal vote in Congress. It provided for "a perpetual union" while limiting the sovereignty of the states in numerous ways. Dickinson's draft authorized Congress to fix the boundaries of states with disputed claims to western lands. It prohibited the states from, among other things, adopting laws in conflict with the Articles of Confederation, as Dickinson called them; conducting foreign affairs or making alliances among themselves without congressional approval; discriminating against citizens of another state; or adopting new laws restricting freedom of religion. Congress could make war or ratify a treaty by a vote of nine states. It was not, however, given the express power to regulate trade, and it could not levy taxes or duties, except as necessary to operate a postal service. The committee deleted the clause on religious liberty, made a few less interesting changes, and submitted its report on 12 July, ironically after Dickinson had left Congress.[5]

The delegates took up the report ten days later and debated the proposed Articles until 20 August, when they ordered a new draft to be printed. Jefferson was eager to return to Virginia, where he would serve in the new House of Delegates, but he took notes on the discussions and, as was his custom, occasionally participated. The debates introduced Jefferson to the constitutional problems that would most perplex Americans over the next dozen years. Four issues proved especially divisive.[6]

Samuel Chase of Maryland argued slaves should not be counted in determining a state's financial obligation to Congress. John Adams, James Wilson, and John Witherspoon, among others, disagreed. Virginia's Benjamin Harrison proposed a compromise: counting a slave as half of a free person. The amendment lost by a vote of 7–5, with Georgia divided. The idea of basing requisitions on population remained controversial however people were counted, and the middle states eventually decided it was not in their best interest. Ultimately, Congress voted to allocate costs based on land values.[7]

According to Jefferson's notes, when the debate reached the matter of voting, "Mr. Chase observed that this article was the most likely to divide us of any one ... under consideration." He was right, at least for the next decade. Large and small states both threatened to leave the Union if they did not get their way, but Jefferson thought they all understood unity was essential if they hoped to secure aid from abroad. Large-state delegates, demanding representation based on population, made strongly nationalistic arguments. The more power the new national government exercised over the people, the more reason they should be fairly represented in its deliberations. "The confederacy," John Adams said, "is to make us one individual only; it is to form us, like separate parcels of metal, into one common mass. We shall no longer retain our separate individuality, but become a single individual as to all questions submitted to the confederacy." It was a bit disingenuous; delegates from the more populous states did not necessarily want to increase federal power. As the debate stretched into 1777, Jefferson, now out of Congress but worried about the congressional stalemate, endorsed a compromise adapted from the Connecticut Plan: acts of Congress should require the approval of

A Friendship Was Formed

representatives of a majority of the people and a majority of the states. There were enough small states, however, to retain the one-state, one-vote rule.[8]

While issues involving slavery, funding the government, and allocating seats in Congress would bedevil American politicians for years, at the moment the question of who would control the territory between the Appalachian Mountains and the Mississippi River produced the bitterest controversy. Seven states, including Virginia, lacked well-defined western borders. Virginia claimed, under an ambiguous colonial charter, huge tracts of land, which it could not govern effectively, stretching north by northwest from Kentucky into modern-day Canada. The state claims frequently overlapped. "Landless" states, led by Maryland, hoped to put the western lands under federal control, so they could be sold to help pay their share of the Revolutionary War debt and provide land bounties for veterans. To complicate a seemingly intractable problem, speculators with political connections and dubious land titles tried to manipulate the process to find a forum friendly to their claims. Out-of-state land companies assumed Congress would be more sympathetic to their interests than the Virginia assembly would be. The Indiana Company, for example, asserted title to two million acres in the West by virtue of a 1768 purchase from the Indians that was probably void under Virginia law.[9]

Relatively early in the debate, Jefferson proposed an amendment invalidating land purchases made beyond state boundaries; it assumed those boundaries were fixed and not subject to modification by Congress. The amendment failed, but opponents of federal jurisdiction got the issue postponed until a provision in the Articles allowing Congress to adjudicate western land claims was deleted. The land issue, apathy, and war-related demands on Congress's attention delayed final action on the Articles for months.[10]

When debate resumed in April 1777, a new delegate, Thomas Burke of North Carolina, raised a new objection that would prove to be momentous but, at the time, not particularly controversial. Burke complained that Article III of the Dickinson draft, giving the states "sole and exclusive" jurisdiction over their internal affairs "in all matters that shall not interfere with the Articles of this Confederation," implicitly conferred broad powers on Congress. Burke wanted it deleted in favor of a new article that provided that "every State retains its sovereignty, freedom and independence, and every power, jurisdiction, and right, which is not by this confederation expressly delegated to the United States, in Congress assembled." Eleven states concurred.[11]

Debate went on sporadically until October, when a worsening financial situation and the need to negotiate a foreign alliance compelled the delegates to put the Articles in final form. Congress sent the document to the states for ratification, which required unanimous consent, in November. It created a far weaker union than the Dickinson committee had envisioned sixteen months earlier. Jefferson seemed satisfied and almost immediately drafted a bill for the Virginia assembly repealing all state laws inconsistent with the Articles. Jefferson's proposal was apparently never introduced, but by June 1778 Virginia and all the other states except Maryland, Delaware, and New Jersey had ratified the Articles. New Jersey approved them in November. Delaware came around in February 1779. Maryland, adamant in its demand for congressional control of the West, held out, and Congress remained in a constitutional limbo, fighting a revolution with the most ill-defined authority.[12]

———

IN SEPTEMBER 1776, Congress voted to send Thomas Jefferson, along with Benjamin Franklin and Silas Deane, to France to negotiate treaties of amity and commerce with the French and the other European powers. Pleading family obligations, Jefferson declined the appointment. Jefferson could happily leave Congress and turn down a diplomatic post in part because he believed the work of creating republican governments would be done mainly within the individual states. As he later put it, "I saw . . . that the laboring oar was really at home," and he thought he could be most useful in Virginia. "Our legislation under the regal government," he believed, "had many vicious points which urgently required reformation." Between 1776 and 1779, Jefferson introduced more bills than any other Virginia lawmaker, making those years arguably the most productive period of a remarkably productive life. One of the most popular members of the legislature, he took on jobs large and small, and although clearly identified with the assembly's liberal element, he enjoyed close friendships with conservatives like Edmund Pendleton. Jefferson saw service in the assembly as an opportunity to implement legal reforms that Virginia's new constitution had failed to achieve. At the same time, he did not expect the opportunity to last long: "From the conclusion of this war we shall be going down hill." The people, he predicted, "will forget themselves, but in the sole faculty of making money."[13]

Jefferson and Madison met for the first time during the fall 1776 session of the assembly. They did not immediately become close. Jefferson recalled the Orange County delegate as being too modest initially to enter into legislative debates. Madison remembered their acquaintance that fall as "very slight" due to "the distance between our ages being considerable, and other

58   *A Friendship Was Formed*

distances much more so," by which he presumably meant Jefferson was then the more highly regarded legislator.[14]

The potential for close collaboration, however, existed from the beginning. They served together on several committees, and Madison's dogged work ethic and skill as a legislative draftsman—traits Jefferson shared—routinely impressed contemporaries. Madison's diligence, intelligence, and integrity, in Jefferson's words, "rendered him the first of every assembly afterwards of which he became a member." Shy and not particularly ambitious, as politicians go, Madison never resented Jefferson's greater public prominence. Besides similar backgrounds among the Blue Ridge gentry, they were both prone to stress-related or psychosomatic illness; Jefferson suffered from migraines, while stomach ailments and epileptic symptoms plagued Madison.[15]

Both men could be stubborn, and both men could be flexible. Where they differed temperamentally—and they did—those differences usually complemented each other. Jefferson possessed a more fertile imagination, a flare for memorable prose, a better feel for public opinion, and broader interests. Madison tended to be more comfortable with political conflict and more pragmatic but deeper and more systematic in his political thought. As we have seen, they both read widely, especially in the law. Madison said of Jefferson, "The Law itself he studied to the bottom, and in its greatest breadth." They both believed the law could be used to promote a republican political order, not simply to solve an immediate problem or to appease a particular constituency. If they took an essentially negative view of liberty as a life lived with a minimum of government interference, they also believed legislation could be used to encourage civic virtue and responsible citizenship.[16]

Of the bills he drafted, Jefferson thought four formed "a system by which every fiber would be eradicated of antient or future aristocracy; and a foundation laid for a government truly republican." They consisted of bills prohibiting entail and primogeniture, his Bill for the More General Diffusion of Knowledge, and his Bill for Establishing Religious Freedom. Of the various assembly committees on which Jefferson and Madison served together, one was the committee on religion.[17]

Similar opinions on the proper relationship between church and state helped bring them together. They viewed state-supported religion as a threat to intellectual freedom generally. Jefferson was privately skeptical of religious orthodoxy as well. Edmund Randolph described him as "adept . . . in the ensnaring subtleties of deism." Madison was less skeptical, or perhaps simply more private, but he feared an alliance of church and state would inevitably corrupt the church and, by converting religious differences into political issues, destabilize the state. Jefferson's papers from the period shed light on his thinking. They include notes from Locke's *A Letter Concerning Toleration* (1689) and from Shaftesbury's *A Letter Concerning Enthusiasm* (1708). From Locke, Jefferson recorded the ideas that God could not respect religious obedience compelled by the law and that "truth will do well enough if left to shift for herself." Jefferson also noted Shaftesbury's claim that reason and science had flourished in classical Greece because the ancients had permitted free inquiry. His own reading persuaded him that Christianity was not part of the common law, contrary to a widespread view, and that the early church had prospered when supported only by the voluntary contributions of its members.[18]

Recent scholarship suggests Virginia's established Anglican Church enjoyed more vigor before the Revolution than historians once believed. The assessment collected to help support the church was often the highest tax paid by Virginians. Only Anglican clergy could perform baptisms and marriages, and the duties of the Anglican vestry combined religious and civil functions: fixing boundary lines; finding homes for orphans; and bringing grand jury presentations for sexual offenses, swearing, and drunkenness. Virginia law required attendance at Anglican services or a licensed dissenting church. Dissenting ministers had to obtain a license from colonial authorities, which could be hard to get, and were sometimes denied the right to conduct funerals in churchyards. Consigned to a relatively low social status by their more boisterous services and lower levels of education, Baptist ministers especially faced discrimination and sometimes vigilante violence. At least half of Virginia's Baptist ministers had served jail time for preaching by 1775.[19] The growing number of dissenters, mainly Presbyterians and Baptists, created pressure for reform. The outbreak of the Revolution further undermined the status quo.

Virginia's Declaration of Rights had proclaimed that "all men are equally entitled to the free exercise of religion, according to the dictates of conscience." The established church's close ties to the royal government made it especially vulnerable to criticism. When the assembly convened for its fall 1776 session, dissenters inundated the delegates with petitions to end what Jefferson called "spiritual tyranny." They provoked, he later recalled, "the severest contests in which I have ever been engaged. . . . For although a majority of our citizens were dissenters . . . a majority of the legislature were churchmen."[20]

Jefferson exaggerated the size of the dissenting denominations. They represented no more than roughly a third of Virginia's white population, but he understood the political dynamics. Combined, dissenters, the unchurched, and nominal or latitudinarian Anglicans like Jefferson and Madison did constitute a majority of the population. The Anglican majority in the assembly, led by conservatives like Robert Carter Nicholas, Archibald Cary, and Edmund Pendleton, hoped to preserve state support for their church by making a few concessions to the dissenters, but if they did too little, they risked compromising the dissenters' enthusiasm for the war effort.[21]

As a member of the committee on religion, Jefferson drafted a series of resolutions calling for the repeal of English laws punishing unorthodox religious beliefs or "any mode of worship" and endorsing the end of the establishment and public support of Anglican ministers but allowing them to retain a life estate in current glebes. Conservative Carter Braxton chaired the committee, however, and its members were so badly divided that, on 9 November, the House of Delegates dissolved it. What happened next is unclear, but ten days later the assembly approved a set of compromise resolutions: acts of Parliament punishing heresy and requiring church attendance would be repealed, and dissenters would be exempted from the parish levy. At the same time, the state would continue to license clergy and regulate religious assemblies, incumbent clergy would continue to receive their salaries, and the established church would retain its property. The delegates appointed a new committee, which included Jefferson and Madison, to prepare an appropriate bill.[22]

Jefferson conceded in the course of the debates that he knew his contemporaries had no stomach for a religious inquisition, but he argued that citizens should not be dependent on the spirit of the times for the protection of their rights. With regard to religious beliefs, individuals should be answerable only to God; the state should limit its concerns to overt acts. He argued state-imposed religious conformity stifled intellectual inquiry of all kinds and pointed out that in countries where Roman Catholicism was the official faith, the state church produced not piety but hypocrisy. The withdrawal of state support, Jefferson argued, would improve the quality of clergy, forcing ministers to be "Industrious" and "Exemplary."[23]

The new committee submitted its report on 30 November. Jefferson had left the assembly the day before. The committee had apparently orchestrated its next step with the other delegates; the assembly adopted new resolutions conforming to a bill the committee had already drafted. It exempted dissenters from the church levy but otherwise generally maintained the status quo. The lower house passed the bill a few days later, after Jefferson had returned and after George Mason had won adoption of an amendment repealing all laws punishing nonconformity, but the law that had established the Anglican Church remained in effect. Mason shared Jefferson's commitment to religious liberty, but as an elder statesman and fairly conventional Anglican, he made reform seem benign. Jefferson called him "a man of the first order of greatness." Relieving Presbyterians and Baptists from the church tax would obviously shift costs to Anglicans, a potentially onerous burden as long as the established church retained its responsibility for poor relief. On a motion by Robert Carter Nicholas, the delegates agreed to a temporary suspension of the church tax until, Nicholas hoped, a "general assessment" could be imposed levying a tax for the support of all Christian denominations.[24]

Jefferson, Madison, and their allies had taken a long step toward separating church and state in Virginia, without getting everything they wanted. As the maneuvering in the assembly demonstrated, no consensus, or even a reliable majority, could be found for a coherent and comprehensive theory of church-state relations, but the traditional establishment was becoming increasingly difficult to defend. In 1779, the suspension of the tax on Anglicans became permanent. In 1780, Anglican ministers lost their exclusive right to perform marriages. The question of a general assessment, however, would linger for a decade. Jefferson drafted his famous Bill for Establishing Religious Freedom, repudiating the principle of state aid to religion, in 1777, but it would not be introduced until June 1779, when Jefferson's election as governor removed him from the legislature. The bill languished there for years, and by the time it was resurrected, leadership on the issue had passed to James Madison.[25] The high point of reform in Virginia, the Bill for Religious Freedom illustrated both the potential and the limits of state politics.

More importantly, perhaps, it united Jefferson and Madison in a common cause. The question of religious liberty would also prove to be critical in shaping Madison's thinking about how to protect individual rights and manage competing interests in a republican society.

———

THOMAS JEFFERSON believed Virginia had a number of advantages as it embarked on its republican experiment. It had a history of self-government. It was already an agrarian society, and Jefferson accepted as an article of faith the idea that economically independent, small farmers made the best citizens. Virginia was also relatively homogeneous; 90 percent of its white population was of British ancestry. Jefferson had some radical ideas, but he did not have a radical temperament. He tolerated different opinions, and he was willing to wait for change to come. He wanted to reform Virginia society, not remake it. His most ambitious goal was to replace what he called "an aristoc-racy of wealth" with "an aristocracy of virtue and talent," and that was a less radical proposal in America than it would be in Europe. Unlike later revolu-tionaries in France and Russia, Jefferson confronted a less-entrenched elite, with more porous boundaries, and he would propose more modest remedies. He typically sought to eliminate artificial barriers to social mobility, not to redistribute wealth wholesale.[26]

On 12 October 1776, the House of Delegates authorized Jefferson to prepare two bills, one to restrict entails and the other to establish a process to revise Virginia's legal code. The English practice of entail, designed to pre-serve large landholdings, allowed a testator to limit the ability of his heirs to divide an estate. An entail could be set aside, or "docked," by the assembly, but the process was cumbersome, and entails were not popular. Jefferson introduced an entail bill on 14 October, and it passed quickly.[27]

To Jefferson the abolition of entail and the end of primogeniture went hand in hand and, along with freedom of conscience and the creation of a public school system, were essential for a truly republican state. As did entails, primogeniture propped up the landed gentry; in cases of intestate succession the estate went to the eldest son. Jefferson drafted a bill to replace primogeniture with an equal division of property among immediate heirs, but it did not pass until 1785; primogeniture, after all, could be defeated by the simple act of making a will and caused fewer headaches than did entails. The end of entail and primogeniture did not produce a social revolution in Virginia, but the emphasis Jefferson put on it suggests something about his frame of mind: his rhetoric occasionally outran the substance of his proposals and made him sound more radical than he was.[28]

If Jefferson was no Jacobin, he was a legislative workhorse. The day after he introduced the entail bill, he proposed another bill to appoint a committee to revise Virginia's laws, many of which, he said, "are founded on principles heterogeneous to the republican spirit" and which were, in fact, an uncoordi-nated hodgepodge of colonial statutes, acts of Parliament, and common-law precedent. The bill passed easily, and when the assembly voted to fill the committee's five seats, Jefferson received more votes than anyone else. He would serve as chair.[29]

Edmund Pendleton, George Wythe, George Mason, and Thomas Lud-well Lee would serve with Jefferson. They met in Fredericksburg in January 1777 to divide the work, but most of it fell to Jefferson, Wythe, and Pendleton, and especially Jefferson and Wythe. Lee died early in the project, and Mason, who was not a lawyer, thought it best to resign after getting a look at the scope of the committee's assignment. Committee members would have to cull the wheat from decades of legal chaff and in some cases prepare entirely new statutes. Where they retained existing acts, Pendleton, the conservative icon, favored thoroughly modernizing their language. Jefferson, the putative radical, preferred more modest revisions, arguing that where meanings had been settled by precedents, rewording statutes would invite litigation. Jefferson was given the task of reviewing early English statutes; he inherited most of the work originally assigned to Mason and Lee, which included the slave code and criminal law; and he included in the committee's report a number a new proposals, including, for example, the ban on primogeniture. In all, he drafted at least fifty-one bills.[30]

The committee submitted its final report, consisting of 126 proposed bills, in June 1779. A few of the measures had already been adopted, and a few more would pass immediately. Many were routine, such as No. 41, "Preventing Infection of the Horned Cattle," and No. 49, "Unloading Ballast and Burial of Dead Bodies from on Board Ships." Others had constitutional significance. No. 57 provided that "no freeman" could be deprived of liberty or property without a jury trial and due process of law. Most of the bills eventually became law, in large measure due to the efforts of James Madison in the 1780s, and his support helped solidify his relationship with Jefferson. Madison called the committee's report "a mine of Legislative wealth." Legal reform, nevertheless, went slowly. The business was important and complicated, and the assembly had other responsibilities.[31]

To Jefferson, none of the committee's proposals had a greater potential for good than No. 79, "A Bill for the More General Diffusion of Knowledge." He explained its purpose in the bill itself. Even the best forms of government can be "perverted . . . into tyranny." To safeguard the people's rights, republican government required informed citizens and educated leaders. "The people at large" needed particularly to be taught history so that from "the experience of other ages and countries, they may be enabled to know ambition under all its shapes, and be prompt . . . to defeat its purposes." A public "liberal education" could also prepare those naturally "endowed with genius and virtue" for political office "without regard to wealth, birth or other accidental condition or circumstance."[32]

Jefferson proposed specifically that "hundred," or primary, schools be established to educate all white children for three years at public expense. The bill required parents to pay a fee if they wanted their children to stay beyond three years. District or grammar schools would offer more advanced instruction; they would charge tuition, but the state would provide the schoolhouse and pay a stipend to talented students. Finally, the state would give the best grammar school graduates scholarships to attend the College of William and Mary. In an age when education was largely a private affair, the bill, despite its limitations, was a truly novel measure.[33]

It was not, however, very popular. The bill guaranteed most children only three years of public education, probably too little and at too early an age to learn enough history to enable them to penetrate the wiles of a demagogue, although contemporary critics found other reasons to complain. The Presbyterian cleric Samuel Stanhope Smith warned Jefferson that his coreligionists resented the favoritism being shown the Anglican William and Mary: "This contest will chiefly lie betwixt the Presbyterians and the Episcopalians. The Baptists and the Methodists content themselves with other kinds of illuminations than are afforded by human science." The secular tone of the bill probably troubled other churchgoers. Virginia's large size and low population density presented practical obstacles to a statewide system of schools accessible to students traveling on foot or by horse or mule. Most damaging to its prospects, the bill would have taxed wealthy planters, who dominated the assembly, to educate poor white children. Debated intermittently from late 1778 until 1786, the Bill for the More General Diffusion of Knowledge never passed the assembly.[34]

Criminal law offered a more fertile field for change. Relying on English statutes and the common law, Virginia before the Revolution did not even have a criminal code. Enlightenment philosophers had promoted the reform of criminal law, and Jefferson, who read Marquis Beccaria's *Essay on Crimes and Punishments* and similar works, embraced the Enlightenment agenda. Jefferson believed criminal law should be "strict and inflexible, but proportioned to the crime." Punishment should be no greater than needed to deter the offense. Overly harsh penalties were difficult to enforce; certainty of punishment, he believed, was more important than its severity in deterring crime. To avoid discrimination among defendants, "the judge should be a mere machine," dispensing sentences as prescribed by the legislature. Jefferson hoped to limit the death penalty to murder and treason and to reduce the number of crimes punished by mutilation, although he supported castration for rape and other sexual offences. Slaves who committed crimes should be deported. Most other crimes could be punished by hard labor.[35]

Service on the law revisers' committee provided an opportunity to implement his ideas. Sending a draft bill on capital crimes to Wythe, he explained his objectives: "I have aimed at accuracy, brevity and simplicity, preserving however the very words of the established law, wherever their meaning had been sanctioned by judicial decisions, or rendered technical by usage." He tried to modernize recent statutes with less judicial gloss. Bill No. 64 of the committee's report limited the death penalty to murder and treason; "rape, polygamy, & sodomy" would now be punished by mutilation. Jefferson found the rule of lex talionis distasteful, but by later standards, he took a narrow view of cruel and unusual punishment. He did not propose a ban on bills of attainder but simply provided that they should not "work corruption of the blood in any case." In a day before the widespread use of prisons, Jefferson proposed requiring convicts to toil in lead mines or "other hard and laborious works" with "heads and beards constantly shaven, and . . . clothed in habits of course materials." The leniency of the proposed code, not its harshness, delayed final legislative action until Jefferson had left Virginia for a diplomatic post in Europe.[36]

A criminal code, of course, assumed the existence of courts to enforce it. Indeed, "the most dramatic institutional transformation in the early Republic," Gordon Wood has written, "was the rise of what was called an 'independent judiciary.'" Here, Jefferson played his part. As chair of a committee to create the courts authorized by Virginia's new constitution, Jefferson drafted five separate bills, one for five separate courts, in the fall 1776 assembly. It was a further display of his legislative diligence; one bill alone ran to forty handwritten pages. His bills provided for a court of admiralty; a general court, a common-law court with original jurisdiction in cases involving ten pounds or more and appellate jurisdiction over inferior courts; a High Court of Chancery, a court of English origins that could exercise original jurisdiction and hear appeals in cases not cognizable under the common law; and a court of appeals, a final appellate court consisting of judges from the admiralty, general, and chancery courts. He also proposed reforming the existing county courts, where judges, who were typically not lawyers, decided a variety of usually minor cases. He inserted other innovations elsewhere. Under English law, chancery courts did not use juries. To limit the chancellor's discretion, which could be considerable, he proposed adding them.[37]

The bill for an admiralty court passed immediately. The other measures encountered opposition. Some planters feared a functioning court system would allow British merchants to collect debts owed them by their Virginia customers. Jefferson's attempt to appease opponents by suspending debt collections for the duration of the war did not reassure them. He persevered, the need was obvious, and the assembly finally approved the general court and chancery bills during its October 1777 session. Legislation establishing

66   *A Friendship Was Formed*

the court of appeals passed the following year. A later amendment deleted the provision for jury trials in chancery court.[38]

Jefferson recommended allowing the county courts to impose a levy for the purchase of law books and requiring justices of the peace to meet when petitions were submitted to them and not on a fixed schedule. The courts were amateurish but powerful bastions of the status quo, and even those minor reforms failed, as did a more ambitious bill permitting voters to select the justices. In all likelihood Jefferson recognized a network of assize courts, local trial courts with broad jurisdiction but no nonjudicial functions, as the real solution. Jefferson appreciated judicial professionalism, and he apparently sensed early on that well-trained lawyers—he was one, after all—could play an invaluable role in maintaining the rule of law in a republican society. He suggested to Wythe, for example, that county court lawyers be barred from practice in the more prestigious general court so a few attorneys could afford to devote themselves to its more complex litigation and develop their expertise. As it was, "an inundation of insects is permitted to come from the county courts and consume the harvest." The assembly saw matters differently, and the county courts conducted business as usual until Virginia adopted a new constitution in 1867.[39]

Frustration in one area did not deter Jefferson from tackling other issues. He drafted a bill to relocate the state capital from Williamsburg to Richmond, a democratic move intended to bring the state government closer to the bulk of the population. Defeated when first introduced in 1776, it became law three years later. In 1779, he authored a citizenship statute that, save for its racial bias, was liberal for its day. It extended citizenship to "all white citizens" born in Virginia and resident for two years and to immigrants who intended to remain in the state. Jefferson's bill recognized a right of expatriation and a right to renounce one's citizenship, then novel concepts to which he was deeply committed. In a provision that gave evidence of Jefferson's nationalistic tendencies, the citizenship law also guaranteed "free white inhabitants" of other states "all the rights, privileges, and immunities" of free citizens of Virginia.[40]

Jefferson preferred long-term reform to managing the exigencies of war, but the conflict could hardly be ignored. In January 1778, he introduced a popular measure that provided for state administration of Tory estates; income from the estates would go to the state treasury. The bill also stipulated that Virginia's paper money could be used to pay British debtors, with the state to hold the payments until the end of the war. The sequestration plan worked poorly, and the next year Jefferson secured passage of a bill simply confiscating Tory property. Neither effort produced much revenue or fit into

Jefferson's program for republican reform, but he disliked Loyalists and the state needed money.[41]

As a member of the House of Delegates, Jefferson strove to make the American Revolution more than a war for independence, and he won notable victories while taking defeat and delay in stride. He by no means achieved everything he wanted, but optimistic by nature, he thought Americans had made a fine start toward establishing their new republic. "With respect to Virginia in particular," he wrote Benjamin Franklin in August 1777, "the people seem to have deposited the monarchial and taken up republican government with as much ease as would have attended throwing off an old and putting on a new suit of clothes. Not a single throe has attended this important transformation." His robust legislative agenda demonstrated his confidence that Virginia could manage its own affairs, a belief that would temper but not erase his support for a stronger national government.[42]

——

JAMES MADISON had lost his bid for reelection to the House of Delegates in April 1777 to Charles Porter, a local tavern keeper. Madison's defeat owed less to his legislative record than it did to his refusal to "treat" the voters with liquor on Election Day. The race took a nasty turn. Madison's supporters, accusing Porter of "bribery and corruption," asked the assembly to set aside the results, but the delegates dismissed their petition for a lack of evidence.[43]

Madison did not long remain out of office. In November, the assembly elected him to one of the eight positions on the governor's council. He took his seat in January 1778; he would spend most of his time in Williamsburg until the end of the following year. The governor and council had little authority, but together they granted pardons, commanded the militia, made interim administrative and judicial appointments when the assembly was not in session, and exercised whatever additional duties the legislature delegated to them. Administration by committee proved cumbersome; Madison later called the council "a grave of useful talents." As always, however, he took his work seriously. The committee met six days a week at 10 A.M., and Madison rarely missed a meeting. Orange County voters presumably appreciated his service. They elected him to the assembly in April 1778, but the house ruled Virginia's ban on dual officeholding prevented a council member from running for another position.[44]

It was probably just as well. Thomas Jefferson succeeded Patrick Henry as governor in June 1779. Working together daily in a small group, Jefferson and Madison, allies at a distance before, bonded almost immediately.

"Our acquaintance there became intimate," Madison recalled after Jefferson's death, "and a friendship was formed, which was for life, and which was never interrupted in the slightest for a single moment."[45]

Shared responsibility and adversity helped bring them together. They enjoyed some victories, in particular George Rogers Clark's successful campaigns against British garrisons in the trans-Appalachian West, but they faced innumerable difficulties. When Congress delayed approving a treaty with France, they wrote the French counsel to assure him of Virginia's support. In light of Virginia's long coastline and extensive river system, Jefferson believed a navy was critical to the defense of the state. The council tried to build a small fleet and to coordinate naval operations with North Carolina, largely for naught. Maritime efforts, he eventually confided to Richard Henry Lee, "have indeed been unsuccessful beyond all my fears." Attempts to mobilize troops for armies to the south, north, and west stretched Virginia's resources. The council confessed to George Washington in November 1779, "We find it very difficult to procure men." Equipping them was no easier. Attempting to implement an act of the assembly, the council contracted with the firm of Penet, Windel, and Company to build "a manufactory of firearms and foundry of ordnance." Imports and existing domestic production had not been sufficient, and neither, as it developed, was the new initiative.[46]

Jefferson, Madison, and their colleagues occasionally quarreled with Congress over scarce resources. In December 1779, the council tried to explain Virginia's decision to seize weapons intended for the Continental army: "Necessity alone dictated the measure . . . no sentiment of disrespect to Congress entered into the transaction." They generally sought to cooperate. When Congress requisitioned $2.5 million from Virginia for 1780, Madison feared it might not be possible to raise the money, but he thought "no exertions," including heavy taxes on every type of property, "ought to be omitted to testify to our zeal to support Congress in the prosecution of the War."[47]

In December 1779, the assembly elected Madison to the Continental Congress, leaving Jefferson to carry on as governor without his closest ally. Chosen annually by the assembly, Virginia's executive was a weak figure. The governor lacked the veto power, could not act without the approval of the council, and, for part of Jefferson's administration, shared power with a board of war and a board of trade, both of which were also appointed by the assembly. Jefferson came to see the need for a stronger executive. He thought the governor should be able to act without the council's consent, and he believed the governor should be able to appoint members of the county courts. Allowing Virginia's voters to select the executive would have made the office less dependent on the legislature and given the governor the prestige that would accompany an electoral triumph, but Jefferson did not then endorse the idea.[48]

As governor, Jefferson, in the words of Dumas Malone, "gave the impression of unfailing zeal and incessant labor. . . . He was enmeshed in details and swamped by paper work."[49] When Congress recommended the states issue proclamations setting aside "a day of publick and solemn THANKSGIVING to Almighty God," Jefferson, the apostle of the separation of church and state, complied. When the assembly, worried about feeding American troops, empowered the governor and the council to impose a temporary embargo on the export of foodstuffs, Jefferson proclaimed an embargo. He complained to the governor of Maryland when officials there seized flour Virginia had tried to buy in Maryland. He issued a warrant to impress supplies for the so-called Convention Army, British soldiers and German mercenaries who had been taken prisoner at the Battle of Saratoga and then interned in Virginia.[50]

Jefferson could authorize strong measures, as when he instructed an army doctor in May 1781 to seize any church or vacant house needed for a military hospital. British troops had invaded Virginia, and Jefferson explained, "Necessity is Law, in times of war most especially." At the same time, he worried about overstepping his legal authority, and he was not predisposed by nature to vigorous executive action. Jefferson explained his philosophy to the American general Baron von Steuben: "We can only be answerable for the orders we give, and not for their execution. If they are disobeyed from obstinacy of spirit or want of coercion in the laws it is not our fault. We have done what alone remained for us to do."[51]

Legislative service suited Jefferson's temperament better than did the governor's office, and he valued a private life of study and reflection above all else. "Public offices are," he thought, "what they should be, burthens to those appointed to them which it would be wrong to decline." He obviously envied the Philadelphia astronomer David Rittenhouse, whom he ranked among "an order of geniuses above that obligation." Many could hold public office; few could advance the cause of human enlightenment. When Jefferson received his copy of François Barbé-Marbois's list of questions about the respective American states, he happily assumed the task of providing Virginia's response to the French diplomat. His answers would evolve into his *Notes on the State of Virginia*, which would include a new draft constitution for Virginia and a commentary on the existing one. The American Philosophical Society elected Jefferson to its executive board during his last year as governor. "The busy scene in which I have the misfortune to be engaged" delayed his response, but he hoped his impending retirement would give him the leisure to make some contribution to science.[52]

During Jefferson's second term as governor, the military and political situation deteriorated. In May 1780, Charleston fell to the British. In July, Jefferson confessed to Samuel Huntington, the president of the Continental Congress, that Virginia, as Madison had feared, would not meet its congressional requisition. Jefferson attributed the failure to the difficulty of coordinating tax collections in a state as large as Virginia: "The time for complying with a requisition expires frequently before it is discovered that the means provided were defective." In August, an American army led by Horatio Gates suffered a crushing defeat at Camden, South Carolina. The poor performance of Virginia's soldiers left Jefferson "extremely mortified." By September, Jefferson governed a state "utterly destitute of money" and lacking the wagons to transport provisions, if it had the funds to buy them. Shortages of muskets, bayonets, cartridge paper, and cartouche boxes persisted into 1781. "It is impossible," he wrote to Madison in Philadelphia, "to give you an Idea of the Distress we are in for want of Lead." Near the end of his term, Jefferson suggested some remedial measures to the assembly, including the construction of river galleys and earthworks and the use of slaves to build fortifications, but he deferred to "the Wisdom of the Legislature."[53]

Jefferson also called for stricter discipline within militia units and relayed to the assembly complaints from American commanders about their lack of authority over civilians near the opposing armies. George Washington and Nathanael Greene had written him to bemoan the unreliability of poorly trained, part-time soldiers, and Jefferson had learned from experience that militiamen, worried about their families and farms, would not stay in camp when their own counties were threatened: "They desert and carry off their arms."[54] Repeated attempts to mobilize the militia and efforts to recruit soldiers for the Continental army aggravated disaffection and provoked an occasional riot. Jefferson professed himself "perfectly happy" with public support for the Revolution, but he admitted Virginia contained substantial pockets of discontent from "Montgomery County along our Southern boundary to Pittsylvania and Eastward as far as the James River."[55]

Jefferson decided not to seek—or, perhaps more accurately, not to accept—a third term as governor. Madison lamented his friend's decision to retire "in the present crisis," but confident Jefferson had "weighed well the reasons on which it is grounded I shall lament in silence."[56] A British raid led by the erstwhile American hero Benedict Arnold in late 1780 had caught Virginians by surprise and reached as far inland as the new capital at Richmond. Confused by poor intelligence, Jefferson had hesitated to call out the militia. Worse was yet to come. In April 1781, Lord Cornwallis and a British army of 7,500 men marched into Virginia from North Carolina. The invasion disrupted the state government. Jefferson's term expired on 2 June before the assembly, which was forced to convene in Staunton, could elect a successor. On 4 June, Jefferson narrowly escaped capture, fleeing on horseback just as British dragoons from Colonel Banastre Tarleton's notorious command reached Monticello.[57]

Not until mid-June did separate American armies under the Marquis de Lafayette, "Mad Anthony" Wayne, and Baron von Steuben rendezvous in Virginia and begin to offer effective resistance. On 12 June, the assembly elected Thomas Nelson to replace Jefferson and, on a motion from George Nicholas, authorized an inquiry into Jefferson's performance. The motion implied that Jefferson, despite the lapse of his formal authority, should not have abandoned his position. It also seemed to question his physical courage. The delegates, who met for only five days, postponed the matter to the fall assembly, which, when it convened, quickly passed a brief resolution vindicating Jefferson. Once the crisis had passed, all concerned seemed to have decided he could not have done much more. Nicholas's motion stung Jefferson more than any other affront he suffered in his long political career, and his Federalist enemies would use the affair against him in the 1790s and early 1800s. Ironically, had he simply served a third term and held office until Cornwallis's surrender at Yorktown in October, his governorship probably would have been remembered as a relative success.[58]

Instead, it had been a painful ordeal. Virginia's efforts to support Congress and the Continental army while defending its own borders, which at least theoretically extended to Canada and the Mississippi River, severely taxed its resources. Congress offered limited help. Yet, rather remarkably, the struggles of the war years did not shake Jefferson's confidence in the basic soundness of the Revolutionary political order. Only on a handful of issues did he come to see a need for constitutional reform of continental dimensions.

———

One issue had to be addressed before reform could proceed: the fate of the vast domain west of the Appalachians, and in particular the territory north of the Ohio River. State claims there overlapped, Virginia could not effectively govern the area it claimed, and if it could have, it would have fostered bitter resentment among the "landless" states. The Articles of Confederation

A Friendship Was Formed

left the western problem unresolved, and that omission alone delayed their ratification until February 1781 when Maryland, under pressure from French officials who wanted a united ally as the war reached a critical stage and after Virginia had shown a willingness to compromise, reluctantly approved them. The controversy over control of the West raised fundamental constitutional issues. Who had jurisdiction to resolve the conflicting claims? If Congress attempted to impose a solution, would it jeopardize the union, or at least doom any effort to create a more dynamic national government? Assuming states like Virginia eventually surrendered their claims to Congress, how would the territories be governed?[59]

Speculators saw land in the West as a source of potential profits; most politicians dreamed it could be used to finance the Revolution. Jefferson, above all else, wanted to settle the land with sturdy yeoman farmers. To him, expansion and republicanism complemented one another, and he considered expansion virtually inevitable. "They will," he said, "settle the land in spite of everybody." Although he later proposed a more politically feasible course, he initially preferred giving the lands away, arguing taxes paid by new settlers should be sufficient to pay the Continental debt.[60]

As a state legislator, Jefferson had worked with George Mason to develop a legal framework for orderly development. In January 1778, they produced a bill to settle private claims within Virginia's borders and a companion bill establishing a land office to sell "waste and unappropriated lands." The land office bill—primarily, it seems, Jefferson's work—retained the colonial head-right system, gave 75 acres to native Virginians upon marriage, and provided that purchases of land not exceeding 400 acres could be made through the local county clerk. Larger purchases went through the state treasurer. Mason took the lead on the title bill; it confirmed royal grants to land companies with properly surveyed claims, granted squatters 400 acres and the right to purchase up to 2,000 acres, and established a commission to decide title disputes. The commission would function without a jury and with no right of appeal, which, coming from Jefferson and Mason, seemed uncharacteristically autocratic, but Jefferson argued the commission should be given broad discretion because there was no relevant law to apply.[61]

Opposition came from Tidewater aristocrats who feared western expansion as a threat to the privileged position of the East and from conservatives with ties to the land companies. Neither bill passed until June 1779, as Jefferson was starting his first term as governor. The assembly made substantial amendments to the land office bill, eliminating the provisions for headrights and for land grants to newlyweds and requiring all purchases to go through the state treasurer, which made transactions more difficult for small frontier farmers. Those, and other amendments, favored the speculators.[62]

The land bills were obviously an assertion of Virginia's jurisdiction in disputed territory. In the fall of 1779, Congress decided to consider a petition from the Indiana and Vandalia land companies to validate their claims in what is today West Virginia and asked Virginia to delay opening its land office. Mason responded, on behalf of the assembly, with a stout defense of Virginia's sovereignty. Madison, aided by fellow Virginia congressman Joseph Jones, presented the state's case to Congress, arguing that body had no legal authority to determine title to land within Virginia's borders. Mason's rebuttal stifled the opposition for months.[63]

Jefferson hoped revenues from the land office, the confiscation and sale of Loyalist property, and new taxes would put Virginia on a sound fiscal footing and allow it to "cooperate with our sister states" in reducing the amount of deflated paper money in circulation. "Every other remedy is nonsensical quackery," he opined. Yet the travails of the land office bill may have predisposed Jefferson and Mason to support a cession of the trans Appalachian West to Congress on the theory the national government would manage the territory more responsibly than would the Virginia assembly. In any event, Jefferson, Mason, Madison, and Jones all favored a compromise. Jefferson advised David Shepard, a Virginia county lieutenant in territory also claimed by Pennsylvania, to encourage Virginians there to "neglect little circumstances of irritation" and avoid provoking an interstate confrontation that could "shipwreck the general cause." Jefferson also reassured Samuel Huntington, the president of Congress, that the land office bill would not take effect for a year, which would give Virginia time to negotiate a settlement of the Pennsylvania border dispute and, by implication, other issues.[64]

The New York legislature helped create momentum for a settlement in February 1780 when, hoping to win support for its claim to Vermont, it voted to cede its rights to land farther west if doing so would expedite ratification of the Articles of Confederation. Mason, meanwhile, steered a bill settling his state's dispute with Pennsylvania through the assembly. Mason, Jones, and Madison—undoubtedly with Jefferson's blessing—also agreed on terms for a Virginia cession to Congress: new states would be carved out of ceded territories in the Northwest; Virginia would be reimbursed for the costs of George Rogers Clark's western campaigns; promised land bounties to Virginia's veterans would be honored; western lands would be held for the common benefit of the United States; and private purchases of land from Native Americans would not be recognized. The last two points targeted the land companies; their titles often derived from unscrupulous dealings with hard-pressed tribes, and the more land the speculators could secure, the less revenue the cession would generate for Congress.[65]

Madison and Jones sought to promote a cession on Virginia's terms in Congress while Mason urged his fellow assembly members to compromise. On 10 October 1780, Congress approved a generally favorable committee report but refused to reimburse Virginia for the costs of its western military operations or to repudiate private purchases of Indian lands. The result embarrassed Madison because he could not deliver Virginia's vote; Jones had left Philadelphia to lobby the Virginia assembly, and Madison's remaining colleagues, John Walker and Theodorick Bland, voted with the land companies. Representatives of the Indiana Company, Madison reported to Jefferson, had used "every art ... to extend their influence and support their pretensions."[66]

Madison and his allies had won only a partial victory, and the western issue had hardly been resolved, but a consensus was beginning to emerge around three crucial points. The states would cede their lands to Congress voluntarily through negotiations between equals. Western lands were to be managed for the common benefit of all American citizens, and at some point new states with republican governments would be created in the ceded territories. In January 1781, the assembly approved Mason's conditions for a surrender of Virginia's claims to land north of the Ohio River. Congress did not immediately accept it. With the matter stalled in Philadelphia, Madison confided to Jefferson that state lawmakers might be justified in suspending or revoking the cession if they presumed "the present Union will but little survive the present war," but he urged restraint. The assembly, he wrote, "ought to be as fully impressed with the necessity of the Union during the war."[67] In other words, Madison premised the survival of the union, even in the short term, on a mutually agreeable solution to the western problem, and in time, it would come. Congress would respect the territorial integrity of the states, creating space—although no one may have realized it at the time—to strengthen the national government.

—

The viability of western settlements, whoever controlled them, depended in large measure on American access to the Mississippi River. When the Revolution began, Great Britain owned the east bank of the river and navigation rights to it. Spain controlled New Orleans and the mouth of the Mississippi. Spain declared war on Britain in 1779 but did not enter into an alliance with the United States. In August 1780, after the American defeats in South Carolina, John Jay, Congress's representative in Madrid, asked for instructions. Jay thought the United States needed Spanish assistance; he did not know what he could give up to get it.[68]

The Virginia assembly had resolved that any treaty with Spain should guarantee American access to the Mississippi, and Joseph Jones wrote a report for Congress asserting the American claims. After Jones left Congress in September, the task of drafting Jay's instructions fell to Madison. In his first major public paper on foreign affairs, Madison argued that the Treaty of Paris of 1763, which ended the French and Indian War, had fixed the border between British and Spanish territory and that the United States had inherited Britain's rights. He also made practical arguments: the river marked a natural boundary, American states had claims in the West, and American citizens had begun to settle the area. Americans, he noted ominously, might cause problems if anyone attempted to exclude them from the region. The United States, he added, needed the resources of the West to support its war against Great Britain.[69]

If the United States had succeeded to the rights of Great Britain, it might logically follow that title to the West had devolved on Congress, not the individual states, a position inconsistent with Virginia's western claims. Madison tried to ignore that problem, and in fact he had a better argument on the more salient issue: navigation rights on the Mississippi River. Here he again asserted the rights of the United States as the successor to the 1763 treaty, but he also appealed to natural law and the law of nations. Closing the river to American traffic would "contravene the clear indications of nature and providence, and the general good of mankind." Citing Emer de Vattel, Madison argued international law should merely allow Spain to impose a tax on American commerce. He also appealed to Spain's self-interest. Predicting rapid growth in the West, Madison predicted as well that if American goods could not travel down the Mississippi, they would go up the St. Lawrence, increasing U.S. trade with Great Britain at the expense of Spain and its ally France.[70]

Benedict Arnold's defection had horrified Madison, and his invasion of Virginia forced the Virginia assembly to reconsider its position. In Congress, states with no western claims seemed willing to make concessions to Spain as the price of an alliance. Congress enlisted a reluctant Madison, who was apparently becoming a congressional expert on western diplomacy, to draft new instructions to Jay. The American diplomat could now "recede" from his previous directive regarding the Mississippi "so far as it insisted on their [the United States'] claim to the navigation of that river below the 31st degree of Latitude, and to a free port or ports below the same." As luck or providence would have it, the new instructions took months to reach a wary Jay, who made only a half-hearted effort to negotiate with the Spanish, with the result that nothing had been settled when the Franco-American victory at York-town made the issue of a Spanish alliance virtually moot.[71]

Jefferson and Madison often reached for more in the West than they could grasp. Military operations beyond the mountains taxed Virginia's re-sources to the breaking point and impaired the state's ability to defend itself. Why were they willing to take on so much? Popular support goes a long way in explaining their western ambitions. As the leading student of the Revolution in Virginia has noted, "Authorities had noticeably less difficulty recruiting troops for the conquest and defense of the West than for reinforce-ment of Washington in the North." Moreover, the virtuous farmers on whom the survival of republican government depended, as Jefferson and Madison saw it, would need land, and they would need access to the Mississippi to send their crops to market. If Jefferson and Madison had their failures, their successes and the positions they staked out helped the United States secure clear title to the West when the 1783 Treaty of Paris ended the Revolutionary War.[72] Creating a central government capable of exploiting that advantage would become another reason for constitutional reform.

———

The greatest threat to the success of the American Revolution was an in-ability to pay for it. The value of Virginia's currency had begun to fall by the time Jefferson became governor. In May 1779, the assembly had authorized the payment of taxes in commodities, but collection was difficult and pay-ment in kind exacerbated the shortage of transportation. When the assem-bly raised taxes or printed more money, inflation negated any real increase in state revenues. Jefferson, who wanted to reduce the amount of money in circulation, complained to Richard Henry Lee that inflation may do what "a powerful enemy could not." By the fall of 1779, Madison had concluded that the sale of Loyalist estates and western lands would not generate enough rev-enue to finance the war effort. Taxation, he thought, offered a better option, but he feared that as far as Continental expenses went, Congress had asked the states for all it "prudently" could.[73]

Elected to Congress in late 1779 but confined to Montpelier by bad weather, Madison spent part of the winter, as he put it in his autobiography, "making himself acquainted with the state of the Continental affairs, and particularly that of the finances which, owing to the depreciation of the paper currency, was truly deplorable." Madison reduced his thoughts to a brief philosophical essay of the kind for which he would become famous. In his "Money" essay, Madison addressed the causes of inflation. He rejected the arguments of Montesquieu and Hume that the amount of money in circulation determined its value. He emphasized instead the creditworthiness of a nation. British bills or notes were payable on demand in specie and held their value. American notes provided holders with no such certainty: "In the emissions of Congress, no precise time has been stipulated for their redemption, nor any specific provision made for that purpose." The war itself undermined public confidence. Madison explained the problem: "a train of sinister events during the early stages of the war likewise contributed to increase the distrust of the public ability to fulfill their engagements." Increasing the amount of money appeared to decrease its value simply because the more paper in circulation, the more difficult it would be to redeem. Monetary stability, Madison implied, would require the restoration of public confidence through conservative fiscal policies.[74]

On 3 March 1780, the day Madison arrived in Philadelphia, Congress adopted a new plan to stabilize the currency. Congress would relinquish its right to print money, leaving that power to the state governments. Existing Continental dollars would be retired at a rate of 40 to 1 to new bills, which would be redeemed in specie in six years. As the states collected the old Continentals in taxes, they would be sent to Congress for destruction, and a $200 million national debt would be reduced to $15 million dollars. For every $20 returned, the states could print $1, which would produce $10 million dollars, 40 percent of which would go to Congress. New notes were to be redeemed by state taxes paid in specific commodities, with Congress pledging to make good any shortfall by an individual state.[75]

Madison predicted the new plan "will probably create great perplexity and complaints in many private transactions." With the army near collapse, the treasury empty, and Congress's credit exhausted, Madison warned Jefferson that "a total stagnation [was] in prospect" during the transition to the new currency system. By May, Madison could report to Jefferson that the currency, both old and new, had depreciated rapidly. Everything now depended on the states, and Madison feared they might be slow in providing the requested supplies. All concerned understood that the financial crisis imperiled the ability of both Congress and the states to carry on the war. Anthony Wayne's Pennsylvania troops, ordered south to confront the British, were delayed for weeks by "the want of money." Virginia continued to issue large amounts of paper money but remained unable to supply its soldiers adequately. As Jefferson described the situation in November, "Clothing, blankets, and transportation are objects of immense difficulty, and money is necessary to set every wheel in motion."[76] Madison, in turn, sent to Richmond reports of mutinies among poorly paid and ill-fed Connecticut and Pennsylvania regiments.[77]

Living in expensive Philadelphia on a congressional salary rendered inadequate by inflation, Madison felt the economic crisis more personally than did Jefferson, who could still retreat to Monticello. In 1780, Madison spent well over $6,000 simply to stable his horses. In November, the Virginia delegates complained to Governor Jefferson that the state had to find a better system "for supplying us with money. Other wise we shall not be able to exist." By the spring of 1781, Madison and his Virginia colleagues were talking about selling "what little property we possess here" or going home. There were undoubtedly many reasons why Madison was interested in constitutional reform; surely his personal ordeal in Philadelphia played some small part.[78]

———

Despite frustrations great and petty, James Madison emerged as a national leader during the spring and summer of 1780. He served on almost every major congressional committee, and as his political stature grew, even his health seemed to improve. He set a record for regular attendance no other delegate to the Continental Congress ever surpassed.[79] Ironically, the status of Congress had begun to decline dramatically just as Madison began his legislative service, and he knew it. By relinquishing the power to print money, Congress, he told Jefferson, had made itself entirely dependent on the states. Ratification of the Articles of Confederation in early 1781 may have weakened Congress yet again. Before the Articles took effect, Congress, with considerable popular support and a war to manage, could attempt to do virtually anything the states seemed willing to accept. Ratification, however, imposed precise limits on congressional authority.[80]

Madison repeatedly supported efforts to strengthen the central government, with limited success. The Articles provided that routine matters could be decided by a simple majority. Madison argued unsuccessfully that the requirement meant a majority of states present. The majority of delegates read it to mean a majority of all the states, which made it much more difficult to pass anything since absenteeism was common, and a state had to have at least two delegates present to cast its one vote. Madison proposed giving Congress the power to authorize the impressment of supplies and to impose an embargo; state officials who refused to enforce trade restrictions, Madison suggested, should be dismissed, although he was willing to leave that step to the state courts. He authored a proposal to create a national system of admiralty courts, again using state court judges. He had more success persuading colleagues to put crucial departments under a single individual rather than under a committee; the Pennsylvania financier Robert Morris, for example, became superintendent of finance.[81]

The most sensible reform debated while Madison was in Congress was an amendment to the Articles that would have allowed Congress to impose a 5 percent duty on imports. Madison supported it enthusiastically, and the impost had broad appeal, even though the states could never quite agree on the details of the provision. In an apparent fit of desperation, Madison authored one amendment that, if adopted, might have provoked a civil war. He believed Congress possessed "an implied right of coercion" to enforce its decisions. Why would the Articles confer a power on Congress if lawmakers could not compel obedience? To remove all doubt, Madison drafted an amendment authorizing the use of force against recalcitrant states. As he explained his thinking to Jefferson, should a state refuse to abide by an embargo or fail to meet a congressional requisition, a small naval force could blockade its major ports and, with little or no violence, force the state to submit to the will of Congress. Madison admitted that failure of the amendment would discredit his theory of an implied power of coercion—the states would have expressly rejected the idea of coercion—but he argued, "It is . . . most consonant to the spirit of a free constitution" that powers and sanctions "be clearly promulgated and understood." The amendment had some friends in Congress but, wholly inconsistent with the political tenor of the times, never came close to passage.[82]

Madison had asked for Jefferson's opinion of his amendment. There is no record of a reply. Perhaps Jefferson tactfully ignored the request. Jefferson did write a few days later that he had lost most of his papers during "the visit which was made by General Arnold to this place." Perhaps the outgoing governor overlooked Madison's inquiry in the tumultuous final days of his administration. In any event, Jefferson was not ready to endorse such draconian methods, although he eventually would. In June 1778, when Congress probably enjoyed greater prestige than it would later in the war, Jefferson told Richard Henry Lee that he did not think the Virginia legislature would approve enlarging the powers of Congress. Lee, a congressional veteran, had apparently suggested some unspecified enhancements. Madison's national service likewise convinced him of the need for constitutional reform, but for the moment, a more skeptical Jefferson, at home in Virginia, possessed the keener political instincts.[83]

A Friendship Was Formed

FOUR

All the World Is Becoming Commercial

1781–1785

IN THE FALL OF 1781, the General Assembly elected Thomas Jefferson to Congress. He declined the appointment. Still bitter at the legislative inquiry into his conduct as governor, Jefferson told James Monroe that "every fiber" of political ambition had been "thoroughly eradicated" from his system. If he had ultimately been vindicated, "in the meantime I had been suspected & suspended in the eyes of the world." Jefferson hoped that, after devoting much of his life to public service, "I shall be permitted to pass the rest in mental quiet."[1]

Martha Wayles Jefferson's death, after a difficult pregnancy, in September 1782 changed everything. The loss of his wife plunged Jefferson into a deep depression and, as he put it, "wiped away all my plans and left me a blank which I had not the spirits to fill up." Jefferson's retirement had worried James Madison. Sensing an opportunity to make the best of a tragedy, Madison secured Jefferson's appointment to the commission charged with negotiating a peace treaty with Great Britain. Bad weather delayed Jefferson's voyage to Europe until his services were no longer needed, and Congress canceled his mission in April 1783, but Jefferson had made clear his willingness to return to the political fray.[2]

Jefferson and Madison were growing closer. They stayed in the same Philadelphia boardinghouse for a month while Jefferson prepared for his abortive trip to Europe. Jefferson tried to console Madison when his fiancée, Catherine Floyd, the sixteen-year-old daughter of a New York congressman, unexpectedly broke off their engagement. Jefferson and Madison met again in Philadelphia in the fall of 1783 when term limits forced Madison to retire from Congress; Jefferson agreed to replace him. Jefferson made a quick trip to Princeton, where Congress was meeting temporarily before deciding to adjourn to Annapolis. Madison traveled to Maryland with him before going home to Montpelier. By the end of the year, Madison had solidified his position as Jefferson's principal political confidant. In letters and conversation, they discussed Madison's legal studies and constitutional reform in Virginia. Jefferson sent Madison his latest draft of a new state constitution, and Madison agreed to support the law revisers' report in the state assembly.[3]

The more vivid personality, Jefferson would eventually inspire more fervent loyalties and more bitter antagonisms. Merrill Peterson has written that "men respected Madison, even in opposition. They worshipped, or hated Jefferson." Usually seen as the senior partner in the relationship, Jefferson also seemed to be the more emotionally dependent, or controlling, as when he invited Madison, whose Montpelier estate was only thirty miles from Monticello, to buy land closer to him. Jefferson had extended similar invitations to Monroe and William Short. "With such a society," he wrote Madison, "I could once more venture home and lay myself up for the residue of life."[4]

Meanwhile, Madison and his congressional colleagues grappled with new issues raised by the end of the Revolution. George Washington recommended that Congress maintain three or four regiments to garrison West Point and a few frontier posts and coastal batteries, but Madison worried that the Articles of Confederation did not allow Congress to support a peacetime military. Congress also had to choose a permanent capital for the new nation, a task that provoked bitter sectional rivalries. The delegates temporized and compromised, eventually agreeing in the fall of 1783 to establish two permanent "federal towns," one near Trenton and the other along the Potomac, and alternate between Annapolis and Trenton in the interim. Madison supported one tentative decision that set a lasting precedent: the national capital ought to be fixed in a federal district "to be entirely exempted from the authority of the State ceding the same." That position, however, raised another issue. Could Congress accept a gift of land from a state to exercise a power—creating a federal district—not authorized by the Articles? It all led Madison to complain to Edmund Randolph that Congress would seem to be "incompetent to every act not warranted by that instrument or some other flowing from the same source."[5]

All the World Is Becoming Commercial

His congressional service ended with one final indignity. A mutiny by unpaid Continental soldiers had forced Congress to abandon Philadelphia for Princeton. Madison had enjoyed Princeton as a college town. Yet as an ersatz capital, it was, he thought, wholly inadequate. Forced to share a room "not ten feet square" with his rotund Virginia colleague Joseph Jones, and "without a single accommodation for writing," he complained to Jefferson, "I am obliged to write in a position that scarcely admits the use of any of my limbs." The Princeton Congress accomplished very little, and once the danger passed, the delegates spent weeks deciding whether they wanted to return to Philadelphia or to seek refuge elsewhere. "The picture of our affairs is not a flattering one," he admitted to Jefferson, but he added hopefully that previous ills had produced "their own remedy."[6]

Madison's congressional term officially expired on 2 November 1783. Term limits aside, "the idea of protracting my service in Congress," he had written Randolph in June, "does not coincide with the plans which I have in view," which at that point apparently included marriage to Kitty Floyd. Madison left office as a strong nationalist, up to a point. He had given a broad interpretation to Congress's power to make war. Madison had written a report for Congress proposing to use military force to prevent Americans from trading illegally with the British. Congress called on the states to stop the illicit commerce but deleted Madison's references to the use of force. He believed Congress possessed an implied power to compel the states to provide it with troops and money, and he thought the Articles of Confederation had been intended to create a "perpetual Union." At the same time, he defended Virginia's right to cede its western lands to Congress on its own terms. When New Jersey authorities refused to exchange two Loyalists for American prisoners of war, he acquiesced, although the issue appeared to fall within the congressional war power. He voted most reluctantly to charter Robert Morris's Bank of North America; he took some comfort in compromise language calling on the states to adopt legislation giving the bank "all the necessary validity within their respective jurisdictions." He hoped the "tacit admission" that Congress lacked the power to charter a bank would "be an antidote against the poisonous tendency of precedents of usurpation."[7]

Returning to Virginia, Madison had reasons for modest optimism, or at least pride in his own performance. After entering Congress as a relative unknown, he left as a leader of the body's moderate nationalists and as something of an expert on territorial, fiscal, and foreign policy issues. Madison recognized determining the original intent behind the Articles of Confederation could be difficult because the document's authors had not always been of one mind. He spent four years in Congress, longer than anyone else, and his tenacity, unassuming personality, and attention to detail earned him wide respect.[8]

Jefferson succeeded him in a Congress that, despite the coming of peace, confronted several vexing issues, including the disposition of western lands and chronic financial woes, as it struggled simply to maintain a quorum. Major decisions required the concurrence of nine states, and under the Articles, a state had to have two delegates present before it could vote. Typically only seven or eight states were present, and most of them had only two delegates, creating the possibility of a deadlock within a delegation or the loss of a state's vote by a temporary absence. In February 1784, Jefferson reported to Madison that two delegates were confined to their quarters by gout. Jefferson thought that if all the states could have three delegates present at the start of a session, Congress could manage its affairs by meeting not more than two or three months a year. As it was, Congress could do nothing but "waste our time, temper, and spirits."[9]

Jefferson blamed the delegates' poor attendance on the simple fact "that their states do not furnish them with money." Lack of means drove "spirited members" to go home, and "thus we are kept with a house incompetent to business." He complained to Madison that he had been in Congress for months and incurred $1,200 in expenses "before I received one farthing" from the state of Virginia. Madison undoubtedly sympathized with his plight; Madison's 20 paper dollars per day were worth mere pennies while he served in Congress.[10]

The American economy struggled in the 1780s; historians disagree about how well the states handled the postwar recession. Most of the states adopted resolutions to curb British imports, raised taxes to pay off wartime debts, and attempted to satisfy congressional requisitions. In the seven states that had made paper money legal tender by 1786, the currency's value generally remained stable. Some states, or course, performed worse than others. Massachusetts did little to help cash-strapped farmers. Rhode Island became notorious for the profligate printing of paper money. Georgia made no contribution to Congress's financial needs, even though requisitions seemed reasonable. George William Van Cleve has calculated they averaged fewer than five dollars per household a year between 1781 and 1786. They were not, however, popular, and the requisition system never provided Congress with sufficient revenue.[11]

Jefferson fumed as Congress waited weeks to assemble the nine states necessary to ratify the peace treaty with Great Britain, but he opposed a

All the World Is Becoming Commercial

proposal to allow the seven states present to approve the agreement. Finally, on 14 January 1784, nine states assembled to approve the Treaty of Paris. Jefferson feared the news of ratification would not reach Europe by the deadline set by the peace commissioners; Madison assured him the delay would be immaterial. His prediction proved correct, but Congress's embarrassments persisted. Congress could not pay a courier to deliver the instrument of ratification, so the French minister Anne-César, Chevalier de la Luzerne, paid a British sea captain to take it to England and France.[12]

Even when Congress had funds, its procedural rules continued to stifle action. Under the Articles, appropriations bills required the votes of nine states. Jefferson thought that once a budget was approved, "trifling money propositions" should require only a simple majority. Madison agreed; if not, "the Secretary of Congress could not buy quills or wafers without a vote of nine States." Often, of course, the funds were lacking. "Virginia," Jefferson thought, "must do something more than she has done to maintain any degree of respect in the Union and to make it bearable to any man of feeling to represent her in Congress."[13] Jefferson favored the creation of a "committee of the states" to function during a congressional recess. Congress tried the experiment in the summer of 1784, but the committee split into factions, several New England members went home, and the plan collapsed.[14]

Jefferson ultimately judged the Articles of Confederation to be a failure. Once peace came, Americans became preoccupied with their own affairs, and "less attention was paid to the calls of Congress." The central government, such as it was, suffered because there was no separation of powers and because Congress lacked a reliable source of revenue, but Jefferson concluded that "the fundamental defect of the Confederation was that Congress was not authorized to act immediately on the people," a view Madison shared.[15]

Through it all, however, Jefferson typically seemed more sanguine than Madison and more confident that whatever obstacles the nation faced, they would eventually be overcome. Writing from Annapolis to his friend, Jefferson admitted the mutiny in Philadelphia had created "great doubts of the stability of our confederacy" in Europe, but he dismissed the reports of disorder in America as "greatly exaggerated." He usually presented the best face possible when he discussed American politics with Europeans. In early 1784, he assured the Frenchman Chevalier de Chastellux that, while Congress labored to requisition money from the states and while the Articles of Confederation would need to be amended, "as yet everything has gone smoothly since the war." For all its flaws, he found Congress to be "a good school for our young statesmen." In the national legislature, "they see the affairs of the Confederacy from a high ground; they learn the importance of the Union." When the lower house of the Massachusetts assembly passed a bill to give Congress the power to regulate commerce, Jefferson thought the vote illustrated a strong and growing conviction that "nothing can preserve our Confederacy unless the band of Union, their common council be strengthened."[16]

Jefferson's return to Congress lasted a year, and then he accepted a diplomatic post in Europe, leaving, like James Madison, as a respected Virginia nationalist. David Howell of Rhode Island thought Jefferson had been "one of the best members I have ever seen in Congress." In May 1784, Jefferson bid farewell to the Virginia House of Delegates. He had, he told them, "made the just rights of my country," by which he meant Virginia, "and the cement of that union in which her happiness and security is bound up, the leading objects of my conduct."[17]

Madison would keep Jefferson apprised of conditions at home. After a trip to Philadelphia and New York in the fall of 1785, Madison reported to his friend in Paris, "Congress has kept the vessel from sinking, but it has been by standing constantly at the pump, not by stopping the leaks which have endangered her." He blamed the selfishness of its constituents for blocking Congress's efforts at reform.[18] Three issues in particular tested that union throughout the 1780s: the challenge of governing the West and ensuring American access to the Mississippi River; the problem of paying the nation's Revolutionary War debt and financing its modest central government; and the task of promoting American commerce abroad, especially in the British West Indies. Each deserves further attention.

———

Virginia's cession of its claims to land north of the Ohio River languished in Congress for years. Speculators opposed the conditions Virginia had attached, including its ban on private purchases of Indian land. Madison believed New Jersey, Pennsylvania, Delaware, and Maryland were motivated "principally by the intrigues of their citizens who are interested in the claims of land companies." New York claimed most of the same territory, and Connecticut asserted title to a strip of land south of Lake Michigan. State claims rose and fell on a confusing sea of colonial charters, Indian treaties, and royal grants and decrees. Nationalists could argue that "vacant country," as Madison called it, was already part of the national domain. In 1781, a congressional committee had issued a report sympathetic to New York's position. Arguing that Congress lacked jurisdiction to determine a state's borders, Virginia had refused to provide the committee with evidence of its title. The

All the World Is Becoming Commercial

opposition left Madison irritated and pessimistic, although he and Jefferson remained committed to the eventual transfer of land in the West to Congress. As Jefferson put it, "This separation is unacceptable to us in form only and not in substance."[19]

After Yorktown, pressure for a settlement grew. Congress needed the revenue a newly acquired national domain could provide, and it needed land for the enlistment bounties it had promised veterans. George Washington warned Jefferson that, if the cession issue were not resolved, squatters would settle the West to the detriment of both Virginia and Congress. Jefferson worried about Patrick Henry's proposal to establish independent republics in the disputed territory. In the summer of 1783, however, a congressional committee issued a new report that Madison believed offered "a fit basis for compromise" because "it tacitly excludes the pretentions of the [land] Companies." After Congress indicated a willingness to compromise, the Virginia assembly passed a new cession act that only implicitly asserted its authority over existing private claims. The vagueness satisfied Congress, and on 1 March 1784, Virginia presented Congress with a deed to the territory.[20]

Madison had helped to begin the process of transferring the trans-Ohio region to national control. Jefferson continued it. In December 1783, Jefferson had been made chair of a committee to draft a plan for a temporary government in the West. Beginning with the idea of creating a single western colony, Jefferson changed his mind as he worked on the project, deciding instead to recommend the creation of several new states. Struggling to fix the new state boundaries, the committee left behind a confusing paper trail but ultimately came to some reasonably clear conclusions.[21]

On the day the cession was completed, Jefferson, on behalf of the committee, introduced what would become the Ordinance of 1784. Although the report was not specific, he apparently envisioned dividing the territory into fourteen states, arranged longitudinally in three tiers. He ignored physical features; the Virginia cession had said the new states should be 100 to 150 miles square. To much ridicule from later historians, he gave his proposed states Indian names with classical endings. Cherroneus was one. All free white men could vote in a process designed to move quickly from a temporary government to a constitutional convention to statehood, when the new states would enjoy all the rights of the original thirteen. The Virginians had insisted on equality among the states.[22]

Under Jefferson's proposal, settlers would possess considerable autonomy, but the provisional governments would remain under congressional oversight. The new state governments had to be republican, they would be assigned a portion of the national debt, and they were required to remain in the union. After 1800, slavery would be prohibited in the region and in any additional territory acquired by the United States. The ban on slavery fell one vote short of the seven votes needed for passage. An ailing John Berry of New Jersey was absent, which left his state, an almost certain antislavery vote, with only one delegate and therefore unable to vote. Congress also deleted Jefferson's fanciful state names.[23]

Almost simultaneously, Jefferson drafted a proposal for a land office to sell plots in the newly ceded territory. He had hoped free land could be made available to settlers, but he bowed to financial necessity and, as he often did, made the best of it. After reaching Paris in the fall of 1785, he assured the English diplomat David Hartley that the sale of western land would shortly "rid us of our domestic debt, which is four fifths of our whole debt. Our foreign debt," he added, "will then be a bagatelle."[24]

Much of the Ordinance of 1784 would soon be superseded by the more famous Northwest Ordinance of 1787, which, reflecting pressure from eastern conservatives and, in all likelihood, political reality, tightened congressional authority over the West. Yet in managing the legal and constitutional issues raised by the existence, from a white perspective, of unappropriated lands in the West, Madison and Jefferson had helped establish three precedents. Congress would respect the territorial integrity of the states, even when their borders were ill defined. Ceded regions would eventually become full-fledged states. And finally, congressional power would be liberally construed when it came to acquiring and governing new territories; the Articles did not specifically authorize Congress to do what it had done.[25]

Jefferson also favored Virginia's cession of Kentucky because he feared Kentucky might break away unilaterally and take all the land west of the Alleghany Mountains with it. He hoped to maintain Virginia's control of the Great Kanawha River in what is today West Virginia partly because he thought the river could be made navigable, thereby connecting the Ohio and Potomac Rivers and giving Virginia access to both western and Atlantic commerce. In fact, Kentucky remained part of Virginia until achieving statehood in 1792. Jefferson and Madison shared a vision common among Virginians: state-supported internal improvements and navigation projects could open new trade routes and give Virginia's planters and farmers access to land in the West. State and national governments could cooperate in promoting commerce. Congress could provide law and order in frontier regions beyond the effective reach of Virginia authorities and help secure markets in Europe and the West Indies for America's agricultural surplus.[26]

In that vein, Madison complained to Jefferson when the British refused after the Revolution to abandon a string of forts along the frontier. Madison suspected, correctly, that they, or the Canadians, hoped to monopolize the fur trade in the Northwest. A far more serious threat to America's commercial interests came from Spain. Madison had reported to Jefferson in May 1783 that the Spanish had been cooperative in fixing the American border with West Florida, but he added, "The navigation of the Mississippi remains to be settled." In 1784, Spain, hoping to stem the tide of American settlers who seemed destined to someday overflow its borders, closed the river to U.S. traffic. Madison considered Spain's strategy misguided, writing Jefferson that Spanish security really depended on "the complexity of our federal government and the diversity of interests among the States" or, in other words, on the inability of the Americans to reach the consensus necessary for action under the Articles. In that case, Madison concluded, Spain would benefit from American expansion. New states would make concerted action even more difficult.[27]

In the summer of 1785, John Jay, then Congress's secretary for foreign affairs, began talks in New York with the Spanish minister Don Diego de Gardoqui over the Mississippi issue, while Madison, now a member of the Virginia assembly, launched his own campaign to reopen the river. He laid out the American argument in a long letter to the Marquis de Lafayette. Congress needed to sell public land in the West to retire its Revolutionary War debt, much of which was owed to France, and the value of the land depended on access to the Mississippi. "Nature has given the use of the Mississippi to those who may settle on its waters," and nations are most successful when they abide by the laws of nature. Spain could slow but not stop American expansion. Attempting to confine the United States to the Atlantic Seaboard would only encourage the development of an American navy, which could not be in Spain's best interest.[28]

Madison hoped Lafayette could influence the French government to pressure Spain to reconsider its decision. "The chief advantages expected in Europe" from American independence, he wrote, "center in the revolution it was to produce in the commerce between the new and old world." An expanding, agricultural United States would be a lucrative market for European manufactured goods and a bountiful source of raw materials. Confined to the coast, Americans would turn to subsistence agriculture and domestic industry, depriving Europeans of a profitable trade. European governments did not necessarily agree, and neither did many northern members of Congress. Use of the Mississippi meant far more to southerners like Madison and Jefferson than it did to New Yorkers or New Englanders, and sectional differences over the relative importance of the river would do more than any other issue to undermine national unity in the years preceding the Constitutional Convention.[29]

———

THOMAS JEFFERSON concluded late in life that among the weaknesses of the Articles of Confederation, none was "more distressing than the utter impossibility of obtaining from the states, the monies necessary for the payment of debts, or even for the ordinary expenses of government." In February 1781, Congress had asked the states for an amendment to the Articles that would have allowed it to impose a duty of 5 percent on imports. Twelve states approved the measure, but it died in November 1782 when Rhode Island rejected it.[30]

Madison had feared the impost of 1781 would fail. With Congress unable to pay its bills, soldiers and creditors looked to the states for relief, and when New Jersey, in 1782, promised to pay New Jersey troops in the Continental line, Madison considered it a threat to "the federal constitution." The Virginia assembly's decision to repeal its ratification of the impost after Rhode Island had defeated the levy perplexed and embarrassed him. Confident "that with the same knowledge of facts which my station commands, my Constituents would never have passed that act," Madison continued to work in Congress for what he often called "a general revenue."[31]

On 28 January 1783, Madison delivered a major speech in support of a new impost proposal. "The idea," he told his fellow delegates, "of erecting our national independence on the ruins of public faith and national honor must be horrid to every mind which retained either honesty or pride." Public creditors must be paid, and Madison favored a general revenue sufficient to free Congress from its financial dependence on the states. Without it, the states would pay their own citizen-creditors and veterans, assume the Continental debt, undermine the authority of Congress, and weaken the union. Madison dismissed objections that giving Congress an independent source of revenue would violate the republican maxim against combining in one body "the constitutional authority over the purse as well as the sword." That bridge had been crossed when the Articles of Confederation gave Congress the power to make requisitions on the states.[32]

In February, Madison reported to Jefferson that Congress had reached an impasse in trying to allocate costs among the states. The Articles said requisitions were to be based on land values, but Congress could not agree

All the World Is Becoming Commercial

on an appraisal process, and Madison did not think the states would approve any alternative source of funds.[33] Madison had expressed a willingness to compromise in his January speech, and he was forced to make concessions to his less nationalistic colleagues. On 19 February, Congress voted to allow the states to appoint the collectors of the impost. The next day members voted to limit the impost to twenty-five years, and they eventually agreed to base a state's share of the federal debt on its white population.[34]

The indefatigable Madison accepted the changes and, with the support of Alexander Hamilton, James Wilson, and Robert Morris, continued to urge the other delegates to endorse a revenue amendment of some kind. Such a measure "could not be deemed inconsistent with the spirit of the federal constitution," he told them, although public opinion required any national levy be limited to "duties on commerce." Congress needed more money than an impost could produce, but Madison would now allow each state to make up its share of the deficiency however it saw fit.[35]

Appointed to a committee to draft a comprehensive revenue plan, Madison presented a new proposal to Congress in March. It called for a 5 percent ad valorem tax on most imports and for specific duties on salt, wine, rum, brandy, sugar, and tea. Levies would remain on the books for twenty-five years. Proceeds would be earmarked for the payment of the Revolutionary War debt. Tax collectors would be appointed by the states but could be dismissed by Congress. States would be asked to raise an additional $1.5 million. To avoid the problem of valuing land, a state's total revenue obligation would be based on its population, with a slave counted as three-fifths of a free person. To give the plan broad appeal, Madison included several provisions that were not, strictly speaking, revenue measures. States would receive a credit, or abatement, for war-related damage; Congress would assume reasonable state war debts; and, to entice "landless states," states with land in the West would be urged to complete their cessions of territory to Congress. Madison thought Virginia and the other southern states should support the plan because, as he told Jefferson, they were "likely to enjoy an opulent and defenceless trade" and would need a strong central government to protect them "agst. the maritime superiority of the E[astern] States."[36]

Congress approved an amended version of Madison's plan on 18 April 1783. But the delegates separated the various provisions and then defeated his proposals for an abatement for war-torn regions and the assumption of state debts. Madison and Jefferson believed the changes would make the surviving amendments less attractive to Virginians. Madison nevertheless remained cautiously optimistic, and Jefferson, passing through Richmond, lobbied state lawmakers to support the impost. To his mild surprise, Patrick Henry endorsed it, although he does not appear to have made much effort on the measure's behalf.[37]

Madison, by contrast, prepared a congressional address to the states in support of the revenue plan. Voluntary requisitions from the states, as authorized by the Articles, were too slow to allow Congress to make timely interest payments on the national debt. The proposed amendment was as minor a change as possible, he argued, and a tax on consumption was the least burdensome tax imaginable. A secure revenue stream, moreover, would improve the nation's credit rating and reduce costs in the long run. If the plan seemed convoluted, "the strict maxims of public credit gave way to the desire of Congress to conform to the sentiments of their constituents."[38]

Nine states approved the 1783 impost quickly. Then progress slowed. The amendment had not been ratified by the time Jefferson replaced Madison in Congress. Jefferson thought time was of the essence. As new states joined the union, amending the Articles of Confederation would become more difficult. New York and Pennsylvania belatedly approved the revenue plan but with crippling restrictions. In the spring of 1785, as Jefferson's last year in Congress drew to a close, he alternately feared the impost would not be approved in the foreseeable future and was encouraged by reports of growing support for it. By the middle of 1786, however, he knew prospects for eventual ratification were bleak.[39]

——

The new nation faced a host of foreign policy challenges in the 1780s in addition to its conflict with Spain over American use of the Mississippi. Article IV of the Treaty of Paris ending the war provided for the recovery of debts owed by Americans to British creditors. Article V committed Congress to request that the states return confiscated Loyalist property. Yet Congress could enforce neither provision, which gave the British an excuse not to honor their treaty obligation to remove British soldiers from their frontier posts. Even worse, to Jefferson and Madison, were British restrictions on American commerce. Amid the partisan battles of the mid-1790s, Madison wrote publicly that the primary reason for the adoption of the Constitution had been to create a government capable of retaliating against Great Britain for its discriminatory trade policies.[40]

Great Britain had initially seemed open to trade with its former colony on liberal terms. In March 1783, William Pitt, the chancellor of the exchequer, introduced a bill in Parliament that would have permitted U.S. goods aboard

All the World Is Becoming Commercial

U.S. ships in ports in Great Britain and in Britain's American colonies on the same terms as British goods in British bottoms. But British shippers opposed the measure, and Lord Sheffield, in an influential pamphlet, argued that since Congress could not regulate trade, Britain could enjoy all the advantages of American commerce without making any concessions.[41]

Madison served on a committee that considered a proposed commercial treaty with Britain, and he kept Jefferson apprised of its work. The United States wanted to trade directly with the British West Indies and to participate in the carrying trade between the West Indies and other parts of the world, including other ports within the British Empire. Congress, in exchange, would allow British subjects "equal privileges with our own citizens." Madison saw the carrying trade as an issue mainly for New England, but the South, he thought, should want to encourage competition for the right to transport its imports and exports. Madison understood that commercial treaties could have long-term implications; hence they should be of limited duration. He had read Adam Smith's *Wealth of Nations,* and he believed free trade benefited an agrarian society, but as America became more settled, Madison anticipated that Congress might want to adopt regulations to encourage manufacturing and navigation. In a world of mercantilism, truly free trade seemed impractical. He feared trade policy could divide the states; some treaties "may survive the Confederacy itself." At the same time, a treaty that served the interests of all the states "might be a new bond to the federal compact." Yet conscious of the debts that Virginia's planters owed to British merchants, Madison suggested to Edmund Randolph that Virginia might want to reserve certain rights over its own trade in any treaty with Great Britain.[42]

By June 1783, however, prospects for an agreement had dimmed. Madison reported to Jefferson that Robert Livingston, Congress's first secretary for foreign affairs, had resigned, complaining about his meager salary. Congress could not assemble enough members to raise it. Worse yet, in July, with public opinion shifting in England, the Privy Council banned American ships and most American exports from the British West Indies. New restrictions on the American carrying trade followed, and British subjects were forbidden to buy ships built or repaired in the United States since 1776.[43]

Merrill Jensen has argued that smuggling and various legal loopholes greatly reduced the impact of British protectionism, but Madison and Jefferson believed the nation faced a commercial crisis. Congress's inability to either forge a consensus among the states or impose its will on them convinced the British that they could enjoy a robust trade with America, in Madison's words, "without paying any price for it."[44] The two Virginians agreed on the need to retaliate. By April 1784, Jefferson had succeeded Madison in Congress, and he drafted a report recommending that Congress be allowed to prohibit the import or export of goods in ships of countries that had not signed commercial treaties with the United States and to ban foreign merchants from importing goods from any nation other than their own. Congressional inaction, as economic conditions deteriorated, further frustrated Jefferson and Madison. British domination of U.S. trade raised the costs of imported manufactured goods and depressed prices for the nation's staple crops, and Jefferson considered British freight rates to be in essence a tax on American farmers. In November, Jefferson, by then in Europe on his diplomatic mission, lamented to Madison, British "hostility towards us has attained an incredible height." In March 1785, he had concluded nothing but force would lead the British to negotiate. In the meantime, Americans could buy "gee-gaws" anywhere and sell their tobacco around the globe.[45]

Later that year, Madison warned Jefferson that British restrictions on American trade threatened the union; they fell most heavily on merchants in Boston, New York, and Philadelphia. Madison worried the South, enjoying at the time high tobacco prices, might frustrate northern efforts to retaliate against Great Britain. In fact, Madison suspected British policy aimed as much at destroying the union as at monopolizing American trade.[46]

———

"All the world is becoming commercial," Thomas Jefferson told George Washington in March 1784. Jefferson would have preferred to avoid foreign trade, which he thought bred wars, and "to stand with respect to Europe precisely on the footing of China." He realized, however, that complete isolation from the outside world was impractical. An agricultural surplus would eventually force many American farmers to turn to manufacturing or "navigation," and of the two, he preferred maritime trade because he thought sailors made better citizens than factory workers. He hoped America could, for as long as possible, "keep our workmen in Europe." Americans, moreover, would not voluntarily cut themselves off from the emporiums of the Old World; "our citizens have had too full a taste of the comforts furnished by the arts & manufactures to be debarred the use of them." Jefferson recommended accepting the inevitable. Virginia should seek to become a conduit for commerce between Europe and the western frontier, and the United States should build a navy to protect its carrying trade.[47]

Jefferson, Madison, and most American policy makers professed a belief in free trade and in the maxim "Free ships make free goods," or in other

All the World Is Becoming Commercial

words, in a world often at war, neutrals should be able to trade, with a few exceptions, with belligerents. The 1778 Treaty of Amity and Commerce with France reflected those principles. Before the Revolutionary War ended, the United States also signed commercial treaties with Sweden and the Netherlands. Jefferson saw more than economic advantages to such agreements; they also represented "an acknowledgment . . . of our independence and of our reception into the fraternity of nations." Jefferson served, along with Elbridge Gerry of Massachusetts and Hugh Williamson of North Carolina, on a congressional committee charged with drafting instructions for American ministers abroad. Their report embraced free trade and the right of treaty signatories to carry their own produce in their own bottoms to other ports on terms enjoyed by the most favored nation. Even a commercial treaty, however, had political significance. Jefferson, Gerry, and Williamson also recommended that the United States "being by their constitution consolidated into one federal republic . . . be considered in all such treaties and in every case arising under them as one nation."[48]

Madison generally concurred, with a few qualifications. Suspecting that the United States might in the future want to adopt its own protectionist policies, Madison again advocated limiting treaties to modest time periods. He also worried that Congress gave too much deference to its own negotiators.[49] In April 1784, Madison even suggested to Jefferson that Congress suspend its efforts to negotiate new commercial treaties until the central government was given the power to retaliate against Great Britain for restricting access to the British West Indies. Jefferson disagreed. He admitted American trade was suffering "vital agonies" by virtue of the nation's exclusion from the West Indies and from some European ports, but trouble with the British and a few others should not preclude treaties with the rest of the world. He held out some hope that Congress might be able to impose "a uniform measure" to bring the British to terms.[50]

Jefferson found himself at the center of the trade issue. In May 1784, Congress appointed him a minister plenipotentiary, along with Benjamin Franklin and John Adams, to negotiate commercial treaties with the various European powers. Their instructions, which authorized them to begin talks with twenty European and North African states, incorporated language from Jefferson's committee report of a few months earlier. While the committee's desire to open foreign markets to American exports provoked no controversy, the reference to the United States as one nation was, in Jefferson's words, "an extreme delicate point" among "a great party jealous of their separate independence." To appease the critics, Congress had deleted the assertion that the nation was a consolidated, federal republic and, after the reference to America as one nation, added the phrase "upon the principles of the federal constitution."[51]

After Jefferson made a trip north to gather information on possible exports from Pennsylvania, New York, and New England, he and his daughter Patsy left for England in July. There he found "all respect for our government is annihilated on this side of the water, from an idea of its want of tone and energy." The perception of American weakness might well "bring on insults which will force us into war." He did what he could to improve the image of America. Late in 1784, James Monroe chaired a congressional committee that produced another report calling for an amendment to the Articles that would give Congress the power to regulate trade and to tax imports and exports. Opposition came principally from southerners who feared an American navigation act would give the North a monopoly on southern shipping, and the measure died in Congress. Nevertheless, February 1785 found Jefferson reassuring England's Richard Price, a prominent Unitarian minister, that Americans understood Europe was discriminating against their commerce and that "this evil will be immediately redressed and redressed radically" by strengthening the "federal head" of the body politic.[52]

In March 1785, Jefferson replaced Franklin as American minister to France. His experience in Europe heightened Jefferson's sense of American nationalism. It helped him see the need for a national government strong enough to enforce U.S. treaty obligations on the states, to secure America's borders, and to negotiate favorable commercial treaties with the European powers. It also allowed him to test his theory that Congress's treaty-making power could be used to strengthen the union. Jefferson acknowledged that Congress had "no original and inherent power" over commerce and that under the Articles of Confederation, Congress could not prohibit the states from imposing on foreigners the same duties they imposed on their own citizens, nor could it stop a state from prohibiting the import or export of any particular item. But save for those two exceptions, a treaty could preempt state regulation, and as Jefferson wrote James Monroe, "My primary object in the formation of treaties is to take the commerce of the states out of the hands of the states, and to place it under the superintendence of Congress, so far as the imperfect provisions of our constitution will admit, and until the states shall by [a] new compact make them more perfect."[53]

Jefferson believed European governments depended too heavily on import duties to embrace free trade, which made most-favored-nation status the most realistic goal for America's commercial diplomacy, with one caveat:

All the World Is Becoming Commercial

"Access to the West Indies is indispensably necessary to us." It should be, for Europe, "the price of admission" into American markets.[54]

Jefferson did manage to open the French West Indies to some American exports, but adjusting to the demands of French politics, where the concessions were controversial, he concentrated on promoting direct trade between the United States and France. He tried unsuccessfully to end the monopoly on tobacco purchases by the powerful Farmers-General, a French cartel; he did at least see the termination of a monopoly on tobacco sales that the French government had given the American financier Robert Morris. Jefferson also tried to promote the sale of New England whale oil. British duties imposed after the Revolution badly hurt the industry. But French fisheries also wanted protection, and France closed its ports to foreign whale oil. The French consumed large quantities of rice, but Jefferson enjoyed only modest success selling rice; the French palate disliked the American variety. Paradoxically, however, a balance of trade that heavily favored the United States presented the greatest barrier to the expansion of Franco-American commerce. The French exported mainly luxury goods, French merchants were reluctant to extend credit, and French manufacturers struggled to compete with their more efficient British counterparts.[55]

Jefferson enjoyed no more success in the Mediterranean, where the Barbary States of Algiers, Tunis, Tripoli, and Morocco had long preyed on Western shipping. Before the American Revolution, American ships had taken large quantities of flour and dried and pickled fish to Mediterranean ports. Some 80 to 100 ships and 1,200 American seamen had gone there annually under British protection. Left to their own devices after the United States declared its independence, American merchant ships proved vulnerable to piracy. Morocco seized the *Betsy* in 1783; at least two more U.S. ships were taken captive in 1785. Insurance rates more than doubled.[56]

The European states generally placated the Barbary States by paying tribute, and Congress initially authorized Adams, Franklin, and Jefferson to negotiate with the pirates, but it gave them too little money to buy peace. Morocco released the *Betsy* in 1785 and signed a treaty with the United States the following year; the other North African governments were less accommodating. To protect American shipping, Jefferson preferred forming a naval alliance with some of the lesser European powers rather than submitting to what he saw as extortion. John Jay, who was now Congress's secretary for foreign affairs, agreed.[57]

Jefferson understood it was an open question whether war or peace would be cheaper, "but is it a question which should be addressed to our

Honour as well as our Avarice?" He argued America's weakness would soon involve the United States in a naval war with one of the major powers. The forceful liberation of American commerce in the Mediterranean might deter other rivals. Congress had dismantled the navy at the end of the Revolutionary War; rebuilding it, Jefferson hoped, could revitalize the union. A navy would be less menacing than a peacetime army, but it could be used to coerce an uncooperative state, a possibility Madison had raised near the end of the Revolution. Jefferson wanted a single American frigate on a permanent Mediterranean station. To his dismay, Congress lacked the funds to launch a ship, and Jefferson's plans for an international naval armada collapsed.[58]

Jefferson bristled especially at reports in Europe of a depressed American economy, even as Congress cut the salaries of its ministers abroad and as Jefferson's service in France sank him deeper in debt. For foreign audiences, he painted an optimistic picture, arguing at one point that exaggerated stories in English newspapers of American bankruptcies made it more difficult for his nation's merchants to get credit, but tight credit discouraged the purchase of luxuries and forced Americans to trade elsewhere, and the bad publicity deterred immigration, "all of which I consider as advantageous for us." Robert Middlekauff has described America's recovery from the war as "rapid, though uneven." The total volume of foreign trade had fallen from prewar levels, but American exports generally increased in the 1780s. Heavily dependent on European manufactured goods, the United States suffered mainly from an unfavorable balance of trade, which created a demand for new markets and for a government that could secure them. Sharp, short-term downturns had a greater psychological impact than slow but steady growth, and a sense of crisis would soon be widespread.[59]

With Jefferson in Paris and Madison back in the House of Delegates, James Monroe took up the mantle of Virginia nationalism in Congress, and Madison encouraged his efforts to amend the Articles to allow the national legislature to regulate trade. If Congress could not be trusted with new powers, he wrote Monroe, it ought to be restructured to make it more credible. It could be enlarged, or members' terms could be shortened. Passage of trade regulations could require a supermajority, but the defects of the "federal system" ought to be remedied before they threatened the union itself. Why, Madison asked rhetorically, should the people support a government too weak to protect their interests? He dismissed the argument that the economic concerns of the states were too diverse to allow for congressional regulation; by that logic the Articles would never have been adopted. If the votes of two-thirds of the states were to be required to pass a commercial statute, Madison thought it unlikely that so large a majority would support oppressive legislation. He understood some southerners worried New England might try to monopolize the American carrying trade, but he believed a common interest in West Indian markets outweighed all possible "inequalities," and in any event he would rather do business with fellow Americans than with British shippers. Opposition to reform would come from lawmakers "unaccustomed to consider the interests of the State as they are interwoven with those of the Confederacy."[60]

Paris provided a far broader perspective, and from his diplomatic post Jefferson welcomed Monroe's efforts. Jefferson seems to have sincerely overrated the prospects for an amendment empowering Congress to levy an impost or to regulate trade, even suggesting in letters to some of his European correspondents that British trade policies had made constitutional reform in America inevitable. The movement to give Congress jurisdiction over the states' trade had "produced a wonderful sensation in England in our favour," he wrote Madison. Not until it appeared had he "been able to discover the smallest token of respect towards the United states in any part of Europe." Jefferson believed an amendment strengthening the Articles would benefit American trade more than a commercial treaty with Great Britain would.[61]

His optimism was short lived. Congress never submitted Monroe's proposal to the states. By January 1786, if not earlier, Jefferson had concluded that Rhode Island merchants would block that state's ratification of any amendment providing for congressional regulation of commerce. Nor, apart from an agreement with Prussia, had his treaty-making efforts borne much fruit. With access to the West Indies as his first priority, treaties with European nations that lacked American colonies offered limited advantages to the United States. Worse yet, treaties tended to be written so broadly, he complained, that their implementation largely depended on the state legislatures. "Treaties" he wrote the Frenchman Jean-Nicolas Démeunier, "are very imperfect machines for regulating commerce in detail."[62]

———

IN MAY 1784, before Jefferson left for Europe, he asked Madison to oversee the education of his fourteen-year-old ward and nephew, Peter Carr. The request illustrated the closeness of their relationship. Jefferson also asked Madison to send him regular reports on the business of the Virginia assembly and on political developments generally. In return, Jefferson promised to keep an eye out for books that would be of interest to Madison. Madison had attempted to resume his "course of law reading" at Montpelier the previous fall, only to be distracted by what he called "frequent interruptions," but heavy snow that winter reduced the numbers of visitors to the Madison estate and allowed Madison to make real progress, and he asked Jefferson to help him order legal texts and other books from London and Paris.[63]

Madison expressed a particular interest in books on the law of nations and on natural law and on the constitutions and public laws of the various European confederacies. "The operations of our own," he wrote Jefferson, "must render all such lights of consequence." He later added books on the political history of the Americas and works by the less familiar Greek and Roman writers. Jefferson responded with some 200 titles. Madison took his studies seriously, even staying in Richmond after the fall 1784 session of the assembly adjourned to spend time in Edmund Randolph's office "with a view of gaining . . . some insight into the juridical course of practice." When Jefferson invited Madison to visit him in Paris, Madison gave two reasons for saying no: his health and his reluctance to disrupt his current "course of reading." Ironically perhaps, Madison still gave no real evidence of an intention to practice law and not much explanation for his interest in the law generally. He was more likely to have been looking for clues to make the American confederacy work and for arguments to support reform of the republic's political structure. Madison would be the best prepared delegate in Philadelphia when the federal Constitutional Convention assembled there in May 1787, but he embarked on his legal studies long before the convention was a realistic possibility.[64]

While Madison read law in Virginia, Jefferson's experience in France undoubtedly reaffirmed his sense of American nationalism. We have no reason to believe the pro-American propaganda he generated in Europe was wholly insincere, and if it ever was, he surely came to believe it. Despite reports in the London newspapers of "anarchy, discontent and civil war" in America, he still maintained that "there are not on the face of the earth more tranquil governments than ours, nor a happier and more contented people." The disruption of trade within the British Empire by the Revolution, before new markets could be found elsewhere, had caused economic "stagnation" in America, but except for a certain lack of "frugality," he would accept few other serious criticisms of life in the new republic. He did admit the need for one "great reformation . . . in our manners and our commerce." Americans relied too heavily on merchants—usually British—who offered credit but at high prices. He put much of the blame on the merchants. No one, he complained, had a right to enter a "calling" that would "ruin many better men than himself."[65]

All the World Is Becoming Commercial

Europe suffered by comparison. "I find the general fate of humanity here, most deplorable," he wrote to one correspondent. He agreed with Voltaire: "Every man here must be either the hammer or the anvil." Jefferson admired France's accomplishments in the arts and appreciated French manners, noting, "Here a man might pass a life without encountering a single rudeness." At the same time, he found their morals revolting. The wealthy were corrupt, and "conjugal love having no existence among them, domestic happiness, of which that is the basis, is utterly unknown."[66]

The extremes of wealth and poverty appalled him. Walking near Fontainebleau in the fall of 1785, Jefferson encountered an elderly peasant woman who told him she was often unemployed and without bread. After she had guided Jefferson for several miles, they parted ways. When he gave her twenty-four sous, she burst into tears. Her plight "led me into a train of reflections on that unequal division of property which occasions the numberless instances of wretchedness which I have observed in this country & which is to be observed all over Europe." A very few owned much of the land, and while they employed servants and laborers, many others were left destitute and without work. The aristocracy had land they kept as uncultivated game preserves. The rich were so wealthy they had little interest in more productive activities.[67]

Jefferson considered complete equality to be impractical, and in order to promote enterprise, societies had to respect property rights, but "whenever there is in any country, uncultivated lands and unemployed poor, it is clear that the laws of property have been so far extended as to violate natural right." Lawmakers should do what they could to mitigate economic inequality. Property should be divided equally among a decedent's heirs. Taxes should be progressive, and property below a certain level should not be taxed. Some provision should be made for those without land. Thankfully, inequality in the United States had not reached European proportions, but American lawmakers should use "every possible means" to keep the number of landless poor "as few as possible."[68]

The comparison between France and America undoubtedly helps explain why Jefferson viewed constitutional reform in America as less urgent than Madison saw it. In any event, with Thomas Jefferson preoccupied in France, the cause of reform in Virginia would fall, in large part, to James Madison.

FIVE

Confusion . . . Must Stifle All Enterprize

1784–1786

JAMES MADISON RETURNED to the House of Delegates in May 1784 with an ambitious agenda. He hoped to complete the revision of Virginia's legal code that Thomas Jefferson had begun in 1776 and to secure adoption of a new state constitution, another of Jefferson's long-held objectives. As did Jefferson, Madison also supported efforts to meet congressional requisitions and to give Congress the power to tax and to regulate commerce, and he wanted Virginia to honor American obligations under the Treaty of Paris to allow the collection of prewar British debts. Madison considered the nation's political situation to be dire, in part because with an almost impotent Congress it was, but also perhaps because the new republic seemed to be falling short of the lofty goals of the Revolution. He recalled years later that he had felt obligated to return to the assembly to do what he could to prevent a political disaster. He hoped, he said, that he could help bring "about a rescue of the Union and the blessings of liberty staked on it, from an impending catastrophe."[1]

It made sense for Madison to return to the assembly. In the decentralized political system created by the Articles of Confederation, real political power rested with the states, and Virginia was far and away the largest and most influential of the states. Madison's experience and ability, and his dedication to his work, would immediately put him among the top tier of lawmakers. He could logically expect to accomplish more in the Virginia assembly than he could in Congress. Yet he would be disappointed. The state's most popular politician, Patrick Henry, generally opposed reform; Henry became governor in May 1784 when the assembly met for what would be its last spring session. Madison's fellow lawmakers would present him with even greater obstacles. Reluctant to cede power to Congress, they were too provincial to handle the responsibilities the Articles thrust upon them, and Madison found he could do little to cure the ills of the Confederation from the legislative halls of Richmond. He spent much of his time on the defensive, and ironically, as we shall see, his greatest substantive accomplishment as a state legislator in the 1780s, passage of Jefferson's Bill for Establishing Religious Freedom, illustrated his theory that a national legislature would be less likely to pass bad laws than would a state assembly.[2]

Madison believed that a healthy economy needed some support from the government, and he thought a republican state and a viable union required a reasonably prosperous economy. On neither count did Virginia fare well. Returning home in 1783, he reported to Jefferson that "the commerce of this country" was "even more deplorable than I have conceived it." Virginia paid dearly for its reliance on Philadelphia and Baltimore as conduits for many of its exports and imports. His native state lagged behind more enterprising Pennsylvania in "commercial genius," but even if Virginians had been more industrious, "the confusion" of the nation's political affairs "must stifle all enterprize."[3]

Under the Treaty of Paris, for example, the United States had agreed that British creditors ought to be able to collect prewar debts from their American debtors. Virginians adamantly resisted payment. During the war, the assembly had passed legislation allowing debtors to discharge their obligations by paying into the state treasury paper money worth only a small fraction of the actual debts in pounds sterling. The May 1784 session passed another act simply forbidding suits by British creditors. American intransigence gave Great Britain an excuse not to honor its treaty commitments. During the spring legislative session, Madison had supported a compromise plan providing for payments in installments. In the fall assembly, Madison won passage of a bill approving a schedule for debt payments, but after the senate agreed to a slightly amended version, bad weather in the closing days of the session prevented the house from assembling a quorum to pass the amended bill. Another bill for paying British debts died the next year.[4]

State and congressional finances, even more than private debts, bedeviled Madison during his three years in the assembly. The May 1784 session earmarked part of the state's property tax revenues and a portion of its impost duties for Congress, but as he told Jefferson, it "will be much short of what they need." Acting on a suggestion from Jefferson, Madison proposed appropriating half the proceeds from Virginia's slave tax to Congress, but his colleagues had committed those revenues to the liquidation of the state's war debt. Henry, among others, opposed higher taxes to meet congressional requisitions.[5]

Simply paying the state's bills proved difficult enough. "Nothing," Madison told Jefferson at the end of the May 1784 assembly, "can exceed the confusion which reigns throughout our Revenue department." That fall Madison agreed to a compromise tax bill that postponed some tax collections and allowed for payment in kind, and he permitted himself a brief flurry of optimism. The fall harvest had been good, tobacco prices were high, and he hoped "a few more plentiful years with steadiness in our Councils will put our credit on a decent footing," but he later came to question the wisdom of allowing Virginians to pay their taxes with tobacco.[6]

During his first session back in the assembly, Madison had managed to pass a bill to empower Congress, for fifteen years, to impose economic sanctions on any nation that excluded American vessels from its ports, but the measure could not take effect until it was approved by all the states, and it never was. Madison tried again in the fall 1785 assembly, where he proposed giving Congress, for a period of twenty-five years, authority, upon a vote of two-thirds of the states, to ban or tax ships or goods from nations that did not have commercial treaties with the United States, to impose a 5 percent tariff on imports, and to prohibit state duties on interstate commerce. In addition to dealing with foreign restrictions on American trade and Congress's chronic financial woes, Madison hoped to forestall conflicts among the states: "Without some such self-denying compact it will, I conceive, be impossible to preserve harmony among the contiguous States." At the moment, Connecticut was taxing goods from Massachusetts at a higher rate than foreign imports. Virginia merchants, however, feared that a northern majority in Congress might adopt regulations harmful to the South, and the measure was amended to reduce the term of the grant of power to Congress to thirteen years. Madison opposed the amendment, and the assembly tabled the resolution.[7]

As he explained to George Washington, a partial remedy might undercut support for a permanent solution. "Further experience, and even distress," would probably be required to convince the assembly to give Congress the powers it needed. "Nothing but the peculiarity of our circumstances" during the Revolution "could ever have produced those sacrifices of sovereignty

Confusion ... Must Stifle All Enterprize

on which the federal Government now rests." Relieved from a threat of foreign invasion, Virginia lawmakers hesitated to sacrifice any more sovereignty to Congress.[8]

—

JEFFERSON's most substantive accomplishment in the mid-1780s was the publication of the only book he ever wrote, *Notes on the State of Virginia*. It began as a series of questions that François Barbé-Marbois, the secretary to the French legation in America, had sent to each of the state governors. No one took the assignment more seriously than Jefferson, and *Notes* contains some of his most famous aphorisms and extended commentaries on law, politics, and natural history. Jefferson had been collecting maps, manuscripts, and books about Virginia for years, and the end of his term as governor allowed him to devote more time to the project.

After leaving office in June 1781, Jefferson retired to his Poplar Forest retreat. A fall from a horse and a broken arm extended his stay, and he spent part of his convalescence working on the manuscript. In August, he returned to Monticello, where he could make use of his own extensive library. Jefferson sent Marbois an early draft in December, but he continued to make revisions. Jefferson had originally intended simply to circulate manuscript copies among a small circle of friends—he sent Madison a copy in March 1782—but as the work grew, that became impractical. Unable to get the manuscript printed in Philadelphia before he left for his diplomatic assignment in Europe, Jefferson had *Notes* printed in Paris in 1785 and later in London. Madison was likely the first person he told of the book's publication.[9]

Jefferson wanted to distribute copies of *Notes* to the students at the College of William and Mary, but he feared portions of the book might be controversial, and he asked Madison and others for advice. *Notes* questioned the intelligence and even the emotional maturity of Africans at the same time that Jefferson claimed that his law revisers' committee had prepared a bill to provide for the gradual abolition of slavery in Virginia and the colonization of freed slaves. He devoted even more space to criticizing Virginia's constitution. Jefferson's racial prejudices would offend modern readers, but he worried mainly about the possibility his comments on slavery and the Virginia Constitution could provoke a pro-slavery backlash and further opposition to constitutional reform.[10] Madison consulted with George Wythe and passed on the law professor's advice that *Notes* be placed in the William and Mary library for faculty members to assign to students as needed. As it developed, Jefferson's argument in *Notes* for freedom of conscience caused him more grief than anything else in the book: "It does me no injury for my neighbor to say there are twenty gods, or no god. It neither picks my pocket nor breaks my leg." His political opponents, especially in the presidential election of 1800, would later accuse him of atheism.[11]

Notes, in fact, gave Jefferson space to develop many of the tenets of his brand of republicanism. As his proposal to colonize ex-slaves suggests, he often preferred homogeneity to diversity. "It is for the happiness of those united in society to harmonize as much as possible in matters in which they must of necessity transact together," he wrote. All governments, Jefferson argued, rested on a common consent to certain fundamental ideas. The American system was an unusual "composition of the freest principles of the English constitution, with others derived from natural right and reason." American politics required citizens who understood those principles. He thought no expense should be spared in encouraging the immigration of skilled artisans, and if immigrants "come here of themselves, they are entitled to all the rights of citizenship." Mass immigration, however, should be discouraged because it would mean immigrants would be coming from monarchial states, and they would bring with them monarchial tendencies or run to the other extreme of "unbounded licentiousness."[12]

He also argued in *Notes* that native-born yeoman farmers made the best republicans: "Those who labour in the earth are the chosen people of God, if ever he had a chosen people. . . . Corruption of manners in the mass of cultivators is a phenomenon of which no age or nation has furnished an example." Jefferson romanticized farmers for their independence, writing, "Dependence begets subservience and venality, suffocating the germ of virtue, and prepares fit tools for the designs of ambition." Jefferson welcomed the foreign "carpenters, masons, and smiths" who could serve an agrarian economy, "but, for the general operations of manufacture, let our work-shops remain in Europe."[13]

Such attitudes had profound implications for American foreign policy and constitutional law. They contributed to Jefferson's, and Madison's, embrace of foreign trade. American farmers would need imported, manufactured goods and overseas markets for their produce. As Jefferson explained in *Notes*, "Our interest will be to throw open the doors of commerce, and to knock off all its shackles, giving perfect freedom to all persons for the vent of whatever they may chuse to bring into our ports, and asking the same in theirs." Jefferson believed competition for markets would lead to war, "but the actual habits of our countrymen attach them to commerce," and lawmakers would have to accept that reality. An army would be "useless" in a war for

Confusion . . . Must Stifle All Enterprize

foreign markets, but while the United States could never match the naval strength of the great European powers, it could strive for local superiority. Jefferson envisioned an American navy of eighteen ships of the line and a dozen frigates, which was far beyond the capacity of the Confederation Congress.[14]

If Jefferson's view of foreign trade as unavoidable and war as inevitable predisposed him to support a more energetic central government, when he wrote *Notes* he was more interested in reforming Virginia's constitution. Madison supported his efforts: "I grow every day more and more solicitous to see this essential work begun."[15] As a start, they wanted to make clear the superiority of a constitution over ordinary legislation. Americans in the 1780s were coming to see the dangers of placing virtually all political authority in the state legislatures. Jefferson and Madison wanted to make the assemblies more representative while limiting their ability to infringe on the rights of minorities; they understood that majorities would not always respect minority interests. Constitutions should separate legislative, executive, and judicial functions and establish systems of checks and balances. In the context of the 1780s, this meant, for example, strengthening the state governors.[16]

By the fall of 1782, the movement to revise Virginia's 1776 constitution seemed to be gaining momentum. Thomson Mason, George Mason's younger brother and a highly regarded lawyer, took up the cause. Jefferson stopped in Richmond in May 1783 on his way to Monticello after Congress had canceled his appointment to the peace commission charged with negotiating an end to the Revolutionary War. His conversations with lawmakers convinced him the prospects for reform were promising. Returning home, Jefferson drafted a new constitution in about six weeks and sent a copy to Madison.[17]

Jefferson had exaggerated the support for a new constitution, but he and Madison worked to keep the issue alive. In late 1783, Madison solicited the support of George Mason at his Gunston Hall estate and found Mason to be "sound and ripe" on the question of a constitutional convention. Madison saw reasons for optimism in the May 1784 assembly, and he hoped he could make use of Jefferson's draft.[18]

Jefferson attached a copy of his new proposed constitution as an appendix to *Notes on the State of Virginia* and included a critique of the existing constitution in the text of the book. It "was framed when we were new and unexperienced in the science of government." As the very first American constitution, there was "no wonder then that time and trial have discovered very capital defects in it." He pointed out six.[19]

First, too few Virginians could vote. Only about half the men on the tax and militia roles enjoyed the franchise. Second, seats in the assembly were distributed unfairly. Jefferson estimated 19,000 men in the Tidewater "give law to upwards of thirty thousand" in the rest of Virginia and selected all the principal executive and judicial officers. Third, the senate too closely resembled the lower house to serve the purpose of a bicameral legislature. Different houses should "introduce the influence of different interests or different principles."[20]

His fourth complaint went to the core of the postwar, republican dilemma: virtually all power resided in the legislature. This, Jefferson wrote, "is precisely the definition of despotic government." It made no difference "that these powers will be exercised by a plurality of hands, and not by a single one. 173 despots would surely be as oppressive as one." The 1776 constitution had tried to separate executive, judicial, and legislative functions by prohibiting dual officeholding, but failing to give the governor or the courts the means to the check the legislature, it had not gone far enough. In perhaps a nod to legislative sensibilities, Jefferson acknowledged that the integrity of Virginia's lawmakers had prevented serious abuses of legislative discretion, but the assembly should anticipate "a time, and that not a distant one, when corruption in this, as in the country from which we derive our origins, will have seized the heads of government, and be spread by them through the body of the people.... The time to guard against corruption and tyranny, is before they shall have gotten hold on us."[21]

Jefferson considered his fifth complaint to be of at least equal weight, although his concerns were not yet widely shared. He believed the legislature could lawfully violate the 1776 constitution because it was not a real constitution. When voters elected delegates in April 1776, they did not anticipate the convention would declare independence and write a new constitution. Virginia needed only a temporary government to carry on the war against Great Britain, and the convention had no authority to bind a future legislature. Jefferson conceded Virginians had accepted the constitution, but as colonists they had also accepted various acts of Parliament, a fact that had complicated the American case when Britain tried to tax them.[22]

Jefferson's sixth and final complaint seems minor by comparison, although it was the kind of parliamentary technicality that could alarm eighteenth-century civil libertarians: the 1776 constitution allowed the assembly to determine its own quorum. The common law defined a quorum as a majority of a body's membership. During one British invasion of Virginia, the assembly had fixed its quorum at forty, which was less than a majority. Jefferson worried its wartime act could become a precedent for setting the quorum so low that the legislature would cease to be representative.[23]

Confusion ... Must Stifle All Enterprize

Experience, in particular Jefferson's difficult two years as governor, led him to recommend some revisions to the constitution he had proposed, with little success, in 1776 and more changes to the constitution that had been adopted. His 1783 draft provided that senators would be elected from special senate districts by electors chosen by the voters, not by the lower house, and they would serve two-year terms. House members would continue to represent individual counties for one-year terms, but as he had proposed in 1776, house seats should be allocated based on the number of voters in each county. "All free male citizens" resident in a county for one year or who owned an unspecified amount of property or who had been on the militia rolls for a year would be allowed to vote. Jefferson had long advocated expansion of the franchise.[24]

Jefferson reduced the legislative quorum from the two-thirds required in his 1776 draft to a simple majority and fixed the lawmakers' compensation: hard currency equal to the value of two bushels of wheat for each day of a legislative session. Military officers, certain executive officials, and "ministers of the gospel" were banned from state office. Although his new constitution did not include a separate bill of rights, it did provide that the General Assembly could not restrict religious freedom or assess a tax to support religion, and it could not impose the death penalty except for murder, treason, or offenses committed in military service. Jefferson also proposed banning ex post facto laws, bills of attainder, and torture "in any case whatsoever." The further importation of slaves into Virginia would be prohibited, and all people born after 31 January 1800 would be declared free. Separate provisions recognized the right to habeas corpus and guaranteed that "printing-presses shall be subject to no other restraint than liableness to legal prosecution for false facts printed and published."[25]

The assembly would appoint the state attorney general, treasurer, and certain other officials, as well as senior military officers. In a symbolic gesture, Jefferson's executive, whom he had called the "administrator" in 1776, was now granted the loftier title of "governor." Jefferson wanted to make the governor more independent of the legislature without creating a strong executive; fear of monarchs and royal governors lingered. The assembly would continue to elect the governor, but his term would be extended from one year to five, a significant departure from Jefferson's 1776 draft and existing law. Jefferson's governor could not seek reelection and exercised little authority. "We give him, Jefferson wrote, "those powers only, which are necessary to execute the laws (and administer the government) and which are not in their nature either legislative or judicial." Jefferson retained the council of state, which he and Madison agreed had created an unnecessarily cumbersome executive, but apparently Jefferson thought it should serve in a purely advisory capacity.[26]

Jefferson's constitution provided for the creation of superior courts and courts of appeal and empowered the assembly to create county and inferior courts. The issue of judicial independence loomed larger for Jefferson's generation than did questions of jurisdiction or the structure of a court system. To that effect, superior court judges would serve during good behavior, and their salaries could not be altered while they were in office. Protecting the autonomy of juries rivaled an independent judiciary in importance; Jefferson expressly provided that questions of fact were to be decided by a jury. All parties to a lawsuit, moreover, would be allowed the right to counsel and the right to subpoena witnesses on their own behalf.[27]

Searching for an additional check on the assembly, wary of executive power, and unfamiliar with the modern practice of judicial review, Jefferson proposed the creation of a council of revision, an idea he may have borrowed from the New York Constitution. Composed of the governor, two members of the governor's council, and one judge from each of the three superior courts, the council of revision could veto legislation. Its veto could be overridden by a two-thirds vote of both houses of the legislature. In what would be a significant omission as American constitutional law developed, Jefferson did not provide a method by which the new constitution could be ratified by the voters. He did, however, create a process for amendments, which presented another troublesome procedural issue: a two-thirds vote of two of the three branches of government could call a constitutional convention to consider amendments. In sum, Jefferson's constitution was a progressive, but not a radical, document.[28]

When, in June 1784, the assembly considered calling a constitutional convention, Madison made the case for constitutional reform to the House of Delegates. While Jefferson prepared to leave for his new diplomatic assignment in Europe, his influence, or at least the similarity between his thinking and Madison's, was obvious. If Madison followed his notes, he told his fellow lawmakers that Virginia's existing constitution had been adopted "without due power from the people." Written by a convention that had not been elected for that purpose, the constitution had not even been submitted to the voters for ratification. As a wartime expedient, its legitimacy rested on popular "acquiescence," which he dismissed as a "dangerous basis" for fundamental law. Madison's notes list ten more specific complaints, several of which revolved around an inadequate separation of powers. The executive

Confusion ... Must Stifle All Enterprize

and judiciary depended on the legislature for their salaries. The "Privileges & wages" of legislators were not defined. The senate was "badly constituted & improperly barred" from initiating legislation. The constitution failed to protect the right to petition for a writ of habeas corpus. Counties were not guaranteed equal representation. Voting rights were not secure; Madison's notes suggest he thought the constitution might permit the disenfranchisement of Catholics.[29]

Madison believed the fate of any new constitution rested with Richard Henry Lee and Patrick Henry; Mason, plagued by gout and less consumed by politics than was Madison, did not attend the session. Pessimistic about the prospects for a constitutional convention, Madison hesitated to raise the issue until a petition for a convention arrived from voters in Augusta County. Lee favored a constitutional convention, but he fell ill the day before the proposal came to a vote, and Henry "shewed a more violent opposition than we expected." On 21 June 1784, the delegates, voting as a committee of the whole, decided by a vote of 57 to 42 not to call a convention. By the end of the year, Jefferson found himself trying to make the best of the disappointment, writing Madison from Paris that a constitutional convention might have done more harm than good: "While Mr. Henry lives another bad constitution would be formed, and saddled for ever on us." Blaming Henry for frustrating one reform after another, he told Madison, "What we have to do I think is devoutly to pray for his death."[30]

Madison's defeat stymied the cause of constitutional reform in Virginia for almost half a century. He confessed to Jefferson that efforts to amend the constitution "seem to interest the public much less than a friend to the scheme would wish." At the same time, developments elsewhere kept Madison focused on the problem of creating a functioning republican regime. In 1785, an old Princeton classmate, Caleb Wallace, who had become a lawyer and moved to Virginia's Kentucky district, asked Madison's advice on a proper state constitution should Kentucky achieve statehood. Madison responded with a letter that both reflected concerns he and Jefferson had long held and raised some new ones. Madison began with a common complaint against "all our republics": in republican theory, the senate was intended to "give wisdom and steadiness to legislation," but America's constitutions had created senates too much like the lower houses of the state legislatures to serve as a check on them. Yet Madison was not ready to abandon the institution. Virginia's senate, "bad as it is, . . . is often a useful bit in the mouth of the house of Delegates." To help distinguish the house from the senate, he recommended one-year terms for house members and four- to five-year terms for senators. He saw no need for term limits.[31]

The lower house, Madison went on, ought not to be "too numerous," and its privileges, compensation, and quorum—presumably a majority of the membership—should be fixed in the constitution. On the delicate issue of defining the legislature's powers, Madison favored a specific enumeration but feared it would be impractical. Instead, the constitution would have to state what the legislature could not do: abridge religious freedom or freedom of the press, the rights to a jury trial and habeas corpus, the privilege against self-incrimination, or the right to vote. Private property should not be taken without just compensation. Madison also included in his de facto bill of rights a ban on the slave trade and on state laws inconsistent with the Articles of Confederation.[32]

To Madison, suffrage was of "critical importance." Limiting the franchise to landowners would, as the population grew and land became more dear, eventually exclude too many citizens from the political process. But extending the suffrage too broadly would enfranchise people who would abuse the right or sell their vote. He found a happy medium in an expanded suffrage for elections to the lower house and, following North Carolina's example, a property requirement for senate elections. He admitted that a property requirement might "offend the sense of equality which reigns in a free Country," but he saw "no reason why the rights of property which chiefly bears the burden of Government & is so much an object of Legislation should not be respected as well as personal rights in the choice of Rulers." Madison seemed to want to protect property rights without creating a legally entrenched aristocracy. He conceded that property gave its owners a certain influence, and with a few safeguards their estates ought to be secure.[33]

As Jefferson had advocated in his 1783 draft constitution, and as Madison had apparently argued in his June 1784 speech to the Virginia House of Delegates, Madison recommended to Wallace that counties be allocated seats in the assembly based on population. He also anticipated a need, as population centers shifted, to reapportion seats, without, however, providing a mechanism to force reapportionment. Madison diverged from Jefferson on one very practical detail. Jefferson's constitution had specifically authorized the practice of oral voting. It was traditional, cheap, and convenient for illiterate voters. Madison insisted voting be by secret ballot as "the only radical cure for those arts of Electioneering, which poison the very fountain of Liberty." Only in states that used ballots were "elections tolerably chaste." Madison had more experience in postwar electoral politics than Jefferson

Confusion . . . Must Stifle All Enterprize

did, and Madison's generally darker view of the nation's political health may owe something to his doubts about the integrity of American elections.[34]

As a barrier to ill-considered or unconstitutional legislation, Madison recommended, as had Jefferson, replicating New York's Council of Revision. He called it "a further security against fluctuating & indigested laws." The political amateurs who largely populated the state assemblies also needed technical assistance. A standing committee "composed of a few select & skillful individuals," who held no other public office, could draft bills on the lawmakers' behalf before and during a session. Virginia's legislators, he lamented, "give almost as many proofs as they pass laws of their need of some such Assistance."[35]

He gave the executive branch little thought and little respect: "Though it claims the 2nd place [it] is not in my estimation entitled to it by importance, all the great powers which are properly executive being transferred to the federal Government." Presumably, Madison had in mind the management of foreign policy. He expressed no opinion on whether the executive should be elected by the people or by the legislature or whether the position should consist of one person or a committee, although he did complain that Virginia's executive branch, with a governor serving for one year and a council, all chosen by the assembly, was "the worst part of a bad constitution." He would impose term limits on members of the executive branch, especially on the governor, if they were not subject to "frequent" popular elections.[36]

The judiciary, by contrast, "merits every care." In Great Britain, he wrote Wallace, "it maintains private Right against all the corruptions of the other two departments" and gave the British government a better reputation than it deserved. Here, however, Madison followed Jefferson and conventional wisdom. The constitution could identify the state's more important courts and leave it to the legislature to create inferior tribunals, with the hope that lawmakers would not recreate Virginia's oligarchic and self-perpetuating county courts. Judges should serve during good behavior and enjoy fixed and liberal salaries sufficient to recruit distinguished attorneys. Otherwise "the bar will be superior to the bench."[37]

Madison echoed Jefferson's proposal that a majority of two of the three branches of government ought to be able to call a constitutional convention to consider amending the constitution, but he added a caveat that reflected one of his more telling differences with his fellow Virginian: Madison did not think a constitution should be subject to revision on a regular basis. While he recognized amendments would be needed, he suggested that Kentucky, after it had achieved statehood, wait fifteen to twenty years to pursue them. Time would better expose the constitution's defects. And whether he thought of the argument now or later, Madison would say elsewhere that a constitution's legitimacy rested in part on its longevity.[38]

———

JEFFERSON AND MADISON agreed that African slavery raised issues of constitutional dimensions. In his *Notes on the State of Virginia*, Jefferson had treated Africans with condescension, and in places he had made slavery sound almost benign: "Under the mild treatment our slaves experience, and their wholesome, though course food, this blot in our country increases as fast, or faster, than the whites." Most white northerners in the 1780s would have found Jefferson's racial attitudes unremarkable. More striking, for a Virginia slave owner, were his criticisms of slavery.[39]

He lamented the "unhappy influence on the manners of our people produced by the existence of slavery among us. The whole commerce between master and slave is a perpetual exercise of the most boisterous passions." Witnessing the abuse of enslaved Africans, white children learned to be bad tempered and violent. Slavery destroyed white morals and crushed the spirit of blacks. It undermined the white work ethic, hurt the economy, and subverted the idea that liberty was a gift from God. "I tremble for my country when I reflect that God is just. . . . The Almighty has no attribute which can take sides with us" in a struggle to preserve slavery. Despite all the evils he attributed to slavery, when Jefferson wrote about the institution, he typically found reasons for optimism. The American Revolution had unleashed new, humanitarian impulses: "The spirit of the master is abating, that of the slave rising from the dust, his condition mollifying, the way I hope preparing, under the auspices of heaven, for a total emancipation."[40]

His views on the morality of slavery never changed fundamentally. Years later Jefferson wrote in his autobiography that "nothing is more certainly written in the book of fate than that these people are to be free," but he remained convinced that whites and free blacks could not live together: "Nature, habit, opinion has drawn indelible lines of distinction between them." To avert a slave insurrection, he hoped whites would act while they could control the process of emancipation, liberating slaves gradually so they could be replaced by free white workers.[41]

In contrast to Jefferson, Madison usually eschewed public statements about controversial topics like slavery or religion when they could be avoided. The scant evidence he left behind suggests attitudes similar, but not identical, to Jefferson's: a philosophical opposition to slavery as perhaps a greater

Confusion . . . Must Stifle All Enterprize

burden on whites than on blacks. Madison's father was one of the largest slave owners in Orange County, and tax rolls from the mid-1780s show Madison himself held title to sixteen people. Madison had worried during the Revolution when Lord Dunmore offered freedom to slaves who would fight for the British, and he objected when the Virginia assembly considered offering a slave as a bounty to white recruits. "It would certainly be more consonant with the principles of liberty," he wrote Joseph Jones, to free slaves willing to fight for the American cause.[42]

He was, to be sure, hardly an abolitionist. Serving in Congress while it was meeting in New York, he promised to help Edmund Pendleton recover a runaway slave who was traveling north with the French army after the Battle of Yorktown. He excoriated British commanders for taking fugitive slaves with them, in violation of the Treaty of Paris, when they withdrew from American cities at the end of the war. Privately, however, in 1785, when he was reading law and speculating modestly in upstate New York farmland, Madison confided to Edmund Randolph that he hoped to earn "a decent and independent subsistence" and "to depend as little as possible on the labour of slaves." While Madison was serving in Philadelphia, Billey, a slave who had been with Madison since they were both boys, escaped and was recaptured. Madison sold him there, where under Pennsylvania's newly enacted emancipation act, Billey would be freed within a few months. Madison said he could not send Billey back to Virginia "merely for coveting that liberty" the Revolution was fought to defend.[43]

Neither Jefferson nor Madison ever made much real effort to abolish slavery or free their slaves, but Madison acquired a reputation as a benevolent master, avoiding corporal punishment or even the public embarrassment of slaves and trying to keep black families together. By 1789, if not earlier, Madison had embraced the "enlightened," moderate position on slavery: it should be abolished gradually and freed slaves should be colonized away from white settlements, probably in Africa. After 1820 and the controversy over Missouri's application to enter the union as a slave state, Madison become more protective of slavery, opposing federal interference with the institution. He even expressed doubts whether free blacks were better off than slaves, but he never questioned the innate intelligence of Africans, and he attributed the struggles of free blacks, at least in part, to the hostility they encountered from whites.[44]

Jefferson's campaign, such as it was, against slavery began in 1769, when, as a newly elected member of the House of Burgesses, he drafted a bill that would have allowed slave owners to free their slaves without the approval of the governor and council. He then persuaded Richard Bland to introduce it. The measure failed. Jefferson criticized the African slave trade in *A Summary View of the Rights of British America* and claimed widespread support in the colonies for the end of slavery. The constitution he drafted for Virginia in June 1776 provided that "no person hereafter coming into this country shall be held within the same in slavery under any pretext whatever." The convention that adopted a new constitution rejected the provision and, even before Jefferson drafted the Declaration of Independence, set a precedent for defining "equality" to exclude slaves. As we have seen, Jefferson's draft of the Declaration included an attack on George III for allowing the foreign slave trade to continue, but the Continental Congress deleted it. Although as John Miller has noted, Jefferson's omission of property from the Declaration's trilogy of inalienable rights created an opening for opponents of slavery, there is no evidence that was his intent.[45]

In 1778, the Virginia assembly passed a bill banning the further importation of slaves. Jefferson took credit for the measure and considered it one of his greatest accomplishments. He had certainly encouraged the idea, and he may have drafted the measure, or at least an earlier version of it, but he did not sponsor the bill. The slave trade ban passed in October. Jefferson did not arrive in Williamsburg for the fall session until the end of November. More significantly, Jefferson and his contemporaries, who seem not to have fully appreciated the potential for the American slave population to expand naturally, put great hope in the end of the slave trade. It "will in some measure," he believed, "stop the increase of this great and moral evil, while the minds of our citizens may be ripening for a complete emancipation."[46]

In 1782, the Virginia assembly finally passed a bill to authorize private manumissions. The state's lawmakers would adopt no further antislavery measures. Jefferson apparently concluded later that the manumission bill aggravated white anxieties because the growing number of free blacks supposedly increased the potential for miscegenation. The state constitution he drafted in 1783 provided that the General Assembly could not "permit the introduction of any more slaves to reside in this state, or the continuation of slavery beyond the generation which shall be living on the 31st day of December [1800]; all persons born after that day being hereby declared free." Jefferson also intended that freed slaves would leave Virginia, but the constitutional convention that Jefferson hoped would consider his proposals never met.[47]

According to Jefferson's autobiography, his law revisers' committee prepared a bill on slavery that was "a mere digest of the existing laws" with the intent that, when the bill came before the assembly, an amendment would be offered freeing slaves born after a certain date and providing for their deportation. The amendment never materialized. During the 1785 assembly, Madison took up Jefferson's antislavery campaign, but it was all he could do to prevent a repeal of the law allowing owners to free their slaves without state approval.[48]

In December, the House of Delegates adopted a resolution to repeal the act. Madison privately called it a "retrograde step" that would embarrass Virginia and provoke antislavery activists. More than 1,500 people, mainly from south of the James River, had signed petitions calling for the law's repeal. They warned of the "Rapes, Murders and Outrages" likely to be committed by freed slaves. God created slavery, they said, as a way to maintain law and order. Meanwhile, Methodist and Quaker groups had submitted petitions calling for gradual emancipation, which only increased the tensions. Their petitions, Madison reported to Jefferson, "were not thrown under the table, but were treated with all indignity short of it." In the end, the delegates defeated a repeal bill by a vote of 52–35. An emancipation bill did not get a single vote.[49]

Congress offered opponents of slavery a more hospitable forum. In 1777, Vermont, not yet recognized by the original thirteen as a state, adopted a constitution outlawing slavery. In 1780, Pennsylvania adopted a gradual emancipation law. Connecticut and Rhode Island followed suit in 1784. In the 1780s, Massachusetts courts began to interpret their state constitution to condemn slavery. With public opinion in the North turning against slavery, Jefferson's attempt, in the Ordinance of 1784, to bar slavery in all the nation's western territories failed by one vote.[50]

The mid-1780s represent a critical moment in Jefferson's and Madison's— and the nation's—relationship with slavery. For a time, Jefferson, with no objection from Madison, considered the expansion of slavery an issue that Congress, not white settlers, ought to resolve, and when it came to congressional authority over slavery in the West, he interpreted the Articles of Confederation loosely. Among southern delegates, however, only Hugh Williamson of North Carolina supported Jefferson's ban on slavery throughout the West. With virtually no support for abolition in the South, Jefferson and Madison both seem resigned to live with slavery for the foreseeable future. Jefferson, while still in his early forties, began to speak of emancipation as the task of a new generation of political leaders: "We must await with patience the workings of an overruling providence, & hope that that is preparing the deliverance of these, our suffering brethren."[51]

The broad outlines of a constitutional settlement on slavery had emerged well before the federal Constitutional Convention met in Philadelphia in May 1787. The question of abolition within a state would be decided by the state. In the West, slavery would expand south of the Ohio River, but not to its north. The days of the legal African slave trade were numbered. The seeds of the controversial three-fifths clause, counting a slave as three-fifths of a free person for purposes of taxation and representation, had been sown. Madison had helped broker a compromise in which the three-fifths ratio would be used to determine a state's financial obligation to Congress under the Articles.[52] Important details remained to be decided. Would, for example, the national government involve itself in the recovery of runaway slaves? But they were details. And to the dismay of Jefferson and Madison, Virginia, by 1785, would do no more to put slavery on the road to extinction than it had already done.

Virginia seemed more open to reform elsewhere, but change came slowly, if at all, and sometimes Madison overreached. In the spring of 1784, as chair of the house committee on commerce, he sponsored a bill to limit ships to the ports of Alexandria and Norfolk. He hoped the Port Bill, as it came to be known, would encourage the rise of Virginia seaports to rival Baltimore and Philadelphia, as well as the development of local maritime, mercantile, and banking operations. In order to attract white sailors, for example, the law provided that only a third of the crews of coastal and inland vessels could be slaves. It was also intended to better control smuggling and expedite the collection of import duties, which seems to have been especially attractive to Jefferson when he learned of the bill. Madison's primary goal, however, was probably to break the British monopoly on Virginia's trade. British vessels had long plied coastal waters, sailing upstream to deal directly with local merchants and planters. They also extended credit, ensnaring Virginians in debt. If, Madison reasoned, ships were confined to major ports, the British traders would lose the advantage of that long-standing custom, thereby creating opportunities for other European vessels and for merchants less willing to trade on credit.[53]

Despite all its supposed benefits, the Port Bill proved vulnerable on multiple points. Predictably, representatives of the smaller ports objected, as did the planters and British agents whose traditional ways of doing business

Confusion . . . Must Stifle All Enterprize

would be disrupted. Madison had originally wanted to limit international trade to Norfolk but elected to add Alexandria and then was forced to accept amendments adding York, Tappahannock, and Bermuda Hundred. Another amendment exempting Virginians from its provisions created a loophole that gave the bill a xenophobic edge Madison had never intended.[54]

The bill passed as amended, but it was in trouble from the start. Virginia had neither the bureaucracy nor the physical resources—smaller craft would be needed to distribute goods entering the designated ports—to implement it, and the legislature delayed its effective date until June 1786. Long before then, Madison would conclude that problems related to foreign trade would have to be dealt with at the national level. The Port Bill survived initial efforts to repeal it in part because some lawmakers hoped that if it improved the collection of import duties, taxes on real property could be minimized. But by December 1785, Madison confided to George Washington that the fate of the bill was very "precarious."[55]

The Port Bill separated Madison from some of his traditional allies and contradicted ideas he and Jefferson had expressed elsewhere. George Mason published a devastating critique. He noted the damage the bill would do to many localities and raised philosophical objections: "Is there any greater, or more dangerous error in government, than that of governing too much?" The bill would deprive landowners of "a just right to the natural advantages" of living close to a navigable waterway. As to encouraging the rise of bustling seaports, "will not the vice, the depravity of morals, the luxury, venality, and corruption, which invariably prevail in great commercial cities, be utterly subversive" of the virtue required for a republican government? The October 1787 session of the assembly finally repealed the law.[56]

Mason had made some telling points. Madison had based the American claim to access to the Mississippi River on the law of nature; proximity to a river conferred certain natural rights, but not apparently in Virginia. Nothing was more fundamental to Jefferson's and Madison's political thought than a belief in the moral superiority of yeoman farmers over the urban masses, yet the Port Bill envisioned the creation of seaport cities in Virginia itself. They also both claimed to support free trade, not government direction of the economy. The Port Bill illustrates the extent to which Madison, and to a lesser extent Jefferson, would compromise certain principles to end America's economic dependence on Great Britain.

The Port Bill was only one of Madison's statutory initiatives. In the fall of 1784, the House of Delegates appointed Madison chair of its committee on courts, and Madison promptly introduced a bill establishing a system of assize, or circuit, courts that Edmund Pendleton had drafted for the law revisers' committee in 1776. Under the existing law, appeals went directly from the county courts to the superior courts in Richmond, which cost money and wasted time. Jefferson estimated that before the Revolution, the clogged judicial system took twenty years to resolve some cases, although matters had improved since the war. Assize courts, staffed by professional judges, would exercise broad jurisdiction and hear appeals from the county courts. The bill passed, but a later assembly repealed it before it could take effect. The county court justices opposed the circuit courts as a threat to their authority, and John Marshall, then a member of the House of Delegates, thought the bill also drew opposition from poorly trained lawyers who practiced in the informal county courts but who knew they would be incompetent to try cases in a circuit court.[57]

Madison and Jefferson exchanged letters about other portions of the law revisers' report that had not become law and that remained relevant. "I am not without hopes," Madison wrote in November 1785, "of seeing it pass this session with as few alterations as could be expected."[58] That fall, Madison introduced 118 bills. The process went smoothly until the assembly reached No. 64 on crime and punishment; it drew criticism for drastically reducing the number of capital offenses. Jefferson's proposal to end state support for organized religion also provoked, as we shall see, extended debate. The legislature ultimately passed 35 bills in 1785, roughly two dozen at its session the next year, and a few more thereafter until it completed a comprehensive, revised legal code in 1792, but interest in reform had waned by the end of 1785, and national issues soon came to preoccupy Madison. Code revision took far longer and produced less real change than Jefferson and Madison had envisioned it would when the work began in 1776.[59]

One bill, Jefferson's Bill for Establishing Religious Freedom, stands out. The only bill passed in the fall 1785 session after the delegates hit an impasse over the criminal code, it reflected a lifelong commitment Jefferson and Madison shared, and one that was of incalculable importance in the forging of their political alliance.[60] The bill had languished in legislative limbo since 1779, when Virginia permanently abolished its tax for the support of the Anglican Church. By the end of the American Revolution, Virginia had become far too religiously diverse to support a single state church, but the idea of a "general assessment," or a tax to be levied for the denomination of a taxpayer's choice, enjoyed considerable popularity. Most Americans saw Protestantism as a bulwark of civic virtue, and many assumed churches needed state support. Episcopalians and Presbyterians for the most part supported a general

Confusion ... Must Stifle All Enterprize

assessment for "teachers of the Christian religion," as did some influential political leaders, chief among them Patrick Henry and Richard Henry Lee. In November 1784, the Virginia assembly approved a resolution endorsing the concept.[61]

Jefferson's bill, by contrast, began with a long paragraph making the case against the necessity and propriety of state assistance. Compelling support for a particular faith or punishing dissenters only encouraged hypocrisy and tended to corrupt pure religion. "It is time enough for the rightful purposes of civil government for its officers to interfere when principles break out into overt acts against peace and good order. . . . Truth is great and will prevail if left to herself." A much shorter substantive paragraph provided simply that "no man" would be forced to support "any religious worship, place, or ministry whatsoever" and that no one could be punished in any way for his or her "religious opinions or belief."[62]

Eighteenth-century notions of the separation of church and state differ from modern ones. The law revisers' report also included a bill, passed in 1785, prohibiting work on Sunday except for "ordinary household offices of daily necessity, or other work of necessity or charity."[63] One of the most striking features of the Bill for Establishing Religious Freedom is the extent to which Jefferson rested freedom of conscience on a theological basis. He began with the assertion that "Almighty God hath created the mind free" and that any attempt to shape religious beliefs by law "are a departure from the plan of the holy author of our religion, who being lord both of body and mind, . . . choose not to propagate it by coercions on either." Government attempts to support religion frustrated the divine will and had "established and maintained false religions over the greatest part of the world through all time." While Jefferson avoided explicit references to Christianity, the Christian, or at least theistic, tenor of the bill is inescapable. Although he doubted the supernatural claims of Christianity, Jefferson believed in a deity and professed to be "a Christian, in the only sense he [Jesus] wished any one to be," which was as a follower of the ethical teachings of the Gospels. "His system of morality," Jefferson later wrote, "was the most benevolent & sublime probably that has ever been taught."[64]

The general assessment had other opponents, in particular Virginia's Baptists, who had suffered at the hands of the established church. Madison managed to delay final action on the measure until the fall 1785 session, partly by appeasing the Episcopalians with his support for a bill to incorporate the Episcopal Church. The incorporation act probably involved the state more deeply in the governance of the church than Madison would have preferred, but it met a legitimate need to create a legal entity that could hold title to church property. It also helped buy time for Madison and his allies to rally public opinion against the assessment, and of critical importance, the incorporation act aggravated festering hostilities toward the Anglican Church. Some non-Anglicans saw it as an attempt to restore the old establishment in a new guise. Tensions among denominations served Madison's purposes, and he knew it. Presbyterians withdrew their support for the assessment. As Madison wrote Jefferson in August, "The mutual hatred of these sects has been much inflamed by the late act. . . . I am far from being sorry for it as a coalition between them could alone endanger our religious rights."[65]

Madison would not, however, depend entirely on denominational rivalries to defeat the assessment bill. Its opponents spent the summer between legislative sessions preparing petitions to the assembly, and Madison joined the effort with his "Memorial and Remonstrance against Religious Assessments," which Irving Brant called "the most powerful defense of religious liberty ever written in America." In the first of fifteen substantive paragraphs, Madison quoted from the Virginia Declaration of Rights: "Religion or the duty which we owe to our Creator and the manner of discharging it, can be directed only by reason and conviction, not by force or violence." Society had no authority over a person's faith, and if the broader community did not, "still less can it be subject to that of the Legislative body." Americans had learned from their history "to take alarm at the first experiment on our liberties," and if the state could make Christianity the established faith, it could "establish with the same ease any particular sect of Christians, in exclusion of all other Sects." The general assessment on its face discriminated against certain groups; Quakers, Mennonites, and others considered "a compulsive support of their Religions unnecessary and unwarrantable."[66]

Drawing on history and philosophy, Madison next explored the relationship between church and state. He denied "that the Civil Magistrate is a competent Judge of Truth" and denounced the idea that government "may employ Religion as an engine of Civil policy" as "an unhallowed perversion of the means of salvation." True religion had existed before governments had been formed and had flourished without state support. Where Christianity had been the official faith, however, the results had been "more or less in all places, pride and indolence in the Clergy, ignorance and servility in the laity, in both, superstition, bigotry and persecution." Madison and Jefferson worried much about the political abuse of ecclesiastical authority. "A just Government," Madison wrote, had no more need for the sanction of an official church than the church needed state support. State churches had established

Confusion . . . Must Stifle All Enterprize

"spiritual tyranny" over weak governments or upheld "the political tyranny" of stronger ones, but "in no instance have they been seen the guardians of the liberties of the people."[67]

The "Memorial and Remonstrance" also included more mundane arguments against the general assessment. It would discourage immigration into Virginia and encourage outmigration, it would inflame tensions among churches as they competed for state funds, and it would be difficult to enforce in the face of widespread popular opposition, thereby undermining respect for the rule of law. The general assessment, moreover, was "adverse to the diffusion of the light of Christianity." By discouraging the immigration of non-Christians, "it at once discourages those who are strangers to the light of revelation from coming into the Region of it" and, by example, justified nations "who continue in darkness" in "shutting out" those who might bring them light.[68]

Madison had added several new arguments in favor of the rights of conscience to the ones Jefferson had made in *Notes* and in his Bill for Establishing Religious Freedom, but nowhere did he contradict the letter or the logic of Jefferson's writings, although Madison displayed a more explicit Christian bias. Only on one notable point did they diverge. The third and final paragraph of Jefferson's bill conceded that if the bill became law, it could not, as a mere statute, prevent future lawmakers from repealing it, but if they did, "such an act will be an infringement of natural right." The "Memorial and Remonstrance" recognized freedom of religion as a natural right, but Madison ended with an appeal to the Virginia Declaration of Rights: if religious liberty could be abridged by the assembly, all the rights guaranteed by the Declaration would be in jeopardy, a prospect that led Madison to conclude the legislature had "no such authority." While the great majority of Madison's supporters surely agreed, the argument did not flow logically from Madison's and Jefferson's belief that Virginia's 1776 constitution was not a literal constitution and could not bind the legislature. Jefferson rested the Bill for Establishing Religious Freedom on natural law alone and avoided that dilemma.[69]

By the time the fall 1785 session convened, public opinion had shifted so decisively against the general assessment bill that it was not brought up for a vote. Instead, the assembly, after making a few revisions to Jefferson's preamble, passed his bill. It was one of Madison's greatest legislative triumphs. "I flatter myself [we] have in this country," he wrote to Jefferson in Paris, "extinguished for ever the ambitious hope of making laws for the human mind."[70]

Despite its embrace of religious liberty, the Virginia assembly had not redeemed itself in Madison's mind. He had argued in the "Memorial and

Remonstrance" that representative democracy would not necessarily safeguard freedom of conscience because "the majority may trespass on the rights of the minority." Presumably other rights faced equal risks. Madison suspected the general assessment failed not primarily because of the force of his logic but because of divisions among the state's various denominations. The debate over the general assessment vividly illustrated a point Madison had heard from John Witherspoon and read in other Enlightenment thinkers: lawmakers operating in an extended sphere and representing an array of factions could not easily form a majority to pass bad laws. Perhaps on other issues, Virginia was too small a sphere.[71]

———

MADISON's road to a larger sphere took a circuitous route. Shortly before Jefferson had left for Europe, Madison had mentioned to him a jurisdictional dispute between Virginia and Maryland over regulation of the Potomac River. Madison suggested commissioners from the two states meet to compromise their differences. Jefferson liked the idea and passed it along to Thomas Stone, a member of Congress from Maryland, who seemed receptive.[72] In June 1784, the Virginia assembly, apparently at Madison's urging, appointed him, Edmund Randolph, George Mason, and Alexander Henderson to meet with representatives of Maryland. The project moved slowly. Not until the end of the year did the assembly adopt resolutions, drafted by Madison, clarifying its agents' authority. When the Maryland delegates wrote Governor Henry to suggest a meeting place and time, Henry failed to notify the Virginia delegation.[73]

At the last minute, Mason, who had not received his instructions, learned from his Maryland counterparts that they intended to be in Alexandria in March 1785. Making the best of an awkward situation, he recruited Henderson, who lived in Alexandria, to join him in the negotiations. George Washington had long been interested in promoting use of the river, and he invited the commissioners to reassemble at nearby Mount Vernon; hence the ensuing agreement became known as the Mount Vernon Compact.[74]

All concerned seemed pleased with the results of the Mount Vernon conference, its improvised nature notwithstanding. The Maryland legislature approved the compact early in December 1785; Virginia lawmakers approved it later in their fall session. The Mount Vernon commissioners had recommended Virginia and Maryland adopt uniform regulations on other issues, including foreign trade, and the Maryland delegates suggested inviting Pennsylvania and Delaware to subsequent talks, and they would in all likelihood

Confusion . . . Must Stifle All Enterprize

want to include their neighbors. Accordingly, John Tyler introduced a resolution calling for a meeting of all the states to consider commercial issues.[75]

Still hoping to win approval of an amendment to the Articles of Confederation giving Congress the authority to tax and regulate trade, Madison greeted the proposal for a commercial convention of the states with no enthusiasm. He doubted a convention would agree to give Congress the authority the state legislatures had denied it. The failure of the House of Delegates to pass an amendment left Madison with few options. As an aged Madison explained the assembly's action years later, the states' inability to expand the powers of Congress, to provide for the payment of Revolutionary War debts, or to retaliate against Great Britain for discriminating against American trade led the assembly on 21 January 1786, the last day of the session, to issue a call for a commercial conference of all the states. Madison, Edmund Randolph, and St. George Tucker were appointed to represent Virginia. The conference would be held in Annapolis, Maryland, in September.[76]

Madison later recalled approaching the Annapolis conference with more "hope" than "confidence." At the time, both were in short supply. The meeting "will probably miscarry," Madison wrote James Monroe the day after the assembly issued its call; "I think however it is better than nothing."[77] In fact, it would be the first step toward a national, constitutional convention.

SIX

A New Government Must Be Made

1786–1787

THOMAS JEFFERSON'S YEARS IN EUROPE confirmed his belief in America's moral and material superiority over the Old World.[1] That belief, coupled with a more optimistic temperament, allowed him to view the national travails of the 1780s with an equanimity James Madison could not muster. Jefferson did worry about America's image abroad, and Madison sent him good news and bad. Madison's "Memorial and Remonstrance against Religious Assessments," Jefferson predicted, "will do us great honor" among "the wisest part of Europe." Much from the fall 1785 assembly session offered less encouragement. Virginia's unfavorable balance of trade led to a loss of hard currency and created, in Madison's words, "a considerable itch for paper money," along with a new law postponing tax collections. "The wisdom of seven sessions," Madison lamented, "will be unable to repair the mischiefs of this single act."[2]

Jefferson conceded Americans' inability to pay their foreign creditors and "the want of energy in our government" had embarrassed the nation, but even here he found a silver lining. Unpaid bills made it more difficult to get credit, and without credit, American consumers could not indulge their tastes for the luxuries that would otherwise threaten "the loss of those manners which alone can preserve republican government." The feebleness of the national government, meanwhile, complicated America's westward expansion. While Madison fretted about securing access to the Mississippi

126

River, Jefferson feared that Spain might lose control of the region before the United States was ready to seize it.[3]

Writing an article on the United States for Jean-Nicolas Démeunier's *Encyclopédia Méthodique*, Jefferson called the Articles of Confederation "a wonderfully perfect instrument considering the circumstances under which it was formed." He acknowledged a need for only three amendments. The admission of new states should require less than the unanimous consent of the existing states. Requisitions on the states should be based on population, with a slave counted as three-fifths of a free person. And Congress should be empowered to fix uniform duties for imports into all the states and, more generally, to regulate trade so as to "oblige" America's trading parties "to concur in just & equal arrangements of commerce." Jefferson now argued, as had Madison earlier, that the Articles granted Congress an implied power to compel the states to comply with its demands, and he thought a naval force would be equal to the task. Conceding that American governments rarely acted with such vigor, Jefferson invited his European readers to compare the wrongs done by weak states to those done by more powerful regimes: "The last will be found most numerous, most oppressive on the mind, and most degrading of the dignity of man."[4]

Privately, Jefferson seemed slightly less sanguine. As early as February 1786, if not before, he saw a need for fundamental reform. He wrote Madison from Paris, "The politics of Europe render it indisputably necessary that with respect to every thing external, we be one nation only, firmly hooped together. Interior government is what each state should keep to itself." If the states would approve an amendment giving Congress explicit authority to regulate commerce, "it would produce a total revolution in . . . [Europe's] opinion of us." A lack of respect for the United States, Jefferson warned Madison, made war more likely, and unless Congress got control of the nation's foreign policy, an obstreperous state might provoke a conflict.[5]

In later years, Jefferson ruminated frequently on the failure of the Articles. The American Revolution had produced among Americans "a universal conversion to republicanism," but they had failed to exploit fully the opportunities created by independence. "Novices" in the art of self-government, they had organized a central government too weak to manage the nation's foreign affairs. Patriotism and martial ardor compensated for the defects of the Articles during the war, but when peace came, Americans became preoccupied with their own affairs and ignored the demands of Congress. Within the states, progress occurred. Jefferson lauded the state constitutions for expanding popular sovereignty and protecting individual rights, including freedom of religion, freedom of the press, and the "right and duty to be at all times armed." Creating a functioning central government took longer.[6]

As American minister to France, Jefferson worked to enhance the republic's international reputation and to negotiate commercial treaties that would open new markets to U.S. ships and goods. In March, Jefferson went to London to help John Adams negotiate an agreement with the British government. The talks went nowhere. British officials believed, Jefferson concluded, that British ships could dominate the American carrying trade and that British merchants could enjoy all the advantages of the American market without a treaty and without making any concessions to the United States. Jefferson and Adams had more cordial talks with British merchants. Although they disagreed on details, all concerned agreed that American state courts, as anticipated by the Treaty of Paris, ought to be open to British creditors trying to collect debts from their American customers. Congress could not, however, make the states cooperate. In fact, the British government, citing the debt issue and America's harsh treatment of Loyalists, had announced in February that it would not honor its treaty commitments to remove its troops from the American Northwest. After six frustrating weeks, Jefferson returned to Paris. The futile mission to London surely reinforced his doubts about the Articles, but in Jefferson's mind, British stubbornness and pride shared roughly equal blame for the diplomatic stalemate. Jefferson summed up his country's dilemma: "The English, their ministers, & esp. the king hate America."[7]

By the spring of 1786, virtually no one expected the states to approve any of the various amendments that had been proposed to strengthen the Articles of Confederation. Madison spent much of that spring wading through the almost 200 volumes of historical works and philosophical treatises that Jefferson had sent him from France. He hoped to find a solution to America's political dilemma. His research produced a long memorandum, "Of Ancient and Modern Confederacies," that, while it would prove invaluable in the debates ahead, mainly confirmed what he already believed: "Ancient and modern [confederacies] all tended to fly apart for lack of a supreme authority." Historically, even monarchies seemed to command more popular support than republics. Commenting on the power of the stadtholder in Holland, Madison complained that "men too jealous to confide their liberty to their representatives, who are their equals, abandoned it to a Prince, who might more easily abuse it."[8]

Madison did not, it might be noted, expect a stronger central government to solve all the nation's woes. Responding to Jefferson's observations on

A New Government Must Be Made

Europe's poor, Madison expressed the opinion that a surplus of labor and "a certain degree of misery" were inevitable in a densely populated state, even if it had a republican government. For some, life might actually be worse. A more egalitarian society would need fewer workers manufacturing the "superfluities" consumed by the rich and fewer domestic servants. A "juster government" would also require fewer soldiers.[9]

In the spring and summer of 1786, however, the nation faced more immediate problems. As Madison wrote to Jefferson, "The scarcity of money, the low price of Tobacco, and the high price of bread continue to be the topics of complaint." The states had never fully complied with the requisitions of Congress, and Madison predicted revenues received in 1786 would be less than those of the previous year. Virginia, the largest state, "will not supply a single shilling," leaving Congress unable to pay the interest on its foreign debt or even its current expenses.[10]

Madison believed everything was intertwined: "Most of our political evils may be traced up to our commercial ones, as most of our moral [evils] may be to our political." An unfavorable balance of trade drained specie out of the United States, which in turn fueled a demand from cash-strapped consumers for debt relief, paper money, and the postponement of taxes. To Madison, those remedies made matters worse. Debt relief defrauded British creditors and prevented enforcement of the Treaty of Paris. When Virginia delayed collecting taxes, as it did in 1786, Madison argued the delay meant more money would go to England to pay for imported goods. Tax revenues would have stayed in Virginia. Worst of all was "the general rage for paper money." What Madison called "fictitious money" depreciated rapidly, hurt lenders, and, he feared, risked new tensions among the states if they began to quarrel over whether to accept each other's currency. Only federal regulation of trade, Madison concluded, could stabilize the nation's economy.[11]

At the same time, he approached the Annapolis convention with no great optimism. Annapolis had been chosen as the site of the meeting so the delegates would not appear to be the captives of Congress or of mercantile interests in the larger commercial cities, but opposition to the convention persisted. "We have," Madison wrote James Monroe, "both ignorance and iniquity to control." Madison thought some of the critics meant well; Maryland, for instance, refused to participate for fear a special convention might undermine Congress. He would have preferred an assembly to consider more sweeping reforms, but in the summer of 1786 he thought only a commercial amendment would have a chance of success, and "to speak the truth," he wrote Jefferson, "I almost despair even of this." If, however, the Annapolis convention could launch a movement that culminated in the adoption of an amendment empowering Congress to regulate trade, it could, he hoped, become a precedent for further reform.[12]

Madison had ample reasons to be pessimistic. He worried that "if the present crisis cannot effect unanimity" among the states on the necessity of giving Congress more authority, he could not envision what would. Delay would create new obstacles. Madison dreaded foreign intervention in American politics, and as new states entered the Union, consensus for constitutional reform would become even more elusive. If the Annapolis convention failed, Great Britain and the rest of the world, he feared, would conclude America need not be "apprehended as a nation in matters of Commerce."[13]

Nothing in the months leading up to the Annapolis convention presented a greater obstacle to Madison's efforts to revise the Articles than John Jay's negotiations with Don Diego de Gardoqui over American access to the Mississippi River. In late August 1786, Congress authorized Jay to continue talks aimed at securing commercial concessions from Spain in exchange for closing the river to American trade for twenty-five to thirty years. Madison's own conversations with Gardoqui convinced him a treaty would not be forthcoming in the near future, and there was the manner of arithmetic. Seven states had supported Jay's new instructions, but under the Articles nine votes would be required to approve a treaty, a hurdle Jay was unlikely to clear. Nevertheless, the political damage had been done. How could Madison convince Virginians to grant additional powers to Congress when a northern majority seemed willing to sacrifice a vital southern interest?[14]

Madison and the other Virginia delegates, Edmund Randolph and St. George Tucker, dutifully attended the Annapolis conference, but when the meeting convened on 11 September, the only other states present were New York, New Jersey, Pennsylvania, and Delaware. With so few states represented, the delegates decided to adjourn, but not before taking advantage of some broad language in New Jersey's instructions to its delegates. They had been authorized to consider a "uniform system in their commercial regulations and *other important matters*." Alexander Hamilton, representing New York, drafted a skillful address for the convention that recognized that the New Jersey instructions were "an improvement on the original plan." Effective commercial regulations "may require a correspondent adjustment of other parts of the Federal System." Hamilton did not go into detail about current "embarrassments" in the nation's foreign and domestic affairs; to do so "would be an useless intrusion of facts and observations." Instead, the address

A New Government Must Be Made

simply recommended a convention be held in Philadelphia next May "to devise such further provisions as shall appear to them necessary to render the Constitution of the Federal Government adequate to the exigencies of the Union." Madison apparently persuaded Hamilton to eliminate from his first draft some harsh criticism of Congress and the state governments. It was the beginning of a collaboration that, for the next two years, would be even more productive than Madison's relationship with Jefferson.[15]

Jefferson took the news from Annapolis in stride. If it led to a "full meeting in May, and a broader reformation, it will still be well." By the end of the year, he had formulated his own goals for constitutional reform. The convention should create a separate executive and "make us one nation as to foreign concerns, and keep us distinct in Domestic ones."[16]

———

Armed protests by struggling farmers in Massachusetts helped, ironically, to create momentum for what Madison later called "a salutary Reform of the pol. System." Known to history as Shays's Rebellion after one of its leaders, Revolutionary War veteran Daniel Shays, the movement had been triggered by high taxes and debt-foreclosure actions. In August 1786 rebels stopped a court session in Northampton; in September they disrupted a session of the state supreme court at Springfield. At one point the federal arsenal at Springfield appeared threatened. Meanwhile, Congress's secretary of war, Henry Knox, circulated alarmist accounts of the rebels' strength and intentions.[17]

The affair certainly rattled Madison and confirmed his prediction that the "Dissolution" of the confederation, if it were not reformed, was imminent. Madison thought the Shayites wanted to redistribute the state's wealth, and he dreaded the prospect that the rebellion might spread to New York. It is fair to say Madison overreacted and used the episode to advance his own agenda, but Massachusetts militia under General Benjamin Lincoln did not suppress the revolt until February 1787; its duration was understandably unnerving. The possibility the farmers might achieve their goals lawfully, however, also unnerved Madison. By the spring of 1787, he was complaining to Jefferson and to George Washington that some of the rebels had been elected to "local offices of trust and authority" and that the new governor, John Hancock, sympathized with their demands, which included debt relief and paper money.[18]

Jefferson responded differently. In October 1786, decrying criticism of America in "the lying newspapers of London," he had written Maria Cosway, an English painter with whom he had enjoyed a brief romance, that "there is not a country on earth where there is greater tranquility, where the laws are milder, or better obeyed: where everyone is more attentive to his own business, or meddles less with that of others." John Adams initially advised Jefferson not to be "alarmed by the late Turbulence in New England," but Abigail Adams was soon sending him less reassuring reports. She called the rebel leaders "ignorant, wrestless desperados, without conscience or principals [sic]," and blasted their followers as "a deluded multitude" whose grievances "have no existence but in their imaginations." Jefferson deplored the violence, but he seems to have found Shays's Rebellion encouraging: it demonstrated that Americans could break out of their postwar apathy and protest if they felt themselves oppressed.[19]

Sensitive though he was to the nation's reputation, Jefferson dismissed the notion that Shays's Rebellion had damaged America's image in Europe. He hoped the rebels would not be punished "too severely," lest "the only safeguard of the public liberty"—or in other words, the potential for popular protest—be lost. Shays's Rebellion produced some of Jefferson's most famous aphorisms and hyperbole. To prevent future disturbances, the people should be kept informed through the newspapers. "Were it left to me to decide whether we should have a government without newspapers or newspapers without a government, I should not hesitate a moment to prefer the latter." Or, as he wrote Madison, "I hold it that a little rebellion now and then is a good thing, and as necessary in the political world as storms in the physical." Jefferson could tolerate, in short, a level of popular political participation and, at least theoretically, a degree of instability that Madison could not abide.[20]

———

JEFFERSON thought that the possibility Congress might accept Spain's closure of the Mississippi River was a greater threat to the Union than some disgruntled farmers in Massachusetts. Westerners might well abandon the confederacy and take with them the western lands that Jefferson hoped could be sold to pay the national debt. Madison, in his calmer moments, agreed. As a delegate to the fall 1786 session of the Virginia assembly, he secured passage of a resolution demanding American access to the river. He hoped to reassure representatives from Virginia's Kentucky district. He knew they were especially anxious about the course of the Jay-Gardoqui negotiations. He also understood that the Mississippi issue had alienated Patrick Henry, Virginia's most popular politician, from the cause of constitutional reform. Renewing Virginia's determination to keep the Mississippi open, coupled with anxiety over Shays's Rebellion, helped Madison persuade the assembly to approve the call of the Annapolis convention for a general meeting of all the states. "The unanimous sanction given by the Assembly" to the Philadelphia convention, he wrote Jefferson, "marks sufficiently the revolution of sentiment which the experience of one year has effected in this country."[21]

Madison also helped defeat, by an impressive 85–17 vote, a proposal to issue paper money. For the most part, however, the fall session did little to restore Madison's faith in state politics. Lawmakers rejected Jefferson's education bill that had first been proposed in the law revisers' report. The bill to reform the criminal law, with its provisions to eliminate the death penalty for all but the most serious crimes, failed by one vote. "The rage against Horse stealers," Madison told Jefferson, was too much. A bill Madison had introduced to establish a district court system also lost by a single vote. An effort to repeal Madison's controversial port act failed, but the assembly added two more towns to the list of legal entry points, which further weakened an already diluted statute. The assembly approved new taxes, but only as a response to a fiscal crisis. As Madison described the situation to Jefferson, "Our Treasury is empty, no supplies have gone to the federal treasury, and our internal embarrassments torment us exceedingly."[22]

In February 1787, Madison arrived in New York City for another session of Congress. It did nothing to improve his morale. He complained to Edmund Pendleton, "No money is paid into the public Treasury; no respect is paid to the federal authority. . . . It is not possible that a Government can last long under these circumstances." In March, he reported to Jefferson that "Congress have continued so thin as to be incompetent to the dispatch of the more important business before them." Members could not agree on a plan for the sale of western land and made no progress on the settlement of financial accounts between the states and Congress that were left over from the Revolutionary War. Congress had endorsed the call for a constitutional convention, but its prospects were uncertain. Madison had been a virtually inevitable choice for the Virginia delegation. Washington, however, had not yet agreed to accept his commission, and Henry had flatly refused to serve. Madison suspected Henry wanted to be free to oppose the convention if the Mississippi controversy ended badly.[23]

Madison proposed that Congress transfer the negotiations to Madrid and authorize Jefferson to represent the United States. Jay blocked the attempt to circumvent his authority as secretary for foreign affairs, but he knew only seven states supported his plan to trade access to the Mississippi for access to certain Spanish ports, and Madison suspected the New Yorker was too cautious to agree to a treaty that would not enjoy broader support. If sectional animosities aroused by the affair would linger and hamstring Madison's struggle for a stronger national government, the real danger had passed. As Madison put it in a letter to Jefferson in March 1787, "The Spanish project sleeps."[24]

Reports of growing support for an emission of paper money in Virginia would haunt Madison throughout the spring and into the summer, but by the middle of March he at least expected the Philadelphia convention to be well attended. Only Rhode Island had refused to appoint delegates. Madison later attributed the state's refusal to "an obdurable adherence to an advantage which her position gave her of taxing her neighbors thro' their consumption of imported supplies, an advantage which it was foreseen would be taken from her" by a reformed national government. Rhode Island was also a notorious source of paper money.[25]

Service in a somnolent Congress gave Madison time to think, and he began to consider what he wanted the upcoming convention to do. He later said that his first outline of a new constitution appeared in a letter to Edmund Randolph early in April, but a March letter to Jefferson anticipated much of what he would tell Randolph. The "new system" would have to be ratified by the people, not by the state legislatures, "to render it clearly paramount to their Legislative authorities." In addition to the power to regulate trade, Congress should be given "a negative *in all cases whatsoever*" in order to protect its jurisdiction from the states, to protect the states from each other, and to protect minorities within the states from "paper money and other unrighteous measures." Representation in Congress would have to be based on population. Madison understood that abolishing the one-state, one-vote rule would be controversial, but he minimized the difficulty of the task. The northern states would embrace it, he predicted, because they contained a majority of the population. The South would accept it because southerners expected their region to grow more rapidly. The small states could not resist a solid phalanx of larger states, and once the big states were assured of a greater voice in Congress, they would support enhancing the power of the central government. Finally, the concentration of authority in Congress would be replaced by a separation of powers among different branches of the national government.[26]

Madison elaborated on his plans in his April letter to Randolph and largely recapitulated them in a letter to George Washington a few days later. He acknowledged it would "be well" to retain as much of the Articles of Confederation as possible, but he preferred incorporating parts of the old

A New Government Must Be Made

system into a new constitution to amending the Articles. In addition to proportional representation in Congress and a congressional veto over state laws, Madison believed the national government must have "positive and complete authority in all cases where uniform measures are necessary." He envisioned a national court with jurisdiction over cases involving foreigners, citizens of different states, and admiralty issues. Congress should be divided into two houses, with its acts subject to the veto of a "council of revision." One house would be smaller than the other, and its members would serve longer terms. His thinking on a national executive had not evolved since he wrote Jefferson; he admitted to Randolph he did not know how the office would be constituted or what it would do. He proposed the "tranquility" of the states be guaranteed "against internal as well as external dangers," surely a reference to Shays's Rebellion and possibly to a slave revolt. Madison also repeated his call for popular ratification of the convention's handiwork.[27]

His design for a national government was conservative to the extent it reflected structures and procedures, among them bicameral assemblies and popular ratification, that had become commonplace in the states by 1787. Even his council of revision was borrowed from New York. In other respects, Madison's ideas were both radical and reactionary. He claimed to be searching for "some middle ground" between state and national authority, but he clearly considered the states to be unavoidable nuisances. "No material sacrifices," he wrote Randolph, "ought to be made to local or temporary prejudices." The states could not be eliminated, so he would "leave in force the local authorities so far as they can be subordinately useful." He understood the sweeping nature of his proposals, telling Randolph, "My ideas of reform strike so deeply at the old Confederacy, and lead to such a systematic change." He did not, however, fully understand their political implications. Besides miscalculating the opposition his proposal for proportional representation would provoke, Madison had resurrected two especially unpopular ghosts from America's colonial past. He had patterned his "congressional negative" after the veto wielded by the royal governors, and the phrase "in all cases whatsoever" had appeared in the infamous Declaratory Act, in which Parliament had asserted its right to tax the colonies "in all cases whatsoever."[28]

Madison's thinking had changed dramatically. In the early 1780s, he had chiefly criticized the structural flaws of the Articles of Confederation and that document's failure to empower Congress to impose taxes or regulate commerce. Now he aimed his ire at the states. Jack Rakove has observed that national issues alone "could never have generated the sense of crisis that gave the struggle over the Constitution its urgent tenor."[29] That was certainly the case with Madison. The Articles of Confederation had left sovereignty in the states, and years of frustration with state politics, which went back to 1776 and the ad hoc process by which Virginia had adopted its constitution, had convinced Madison the states were not equal to their responsibilities. Constantly shuttling back and forth between an impotent Congress and a parochial state assembly, as Madison did throughout the 1780s, had immersed him in the failings of both in a way that relatively few of his contemporaries, including Jefferson, had experienced.

Madison's letters to Jefferson, Randolph, and Washington reflected a fundamental critique of the political order. As was his custom, Madison reduced his thoughts to writing, in this case a memorandum he titled "Vices of the Political System of the United States," which he wrote in April 1787 while rooming at Vandine Elsworth's boardinghouse on Maiden Street, near New York's city hall, where the Confederation Congress was meeting. "Vices" consisted of twelve numbered allegations against the system, almost all of which implicated the states. Madison complained, predictably, of the states' refusal to comply with congressional requisitions and, somewhat less predictability, of state actions, such as the Mount Vernon Compact, that encroached "on the federal authority." The states had violated the nation's international obligations, including the Treaty of Paris of 1783. They had also violated each other's rights with their emissions of paper money, debt-relief measures, and trade regulations.[30]

The nation needed uniform laws to regulate naturalization and intellectual property and to establish "national seminaries" and corporations, although oddly he did not specifically mention interstate commerce. Still shaken by Shays's Rebellion, Madison believed the states needed protection against internal disorder and help maintaining republican governments. A minority with "the skills and habits of military life" might impose its will on a majority. A minority of the electorate might seize power with the support of those "whose poverty excludes them from a right of suffrage." Here he added cryptically, "Where slavery exists the Republican Theory becomes still more fallacious."[31]

Congress could not enforce its decrees on the states, and politics within the states made voluntary compliance unlikely. "Every general act of the Union must necessarily bear unequally hard on some particular member or members of it," Madison observed. The "courtiers of popularity" within the affected state or states would resist such measures to advance their own careers. State jealousies added another impediment: "A distrust of the voluntary compliance of each other may prevent the compliance of any." Madison

A New Government Must Be Made

also argued that because the Articles had not been ratified by a vote of the people, an act of Congress was arguably inferior to a subsequent act of a state legislature and, "from the doctrine of compacts," a breach of the Articles by one party relieved all the other members of the Confederation from their obligations under them. Approval of the Articles by a state legislature did not transfer sovereignty to Congress.[32]

State lawmaking, more than anything else, Madison thought, had created the current crisis. State legislatures passed too many laws and changed them too frequently: "We see daily laws repealed or superseded, before any trial can be made of their merits; and before even a knowledge of them can have reached the remoter districts within which they were to operate."[33]

Madison devoted the longest section of "Vices," the eleventh, to the "injustice of the laws of States," which "brings into question the fundamental principle of republican Government, that the majority who rule in such Governments, are the safest Guardians both of public Good and of private rights." In the most crucial passage in the entire memorandum, Madison attempted to explain why state assemblies had failed and what might be done about their almost inevitable shortcomings. He began with the lawmakers themselves, who could be motivated by ambition, personal interest, or the public good. "Unhappily the two first are proved by experience to be the most prevalent," and the ambitious and the interested are often "the most industrious." Even "the honest but unenlightened representative" frequently becomes "the dupe of a favorite leader, veiling his selfish views under the professions of public good."[34]

"A still more fatal if not more frequent cause" of unjust laws, Madison went on, "lies among the people themselves." Societies naturally divide into interests or factions, and when "an apparent interest or common passion" unites a majority, it is apt to transgress the rights of the minority. Considerations of the public interest are "too often unheeded." Neither a concern for public opinion in the larger world nor religious scruples can be relied upon to prevent injustice. However, in a political sphere larger than an individual state, "a common interest or passion is less apt to be felt and the requisite combinations less easy to be formed." A multitude of factions "could check each other." In an enlarged republic, the government should be "sufficiently neutral between the different interests and factions, to controul one part of the Society from invading the rights of another," and sufficiently controlled itself so as not to act in its self-interest. Elections to a national assembly with real authority would, moreover, "most certainly extract from the mass of the Society the purest and noblest characters which it contains."[35]

Madison ended "Vices" anticlimactically, with an unexplained twelfth count labeled simply "Impotence of the laws of the States." Perhaps he had exhausted himself. He had already laid out the argument he would make throughout the Constitutional Convention and the ratification debate: power could safely be conferred on a national government because in a republic of continental dimensions, no single faction was likely to form a majority hostile to the general welfare.[36]

———

MADISON arrived in Philadelphia on 5 May, making him the first delegate on the scene except for the Pennsylvanians. He wrote his initial report on the convention to Jefferson on a Tuesday, ten days later. The convention had been scheduled to begin on Monday, but mainly because of bad weather, the delegates were still trickling in. Of the Virginians, Edmund Randolph, John Blair, and James McClurg had arrived a few days earlier. George Washington reached Philadelphia on Sunday. George Mason was expected shortly. The convention would not command a quorum until 25 May. The delay frustrated Madison, but it allowed the Virginians time to agree on an outline for a proposed constitution, the Virginia Plan, which was largely Madison's work, and to consult with the sympathetic and nationally minded Pennsylvania delegation.[37]

Despite expressing optimism about the convention's prospects for success, Jefferson had modest expectations. He blamed much of the unease in the nation simply on Americans' tendency to live "so far beyond our income."[38] He confessed, "I do not go as far in the reforms thought necessary as some of my correspondents in America," but he seemed willing to defer to the judgment of the convention.[39] Jefferson hoped the national government would be given exclusive jurisdiction over American diplomacy, including the regulation of foreign trade; a peaceable means of enforcing its decisions on the states; and a reliable source of revenue. The power of the new government, Jefferson thought, ought to be divided among separate legislative, judicial, and executive branches while the states continued to manage their internal affairs. With only a few reforms, he wrote George Washington, Americans would find themselves "in the happiest political situation."[40]

Madison sent Jefferson a second report on 6 June, the day on which, as we shall see, Madison delivered one of his most important speeches of the summer. By then the delegates had elected Washington to serve as president of the convention. They had also agreed to deliberate behind closed doors and to keep their debates confidential. Madison could, as a result, provide

A New Government Must Be Made

Jefferson with no further details, but the identity of the delegates was no secret, and Madison could comment on them. "The names of the members will satisfy you that the States have been serious in this business. . . . The whole community is big with expectation," he noted. In fact, some of the nation's most prominent politicians were absent, skeptical of the proceedings or preoccupied with state affairs or other business. The missing included, besides Patrick Henry, Richard Henry Lee of Virginia, New York's powerful governor George Clinton, and Sam Adams and John Hancock of Massachusetts. John Adams remained at his diplomatic post in London. Nevertheless, the delegates as a whole brought considerable prestige and experience to their task. Forty-two of the fifty-five men who served in the convention had also served in Congress.[41]

On 29 May, Randolph presented the Virginia Plan to the convention. While the other members sat as state delegations at separate tables, Madison had earlier positioned himself in front of the presiding officer to hear the debates more clearly. Struck by the paucity of records on the origins of previous confederacies, he had decided to take shorthand notes of the Philadelphia proceedings and write them out more fully at night. The Virginia assembly's commission to its delegates, which Madison may have written, did not anticipate a complete abandonment of the Articles of Confederation, but the Virginia Plan did. It called for the creation of a bicameral legislature with representation based on "the Quotas of contribution, or the number of free inhabitants, as the one or the other rule may seem best in different cases." Quotas of contributions would reflect wealth and, juxtaposed against free inhabitants, sounded like a euphemism for slaves. One branch would be elected by the people for terms yet to be determined. The other branch would be selected by the first "out of a proper number of persons" nominated by the state legislatures for terms "sufficient to ensure their independency." The national assembly could "legislate in all cases to which the separate States are incompetent." It could also negate state laws "contravening . . . the articles of Union." Presumably, the other Virginia delegates had persuaded Madison to forgo his proposal for a congressional veto extending to "all cases whatsoever."[42]

The Virginia Plan provided for a national executive chosen by the legislature, and although Madison had not yet decided how long a chief magistrate should serve, no second term would be allowed. The executive and some number of federal judges would constitute a council of revision that could veto acts of the legislature, but lawmakers could override its veto by an unspecified majority. The plan envisioned a national court system, as Madison's preconvention correspondence suggested, but with its jurisdiction expanded to include cases of impeachment and "questions which may involve the national peace and harmony." Other provisions guaranteed each state its territorial integrity and a republican government, allowed for the admission of new states, required state officials to swear loyalty to "the articles of Union," required those articles to be approved by Congress and by state conventions before they could take effect, and created a process for later amendments.[43]

Given its scope and the controversies to come, the initial response to the Virginia Plan was surprisingly muted. During the debates of 31 May, Madison told his colleagues he would prefer to enumerate specifically the powers of the legislature, but he doubted an enumeration was practical. By a yes vote of nine states, with one divided, the delegates agreed to allow a new congress to make laws in all cases "to which the states are not competent."[44]

Madison beat some hasty retreats, made a few early compromises, and in some cases made matters worse. He quickly dropped one of his pet projects: explicitly authorizing the national government to use military force against an uncooperative state. When he saw that South Carolina and Georgia would oppose the use of "free inhabitants" as one basis of representation, he moved to strike the phrase. When John Rutledge and Pierce Butler of South Carolina moved to use "quotas of contribution" to allocate seats in what would become the House of Representatives, Madison suggested simply basing representation on population and counting a slave as three-fifths of a free person. Quotas of contribution went by the wayside, and the Three-Fifths Compromise passed, nine states to two. At other times, his colleagues surely found him less helpful. He favored a council of revision because he thought the executive, acting alone, would dare not veto an act of the national legislature. The idea never had much support; the convention also struggled initially over the size of the majority needed to override the council's veto. On 4 June, after defeating a motion to give the executive "an absolute negative," Elbridge Gerry of Massachusetts proposed the executive alone be granted the veto subject to a two-thirds vote of the legislature. That appeared to be progress. Then, when Madison attempted to revive the council, the emerging consensus collapsed, and the issue remained unresolved.[45]

Madison's proposal for proportional representation in both houses of the legislature would prove to be the most divisive issue of the convention. The small states insisted that the states have equal representation in at least one house. To complicate the issue, Madison never explained clearly how senators, to use the term that emerged during the course of the debates, would be elected. Nor could he explain how, if representation in the upper

A New Government Must Be Made

house were to be based on population, the Senate could remain the cozy, deliberate body that he hoped it would be.[46]

Accordingly, on 30 May, the delegates voted to postpone a decision on the question of representation and shortly thereafter took up the issue of selecting members of the lower house. The debate deserves note for two reasons. First, Madison opposed a proposal to allow the state assemblies to select members of the national legislature, as they had done under the Articles. He wanted the new congress to be independent of the states, and while he hoped to curb ill-conceived popular impulses, he did not want to eliminate popular participation in the new government entirely. "He was an advocate," he said, "for the policy of refining the popular appointments by successive filtrations, but thought it might be pushed too far." Second, the debate occasioned Madison's first major speech of the convention. Speaking on 6 June, Madison began by saying he "considered an election of one branch at least of the Legislature by the people immediately, as a clear principle of free Gov't." He quickly pivoted, however, to point out one of the reasons for the convention: to protect individual rights. "Interferences with these were evils which had more perhaps than anything else produced this convention." He then unveiled his theory of factions and his remedy for them: "to enlarge the sphere as far as the nature of Govt. would admit. This was the only defense agst. the inconveniences of democracy consistent with the democratic form of Govt." Madison prevailed by a vote of eight states to three.[47]

He enjoyed less success over the next two days. On 7 June, Delaware's John Dickinson proposed the upper house be selected by the state legislatures. Madison objected, arguing that if state lawmakers selected the upper house, the principle of proportional representation would have to be abandoned or the Senate would be so large as to take on the "vices" of the lower house. Election by the state legislatures would also frustrate the goal of putting a check on state governments. Despite Madison's opposition, Dickinson's motion passed unanimously. The next day, Charles Pinckney of South Carolina moved to expand the congressional negative to all state laws. Madison seconded the motion, defending it as "the mildest expedient that could be devised" for preventing the abuse of power by the state legislatures. The motion lost with three yes votes, seven nos, and one delegation evenly split.[48]

On 11 June, the delegates resumed debate on the thorny issue of representation. Roger Sherman of Connecticut began the day by proposing what would evolve into the Great, or Connecticut, Compromise: "Suffrage in the 1st branch should be according to the respective numbers of free inhabitants; and that in the second branch or Senate, each State should have one vote and no more." Madison bitterly opposed state equality in either branch, and from his perspective, Sherman's motion failed on an ominously close vote: five states favoring it and six states opposed.[49]

The debate then turned to the less weighty issue of the lawmakers' terms. Madison supported terms that were long by the standards of the day but neither revolutionary nor reactionary: three years for members of the lower house and seven years for senators. His arguments were noteworthy mainly for the light they shed on his attitude toward public opinion and the capacity of representative assemblies. When Elbridge Gerry asserted that his Massachusetts constituents would never surrender their right to the traditional annual election, Madison replied that "if the opinions of the people were to be our guide, it wd. be difficult to say what course we ought to take." No one could say what public opinion was now, what it would be in six to twelve months, or what it would be if the people had the same information as their representatives. In defending seven-year terms for senators, Madison expressed the hope that the Senate could give the national government "stability," but "his fear was that the popular branch would still be too great an overmatch for it."[50]

On 13 June, the convention, sitting as a committee of the whole, approved nineteen resolutions that essentially ratified the Virginia Plan, with a few amendments and some modifications. Representation in both houses of the national assembly would be based on population, with a slave counted as three-fifths of a free person. Voters would elect members of the first branch for three-year terms; the state legislators would choose senators for seven years. The national legislature could make laws in all cases in which the states were incompetent, and Madison's congressional negative survived. The executive, not yet denominated the president, could veto legislation subject to a two-thirds vote of the legislature. The Senate could appoint federal judges, who would serve during good behavior. The resolutions provided for amendments and for popular ratification of the constitution by state conventions. No mention was made of Madison's council of revision, and he opposed, as we have seen, letting local politicians select members of the upper house of a national legislature. On balance, however, Madison had succeeded brilliantly in shaping the debates, but the question of representation was not really settled, and the convention was far from over.[51]

——

"You see the consequences of pushing things too far," John Dickinson told Madison on Friday, 15 June, after Governor William Paterson of New Jersey

A New Government Must Be Made

presented the small states' alternative to the Virginia Plan. The New Jersey Plan authorized Congress to collect import and postage duties; to regulate foreign and interstate trade; and to compel the payment of congressional requisitions, which would be based on the number of a state's free inhabitants and three-fifths of its enslaved population. Congress would elect an executive, who would serve a single term, to enforce federal law and supervise military operations. The New Jersey Plan created a "supreme Tribunal" with original jurisdiction in impeachment cases involving federal officials and appellate jurisdiction in cases involving federal or international law. Paterson also proposed that federal law and treaties "shall be the supreme law of the respective states so far . . . as those Acts or Treaties shall relate to the said States or their Citizens, and that the Judiciary of the several States shall be bound thereby." The structure and mode of representation in Congress would not be altered.[52]

The New Jersey Plan included everything, and more, that Madison could have wanted—five years earlier. Now, he bitterly opposed it as woefully inadequate. Paterson presented it as a set of amendments to the Articles, thereby avoiding any qualms about the convention's legality. Madison tried to brush that argument aside. The Articles represented a mere treaty among the states; when a state breeched it by refusing Congress's demands for money, as many had, the other states were released from their own commitments. "A new government," Madison said, "must be made." Drawing on his research on ancient and modern confederacies and citing the example of the Amphictyonic League and others, Madison argued the New Jersey Plan would not bring the states to heel. In a speech on 19 June, Madison seemed to be reading from "Vices of the Political System of the United States" with its catalog of state misdeeds, which Paterson's amendments would not prevent. He conceded, however, that "the great difficulty lies in the affair of Representation; and if this could be adjusted, all others would be surmountable." The delegates then proceeded to reject the New Jersey Plan by a 7–3 vote with one state, Maryland, divided.[53]

The next day, Jefferson began a letter to Madison from Paris. The American minister was "uneasy" about Congress's delay in making western lands available for sale and feared the Mississippi controversy would encourage separatist movements in the West. He nevertheless dismissed Madison's suggestion that he go to Madrid to negotiate with the Spanish. Jefferson doubted he could be of much help and suspected his intervention would unwisely irritate John Jay, his nominal superior. Removed though he was from the American scene, Jefferson's political judgment often surpassed Madison's.

Jefferson approved of Madison's proposal to create an executive independent of Congress, but he saw the flaws in the congressional negative: "Prima facie I do not like it. It fails in an essential character, that the hole and the patch should be commensurate." No more than one in a hundred state laws should concern Congress, but politicians being politicians, Congress would want to debate everything. He admitted the need for a check on the states, but in a rather prescient prediction of the development of the doctrine of judicial review, Jefferson suggested a more efficient and less intrusive alternative: "An appeal to a federal court sets all to rights."[54]

If the delegates had rejected the New Jersey Plan, they could not forget it. Connecticut's William Johnson began the 21 June session by observing that "on a comparison of the two plans which have been proposed from Virginia & N. Jersey, it appeared that the peculiarity which characterized the latter was its being calculated to preserve the individuality of the States." Specific issues often raised the more general issue of the proper division of authority between the national and state governments, and Madison repeatedly reminded the other delegates that history and their own experience taught that confederacies typically degenerated into anarchy because of the weakness of "the federal head."[55]

More particularly, Madison's speeches toward the end of June—and he took the floor repeatedly—demonstrated his fear of a populist democracy and his desire to defend proportional representation. After the delegates had voted, over his objections, to trim the terms of House members from three years to two, Madison spoke in favor of longer terms and a high age requirement for senators. America needed a strong Senate to protect the people from the lower house and from their own rash impulses. He hoped the Senate would consist of "a portion of enlightened citizens, whose limited number, and firmness might seasonably interpose agst. impetuous counsels."[56]

Above all else, Madison tried to rebut the demand of the smaller states for equal representation in Congress. Ignoring their concern that under proportional representation individual small states would lose influence, he tried to reassure them that, as a bloc, they would be no worse off. The large states, which meant primarily Massachusetts, Pennsylvania, and Virginia, had no common interest that would unite them against their smaller neighbors. A confederacy based on state equality could not long endure, presumably because it would not command the allegiance of citizens in the more populous states. Then, to defend themselves, the small states would become garrisons with peacetime armies and powerful governors, to disastrous consequences. "A standing military force, with an overgrown Executive will not long be safe

A New Government Must Be Made

companions to liberty," Madison warned. "The means of defence agst. foreign danger, have always been the means of tyranny at home."[57]

Madison's invocation of the dangers of militarism repeated sound republican theory, but even some of the large state delegates, chiefly Benjamin Franklin and George Mason, saw the need for compromise. Madison could not stop the growing momentum behind a motion by Connecticut's Oliver Ellsworth to give each state an equal vote in the Senate, while the lower house would be apportioned based on population. He made a last major effort on Saturday, 30 June. "The States," he said, "were divided into different interests not by the difference of size, but by other circumstances; the most material of which resulted partly from climate, but principally from the effects of their having or not having slaves." Madison then suggested a compromise of his own: allocate seats in both houses of Congress according to population, but count slaves only in one house. His argument, however factually accurate, contradicted the picture Madison had painted only a few days earlier of an extended republic with multiple factions.[58]

On Monday, the convention voted on Ellsworth's motion and split 5–5 with Georgia divided. Connecticut, which had voted against the New Jersey Plan, now supported state equality. Personnel changes ended a deadlock in the Maryland delegation and made it a yes vote. South Carolina's Charles Pinckney immediately recommended a committee, consisting of a member from each state, be appointed to find a way out of the impasse. Roger Sherman agreed: "We are now at full stop, and nobody he supposed meant that we should break up without doing something." Madison, perhaps sensing the drift of the convention, opposed referring the issue of representation to a committee as an unnecessary delay, but he was overruled on a 9–2 vote, and when the Grand Committee was appointed, Mason, not Madison, was chosen to represent Virginia.[59]

On 5 July, Elbridge Gerry, chair of the Grand Committee, submitted its report: representation in the lower house should reflect a state's population; each state should have an equal vote in the upper house; and in an apparent concession to some of the large state delegates, or at least to Mason, all bills for raising or appropriating money should begin in the lower house and could not be amended in the Senate.[60]

Over several days of debate, Madison opposed the compromise. He responded immediately that the less populous states had given up little with the origination clause. A senator who wanted to initiate a revenue bill could find a House member to introduce it. The Senate could refuse to approve a tax or spending bill until it got the amendments it wanted from the lower house.[61]

In a speech on 14 July, Madison unleashed a series of objections. State equality implied states were represented in Congress, which they need not be since Congress would not make laws for the states. It was an awkward claim given his oft-expressed desire to rein in state legislatures. He argued more plausibly, but wrongly as time would tell, that the populous states would not support a national government in which they were not fairly represented. He also argued, correctly as time would tell, that the inequity would increase as thinly settled western states entered the Union. More relevant perhaps was the divide between North and South, and here again Madison's crystal ball failed him. With the current eight northern states and five southern states, the advantage that state equality in the Senate would give the North constituted "a serious consideration." Proportional representation also favored the North at the moment, but as the South grew, "every day would tend towards an equilibrium." Unable to foresee that free state populations would grow faster than those of the slave states, Madison never imagined that a Senate in which the states were equal would become, as it did, a bastion of southern political power.[62]

Despite Madison's entreaties, on the morning of 16 July, a Monday, the convention approved the Grand Committee's Great Compromise by a 5–4 vote, with Massachusetts divided. Caleb Strong and Elbridge Gerry had voted for the agreement, creating the deadlock within that state's delegation. The result seemed unlikely to be undone; New Hampshire's delegates had yet to arrive, and they would undoubtedly support the compromise. The result so shocked Madison, and apparently some of the other large state delegates, that when Edmund Randolph suggested the convention adjourn, and William Paterson seconded the motion, Charles Cotesworth Pinckney asked if Randolph meant to adjourn permanently. As tempers cooled, Randolph explained he had intended to suggest only that they adjourn for the day. At a meeting of mainly large state delegates before the convention resumed Tuesday morning, Madison seemed willing to continue the fight for proportional representation even if it broke up the convention, but with few of the other delegates ready to take that risk, he agreed to accept the majority's decision.[63]

———

The Great Compromise settled the convention's most divisive issue, but several critical, if less controversial, questions remained to be resolved. A day after approving the compromise, the delegates resumed debate on the congressional negative. Gouverneur Morris of Pennsylvania spoke first. Usually a reliable nationalist, Morris condemned the negative "as likely to be terrible

A New Government Must Be Made

to the States, and not necessary, if sufficient Legislative authority should be given to the Genl. Government." Roger Sherman and Luther Martin agreed. Sherman thought the negative "unnecessary" since the courts "would not consider as valid any law contravening the Authority of the Union." Only Madison and Charles Pinckney defended the measure, and it went down to defeat on a 7–3 vote.[64] Madison could resign himself to the rebuff with the observation, made a few days later during a speech in favor of popular ratification of the Constitution, that "a law violating the Constitution established by the people themselves would be considered by the Judges as null & void."[65]

When Madison wrote Jefferson again on 18 July, he could not, because of the convention's decision to keep its debates confidential, provide him with details. He promised, however, "if I ever have the pleasure of seeing you," a full report. "I have taken lengthy notes of every thing that has yet passed, and mean to go on with the drudgery, if no indisposition obliges me to discontinue it." No end was in sight. The people were curious and growing impatient, but no one, he wrote, had complained about the convention's secrecy. In reality, it irritated Jefferson. He conceded the delegates' stature and good intentions but confided to John Adams that he was "sorry they began their deliberations by so abominable a precedent as . . . that of tying up the tongues of their members." For his part, Madison's report to Jefferson dwelled on the wickedness of paper money. Some Philadelphia merchants had almost provoked a riot when they temporarily refused to accept the state's badly depreciated currency. "Nothing but evil," he told Jefferson, "springs from this imaginary money wherever it has been tried."[66]

No issue proved more vexing than how to select the president, not because it split the states into rival camps but because the delegates had no working model of a republican executive on a continental scale. Madison had originally supported an appointment by Congress with no opportunity for reelection. Events overtook him. Approval of the Great Compromise undermined his faith in the national legislature, and then the convention voted to allow the executive to serve a second term, which, Madison believed, would make the president subservient to the lawmakers. To address that concern, James McClurg actually suggested the executive serve during "good behavior," or essentially for life. Madison treated the proposal respectfully, perhaps to save McClurg, a respected physician but a political novice, from embarrassment, or perhaps as a ploy to emphasize the need for an independent executive.[67]

In a speech on 19 July, Madison made the case again for the separation of the executive and legislative functions and explored the dilemma confronting the delegates. Appointment by Congress, even if the president served a single term, "would be attended by intrigues and contentions." He preferred, he said, a popular election. The people would vote for "some Citizen whose merits had rendered him an object of general attention & esteem." Yet a national popular vote presented a problem: the suffrage "was much more diffusive" in the North than in the South; the South would be penalized by its large number of African Americans, who could not vote. The use of electors, he concluded, seemed to be the best solution. Accordingly, the delegates voted to allow electors chosen by the state legislatures to select the president.[68]

Every option seemed to present new difficulties. Less than a week later, William Churchill Huston of New Jersey began the day's debate with a motion that the legislature select the executive, as the Virginia Plan had anticipated. Huston "dwelt chiefly on the improbability, that capable men would undertake the service of Electors from the more distant States." After a relatively brief discussion, the convention approved Huston's motion.[69]

That result had Madison back on the floor on 25 July with one of his longest speeches of the convention. He rehearsed every possible option. Selection of the president by the federal judiciary seemed to be "out of the question." Selection by Congress would be divisive, undermine the independence of the executive, and invite foreign intrigue. Selection by the state legislatures would defeat the purpose of giving the president the veto power: to stop "pernicious measures" should Congress be "infected" by the ills that characterized the state assemblies. No one proposed state judges be allowed to choose the president, and if that power were given to the governors, they could be expected to collude with the candidates and with foreign powers.[70]

An electoral college seemed the preferable alternative. Electors would meet only once, which minimized the opportunities for corruption, but the delegates had rejected that approach. A direct poplar vote, Madison concluded, was the best remaining option. Or was it? He closed with two caveats. The people could be expected to vote for their state's favorite son, a disadvantage to the small states, and he repeated his observation that a popular election would favor the North. Was he trying to move the convention back to the idea of an electoral college by subtly undermining support for a direct election? Perhaps, but perhaps not. He did predict that the South would liberalize its voting laws and that its population would grow, which he sincerely believed. In any event, "local considerations must give way to the general interest." As a southerner, he said, "he was willing to make the sacrifice."[71]

On 31 August, in the convention's closing weeks, the question of presidential selection was referred to the aptly named Committee on Postponed

Parts. Madison was a member. Despite his opposition, the committee seemed ready to recommend the national legislature pick the executive. Just as it was concluding its work, John Dickinson, who had been ill, arrived. Dickinson objected that the people would not support a strong chief executive if they had no voice in the selection process. Dickinson's reservations gave Madison a second chance to influence the committee, and the Virginian quickly cobbled together a plan incorporating ideas that had already won considerable support and added a few refinements of his own.[72]

He revived the Electoral College and gave state legislators authority to determine how electors would be chosen, thus creating an opportunity for a popular election in individual states. The number of a state's electors would equal the numbers of its House members plus its senators, which was something of a boon to states with smaller populations. To avoid a deadlock among favorite son candidates, each elector had two votes; only one could be cast for a citizen of the elector's state. To discourage an elector from wasting a vote to game the system in favor of the favorite son, the second-place finisher would become vice president. If no candidate received a majority in the Electoral College, the Senate would decide the election. With some modifications, the convention accepted what became the committee report. The House, supposedly the more democratic body, was empowered to resolve an inconclusive election, and to appease the small states, when the House voted, each state was to cast one vote.[73]

As much as he loathed intemperate and self-interested majorities, Madison believed that a republican government had to rest on popular consent. While he favored the "filtration" of public participation through an elaborate system of checks and balances, both formal in the case of the separation of powers and informal in the case of the multiplicity of factions in an extended republic, Madison assumed the people would participate in their government. In a speech on 7 August, Madison opposed allowing Congress to regulate the right to vote, observing, "A gradual abridgment of this right has been the mode in which Aristocracies have been built on the ruins of popular forms." He predicted the time would come when most Americans would not own property, and he acknowledged that a landless majority might threaten "the rights of property & the public liberty" or, more likely, "become the tools of opulence & ambition." He even threw out the suggestion that suffrage in one house of the legislature might be limited to property owners, but class divisions in America had not yet reached a dangerous stage. For America, an enlarged republic "will be found the best expedient yet tried for solving the problem."[74]

Madison favored giving Congress the right to regulate the time, manner, and place of elections, which proved to be a surprisingly controversial issue during the ratification debate, because he did not fully trust the state assemblies to hold honest elections. He opposed allowing Congress to fix property requirements for its members, and he joined with Alexander Hamilton in fighting a lengthy residency requirement before naturalized citizens would be eligible to serve in Congress.[75]

In addition to approving a process to select a president, the convention decided another momentous, but far less contentious, issue in its final weeks: what affirmative powers to grant the new Congress. The Virginia Plan proposed giving Congress a virtual blank check to act wherever the states appeared incompetent. So broad a grant was politically unrealistic. On 23 July, the delegates had passed a motion by Elbridge Gerry to appoint a Committee of Detail to begin translating measures already approved by the convention into an actual constitution. The next day, John Rutledge, Edmund Randolph, Nathaniel Gorham, Oliver Ellsworth, and James Wilson were elected to the committee. They begin work in earnest on 27 July, when the convention started a two-week recess, and took some liberties with their instructions, most notably in replacing the Virginia Plan's broad grant of authority to Congress with a list of enumerated powers.[76]

When the committee presented its report to the other delegates on 6 August, the enumerated powers section engendered relatively little debate. Madison had originally preferred granting Congress wide discretion, but the Great Compromise had dampened his enthusiasm for sweeping legislative authority. Madison now contented himself with trying to expand the list of congressional powers. Most of his suggestions were routine. Empowering Congress to hold property for forts and "other necessary buildings" was one. At least two were not: authorizing Congress to grant corporate charters and to found a national university. They were not adopted.[77]

Two other issues produced more discussion. The Committee of Detail report also recommended that Congress be prohibited from banning the importation of African slaves and required a two-thirds vote to pass a navigation law. Both provisions showed the influence of John Rutledge. Many southern delegates feared that a northern majority in Congress might drive up shipping costs by giving American, or essentially northern, shippers a monopoly on the American carrying trade. History made them wary; Parliament's Navigation Acts had conferred a similar monopoly on British shipping before the Revolution.[78]

A New Government Must Be Made

During the debates of 24 August, Luther Martin of Maryland proposed that Congress be allowed to tax or ban the foreign slave trade. The New Englanders Ellsworth and Sherman defended the committee's report, but the debate continued the next day, when Gouverneur Morris recommended that the slave trade issue and the procedure for passing a navigation act be submitted to a new, special committee. The convention agreed, and on 24 August the committee submitted its recommendations: as an accommodation to the North, only a simple majority should be required to pass a law regulating shipping. The slave trade would be allowed to continue until 1800; Congress would then have the discretion to end it.[79]

Madison stayed out of the debate until Charles Cotesworth Pinckney moved that the slave trade be allowed to continue until 1808. "Twenty years will produce all the mischief that can be apprehended from the liberty to import slaves," Madison complained. "So long a term will be more dishonorable to the National character than to say nothing about it in the Constitution." The extension passed despite Madison's objection. The same day, the delegates considered a possible tax on the trade. Madison protested that "it was wrong to admit in the Constitution that there could be property in men," but he lost again.[80]

Breaking ranks with several of his fellow southerners, most notably George Mason, Madison played a more active role in the debate over a navigation act. In opposing the extension of the slave trade, Madison had not threatened Virginia's economic interests. With a surplus of slaves, Virginia stood to benefit from a ban. At least the value of any slaves Virginia's planters sold to the Deep South would be likely to rise. With regard to a navigation act, Madison simply took an optimistic view of the South's economic future. A navigation act, he conceded, might temporarily raise southern freight rates, but it would stimulate trade, attract sailors to the South, and give Congress the tools to retaliate against nations that discriminated against U.S. commerce. If the North profited more than the South, the nation as a whole would still benefit. Most of the delegates found his argument persuasive. George Mason did not and suspected, with considerable evidence, that a deal had been struck. New England delegates had agreed to support a continuation of the slave trade; South Carolina and Georgia in exchange agreed to support a simple majority for the passage of a navigation act.[81]

Madison wrote his last letter of the convention to Jefferson on 6 September, eleven days before the meeting adjourned. He reported a "universal anxiety" among the public about the work of the convention and confessed no idea as to how the Constitution would be received, although he thought "the public mind will now or in a very little time receive any thing that promises stability in the public Councils and security to private rights." He passed along news of unrest in Virginia and attacks on courthouses in several counties. Presumably because he knew Jefferson would not see his letter until long after the delegates had gone home, Madison ignored the convention's rule of confidentiality and gave Jefferson a fairly thorough summary of the Constitution the delegates had almost completed. The extent of the reforms they recommended "may perhaps surprise you. I hazard an opinion nevertheless that the plan should it be adopted will neither effectively answer its national object nor prevent the local mischiefs which every where excite disgusts against the state governments."[82]

Late in life, after Americans had come to venerate the Constitution, Madison could reminisce "that there never was an assembly of men, charged with a great & arduous trust, who were more pure in their motives," but in the summer of 1787, they had dealt Madison a series of painful defeats. His council of revision was an early casualty of the debates. His congressional veto had been replaced by the Supremacy Clause; taken from the New Jersey Plan, it simply obligated state judges to obey applicable federal law. Proportional representation did not extend to the Senate, and to add insult to injury, senators would be chosen by state legislatures, the very institutions Madison had gone to Philadelphia hoping to control.[83]

When the Philadelphia convention finished its work, Thomas Jefferson, by contrast, would have been satisfied with amendments addressing the structural problems of the Articles of Confederation that had become more than obvious by the early 1780s, specifically Congress's inability to tax or to regulate commerce, especially foreign trade. He had also seen for some time the need for a formal separation of the legislative and executive functions, as the state constitutions had already made. By the fall of 1787, a new federal constitution making only those changes in the existing national government probably could have won ratification in conventions in a large majority of the states without much opposition. Yet James Madison and a few other nationalists had loftier, and far more controversial, goals. Why did Madison take the more difficult route?

At least three biases, or convictions, motivated Madison. First, his experiences as a legislator and his reading of history and political theory had given him a vision of a viable republican state: a strong central government policing parochial local interests, but one beyond the control of a single faction and one checked by its own internal divisions of authority. Second, as a Virginian

A New Government Must Be Made

with a political base to protect, Madison sought to expand Virginia's political influence, a bias that goes a long way to explain his dogged commitment to proportional representation. As the largest state in the union, Virginia stood to benefit the most from it. At the same time, Madison showed no particular desire to promote uniquely Virginian, or southern, economic interests, which brings us to a third conviction. Madison hoped to use constitutional reform to advance a conservative economic policy of sound money and respect for property rights, including contract rights. Critics can argue, with some justification, that Madison's political economy protected the privileged position of an economic elite. Madison believed, with some justification, that it was a formula for prosperity and stable economic growth.[84]

In any event, Jefferson and Madison, for the first time in their careers, had dramatically different views on a great political issue. As we shall see, the debate over the Constitution tested their friendship as nothing else ever had or ever would.

SEVEN

Opposition Enough to Do Good

1787–1788

THE VIRGINIA DELEGATE Edward Carrington had urged James Madison to hurry from Philadelphia to New York City, where Congress was sitting. The Constitution had split the Virginia delegation. Carrington and Henry Lee supported the document; Richard Henry Lee and William Grayson opposed it. Madison's vote would break the impasse. As Madison reported to George Washington in late September 1787, "I found on my arrival here that certain ideas unfavorable to the Act of the Convention which created difficulties in that body, had made their way into Congress."[1]

He should not have been surprised by the opposition. Rhode Island had boycotted the Philadelphia convention. Two of the three New York delegates had walked out in protest. Fifty-five delegates had attended at one time or another, but only forty-two had stayed until the end, and of those, Elbridge Gerry of Massachusetts and two Virginians, George Mason and Edmund Randolph, refused to sign the Constitution. Mason's "Objections to This Constitution of Government" would appear in Philadelphia in early October. Mason, Madison later wrote Jefferson, "considers the want of a Bill of Rights as a fatal objection . . . and most probably of all" opposed the proposed new government because of its "power of regulating trade, by a majority only of each House." Although Madison did not consider Randolph to be "inveterate in his opposition," the Virginia governor harbored reservations about the breadth of federal power and the possibility of collusion between the president and the Senate, and he favored holding a second convention to address objections to the Constitution.[2]

The Philadelphia convention had hoped Congress would bless the Constitution and forward it to the states for their approval, but Richard Henry Lee and the Massachusetts delegate Nathan Dane argued that it conflicted with the Articles of Confederation, which strictly speaking it did, and that Congress could not, therefore, lawfully consider it. Madison and his allies overcame that obstacle. As Madison put it, not to approve the Constitution would imply that Congress considered the document flawed since "Congress had never scrupled to recommend measures foreign to their Constitutional functions, whenever the public good seemed to require it." Richard Henry Lee next proposed amendments, including a bill of rights and a provision requiring proportional representation in the Senate. It must have irritated Madison to defend, in effect, state equality in the upper house, but had Congress made changes to the Constitution, it arguably would have triggered the amendment process of the Articles, requiring the unanimous consent of the state legislatures, and would have doomed the Constitution to defeat. By 28 September, however, the delegates had agreed on a unanimous resolution simply sending the Constitution to the state legislatures for referral to state conventions, which gave the impression that Congress supported the Constitution without actually saying so.[3]

Madison sent a copy of the Constitution to Jefferson around the first of November, weeks after he had mailed copies to other correspondents. "Jefferson," Dumas Malone has written, "may have suspected he was not in Madison's full confidence." Jefferson had never been as critical of Congress and of the state governments as Madison had been. On the same day Madison had finally managed to get the Constitution out of Congress, Jefferson had written John Adams that he thought the Articles of Confederation were superior to any regime that had preceded it, and with regard to the state governments, "it is a misfortune that they [Americans] do not sufficiently know the value of their constitutions and how much happier they are rendered by them than any other people on earth." Madison accompanied Jefferson's copy of the Constitution with one of the longer letters he ever wrote. He may have thought Jefferson needed to be convinced of its merits; the epistle's length helps explain his delay in writing.[4]

All the convention delegates, Madison told Jefferson, wanted to preserve the union. They understood that the states would not comply voluntarily with federal laws, while compulsion would resemble "more a civil war, than the administration of a regular Government." The new government was designed to act directly on its citizens. Madison laid out for Jefferson the four "Great objects" of the convention: establishing "a proper energy in the Executive and a proper stability in the Legislative departments"; dividing power between the states and "the General Government"; reconciling the different interests of different sections of the country; and adjusting "the clashing pretensions of the large and small States." Each was "pregnant with difficulties," and given the complexity of the issues and natural differences of opinion, "it is impossible to consider the degree of concord," a slight exaggeration on his part, "which ultimately prevailed as less than a miracle."[5]

Creation of the presidency proved "particularly embarrassing" in almost every respect. Madison may have expected Jefferson to have his own ideas about the office, and he did, but Madison tried to reassure him that the convention had considered every possible option before settling on selection by an electoral college for a four-year term, with the possibility of reelection. Likewise, the delegates had decided, after debating everything from four-year terms to service during good behavior, that senators should serve six-year terms.[6]

"The second object, the due partition of power, between the General and local Governments, was perhaps of all," according to Madison, "the most nice and difficult." Showing a fairly characteristic stubbornness, Madison spent much of the rest of his letter defending his now dead congressional negative. He continued to argue that only a congressional veto of state laws could protect the jurisdiction of the national government and prevent "instability and injustice" within the individual states. He insisted the federal judiciary could not adequately replace congressional oversight. It was more convenient to prevent passage of a bad law than to contest it in court, a private party might not be able to bear the costs of litigation, and a recalcitrant state might not obey a federal court order. Madison feared that the Constitution's ban on state emissions of paper money and on state interference with contracts, two issues dear to him, could not be enforced.[7]

The congressional negative would have obviously shifted even more authority to Congress in particular and to the national government in general, which logically led Madison back to his idea of the "extended republic," although he apologized for his "immoderate digression." Differing political ideologies or religious opinions or even the popularity of different political leaders could create "artificial" distinctions among voters. Economic interests by contrast formed "natural distinctions." Whatever the source, societies spawned interest groups, and when one interest became a majority, as often

Opposition Enough to Do Good

happened in a small state, an individual interest in the public good, religious scruples, or a concern for one's personal reputation would not prevent members of the majority from oppressing the minority. In a large, diverse republic like the United States, however, "the requisite concert [is] less likely to be formed," and the kind of power represented by the congressional negative could safely be transferred to the national government.[8] Madison would soon repeat the argument publicly, in greater detail, to his everlasting fame.

Madison told Jefferson less about the reconciliation of sectional interests. Some of the delegates had wanted to require a two-thirds majority to pass laws regulating commerce. "S. Carolina and Georgia were inflexible on the point of slaves," and so the foreign slave trade was allowed to continue for another twenty years. Nor did he say much about the issue of representation, which "created more embarrassment, and a greater alarm for the issue of the Convention than all the rest put together." The debate ended in a compromise "very much to the dissatisfaction of several of the members from the large States," by which he principally meant James Madison.[9]

Madison closed with an assessment of the Constitution's prospects; he followed the ratification debate as best he could, given eighteenth-century communications that were always slow and often erratic. New Hampshire, Connecticut, New Jersey, and Maryland seemed supportive, as was the city of Boston. Predictably, "the paper money faction" in Rhode Island and New York governor George Clinton opposed ratification. Pennsylvania was divided. Madison expected South Carolina to vote for ratification and for North Carolina to follow Virginia's lead, but he hesitated to predict the result in his home state. He had thought from the beginning that much would depend on Patrick Henry, and he had learned by the time he finished his letter to Jefferson—it presumably took him a few days to write it—that Henry and other "individuals of great weight" would try to defeat the Constitution in Virginia.[10] A defeat in Virginia would cripple the new government.

———

JEFFERSON received a copy of the Constitution, through the offices of John Adams, in early November, long before Madison's letter arrived in France. Jefferson's opinion mattered. It has been argued that Jefferson timed the American publication of his *Notes on the State of Virginia*, with its commentary on Virginia's constitution and a proposed replacement, to influence the ratification debate. In Paris, he explored the merits of the Constitution with Thomas Paine, the Marquis de Lafayette, and other reform-minded associates. People solicited Jefferson's views, and he expressed himself in letters that circulated among his friends and admirers. Public land sales in the West had not produced the revenues Jefferson had anticipated, and he still struggled to arrange new loans to pay old debts to French banks and French officers and to negotiate commercial treaties favorable to the United States. Empowering a new Congress to tax and to regulate trade, as the Constitution did, would have made Jefferson's tasks easier. At the same time, to maintain America's prestige with the European liberals Jefferson admired, it also needed to secure individual liberties. The absence of a declaration of rights made that goal problematic.[11]

Jefferson read the Constitution with serious reservations. Thanking Adams's secretary William S. Smith for sending him a copy, Jefferson confessed that "there are very good articles in it: & very bad. I do not know which preponderate." He suggested the Constitutional Convention had overreacted to Shays's Rebellion, and he told Adams point-blank the Philadelphia delegates had gone too far: "I think all the good of this new constitution might have been couched in three or four new articles to be added to the good, old, and venerable fabrick [of the Articles of Confederation], which should have been preserved even as a religious relic."[12]

He complained specifically and repeatedly about the president's eligibility for reelection. The civil war in the Netherlands, where the stadtholder had invited Prussian intervention, had heighted Jefferson's fear of the abuse of executive power. Jefferson predicted that a president who could be reelected would serve for life, making the office "on every succession worthy of intrigue, of bribery, of force, and even of foreign interference." The American president, he told Adams, "seems a bad edition of a Polish king." He preferred that the president serve a single, seven-year term.[13]

Further, Jefferson vehemently denounced the omission of a bill of rights. It was "a degeneracy in the principles of liberty to which I would have given four centuries instead of four years." He confided to Smith that "it astonishes me" that the majority of his "countrymen" might consent "to live under a system which leaves to their governors the power of taking from them the trial by jury in civil cases, freedom of religion, freedom of commerce, the habeas corpus laws, and of yoking them with a standing army."[14]

Jefferson initially criticized the House of Representatives as inadequate to address foreign or "federal" issues. After a month's reflection, he suggested to Edward Carrington that Congress ought to be allowed to tax imports but that the imposition of direct taxes should be left to the states. Public land sales and a tax on imports would provide the federal government with sufficient revenues. He stressed, however, the lack of a bill of rights and the lack of

Opposition Enough to Do Good

term limits on the president. Yet despite his reservations, Jefferson admitted the Constitution contained "a great mass of good," and he described himself as "nearly a Neutral" in the ratification debate. By early February 1788 at the latest, Jefferson thought he had hit upon a scheme to preserve the best parts of the Constitution while fixing its defects. As he explained in a letter to the Virginia tobacco broker Alexander Donald, nine states, the minimum required for the Constitution to take effect, should ratify it, while four states should withhold their approval until the needed amendments were added. Jefferson wanted in particular specific safeguards, in the form of a bill of rights, for individual liberties. "These are fetters against doing evil," he wrote Donald, "which no honest government should decline."[15]

By the time Jefferson got a copy of the Constitution and the accompanying letter from Madison, Alexander Hamilton had recruited Madison and John Jay to write what we know as *The Federalist* (or *The Federalist Papers*). Produced over the winter of 1787–88 to promote ratification of the Constitution in New York, most of the eighty-five essays constituting the work first appeared in New York City newspapers. A few of the later entries appeared for the first time when the essays were published in book form in the spring of 1788. Madison wrote twenty-nine of the essays. Jay, hobbled by illness, authored five. Hamilton wrote the rest. Although all *Federalist* essays carried the pseudonymous byline "Publius" and debates over the authorship of some of the individual essays lingered into the twentieth century, Madison's contemporaries suspected early on that he was involved in the project. He sent copies of the essays to George Washington and others, and he confided to Edmund Randolph that "I am in myself for a few numbers."[16]

He did not, however, rush to tell Jefferson about his involvement, probably because he feared that Jefferson would have doubts about the Constitution and perhaps because he anticipated that some of the essays would challenge his fellow Virginian's thinking, at least indirectly. Madison knew that "the principal objection that the opponents bring forward against this Constitution, is the total want of a Bill of Rights." He tried to dismiss the complaint summarily in *Federalist* No. 38, which appeared in the *New York Independent Journal* on 12 January 1788, where he asked rhetorically, "Is a Bill of Rights essential to liberty? The Confederation has no Bill of Rights." In his mind, he had largely disposed of the issue in his first *Federalist* essay, the famous No. 10 of 22 November 1787, in which he expanded on his idea of an extended republic. Not only would a large republic's many factions make it virtually impossible for any single interest to form a ruling majority, but in the extended republic, "it will be more difficult for unworthy candidates to practice with success the vicious arts, by which elections are too often carried." Such a government would protect rights, not threaten them.[17]

Madison returned to the idea of an extended republic in later essays. In *Federalist* No. 14, he tried to reassure readers that, Montesquieu to the contrary, republics did not have to be small. Madison praised the union for minimizing the need for a standing army, a concern for Jefferson and old-school republicans. Should the Confederation collapse, as it seemed destined to do, the smaller states would need permanent military forces to defend them from their larger neighbors. The power of the "general government," moreover, was limited to certain enumerated objects that concerned all the states. Madison suggested future generations could be trusted to deal with any political problems created by expansion into the Northwest. Almost every state would have a frontier, which would give them all an incentive to cooperate in the common defense. Madison closed with two uncharacteristic rhetorical flourishes, appealing to a sense of American nationalism and the American willingness to experiment. "Hearken not to the unnatural voice which tells you that the people of America, knit together as they are by so many chords of affection, can no longer live together as members of the same family." He went on: "Is it not the glory of the people of America, that while they have paid a decent respect to the opinions of former times and other nations," paraphrasing a Jeffersonian sentiment from the Declaration of Independence, "they have not suffered a blind veneration for antiquity, for custom, or for names, to overrule the suggestions of their own good sense?"[18]

In *Federalist* No. 51, Madison sought to explain how the separation of legislative, judicial, and executive functions could provide citizens with "great security" or, in his words, how "ambition must be made to counteract ambition." He again stressed the virtues of the large state: "In the extended republic of the United States . . . a coalition of a majority of the whole society could seldom take place on any other principles than those of justice and the general good."[19]

On 9 December 1787, a day after his fifth *Federalist* essay had appeared in the *Independent Journal*, Madison wrote Jefferson, without mentioning his literary efforts. Madison instead focused on the progress of the ratification debate. All the states, save for Rhode Island, had called conventions to pass judgment on the Constitution. Madison expected Pennsylvania, Connecticut, New Hampshire, New Jersey, and Delaware to support ratification. He considered Massachusetts to be unpredictable, and New York remained "much divided." Anti-Federalists, as opponents of the Constitution were coming to be called, were stronger in Maryland than he had expected.

Most Virginians, he thought, favored the Constitution, but strong pockets of opposition existed in the "middle country" and south of the James River. Madison divided Virginians into three camps. One bloc, led by Washington and Edmund Pendleton, supported ratification without reservations or conditions. Moderate Anti-Federalists, exemplified by Mason and Randolph, would vote for ratification with amendments, primarily the addition of a bill of rights. The more radical Anti-Federalists claimed to want amendments, but Madison believed they really opposed "the essence of the System" and were willing to risk a partition of the union. They looked to Patrick Henry for leadership.[20]

Politically, Madison told Jefferson, one fact set the South apart. In New England, the upper classes almost unanimously supported the Constitution, but in Virginia and farther south, "men of intelligence, patriotism, property, and independent circumstances, are . . . divided." But Madison believed most ordinary Virginians, even poor whites, tired as he thought they were of "the vicissitudes, injustice and follies" of the current regime, were "impatient for some change which promises stability and repose."[21]

The ship that was to carry Madison's letter to France was delayed long enough that Madison included with it a shorter letter, dated 20 December; by then he could tell Jefferson that Delaware had approved the Constitution unanimously and that Pennsylvania had ratified it by a two-to-one margin. The letter is noteworthy in part for illustrating the difficulties of communications in the age of sail. Besides the problem of simply finding a ship to take a letter across the Atlantic, with no national newspapers and no real system for gathering information, Madison had to rely on reports from associates and secondhand stories in local papers to stay abreast of the course of ratification. Neither source was entirely reliable. "I hear from North Carolina," he wrote Jefferson, "that the Assembly there is well disposed" to the Constitution. In reality, North Carolina was a hotbed of Anti-Federalism.[22]

Also on 20 December, Jefferson responded to Madison's long letter of 24 October; when Madison received it, it probably confirmed his fears. Jefferson began tactfully with what he liked about the proposed new government, including its relative independence from the state legislatures and the separation of executive, legislative, and judicial functions. As he had done elsewhere, Jefferson questioned the competency of the popularly elected House of Representatives to participate in the management of foreign affairs, but he understood Congress needed the power to tax and believed the people could be taxed only by their elected representatives. He especially approved of the Great Compromise, ironically the one part of the Constitution Madison liked the least: "I am captivated by the compromise of the opposite claims of the great and little states." Jefferson agreed members of Congress should vote individually and not by states, as the Articles of Confederation had required. He approved of the presidential veto, although he would have preferred to involve the courts in the process, as Madison had originally proposed, or to invest the judiciary "with a similar and separate power." Jefferson slightly outran Madison in anticipating the rise of judicial review.[23]

He had a more substantive list of criticisms, beginning with the lack of a bill of rights. Jefferson wanted protections for the familiar rights of conscience, of the press, and of habeas corpus, but his bill of rights would also have included bans on standing armies and commercial monopolies. In addition, he wanted to guarantee "trials by jury in all matters of fact" under "the laws of the land and not by the law of Nations." As he told Madison, "A bill of rights is what the people are entitled to against every government on earth, general and particular, and what no just government should refuse, or rest on inference." He turned next to "the abandonment in every instance of the necessity of rotation in office," which posed a particular danger in the case of the president. A president who could be reelected, Jefferson argued, would be reelected and become a president for life. History proved the election of a powerful executive invited disorder and foreign intervention: "Experience shews that the only way to prevent disorder is to render them [elections] uninteresting by frequent changes."[24]

Jefferson closed with some cryptic comments. He disapproved of allowing federal appellate courts to consider questions of facts and of requiring all federal officials to swear loyalty to the Constitution. He admitted he did not know how best to secure amendments. He also revealed his fundamental differences with Madison: his greater skepticism about governments and his greater tolerance for protest. As he explained, "I owe I am not a friend to a very energetic government. It is always oppressive." He defended Shays's Rebellion mathematically: "One rebellion in 13 states in the course of 11 years, is but one for each state in a century and a half. No country should be so long without one."[25]

Jefferson's letters caused Madison considerable embarrassment, but he could at least be confident his fellow Virginian would not push his opposition to an extreme. Jefferson promised to submit to the judgment of the people: "After all, it is my principle that the will of the Majority should always prevail." If the Constitution were to be approved "in all its parts," Jefferson pledged to hope cheerfully for amendments whenever the people found it worked badly. Americans would remain virtuous farmers "for many centuries," and if "the

Opposition Enough to Do Good

education of the common people will be attended to," he would trust to "their good sense" to preserve "a due degree of liberty."[26] Madison, meanwhile, continued to worry about the possibility of a second constitutional convention where delegates committed to the union would find themselves divided, "perplexed[,] & frustrated by men who had objects totally different." He now considered "every thing . . . as problematical from Maryland southward" and feared that if North Carolina embraced Patrick Henry's Anti-Federalism, "it will endanger the Union more than any other circumstances that could happen."[27]

One recent Madison biographer believes Madison might have had Jefferson in mind, although he would not have seen his friend's most recent letter, when he returned to work on his *Federalist* essays. *Federalist* No. 37, which appeared in print on 11 January 1788, confessed "a faultless plan was not to be expected." Jefferson, Madison may have thought, did not appreciate the difficulty of establishing a new government. There was the daunting challenge of the task itself: dividing power among the three branches of the national government and then between the national and state governments, reconciling the large and small states, and accommodating other regional interests. The imprecision of language and the limits of human judgment made it impossible to produce a perfect charter of crystal clarity.[28]

A week later, Madison, in *Federalist* No. 40, defended the authority of the Constitutional Convention and the legitimacy of the ratification process. Jefferson had never questioned the legal right of the Philadelphia convention to draft a new constitution, but others had raised the issue, and Jefferson had accused the delegates of going too far. Madison loosely construed the delegates' instructions. Congress had given them the job of "revising the articles of confederation" to establish "a firm national government . . . adequate to the exigencies of government and the preservation of the Union." Once the convention decided the union could not be saved under the Articles, what could the delegates do but jettison the less important charge of revising the Articles in favor of the more important task of preserving of national unity? In any event, Madison claimed, the states retained their sovereignty "in all unenumerated cases," so that "the great principles of the Constitution proposed by the Convention, may be considered less as absolutely new, than as an expansion of principles which are found in the articles of Confederation."[29]

Federalist No. 40 conceded that in recommending the Constitution be submitted to state conventions instead of the state legislatures, the delegates had ignored the procedure for amendments established by the Articles, but "in all great changes of established governments, forms ought to give way to substance." Once again invoking the Declaration of Independence, Madison argued "a rigid adherence" to procedural niceties would nullify the people's right to "abolish or alter their governments as to them shall seem most likely to effect their safety and happiness."[30]

Later essays continued to expose areas of disagreement with Jefferson. In *Federalist* No. 41, Madison argued a standing army was a necessary evil; a national military force could not be significantly restricted by the Constitution because potential threats could not be predicted. Ratification of the Constitution would actually reduce the risk that the country would fall prey to a military despot. A united America would have less need for a standing army than would a divided country. Unity itself could deter aggression. Divided, the states would quarrel among themselves and be tempting targets for the European powers.[31] *Federalist* No. 43 highlighted another difference with Jefferson. There Madison explained Article IV, Section 4, of the Constitution, guaranteeing each state "a Republican Form of Government" and protection from invasion and "domestic violence." Alluding to Shays's Rebellion, Madison noted "a recent and well known event among ourselves, has warned us to be prepared for emergencies of a like nature." Jefferson did not share his concern.[32]

In *Federalist* No. 48, Madison both rebutted Jefferson and invoked his authority. Madison argued that, in a republic, the greatest threat to individual rights came from the legislative branch but that "parchment barriers," including the bill of rights demanded by Jefferson and the Anti-Federalists, would not prevent the abuse of power. For Americans accustomed to thinking the executive, in the form of a monarch or royal governor, presented a graver menace, Madison quoted at length from *Notes on the State of Virginia*, where Jefferson complained Virginia's constitution had concentrated all power in the legislature, which "is precisely the definition of despotic government.... 173 despots would surely be as oppressive as one." The federal Constitution's separation of powers, Madison believed, had addressed that danger.[33]

The *New York Packet* published *Federalist* No. 48 on 1 February 1788. The next day, Madison's *Federalist* No. 49 appeared in the *Independent Journal*. It challenged Jefferson directly. Madison began by observing that the draft constitution appended to *Notes*, "like every thing from the same pen, marks a turn of thinking original, comprehensive and accurate; and it is the more worthy of attention, as it equally displays a fervent attachment to republican government, and an enlightened view of the dangerous propensities against which it ought to be guarded." Yet Madison felt compelled to respond to Jefferson's proposal for maintaining the separation of powers.

Opposition Enough to Do Good

Under Jefferson's plan, whenever two-thirds of any two branches of the state government agreed that the third branch had exceeded its prerogatives, they could call a constitutional convention. The scheme could have been adopted at the national level, but the proposed federal Constitution contained higher hurdles for a convention, and Madison apparently thought they might be an obstacle to its ratification.[34]

Madison saw "insuperable objections" to Jefferson's plan. It did not reach the case where two departments combined unlawfully against the third, and furthermore it would not work: legislators would be the ones most apt to self-aggrandizement, but as experienced office seekers, they would dominate a constitutional convention. More importantly, frequent changes to a constitution would undermine the people's faith in their government and weaken "that veneration, which time bestows on every thing." Madison warned his readers about "the danger of disturbing the public tranquility by interesting too strongly the public passions." Jefferson rarely worried about an excess of public participation. More fundamentally, he and Madison disagreed about the value of stability in the law, and that difference would soon prompt one of their most intriguing exchanges.[35]

Finally, Jefferson had questioned the competency of the House of Representatives. He had not belabored the point, but many Anti-Federalists alleged the House was too small to be truly representative. Accordingly, Madison devoted *Federalist* Nos. 55–58, all of which appeared in mid-February 1788, to a defense of the institution. The number of House members, Madison argued, had to be kept to a certain limit "to avoid the confusion and intemperance of a multitude. . . . Had every Athenian citizen been a Socrates," he advised his readers, "every Athenian assembly would still have been a mob." To those who claimed the House could easily be manipulated by foreign interests, Madison responded that it would be larger than the Confederation Congress, and for all its ills, foreign interventions had not been one of them.[36]

To critics who argued the House "will be too small to possess a due knowledge of the interests of its constituents," Madison replied that federal legislation would deal primarily with commerce, taxation, and the regulation of the militia. Even in a large state, representatives from ten or twelve districts would know enough to represent local interests; they would mainly need to be familiar with their own state's laws, which could not be too demanding a task.[37] Elected by the same voters who selected state legislators, members of the House should feel the same attachment to local interests as members of the state assemblies and should be at least equally distinguished among their fellow citizens. New York, Pennsylvania, Massachusetts, and even New

Hampshire had elected state lawmakers from large districts with no complications. The Constitution's requirement for a decennial census, moreover, created a mechanism for Congress to expand the size of the House as the nation's population increased.[38]

In the course of defending the House, Madison articulated a philosophical point of view that distinguished him from his Anti-Federalist opponents but not from Jefferson: "As there is a degree of depravity in mankind which requires a certain degree of circumspection and distrust: so there are other qualities in human nature, which justify a certain portion of esteem and confidence. Republican government presupposes the existence of these qualities in a higher degree than any other form."[39] No government, in other words, could be formed without a degree of mutual trust between the rulers and the ruled.

———

Many of Madison's Publius essays in no way touched upon Jefferson's concerns about the Constitution, although Madison did not forget him. In the middle of February, Madison sent him another report on the ratification battle. Connecticut, Georgia, and Massachusetts had approved the Constitution since his last letter, but opposition remained in Maryland, New York, Virginia, and North Carolina. Jefferson's reservations were narrowly focused, and he never gave the impression of an irreconcilable opponent who would seize upon any alleged imperfection to defeat ratification, as Anti-Federalists sometimes did. Madison's *Federalist* Nos. 18–20 reused arguments from his "Of Ancient and Modern Confederacies" to demonstrate that history taught that a central government had to have authority over individuals and could not effectively govern through largely autonomous regional governments. He ridiculed the Anti-Federalists for their inability to agree on an alternative to the Constitution or to acknowledge the defects of the Articles of Confederation. They complained that the Constitution, for example, allowed the slave trade to continue for another twenty years, but under the Articles, it could have gone on forever.[40] Jefferson did not disagree.

In *Federalist* No. 42, Madison defended congressional jurisdiction over foreign affairs as "an obvious and essential branch of the federal administration. If we are to be one nation in any respect, it clearly ought to be in respect to other nations." Whatever Jefferson's doubts about the House of Representatives, he had made the larger point many times himself. Jefferson could have echoed Madison's observation on the slave trade compromise. It would have been better had the notorious business been stopped immediately, but

Opposition Enough to Do Good

"it ought to be considered as a great point gained in favor of humanity" that the Constitution brought the end of the trade in sight.[41]

Madison chased some red herrings. He devoted one essay to the Anti-Federalist allegation that the federal district the Constitution authorized as the site of a permanent national capital would become a haven for scoundrels and fugitives from state laws. At the same time he took up issues of enormous future significance. He asserted for Congress a power to admit new states and to regulate unorganized territories in the West, critical tasks the Articles had not addressed. Additionally, he justified the ratification process adopted by the Philadelphia convention. To have required unanimous approval, as the Articles did, "would have subjected the essential interests of the whole to the caprice or corruption of a single member." How could he defend permitting nine states to abrogate the Articles? "By recurring to the absolute necessity of the case; to the great principles of self-preservation; to our transcendent law of nature and of nature's God." Natural law made the "safety and happiness of society" the ultimate object of politics. Madison also resorted to an argument he made repeatedly during the ratification debate. Having been ratified by state legislatures and not by popular conventions, the Articles of Confederation represented a mere compact. A breach by one member—and in Madison's mind the breaches were legion—released the other members from their obligations.[42]

In *Federalist* No. 44, Madison celebrated the Constitution's bans on state emissions of paper money, bills of attainder, ex post facto laws, and laws impairing the obligation of contracts, even though he privately questioned the enforceability of federal prohibitions absent a congressional negative. He defended the language in Article I, Section 8, giving Congress the powers "necessary and proper" to carry out its enumerated functions: "Few parts of the Constitution have been assailed with more intemperance than this . . . [but] no axiom is more clearly established in law, or in reason, than wherever the end is required, the means are authorized." No part of the Constitution gave Madison and Jefferson more grief in the 1790s when Hamilton, as secretary of the treasury, unveiled ambitious plans for a federal fiscal program they had not envisioned, but in 1788, they thought the language of Section 8 innocuous.[43]

The Constitution challenged conventional wisdom and popular misconceptions. With its two-year terms for representatives and six-year terms for senators, the Constitutional Convention had ignored the republican maxim that "where annual elections end, tyranny begins." In reality, Madison pointed out, legislative terms varied widely in England and America, and

House members needed time to travel, to resolve disputed elections, and to learn their jobs. For its part, the Senate could provide stability to the political system; protect the people from "their own temporary errors and delusions"; and, more attuned than the House to "the presumed or known opinion of the impartial world," safeguard America's image abroad.[44]

Anti-Federalists charged that the Constitution did not adequately separate the federal legislative, judicial, and executive functions. The president could veto acts of Congress, and the Senate could try impeachment cases, to name two examples. According to Madison, Montesquieu, the dean of separation of powers theorists, had derived his theories from the British model of kings, lords, and commons, but even the British constitution had never completely separated the functions of government. The House of Lords, for example, heard appeals from regular courts. American practice varied. The Massachusetts Constitution expressly endorsed the separation of powers but gave the governor a limited veto. Madison reinterpreted Montesquieu to say that "the whole power" of one branch could not be exercised by another; a working system of checks and balances required a degree of interaction.[45]

Like the separation of powers, the term "republican government," Madison wrote, "has been used with extreme inaccuracy," and he offered a definition: "a government which derives all its powers directly or indirectly from the great body of the people; and is administered by persons holding their offices during pleasure, for a limited period, or during good behavior." In what became one of the most scrutinized passages in all *The Federalist*, Madison responded in No. 39 to the charge that the Constitution replaced a federal system with a "*consolidation* of the States." In rebuttal, he pointed to the ratification process. It was to be decided "by the people, not as individuals composing one entire nation, but as composing the distinct and independent States to which they respectively belong," and the Constitution would bind only those states that approved it. In reality, the new government combined national features in, to name one, its ability to act on individuals with aspects of a federal system "since its jurisdiction extends to certain enumerated objects only." In one of the most portentous asides in any of his writings, Madison also mentioned that where state and national jurisdiction collided, the Supreme Court could resolve the conflict "to prevent an appeal to the sword, and a dissolution of the compact."[46]

It seems likely that Madison's thinking about the Constitution evolved as he gave voice to Publius. Producing twenty-nine long and erudite essays under tight deadlines over parts of a single winter was grueling work, even if he had minimal duties as a member of a dying Congress. Surely Madison became more emotionally invested in the project, and as he had to explain and defend positions he had opposed in Philadelphia, perhaps he came to better appreciate the need for compromise. Defending state equality in the Senate, he conceded, "It is superfluous to try by the standards of theory" an accommodation of opposing interests that "our political situation rendered indispensable." Nor could the Three-Fifths Compromise have been avoided. Madison added that because "government is instituted no less for the protection of the property, than of the persons of individuals," the three-fifths rule might be seen as a way to protect a certain type of property, although he admitted the argument "may appear to be a little strained in some parts."[47]

If Madison's treatment of the necessary and proper clause of Article I, Section 8, put an interpretive gloss on the Constitution that might support a more expansive view of federal power than he came to favor in the 1790s, he created a fuller record for a more modest government than the one he had anticipated when he went to Philadelphia in May 1787. He devoted *Federalist* No. 45 and No. 46 to the argument that the Constitution did not unduly enfeeble the state governments, and he touched upon it elsewhere. State legislatures managed presidential elections and appointed senators. Members of the House would retain their local prejudices, and the state governments enjoyed broader powers and employed more people than did the national government. Madison had originally hoped to rein in the states, and he had initially opposed allowing state assemblies to elect senators; now he argued the states could serve as checks on federal power. Apart from the authority to regulate commerce, which few opposed in principle, "the change which it [the Constitution] proposes, consists much less in the addition of NEW POWERS to the Union, than in the invigoration of its ORIGINAL POWERS."[48]

By February 1788, Jefferson could express to Madison his satisfaction that the Constitution was moving toward ratification, while he continued to hope four states would withhold their approval until a declaration of rights could be added to "cure it's [sic] principal defect." As he wrote another correspondent, "In this way there will have been opposition enough to do good, and not enough to do harm." In mid-May, Edward Carrington sent Jefferson, via Joel Barlow, the first bound volume of *The Federalist* and identified Madison, Hamilton, and Jay as the authors. Carrington promised to send Jefferson the next volume when it was available. Madison did not mention his role in the project to Jefferson until August, after he learned Carrington had written him and was sending him the second volume. Even then Madison tried to keep some distance from the essays, telling Jefferson that Hamilton and Jay had initiated the undertaking: "Though carried on in concert the writers are not mutually answerable for all the ideas of each other, there being seldom time for even a perusal of the pieces by any but the writer before they were wanted at the press and some times hardly by the writer himself."[49]

The Federalist impressed Madison's allies and enhanced his reputation among supporters of the Constitution.[50] Otherwise, the immediate impact of the essays, despite the canonical status they eventually obtained, ought not to be exaggerated. Not widely circulated outside New York, they appeared too late in many places to influence debate and were too scholarly, and occasionally too pedantic, to attract a broad audience. Madison, Hamilton, and Washington tried to circulate copies in Virginia, but with fewer newspapers, Virginia's printers could not keep pace with their New York City counterparts. In an apparent effort to expand their reach, the first thirty-six Federalist papers went on sale in book form in Norfolk and Richmond in April 1788, after delegates to the Virginia ratification convention had been elected. The second volume did not appear until June, after the convention had begun.[51]

Much to the relief of a sheepish Madison, however, The Federalist impressed Thomas Jefferson, without completely solving Madison's Jefferson problem. "I read it with care, pleasure, and improvement," he wrote Madison from Paris in November. He attributed nothing to Jay and little to Hamilton but crowned the essays "the best commentary on the principles of government which ever was written." Jefferson realized Madison had sometimes made the "best defense he can of positions he does not support" but acknowledged Publius had corrected his thinking on "several points." After praising John Locke, Jefferson told his son-in-law Thomas Mann Randolph: "Descending from theory to practice there is no better book than the Federalist." He took Federalist No. 10 to heart, predicting in 1795 that Montesquieu's theory of the superiority of small republics likely "will be exploded by experience." Instead, he adopted the Madisonian position: "The smaller the societies, the more violent & more convulsive their schisms." In retirement, Jefferson wanted to make The Federalist required reading for law students at the University of Virginia, but in the fall of 1788, Jefferson still supported amending the Constitution to limit the tenure of the president and to add a bill of rights.[52]

—

JAMES MADISON'S last contribution to The Federalist, No. 63, appeared in the Independent Journal on 1 March 1788. He then left New York to campaign for a seat in the Virginia convention called to decide whether his home state would accept the Constitution. Bad roads and bad weather made it a slow trip, and Madison spent two days at Mount Vernon with George Washington. He may also have met with John Leland, a prominent Baptist minister, to assure him he would support amendments after the Constitution was ratified. Virginia Baptists wanted an amendment to protect freedom of conscience. Madison, considering it a conflict of interest, had not intended to serve in the state convention, but he changed his mind as he saw his fellow delegates elected to conventions in their states and as opposition to the Constitution grew. He arrived at Montpelier the day before the election "to find the County filled with the most absurd and groundless prejudices against the federal Constitution." On Election Day, Madison said he had to "mount for the first time in my life, the rostrum before a large body of the people, and to launch into a harangue of some length in the open air and on a very windy day." Madison and a second Federalist candidate won in a landslide.[53]

The future of the Constitution, however, remained in doubt. By the time Orange County voted, Delaware, Pennsylvania, New Jersey, Connecticut, and Georgia had ratified the document. A Massachusetts convention had voted for ratification in February, but only after Federalists there had agreed to support a series of amendments. Madison considered the amendments "a blemish, but . . . in the least offensive form." Also in February, the New Hampshire convention adjourned without reaching a decision. Madison found the news "very disagreeable." On the day of Madison's election to the Virginia convention, voters in a popular referendum in Rhode Island, which Federalists had boycotted, rejected the Constitution by better than ten to one. Maryland and South Carolina would approve the Constitution in the next two months, but New York was divided and North Carolina was hostile.[54]

Much if not all depended on Virginia. The Constitution might well win approval in the nine states required for its implementation without being ratified in New York and Virginia, but without those two—and to add insult to injury, without Rhode Island and North Carolina—the new government would not be an improvement over the Articles of Confederation. The Virginia assembly had scheduled the election of convention delegates for the first court day in March, which varied from county to county, so election results trickled in over several weeks. Much in Virginia depended on the fourteen delegates to be elected from Kentucky, where two issues preoccupied voters: could the new government secure access to the Mississippi River, and would it expedite Kentucky's admission to statehood? On 22 April, when Madison reported the election results to Jefferson, returns from Kentucky had still not arrived. Madison thought the Federalists had won a majority of the delegates elsewhere and had elected the more able politicians.

Edmund Randolph would serve in the convention, but he "is so temperate in his opposition" that he could not be considered an Anti-Federalist. Anti-Federalists were divided, with Henry, Madison claimed once again, leading a radical faction and George Mason drifting into his orbit. The Northern Neck remained a Federalist stronghold while Anti-Federalists dominated the Southside. Madison generally gave supporters of the Constitution an edge in the west, although at the time he underestimated the strength of Anti-Federalism in Kentucky.[55]

In Paris, Jefferson began to moderate his criticism, especially in his conversations with Europeans, and he expressed satisfaction at the progress of ratification. Correspondence with Federalists in America alleviated his concerns about direct taxes. He abandoned his proposal that nine states approve the Constitution while four held out for amendments once he learned Massachusetts had ratified and then recommended amendments. He considered that to be the more prudent approach. Rejection of the Constitution by New York and Virginia—he wrongly expected North Carolina to vote for ratification—at this late stage "would have little effect, and joined with Rhode island would even be opprobrious." He probably recoiled at the idea of being in the same camp as Patrick Henry. Jefferson continued to favor a bill of rights and term limits for senators and, more importantly, for the president. He was disappointed that few state conventions had demanded presidential term limits; he thought the assumption George Washington would be the first president had dulled Americans to the potential for the abuse of executive power, but he trusted Washington and thought the nation had time to adopt the necessary safeguards. "We must be contented," he wrote in May, "to travel on towards perfection, step by step."[56]

The Virginia convention assembled in Richmond on 2 June with a deeply divided but unusually distinguished cast. Madison would lead a Federalist bloc that included Edmund Pendleton, John Marshall, and Edmund Randolph; the Virginia governor had by now abandoned most of his reservations about the Constitution. Patrick Henry, aided by George Mason and James Monroe, would make the Anti-Federalist case and, with his remarkable oratorical skills, dominate the debates. Henry, in fact, talked too much, while Madison and his allies often repeated arguments from *The Federalist*. Despite Henry's rhetorical excesses, the convention had only one major issue to decide: would Virginia insist on amendments to the Constitution as a condition of ratification, or would the delegates approve the Constitution and then recommend it be amended, as Massachusetts had done?[57]

Opposition Enough to Do Good

Madison spoke at length on 6 June and began with one of his overarching themes, the need to approve the Constitution to maintain law and order: "On a candid examination of history, we shall find that turbulence, violence, and abuse of power by the majority trampling on the rights of the minority, have produced factions and commotions, which, in republics, have more frequently than any other cause, produced despotism." He pointed to evidence of popular support for the Constitution. After eight states had ratified it, how could Virginia withhold its consent? More substantively, Madison defended the Constitution's provisions for a peacetime army, a sore spot with old Whigs. An attack on the United States by "disciplined veterans" could not be resisted "when opposed only by irregular, undisciplined militia."[58]

He linked defense needs with the imposition of direct taxes, another sensitive issue for traditional republicans. An impost would be adequate, he predicted, for the routine expenses of the national government, but citizens would have to be taxed directly to pay for the costs of any future war. Requisitions on the states, which some Anti-Federalists still favored, were not sufficiently reliable for wartime exigencies. With a popularly elected House and a Senate elected by the state legislatures, Madison assured his fellow delegates they need not worry that direct federal taxation would destroy the "subordinate authority," or in other words, the states.[59]

As long as the speech was, Madison may not have finished it. Heat, tension, and fatigue apparently brought on an attack of "bilious" fever. Madison was bedridden for the next two days and sick off and on for much of the rest of the convention. He rallied sufficiently on 11 June to speak again in defense of direct taxation, a persistent issue given America's revolutionary history. "The conspiracy agst. direct taxes," he wrote privately, "is more extensive & formidable than some gentlemen suspect." Requisitions, the Anti-Federalist alternative, were unworkable. State legislatures would debate congressional requests based on "peculiar local circumstances." Less vulnerable states would respond less generously, to the disadvantage of southern states with extensive coastlines and smaller populations and "other circumstances . . . which do not apply to the northern states," by which he meant their holding of enslaved Africans. Many Anti-Federalists were ready to give Congress the power to collect internal taxes after a requisition had been rebuffed, but at that point, Madison argued, a tax would be seen as "punishment" that would incite "hatred" against the "general government."[60]

He returned to the theme the next day and worked in an appeal to the Kentucky delegates at the same time. Congress under the Articles of Confederation was too weak to negotiate a treaty with Spain to guarantee U.S.

navigation rights on the Mississippi, and in a stronger new government, the South, with sympathizers in New Jersey and Pennsylvania, would have the votes to defeat any treaty hostile to its interests.[61]

On 17 June, Mason criticized the Constitution for allowing the foreign slave trade to continue while failing to provide specific protections for domestic slavery. Because Virginia had a surplus of slaves, the Constitution could have stopped further importations without much cost to the state, but its economy depended on slave labor. Paraphrasing the Book of Common Prayer, Mason complained the Philadelphia delegates "have done what they ought not to have done, and left undone what they ought to have done." Madison conceded the slave trade clause "to be impolitic, if it were one of those things which could be excluded without encountering greater evils." South Carolina and Georgia would not have signed the Constitution if it had prohibited the slave trade, and as he had argued in *The Federalist*, the Constitution at least empowered Congress to end the trade at some point, which the Articles did not permit. On the other hand, the fugitive slave clause provided for the return of runaways, Congress had no authority to free anyone held in slavery under state law, and more significantly for Madison, "great as the evil [of the slave trade] is, a dismemberment of the union would be worse."[62]

One of Madison's lengthier speeches, a defense of the federal judiciary, came relatively late in the convention. No one, Madison said, objected to allowing federal courts to interpret federal law or treaties or to hear maritime and admiralty cases or cases involving foreign officials. Federal courts, moreover, provided an obvious forum for litigation between states. Anti-Federalists, however, objected to the clause in Article III, Section 2, extending federal jurisdiction to "Controversies . . . between a State and Citizens of another State." Madison told delegates who feared Virginia might be hauled into federal court that the clause applied only if the state were the plaintiff and therefore invoked federal jurisdiction on its own initiative. The Supreme Court would soon take a different view.[63]

Jefferson, Mason, and others had objected more strenuously to the authority of federal courts of appeal to decide questions of fact. They saw such authority as a dangerous intrusion on the historic role of juries. Madison countered that Congress could limit the appellate courts' jurisdiction should the power be abused and could also limit "vexatious appeals," but he did not stay on the defensive. Federal jurisdiction over cases involving citizens from different states would prevent discrimination by parochial local courts, and uniform commercial rules would promote the economy, but federal courts would not "annihilate the state courts." "Ninety-nine out of an hundred" lawsuits would still be decided by state judges. The debate over federal jurisdiction exposed another of the fundamental rifts between Madison and the Anti-Federalists. They "suppose," he said, "the general legislature will do every mischief they possibly can, and that they will omit to do every good which they are authorized to do. . . . I consider it reasonable to conclude, that they will as readily do their duty, as deviate from it." He had to assume "that the people will have virtue and intelligence to select men of virtue and wisdom" to lead them.[64]

Madison usually had a plausible response to his opponents, but he had to navigate an embarrassing incident a few days into the convention. About two weeks before the Virginia delegates met in Richmond, Madison learned that a letter from Jefferson criticizing the Constitution was circulating among delegates to the Maryland convention in Annapolis. On 9 June, Patrick Henry, citing Jefferson's February letter to Alexander Donald, told the Virginia convention "this illustrious citizen advises us to reject this Government, till it be amended," and in particular until a bill of rights could be added. No one in Virginia knew Jefferson had changed his mind about the best strategy to pursue amendments. Anti-Federalist leader Willie Jones would cite Jefferson's earlier letters in the North Carolina ratification convention.[65]

Federalists scrambled to reply. Randolph responded the next day. He had not seen the letter, but he understood Jefferson had urged nine states to ratify while four withheld their consent. Surely Jefferson, he asserted, would have wanted Virginia to be among the nine. Randolph was not particularly convincing, and the Federalists struggled with their Jefferson problem for several days. Madison, who was known to be Jefferson's closest confidant, tried again on 12 June. He appealed to his colleagues' sense of propriety: "Is it come to this, that we are not to follow our own reason? Is it proper to introduce the opinions of respectable men not within these walls?" If it were, Federalists could claim the endorsement of "a character equally great," an obvious reference to Washington. Jefferson would not, Madison argued, want to be drawn into the debate, and in any event, he approved of many parts of the Constitution. "But whatever be the opinion of that illustrious citizen," he maintained, "considerations of personal delicacy should dissuade us from introducing it here."[66]

Pendleton followed Madison and quoted the passages from Jefferson's letter emphasizing above all else Jefferson's desire to avoid "a schism in our Union." Jefferson favored amending the Constitution after it had taken effect. "If then we are to be influenced by his opinion at all," Pendleton noted, "we will ratify it and secure thereby the good it contains." Patrick Henry remained unconvinced. If, he asked, New Hampshire ratified the Constitution, as Federalists had predicted it would, where would the four holdouts be found? And it was more than a matter of mere numbers; the four dissenters would need to include a state of some importance, like Virginia, not "a poor despised place" like Anti-Federalist North Carolina.[67]

The skirmish over Jefferson's letter mainly highlighted the principal issue before the convention: whether to recommend amendments or to make them a condition of ratification. How delegates came out on that issue depended in part on the value they attached to amendments. Madison tried to minimize the usefulness of even one of the most popular, a "specific protection" for freedom of conscience: "There is not a shadow of right in the general government to intermeddle with religion." In the course of the convention, Anti-Federalist delegates introduced a proposed bill of rights plus twenty more structural or substantive amendments. Madison opposed them until almost the end of the convention. Enumerating rights in a Constitution would be dangerous; any freedoms inadvertently omitted might be waived. Amendments that went to the structure or operation of the new government could upset delicate compromises negotiated in Philadelphia, and Virginia could not realistically expect the majority of the states to accept its demands now that they had ratified the Constitution.[68]

Yet the balance of forces at the convention made some concessions almost unavoidable. On 25 June, the day after Madison's attack on the idea of a bill of rights, George Nicholas presented a list of amendments the Federalists could support after the convention approved the Constitution. Four days later, by a vote of 88–80, the convention delegates rejected a motion by Henry to refer a set of amendments to a second national convention. Then, by a vote of 89–79, they approved a motion by George Wythe to approve the Constitution but recommend amendments to Congress.

James Madison, as the Constitution's most dogged defender, deserves considerable credit for the result. Jefferson's letter to Donald created some anxious moments for the Federalists, but it did not alter the political forces at work in the convention. Although ten of fourteen Kentucky delegates opposed the Constitution, its supporters apparently convinced most westerners that a new government could better protect their interests than could the Confederation Congress. The prospect that George Washington would fill the executive office gave Federalists an inestimable advantage. Madison and his allies usually had cogent, if not logically flawless, answers to their opponents, who were divided and unable to offer a creditable alternative to the Constitution without running the risk of disunion. The desire to avoid civil unrest in Virginia seems not to have been a factor. Henry had argued the Old Dominion had experienced no tumult that would justify a change in government. George Nicholas conceded the point but cited disturbances elsewhere, specifically Shays's Rebellion in Massachusetts. By the time the Richmond convention met, moreover, the Constitution had gained political momentum. Before the Virginians adjourned, New Hampshire, after a delay that had frustrated Federalists, became the ninth state to ratify.[69]

After voting for ratification, the Virginia delegates appointed a committee to prepare a list of proposed amendments, which the convention quickly approved. The list included much the Anti-Federalists had demanded, including a declaration of rights, a requirement for a two-thirds majority to adopt laws regulating commerce, and an amendment giving a state the option to determine how federal taxes would be collected within its borders. Madison opposed the tax provision but lost. Many of the amendments, he wrote Hamilton shortly after the convention adjourned, were "highly objectionable." The proposed amendments may not have won over any Anti-Federalists before the vote on ratification, but they may have kept some wavering or nominal Federalists in line, and they undoubtedly helped many Anti-Federalists accept ratification. They also opened a new chapter in the making of the Constitution.[70]

EIGHT

Let Us Secure What We Can

1788–1789

"I AM NOT A FEDERALIST," Thomas Jefferson wrote the veteran Pennsylvania politician Francis Hopkinson, "because I never submitted the whole system of my opinions to the creed of any party of men whatever in religion, in philosophy, in politics, or in anything else where I was capable of thinking for myself. . . . If I could not go to heaven but with a party, I would not go there at all." Yet he added, "I am much farther from . . . the Anti-Federalists." He had, he claimed, tried to stay out of the ratification debate. "My great wish is to go on in a strict but silent performance of my duty, to avoid attracting notice, and to keep my name out of the newspapers." Sensitive to criticism, Jefferson found "the pain of a little censure . . . more acute than the pleasure of much praise."[1]

In reality, Jefferson, despite his reservations about the Constitution, celebrated its ratification with correspondents in Europe and America. To Jefferson, the Constitutional Convention and the ratification process vindicated American republicanism; when Americans saw a problem, they would take steps to correct it. Calling the Constitution "unquestionably the wisest ever yet presented to men," Jefferson believed the "example of changing a constitution by assembling the wise men of the state, instead of assembling armies, will be worth as much to the world as the former examples we have given them."[2] He saw immediate benefits to the United States. Ratification stimulated the interest of European investors in the nation's public debt.

Jefferson thought a stronger union would be better able to maintain American neutrality when the next European war came, but he confided to George Washington that "the tyranny of those nations who deprive us of the natural right of trading with our neighbors" could lead to conflict. Congress would need its new power to tax in order to support a military that could "open by force a market" for American exports in the Western Hemisphere.[3]

He continued to favor a bill of rights and felt confident one would be added, especially after the Massachusetts convention approved the Constitution and then recommended amendments. "The argument is unanswerable," he wrote in July 1788, "that it will be easier to obtain amendments from nine states under the new constitution," the number required by Article V, "than from thirteen after rejecting it." The addition of a bill of rights, he predicted, would reconcile most Anti-Federalists to the new government. And apparently convinced his efforts to limit the president's tenure might be considered unseemly as long as Washington lived, Jefferson abandoned them. He knew that only a minority of Americans shared his views. James Madison wrote him in October 1788 that "no doubt" existed that Washington "will be called to the Presidency," which was hardly a revelation to Jefferson. Even before receiving Madison's letter, Jefferson had complained that Washington's "merit has blinded our country men to the dangers of making so important an officer re-eligible." He hoped, however, a limit on the number of terms a president could serve would be adopted "the moment we can no longer have the same name at the helm."[4]

Closer to the debates at home, Madison continued to fret about the persistence of Anti-Federalism in New York, Virginia, and North Carolina. Tiny and incorrigible Rhode Island mattered less. At the New York convention, meeting in Poughkeepsie, Alexander Hamilton feared New York's Federalists might have to agree to make ratification conditional on the approval of amendments by the other states. Madison, now back in New York City as a member of the Confederation Congress, told him a conditional approval would be "worse than a rejection." On 21 July, delegates meeting in Hillsborough, North Carolina, refused to ratify the Constitution by a crushing 184 to 83 margin. By the end of July, the Poughkeepsie convention had ratified the Constitution unconditionally, but it had also issued a circular letter to the states calling for a second national convention. Patrick Henry and Edmund Randolph supported the idea, but Madison feared, as he told Jefferson, that a second convention "would terminate in discord, or in alterations of the federal system which would throw back *essential* powers into the State Legislatures." With the animosities engendered by the ratification battles and no actual experience under the Constitution, "at present the public mind," he wrote Jefferson, "is neither sufficiently cool nor sufficiently informed for so delicate an operation" as another constitutional convention.[5]

New York's proposal for a second convention, as Jefferson put it to his secretary William Short, "gives uneasiness." He hoped it would be rejected, but Madison warned him that events since the Virginia convention had "somewhat changed the aspect of things." A heated debate in Congress over a temporary site for the new government created more hard feelings. The ultimate choice of New York City, Madison wrote Jefferson, "will give a great handle to the Southern Anti-Federalists who have inculcated a jealousy of this end of the Continent."[6]

—

Despite Jefferson's conversion, more or less, to Federalism, as that term was understood in 1788 and 1789, he and Madison continued their own constitutional debate. When John Brown, an assembly delegate from Virginia's Kentucky district, asked for Madison's views on the draft constitution Jefferson had appended to *Notes on the State of Virginia*, Madison responded with a long memorandum and sent Jefferson a copy. Brown wanted suggestions for a constitution for what he hoped would become the new state of Kentucky. Madison's comments demonstrated his generally, but not consistently, more conservative philosophy. Jefferson had proposed two-year terms for state senators. Madison thought two years too short and six years not too long. The senate, he wrote Brown, "ought to supply the defect of knowledge and experience incident" to the lower house, provide "steadiness in public affairs," and check the popular excesses that could provoke an anti-republican backlash. Madison also objected to Jefferson's proposal for an electoral college to select senators from multicounty districts; he could accept an electoral college, but election by districts promoted an unhealthy "spirit of locality." Madison apparently preferred either a popular or an indirect statewide election.[7]

More importantly, Madison recommended imposing a property requirement on voters in senate elections, with liberal suffrage requirements for voters in house elections, to strike a balance between "the rights of persons and the rights of property." He faulted the Revolution for neglecting property rights, but Americans now understood "that in all populous countries, the smaller part only can be interested in preserving the rights of property."

The landless, he feared, will "become the dupes and instruments of ambition, or their poverty and dependence will render them the mercenary instruments of wealth."[8]

On other issues, Madison's ideology cannot be neatly pigeonholed, and he was not always clearly to the right of Jefferson. Jefferson had recommended viva voce voting; Madison favored voting by ballot, a reform still years away. He disagreed with Jefferson's proposal to ban the clergy from service in the state legislature. Madison questioned Jefferson's desire to limit the death penalty to murder and treason, but unlike Jefferson, he thought convicted criminals ought to be eligible for pardons. Jefferson's draft constitution extended the governor's term from one year to five with no possibility of reelection, but he left the assembly's right to fill the position otherwise untouched. Madison preferred a popular election or selection by an electoral college to make the governor independent of the legislature and to avoid "faction, intrigue and corruption." He also would have allowed the governor to serve a second term.[9]

Additionally, he did not think the council of state, a colonial relic Jefferson had retained as largely an advisory body to the governor, should be appointed by the assembly, as had been the custom. Madison believed as a general rule that the governor should have a free hand in appointing minor officials, along with the right to make major appointments with the approval of the senate.[10]

In an age skeptical of executive power and with few working examples of judicial review, how to set aside oppressive or unconstitutional legislation was a reoccurring problem. Jefferson borrowed the idea of a council of revision from the New York Constitution: the governor and representatives of the council of state and the judiciary could veto acts of the legislature, but the assembly could override the veto by a two-thirds vote. Madison had included a similar provision in the Virginia Plan, only to see it defeated. Now he suggested giving the executive and the courts separate vetoes, which could be overridden by a supermajority in the legislature. If a court struck down a law on constitutional grounds, its decision could also be reversed by a supermajority, but only after the next election. Otherwise, "as the Courts are generally the last in making their decision, it results to them by refusing or not refusing to execute a law, to stamp it with its final character. This makes the Judiciary Dept. paramount in fact to the Legislature, which was never intended and can never be proper."[11]

Jefferson, as far as we know, did not respond to Madison's critique of his draft constitution, but they continued to argue, respectfully, about the new federal charter. In July 1788, Jefferson wrote his friend, "I sincerely rejoice at the acceptance of our new constitution by nine states. It is a good canvas, on which some few strokes only want retouching." Those strokes consisted almost entirely of provisions protecting civil liberties. Jefferson, it might be noted, did not complain about a lack of popular participation in the new government. He did complain about language permitting the suspension of habeas corpus in cases of insurrections and rebellions; he thought English history showed it was rarely justified. He wanted specific guarantees of freedom of the press and freedom of religion and a ban on monopolies, which he apparently defined to include patents. A ban might discourage innovation, but "the benefit of even limited monopolies is too doubtful to be opposed to that of their general suppression." Jefferson wrote at length about the need to limit or prohibit the establishment of a peacetime army. No European nation seemed likely to send a large army to America. By contrast, he admitted defeat in his demand for term limits: "I . . . suppose my opinion wrong when opposed by the majority."[12]

Madison replied in October. "My opinion has always been in favor of a bill of rights," he said, but added a critical qualification: "provided it be so formed as not to imply powers not meant to be included in the enumeration" of the powers of Congress. He listed for Jefferson four reasons why he had not considered the absence of a bill of rights to be "a material defect" in the Constitution. First, the federal government would exercise only specifically enumerated powers, which gave it no authority to transgress fundamental liberties. Second, some rights might be defined too narrowly; Madison mentioned freedom of conscience in particular. Third, the "jealousy" of the state governments would serve as a barrier to federal overreaching. Fourth, he doubted the effectiveness of a bill of rights. In Virginia the general assessment had failed not because it violated the religion clause of the state's Declaration of Rights but because of rivalries among the different denominations.[13]

Madison's last argument reflected a seminal difference with Jefferson: Madison's greater fear of public opinion. In the American system, Madison argued, the principal threat to liberty came not from a government acting against the will of the people but from a government acting as the agent of a self-interested majority. Living in Europe, Jefferson, Madison thought, "contemplated abuses issuing from a very different quarter." In other words, Jefferson clung to an older view of an oppressive regime as a royal government unresponsive to the rights of its subjects.[14]

Yet even as he made the case against a declaration of rights, Madison conceded one could serve two purposes: to express certain "political truths" that might eventually become part of the nation's political culture and to offer "a good ground" for an appeal to the people should the government itself threaten their freedoms. He continued to believe the tumult caused by weak governments could lead to despotism as easily as could the ambitions of power-hungry politicians: "It is a melancholy reflection that liberty should be equally exposed to danger whether the Government should have too much or too little power." That point notwithstanding, Madison's resolve had weakened, although it is not entirely clear when he decided he would support a bill of rights or, more significantly, become its dogged champion. He closed his letter by discussing how a bill of rights might be worded. He preferred a statement of general principles to "absolute restrictions" that would probably be violated in emergencies and hence discredited.[15] Perhaps Madison was trying to convince himself of the need for a bill of rights, and in some respects his October letter reads less like a defense of his position than as an effort to justify his past conduct to Jefferson.[16]

Replying in March 1789, Jefferson rebutted Madison's four points one by one. A bill of rights was necessary to prevent the abuse of the federal government's enumerated powers. A partial "declaration of some essential rights" would be better than nothing; "if we cannot secure all our rights, let us secure what we can." The states needed a declaration of principles by which to "try all the acts of the federal government." If bills of rights were not "absolutely efficacious under all circumstances," they enjoyed "great potency always."[17]

Jefferson also introduced a new consideration into the debate: "In the arguments in favor of a declaration of rights, you omit one which has great weight with me, the legal check which it puts into the hands of the judiciary." The judges, "if rendered independent, and kept strictly to their own department," Jefferson believed, merited "great confidence for their learning and integrity," and he put a rhetorical question to Madison: "What degree of confidence would be too much for a body composed of Wythe, Blair, and Pendleton?"[18] It was a point Madison would not forget.

———

Modern readers take the idea of judicial review—a court's power to strike down a law as unconstitutional—for granted, but eighteenth-century Americans did not. To understand their perspective, we need to look briefly at England's legal history, especially with regard to the protection of civil liberties. The English Declaration of Rights, the most important document of its kind before the American Revolution, was approved by an extralegal assembly after James II had been deposed in the Glorious Revolution. After William and

Mary took the throne, a reconstituted Parliament passed the measure as a statute, hence the term "Bill of Rights." In 1774, the First Continental Congress adopted a Declaration and Resolves, a statement that was printed in New York as "The Bill of Rights," which may have been the first use of the term to describe an American document.[19] In any event, the phrase became common in American political discourse.

A statute like the original Bill of Rights could not bind a subsequent legislature, but declarations of fundamental freedoms could educate people about their liberties and serve a polemical purpose. When most of the American states adopted new constitutions during the Revolution, many of them added bills of rights and began the process of turning political statements and legal proclamations into constitutional law. Edmund Randolph's description of the Virginia Declaration of Rights, for example, illustrates its transitional character. It was intended to protect the people's liberties from the General Assembly but also to be "in all the revolutions of time, of human opinion, and of government, a perpetual standard . . . , around which the people might rally, and by a notorious record be forever admonished to be watchful, firm, and virtuous."[20]

Randolph and his contemporaries expected citizens to defend their rights through the political process, and those rights were as much cooperative or collective as individual. George Mason expressed confidence in 1778 that Virginia had placed "the essential Rights of human nature" on a firm foundation because "the People become every Day more & more attach'd" to their new government, not because those rights could be enforced in court. During the Virginia ratifying convention, John Marshall had dismissed the Virginia Declaration as merely a set of recommendations to lawmakers. As late as 1787, Madison seems not to have thought of a bill of rights as a literal, legal check on the legislature.[21]

In the 1780s, however, American courts were beginning, tentatively, to assert the power of judicial review.[22] The Philadelphia convention had not squarely addressed the issue, but at least some of the delegates had assumed federal courts would refuse to enforce laws that violated the Constitution. Madison had said the Constitution's ban on ex post facto legislation would require judges to declare such laws null and void. In a series of essays in *The Federalist*, Alexander Hamilton had articulated a cogent theory of judicial review. In No. 39, Madison had explicitly acknowledged that "controversies relating to the boundary between the two jurisdictions," or in other words the state and federal governments, would be resolved by the federal courts.[23]

Madison was less explicit about a federal court's jurisdiction over allegedly unconstitutional acts of Congress, the type of case a federal bill of rights could produce.[24] He certainly did not believe courts enjoyed an exclusive right to consider constitutional issues. During the first Congress to convene under the Constitution, the question arose as to the president's power to dismiss officials whose appointments required Senate approval. Madison said then that if an issue "relates to a doubtful part of the constitution, I suppose an exposition of the constitution may come with as much propriety from the legislature as any other department." What Congress decides, he predicted, "will become the permanent exposition of the constitution." In all governments, "there are points which must be adjusted by the departments themselves." Madison's willingness to take up the issue seems to have been influenced by his belief that a case involving the removal power was not likely to come before the courts. On the substantive issue, he concluded that if the Constitution did not expressly require Senate approval, no such requirement could be imposed by Congress.[25]

Jefferson probably meant to suggest to Madison a judicial review of a fairly narrow scope, and given his lamentations about judicial supremacy in his memorandum to John Brown, Madison probably would not have accepted anything more. Jefferson eventually developed his own concurrent or tripartite theory of judicial review in which the three branches of the federal government would make their own constitutional determinations and then negotiate their differences. He also challenged the authority of the federal courts to resolve jurisdictional conflicts between the state and federal governments and proposed referring serious disputes to a convention of the states. Jefferson argued in retirement that federal judges ought to be answerable to a combination of state and national officials. They had become, in his mind, independent not simply of the executive and the legislature but of the nation itself, and as federal officers they were overly disposed to consolidate power in the national government. More often, however, Jefferson criticized Federalist judges for how they decided cases, not for hearing them. Always interested in political stability, an elderly Madison accepted federal court review of state laws to avoid "a trial of strength between the Posse headed by the Marshall [representing national authority] and the Posse headed by the Sheriff [representing state governments]." He also criticized the Supreme Court for not using its right of judicial review to curb the expansion of congressional power.[26]

As much as Jefferson and Madison struggled over the course of their long careers to define the proper role of the federal judiciary, in 1789 they seemed prepared to accept judicial review if an egregious conflict existed between a statute and the Constitution and if the court could not avoid the constitutional issue in deciding a particular case. Of course, in 1789 they had almost no real experience with judicial review, but as Jefferson's March letter to Madison suggested, American courts were beginning to grow in their independence, professionalism, and prestige. Allowing a court to overturn a statute that violated the Constitution commanded a certain logic and offered an immediate political advantage. If Madison could propose a plausible mechanism to enforce a bill of rights, it might help him guide one through a skeptical Congress.[27]

MADISON assumed he would serve in the new government, either as a member of Congress or as a member of President Washington's administration. Patrick Henry and the Anti-Federalist majority in the Virginia assembly wanted to keep him out of the Senate, and Madison finished third behind Richard Henry Lee and William Grayson in the assembly vote to fill the state's two Senate seats. They also gerrymandered his congressional district, putting Orange County in a district with counties with Anti-Federalist leanings, and Anti-Federalists recruited a creditable candidate, his friend and sometimes collaborator James Monroe, to oppose him. Henry and his allies reportedly thought defeating Madison would send a message to the other states that Virginians, despite the vote of the Richmond convention, did not support the Constitution.[28]

Madison claimed to prefer to serve in the House; he seemed to think it would require less entertaining than would the Senate. As a House member, he would not be directly accountable to the Virginia assembly, and Madison probably expected the popularly elected House to be more influential than the upper chamber. He had hoped to spend the winter of 1788–89 in New York, working on an undisclosed project "which needs access to the papers of Congress," and he hated "electioneering." His supporters insisted he come home to campaign. The issue, he wrote Jefferson from Philadelphia on his way back to Virginia, would be the "extent" and "mode" of amendments: Would they be limited to a bill of rights, and would they originate in Congress or with a second constitutional convention? Madison continued to see a second convention as a vehicle to subvert the Constitution, if not the union itself, and he now expressed what would be his primary objective for the next several months: if Congress would approve amendments limited mainly to protections for basic liberties, it would separate "the well meaning from the designing opponents . . . and give to the Government its due popularity and stability."[29]

Madison felt confident the Federalists would enjoy a healthy majority in the new Congress, although he feared, once most of the returns were in, that there would be "a very scanty proportion who will share in the drudgery of business," and he anticipated bitter fights between Federalists and Anti-Federalists and between northerners and southerners. Arriving home he faced more immediate problems. Monroe's supporters circulated allegations that Madison opposed any amendments "whatsoever" and that, worse yet, he had "ceased to be a friend to the rights of Conscience." Madison responded in a letter to George Eve, a Baptist minister, which was perhaps the first and clearest public statement of his new position. He conceded he had never seen the threats to liberty in the Constitution that others had perceived and had feared attempting to amend it before it was ratified would provoke "danger-ous contentions," but, he told Eve, "circumstances are now changed." Amend-ments could now placate "well meaning opponents" and provide additional protections for liberty. He mentioned specifically freedom of religion and of the press, the right to a trial by jury, limits on warrantless searches and "vexatious appeals," and a requirement that the House of Representatives be expanded as the nation's population grew.[30]

Madison also laid out his argument for pursuing amendments in Congress as opposed to another national convention. Congress could take up the issue when it met in March. No one knew when or if a second convention might meet. Congress, moreover, could be expected to act prudently, avoiding radical reform. A second convention would attract "insidious characters . . . too likely to turn every thing into confusion and uncertainty."[31]

Monroe and Madison campaigned throughout the district, often in open-air debates that left Madison with frostbite on his nose. Madison's deep roots in the region; his long record of public service; his unflaggingly serious, if not always popular, positions; and his campaigning, however unpleasant he found it, paid off. He defeated Monroe by a comfortable margin of 1,308 to 972, but he knew the Constitution still had enemies in Virginia. After Madison returned to New York for the first session of the new Congress, Representative Fisher Ames of Massachusetts opined that Madison worried about Virginia's "state politics and . . . his popularity there more than I think he should." To no one's surprise, Washington had been elected president with no opposition. Federalist John Adams defeated Anti-Federalist George Clinton in the vice presidential contest, and the Federalists held large major-ities in the House and Senate, but Madison had promised his constituents he would press for a bill of rights, and he intended to honor his commitment. He had other motives as well. As he explained to Jefferson after arriving in New York, "Some conciliatory sacrifices will be made, in order to extinguish opposition to the system, or at least break the force of it, by detaching the deluded opponents from their designing leaders."[32]

———

From his diplomatic post in Paris, Jefferson witnessed the first stages of the French Revolution. In January 1789, he sent Madison two drafts of the Declaration of the Rights of Man, one by the Marquis de Lafayette and the other by Richard Gem, an English doctor who attended Jefferson while he was in France. Lafayette's draft, Jefferson thought, resembled the Virginia Declaration of Rights "as much" as "the actual state of things here" allowed. Jefferson had encouraged Lafayette, unsuccessfully, to delete references to property rights and the preservation of "honor." Jefferson continued to believe that property was not a natural right but a means to the ultimate end of a just society, human happiness. "Honor" to Jefferson implied aristocratic privilege. He may have influenced Lafayette to add a provision recognizing the right of the people to reform their government. The final version of the Declaration, however, did not go as far as Jefferson wanted to protect liberty of conscience.[33]

He nevertheless viewed the unrest in France with an equanimity that can seem naive in retrospect. "The revolution in this country," he wrote John Adams in May, "has gone on hitherto with a quietness, a steadiness, and a progress unexampled." His own house was robbed three times, but even after the revolution turned violent he could joke with Maria Cosway about awakening in the morning and checking to see if his head was still on his shoulders. He wrote a sympathetic French liberal, "I have . . . observed the mobs with my own eyes in order to be satisfied of their objects, and declare to you that I saw so plainly the legitimacy of them, that I have slept in my house as quietly thro' the whole as I ever did in the most peaceable moments." In reality, the storming of the Bastille in July 1789 disturbed him, and he had predicted weeks earlier, sensibly enough, that if the Estates General, representing France's nobles, clergy, and commoners, could not agree on voting procedures, "it cannot be foreseen what issue this matter will take."[34]

Jefferson, consistent with normal diplomatic protocol, initially attempted to maintain some distance from France's domestic politics, but he clearly sympathized with the reformers, and as the crisis worsened he intervened behind the scenes. He tried to help negotiate a constitution on which the

Let Us Secure What We Can

moderate and conservative elements of the popular party could agree. He assumed if a proper political framework could be established, other reforms would come. He drafted a short "Charter of Rights" providing for a constitutional monarchy, and he urged French liberals to limit their demands to concessions Louis XVI seemed likely to accept: the rights to habeas corpus and trial by jury; freedom of conscience and of the press; and an annual, representative assembly with the power to originate legislation, collect taxes, appropriate money, and oversee the king's ministers.[35]

Jefferson's charter ignored two critical issues: whether all public offices would be open to all classes of citizens and whether the three estates would vote together or as separate bodies. The liberal leaders of the new, self-proclaimed National Assembly took a more assertive course—unwisely, Jefferson believed. Louis vacillated while Marie Antoinette opposed any concessions. Jefferson, exaggerating her influence, later blamed the revolution's bloody turn on the queen's extravagance and intransigence.[36]

Jefferson would soon return to America. His brief encounter with the French Revolution is less relevant for his small role in that cataclysm than for what it suggests about his temperament. By the time he left Paris in September 1789, the revolution had gone farther than he had anticipated, but as it became more radical, so did Jefferson's rhetoric. In 1793, after the Reign of Terror had begun, Jefferson confessed himself "deeply wounded" by the deaths of "some of the martyrs to this cause, but rather than it should have failed, I would have seen half the earth desolated. Were there but an Adam & an Eve left in every country, & left free, it would be better than it is now." Yet his rhetoric notwithstanding, Jefferson usually let political reality temper his conduct. He expected a reformed French government to open new markets to American ships. For all the vitriol he routinely directed at kings and queens, he advised the French to establish a constitutional monarchy. His wry comment on the opening session of the Estates General—"As an opera it was imposing"—suggests he had some sense of the limits of French politics.[37] Nevertheless, Merrill Peterson has written that Jefferson "could be accused of bland insensitivity to the psychology of revolutionary movements." Jefferson's goals for the revolution were reasonable: the creation of a monarchy checked by a representative assembly and the rule of law. Only the political dynamics of the revolution made his hopes unrealistic.[38]

In practice, Jefferson eschewed extremism, but he usually began from an idealistic premise: "I have so much confidence on the good sense of man and his qualifications for self-government, that I am never afraid of the issue where reason is left free to exert her force; and I will agree to stand a false prophet if all does not end well in this country. Nor will it end with this country. Hers is but the first chapter of the history of European liberty."[39]

———

IN JANUARY 1789, George Washington asked for Madison's advice on an inaugural address and sent him a seventy-three-page draft apparently written by Washington's aide David Humphreys. In February, Madison stopped at Mount Vernon on his way to New York for the first session of the new Congress and helped Washington write a much shorter and more modest speech better suited to the president-elect's persona. In deference to Congress, Washington's first inaugural address made only one substantive proposal, an oblique reference to the need to amend the Constitution to protect civil liberties. After Washington delivered the speech, Madison wrote a reply on behalf of the House of Representatives promising the president that "the question arising out of the fifth article of the Constitution, will receive all the attention demanded by its importance." He then prepared a response on Washington's behalf. Madison seemed to be everywhere in the first months of the new administration. He spoke 124 times during the first session of Congress, more than twice as often as any other representative, but his influence was not limited to the House floor. The historian Stuart Leibiger has called him Washington's "prime minister."[40]

Five days after Washington gave his inaugural address, Madison informed the House that he intended to introduce amendments. The ratification conventions in Massachusetts, South Carolina, New Hampshire, New York, and of course Virginia had proposed amendments, as had Anti-Federalist caucuses in Pennsylvania and Maryland. He drew on their recommendations, selecting provisions that appealed to him and that seemed likely to be approved. The existing state bills of rights, which were not comprehensive, proved less useful, although Madison relied heavily on the recommendations of the Virginia convention, which, to the extent they called for a bill of rights, followed the 1776 Virginia Declaration of Rights. He added two amendments no state had requested. One prohibited the taking of private property for public use without just compensation. The other attempted to prevent state governments from impinging upon the right to a jury trial, religious liberty, or the freedom of the press; he later called it "the most valuable amendment on the whole list."[41]

Madison acted when he did to preempt his Virginia colleague Theodorick Bland. Madison knew that Bland intended to present the resolution of

Let Us Secure What We Can

the Virginia assembly asking Congress to call a second constitutional convention. Bland introduced his resolution on 4 May, and a New York representative introduced a similar proposal the next day. The actual introduction of Madison's amendments was "postponed," he reported to Jefferson, "in order that the more urgent business may not be delayed." Congress had to organize a new government, after all, but by late May, Madison assured Jefferson a bill of rights would soon be forthcoming, along with "a few other alterations most called for by the opponents of the Government and least objectionable to its friends." Sending Jefferson a copy of the amendments, he expressed confidence they would satisfy the majority of Anti-Federalists, especially in Virginia. Jefferson liked the nascent bill of rights "as far as it goes; but I should have been for going further." Jefferson recommended mainly technical and procedural elaborations, not all of which would have expanded citizens' rights, and then added, "I have so much confidence in my countrymen as to be satisfied that we shall have further amendments as soon as the degeneracy of our government shall render them necessary."[42]

Madison finally had an opportunity to present his amendments on 8 June. Congress, he said, should consider amendments "to quiet that anxiety which prevails in the public mind" and to "prepare the way for a favorable reception of our future measures." Fearful where the debate might end, Madison did not propose reconsidering "the whole structure of the government," but he did believe that provisions to secure the people's rights would command the support of two-thirds of Congress and three-fourths of the states, as required by the Constitution.[43]

Although Anti-Federalists objected to the Constitution on a myriad of grounds, "the great majority of the people who opposed" ratification, in Madison's analysis, did so because of the lack of a bill of rights. It was a "fortunate" omission because their concerns could be addressed "without endangering any part of the Constitution."[44]

Next came Madison's specific proposals. They included language recognizing the sovereignty of the people; their rights to life, liberty, property, and the pursuit of happiness; and their right to reform their government. Madison recommended expanding the House of Representatives and limiting Congress's ability to raise congressional salaries. A longer section addressed civil liberties: religious freedom, freedom of speech and of the press, the right to assemble and to petition the government, and the right to bear arms. He proposed that "no person religiously scrupulous of bearing arms, shall be compelled to render military service in person," and he wanted to restrict the quartering of soldiers in private homes. For criminal defendants, he included bans on double jeopardy, self-incrimination, excessive bail, and cruel and unusual punishment, and he recognized rights to a speedy trial, to confront one's accusers, to summon witnesses, and to retain counsel. Unreasonable searches were prohibited. In federal courts, jury trials and, in criminal cases, grand juries, as allowed by the common law, were to be protected, and no person should be denied due process of law. As noted above, the taking of private property without just compensation was prohibited, and Madison proposed amending the Constitution to provide that "no state shall violate the equal rights of conscience, or the freedom of the press, or the trial by jury in criminal cases." Finally, Madison recommended giving explicit constitutional status to the separation of powers, and his amendments provided that powers not delegated to Congress or prohibited to the states remained with the states.[45]

After conceding, as everyone knew, that he had never considered a federal bill of rights essential, Madison admitted it "was neither improper nor altogether useless." The English Bill of Rights had been intended to limit royal prerogatives. In America, the legislature wielded greater power than did the executive and presented the bigger threat. An ever-larger menace came from "the body of the people, operating by the majority against the minority." A bill of rights, he said, ought to address those dangers.[46]

He now had to rebut arguments he had made during the ratification debate. Congress's powers were enumerated and not unlimited, but even enumerated powers, he conceded, could be abused. Bills of rights were not always effective, but they had "a tendency" to create a culture of respect for liberty. Madison borrowed one argument from Jefferson: if a bill of rights were to be "incorporated into the constitution, independent tribunals of justice will consider themselves in a peculiar manner the guardians of those rights; they will be an impenetrable bulwark against every assumption of power in the legislative or executive" branches. He had shown no such confidence in the federal judiciary during the Constitutional Convention. His view of the state assemblies, which he had excoriated in Philadelphia, had changed even more dramatically. Jealous of federal authority and armed with a bill of rights, they will "be able to resist with more effect every assumption of power than any other power on earth can do; and the greatest opponents to a federal government admit the state legislatures to be sure guardians of the people's liberty."[47]

Madison's proposals, for two reasons, could not be called a literal bill of rights. First, several of his amendments had little if anything to do with civil liberties. The term "amendments" had been used loosely throughout the ratification debate to include both a bill of rights and proposals to alter the structure and powers of the new government.[48] Second, Madison intended for his amendments to be interspersed throughout the text of the Constitution. He did not envision a separate and highly visible statement of the people's rights, which may explain a subtle but significant revision he made to the language of earlier bills of rights. They had typically spoken in terms of what governments "ought not" to do; Madison used the more emphatic "shall not." He may have thought that if his amendments were to be part of the text of the Constitution, they needed to be cast in the imperative, or he may have wanted to abandon the more deferential language that had its origins in declarations of rights that were addressed to the king. In any event, Madison had taken a step toward wording a bill of rights in a manner that could be applied by a court.[49]

Whatever Madison thought he had done, he struggled even to get a hearing on his amendments. Objecting to considering Madison's proposals, Representative James Jackson of Georgia spoke for many House members when he compared the Constitution to "a vessel just launched, and lying at the wharf." The Constitution ought not to be amended until experience had exposed its real defects. When the House took up the issue again in mid-August, it did not provoke a brilliant debate, and the ensuing deliberations did not shed much light on what Madison's recommendations were intended to mean. Most Federalists considered further amendments unnecessary. Anti-Federalist leaders understood that Madison wanted to win over their more pliable followers without limiting the federal government's more contested powers, including the power of direct taxation. George Mason thought Madison felt compelled to fulfill a campaign promise, but he wrote his son John, "Of important & substantial Amendments I have not the least hope." The South Carolina Anti-Federalist Aedanus Burke complained that the revisions likely to be adopted "are not those solid and substantial amendments which the people expect."[50]

Benjamin Goodhue, a Massachusetts Federalist, granted that Madison's amendments probably went "as far towards quieting the honest part of the dissatisfied, as any friend of an energetic government can go," but other Federalists grumbled about the process. Thomas Sedgwick explained Madison's campaign for amendments by echoing his Massachusetts colleague Fisher Ames: Madison "is constantly haunted by the ghost of Patrick Henry." House speaker Frederick Muhlenberg was "sorry so much Time has been spent in this Business." Robert Morris agreed it was a "waste of precious time." Writing as Pacificus, Noah Webster publicly ridiculed Madison for espousing the notion that the people needed a bill of rights to protect them from their elected representatives; it "is a farce in government as novel as it is ludicrous." Richard Peters, who had served with Madison in the Confederation Congress and who was now Speaker of the Pennsylvania assembly, wrote Madison directly to critique his strategy. Adhering to the Constitution as it was, he argued, would "have silenced Antifederalists sooner than magnifying their Importance" by raising the issue of amendments. Many of them, Peters complained, would never be satisfied.[51]

Madison defended his "nauseous project of amendments" in a letter to Peters that emphasized political necessity. If less apt to be needed in a republic than in a monarchy, a bill of rights was "not improper in itself" because "every Govt. power may oppress," but Madison stressed the need to satisfy the skeptics and rally the nation around the new government. The Virginia convention and those of several other states had ratified the Constitution in expectation of amendments. "As an honest man *I feel* my self bound by this consideration," and Virginia Federalists had repeated that commitment in their congressional campaigns. If he had not introduced a bill of rights, Anti-Federalist delegates would have sponsored their own amendments, but adoption of a bill of rights acceptable to Federalists "will kill the opposition everywhere," make it easier to pass other measures, weaken the movement for a second convention, and expedite North Carolina's entry into the union.[52]

Once the House debate began, the representatives focused, to varying degrees, on amending the preamble to the Constitution, on the location of the other amendments, and on the wording of the clause on the relationship between church and state. On 21 July, the House had appointed a select committee, which included Madison, to consider his proposals. Madison had intended to include his first few amendments, which were general statements of broad republican principles endorsed by the Virginia convention, in an expanded version of the Constitution's original preamble. State constitutions and bills of rights often included such language. Virginia's Declaration of Rights, for example, had called for "a firm adherence to justice, moderation, temperance, frugality, and virtue, and . . . frequent recurrence to fundamental principles." With the other amendments buried in the text of the Constitution, a revised preamble would be conspicuous evidence of Madison's efforts to meet Anti-Federalists halfway.[53]

The select committee eliminated most of Madison's preamble and proposed adding instead the phrase "Government being intended for the benefit of the people, and the rightful establishment thereof being derived from their authority alone" before the preamble's original "We, the People." We can only speculate as to the committee's reasoning. Thomas Paine had written a decade earlier that a bill of rights ought to be simply "a plain positive declaration of the rights themselves." Madison's preamble largely duplicated the natural law principles already embodied in the Declaration of Independence and may have been seen as redundant. One of them recognized the people's right to rebel and to reform their government; after twenty-five years of political turmoil, Madison's committee colleagues may not have wanted to encourage any more unrest.[54]

Even the committee's modest changes proved too much for several House members when the House, sitting as a committee of the whole, debated its report in August. Elbridge Gerry, an Anti-Federalist who probably wanted to disrupt the proceedings, complained the new language was historically inaccurate. Another Anti-Federalist, Thomas Tudor Tucker of South Carolina, objected that since the preamble was not a substantive part of the Constitution, amending it served no purpose. A few members defended the committee's report, but even sympathetic Federalists expressed reservations. Virginia's John Page thought "the words 'We the people' had a neatness and simplicity, while its expression was the most forcible of any ever seen prefixed to any constitution." Roger Sherman agreed; "We the people" said all that needed to be said about popular sovereignty. The amendment to the preamble survived an initial vote in the committee of the whole, but in a final vote on 19 August, the House rejected it.[55]

Sherman, who had served on the select committee, had from the beginning opposed Madison's plan to embed amendments in the existing Constitution. He preferred separating the original text from later amendments. After losing an initial skirmish, the Connecticut Federalist, one of the wiliest parliamentarians in the early republic, persisted until, in another vote on 19 August, he persuaded the House to place their amendments at the end of the Constitution.[56]

Madison's proposed amendment on freedom of religion went through several iterations. He had originally written, "The civil rights of none shall be abridged on account of religious belief or worship, nor shall any national religion be established, nor shall the full and equal rights of conscience be in any manner, or on any pretext, abridged." The select committee shortened it considerably: "No religion shall be established by law, nor shall the equal rights of conscience be infringed." Madison explained the intent of the amendment was to prevent Congress from establishing a national religion, enforcing its obligations, or coercing any particular form of worship. At one point, the House approved a version providing that "Congress shall make no laws touching religion, or infringing the rights of conscience," before sending the Senate a final version that may well have been written by Madison: "Congress shall make no law establishing religion, or to prevent the free exercise thereof, or to infringe the rights of conscience."[57]

The Senate amended the House measure to leave open a door to federal aid to churches; Congress could adopt "no law establishing articles of faith or a mode of worship prohibiting the free exercise of religion." Madison served on the conference committee appointed to resolve differences between the House and Senate amendments, and he always took a fairly absolutist position on the separation of church and state. As a member of Congress he would oppose census-takers asking people their occupation because he did not want the federal government compiling a list of ministers. The final version of the amendment showed his influence: "Congress shall make no law respecting an establishment of religion, or prohibiting the free exercise thereof."[58]

The Senate deleted Madison's amendment affirming the separation of legislative, executive, and judicial powers and another prohibiting appeals of lawsuits involving small claims. The upper house eliminated Madison's proposal to exempt conscientious objectors from military service. Elected as they were by state legislatures, senators had no interest in limiting the states' ability to restrict the press, religious freedom, or the rights to a jury trial, and they also killed that amendment. It was the only issue on which Madison thought he had suffered a meaningful loss.[59]

In the course of the debates, Madison and his allies defeated several proposals introduced by Anti-Federalists, including amendments to limit Congress's ability to supervise elections and to impose direct taxes. They fought off efforts to consider all the amendments recommended by state conventions and an attempt to insert "expressly" before "delegated" into what became the Tenth Amendment, which reserved to the states or to the people "powers not delegated to the United States by the Constitution, nor prohibited by it to the States." Madison spoke out against an unsuccessful effort to allow states to instruct their delegates. If the instructions were binding, what, he asked, was a member to do when they called for an unconstitutional act? And if they were not binding, they served no purpose. Madison's amendments already recognized the right to speak and write and to petition the government.[60]

Congress ultimately approved twelve "Articles of Amendments." The first, expanding the House of Representatives by shrinking the size of congressional districts, was never ratified by the states. The second, providing that no congressional pay increase could take effect until after the next congressional election, did not become law until 1992, when it was finally ratified as the Twenty-Seventh Amendment. All the rest, which in 1791 became the first ten amendments to the Constitution, can be traced in substance to Madison's original proposals. Ironically perhaps, it was Jefferson, as secretary of state, who blandly certified their ratification, along with statutes regulating "certain fisheries of the United States" and reorganizing the post office, in a short letter to the state governors. The adoption of the Bill of Rights by an indifferent if not hostile Congress vividly illustrated Madison's tenacity in the face of repeated delays and tiresome debates, the respect he enjoyed among his peers, and the force of his arguments.[61]

———

PRESIDENT WASHINGTON nominated Thomas Jefferson to be secretary of state on 25 September 1789. The Senate confirmed his appointment the next day, the same day Jefferson left La Havre, France, for what he thought would be a relatively brief visit to America. He was bringing his daughters home so they could complete their education in Virginia. Washington had not consulted Jefferson about the appointment, and he did not want it. Jefferson loved France and hoped to watch the revolution there run its course. He feared that the secretary of state, with a virtually nonexistent federal bureaucracy, would be saddled with a host of mundane administrative duties wholly unrelated to American foreign policy. He may also have dreaded the public attacks likely to accompany a prominent position in the new government.[62]

Jefferson heard rumors of his appointment after his ship docked in Norfolk in late November. A letter from the president reached Jefferson during a visit at Eppington, the plantation home of his sister-in-law Elizabeth Wayles Eppes, on his way to Monticello. He sent Washington an inconclusive reply. Jefferson finally arrived home shortly before Christmas, and Madison made the short ride from Montpelier to Monticello a few days later, reuniting the two friends for the first time in five and a half years. Madison urged Jefferson to accept the secretary of state post and minimized the job's clerical demands. A second letter from Washington applied the finishing touch, and Jefferson agreed reluctantly to become the nation's first secretary of state. Neither the time Jefferson and Madison had spent apart nor their initial differences over the Constitution could diminish their friendship or their mutual respect. Jefferson reportedly described Madison to Benjamin Rush as "the greatest man in the world."[63]

Jefferson had written Madison one of his most famous letters shortly before leaving France, carried it across the Atlantic, and then apparently forgot to give it to him when Madison visited Monticello after Christmas. Jefferson mailed it to him in January. The letter reflected Jefferson's struggles with his own debts and with the persistent inequality he had witnessed in France. He posed for Madison the question "whether one generation of men has a right to bind another." Jefferson believed it "to be self evident, '*that the earth belongs in usufruct to the living,*' and that the dead have neither powers nor rights over it." Heirs took property by the laws of their society, not as a natural right. Nor, he thought, should debts descend from one generation to another lest one person "eat up the usufruct of the lands for several generations to come." Likewise, responsibility for public debt passed from one generation to the next as a matter of "municipal" law, not moral or natural law. Calculating that half of the adults alive at any given time would be dead in nineteen years, Jefferson reasoned that no law or constitution ought to remain in force much longer than that. The ability to repeal a law offered scant protection against wastrel or profligate ancestors. Legislative representation might be "unequal and vicious"; factionalism, bribery, and personal interests could corrupt lawmakers.[64]

Madison saw the obvious flaws in Jefferson's logic, but he responded tactfully. Jefferson had, he conceded, raised a "great"—as in profound—idea that "suggests many interesting reflections to legislators," especially when incurring debts on behalf of the public, but on first impression Madison viewed "the doctrine as not in all respects compatible with the course of human affairs." A constitution "so often revised becomes too mutable to retain those prejudices in its favor which antiquity inspires." Frequent revisions of a government would produce "pernicious factions" and risk an interregnum. Jefferson had forgotten that members of one generation often incurred debts that benefited their successors. "New-modelling" property rights every generation would produce bitter contests between landowners and the landless, depress property values, undermine respect for contractual obligations generally, discourage industry, and encourage speculation. For his part, Madison accepted the notion of "tacit consent." As in a republic where the minority implicitly agreed to be bound by the decisions of the majority, one generation in the normal course of affairs tacitly accepted the bequests of its predecessors.[65]

Madison closed as he had begun, diplomatically acknowledging that lawmakers should be mindful of placing undue burdens on future generations and admitting it was easier to see "little difficulties" in a "great plan" than to recognize its potential benefits. "Our hemisphere," he wrote Jefferson, "must still be more enlightened before many of the sublime truths which are seen thro' the medium of Philosophy, become visible to the naked eye of the ordinary Politician." As a matter of positive law, the idea of making all laws and obligations temporary went nowhere, but Madison and Jefferson never forgot the present's responsibility to the future.[66]

The exchange revealed some of their differences. "Some men look at constitutions with sanctimonious reverence, and deem them like the arc of the covenant, too sacred to be touched," Jefferson wrote in 1816, "but I know . . . that laws and institutions must go hand in hand with the progress of the human mind. As that becomes more developed, more enlightened, as new discoveries are made, new truths disclosed, and manners and opinions change with the circumstances, institutions must advance also, and keep pace with the times." Jefferson's faith in progress and in human reason led him to welcome change. He did not believe in a "living constitution" that evolved through interpretation; Jefferson believed constitutions ought to be literally rewritten from time to time. The more cautious Madison saw greater value in stability; change could bring despotism as easily as it could expand liberty. Jefferson considered government itself to be the chief source of tyranny, although perhaps paradoxically, Jefferson did not share Madison's contempt for the Revolutionary state governments. Madison feared "mob rule" and believed tyranny often came as a reaction to licentious popular passions.[67]

Jefferson was more visionary but less doctrinaire. Confident in the ultimate triumph of reason, Jefferson, in the 1780s at least, could accept defeat and move on, as he did on the question of presidential terms limits. Madison, more invested in a particular model of constitutional reform, defended his ill-conceived congressional veto long after its rejection by the Philadelphia convention. Madison could adjust to political reality, as he did during the ratification debate, but not as easily as Jefferson.

Beyond the inexplicable matter of personal chemistry—and they obviously shared similar backgrounds—their areas of agreement far exceeded their differences. Jefferson and Madison shared a commitment to civil liberties, especially an expansive view of freedom of conscience. Both men saw the need for a stronger central government, one competent to pay its debts, to promote American trade abroad, and to avoid disunion. In a sense, Madison's fulminations against the state legislatures in 1786–87 and the significance the demand for a bill of rights assumed during the ratification debate can distract attention from the critical issue of the late 1780s: Congress's inadequacy under the Articles of Confederation.[68]

Reflecting their status as Virginia planters, Jefferson and Madison subscribed to a vision of an agrarian republic of sturdy yeoman farmers; both deplored the evils of slavery but felt compelled to let future generations address them. Beyond protecting American commercial interests in the West Indies, Europe, and the Mediterranean and expediting American settlement in the West, and in Madison's case policing the state governments, the role they envisioned for the federal government was relatively modest. They might be called small-government nationalists. The Constitution lacked the Declaration's commitment to equality and its appeals to natural law, but Jefferson and Madison saw no conflict between the two documents—in Jefferson's case partly because, as he did in the Declaration, he often engaged in soaring rhetoric that he knew could not easily be reduced to actual, positive law. More importantly, Madison saw first, and Jefferson came to see, that the achievements of the American Revolution could not be preserved without a constitutional revolution.[69]

Let Us Secure What We Can

AFTERWORD

THE ADOPTION AND RATIFICATION of the Constitution and the Bill of Rights ended one phase of America's constitutional history and began another. Situations quickly arose that the Constitution ignored or did not clearly address. Political considerations, as well as pragmatic assessments of the national interest, sometimes made it difficult for Thomas Jefferson and James Madison to maintain a consistent approach to constitutional interpretation. Madison's apparent vacillations have created what historians call "the Madison problem": how to reconcile his early nationalism with his embrace of federalism and states' rights in the 1790s and then explain his return to a modest, nationalist agenda as president. In fact, Madison, unlike Alexander Hamilton, probably never envisioned an American government with the taxing and war-making capacity of a major European power, and Madison had been chastened by the ratification debates of 1787 and 1788. Surprised that almost all the opposition to the Constitution came from critics who claimed it took too many prerogatives from the states, Madison had to defend the new regime as a government of limited and carefully enumerated powers. For most of the rest of his career, he honored the representations he had made during the ratification campaign.[1]

Jefferson also took those representations seriously. Initially skeptical of the Constitution, he proved to be an even more aggressive champion of strict construction and limited government than was Madison. Jefferson privately came to prefer a system of "ward republics" in which different functions were delegated to the lowest feasible level of government. As always, however, his differences with Madison did not impair their friendship or their ability to collaborate.[2]

Issues of constitutional interpretation arose in the first session of the first Congress. Madison assumed that Congress had a responsibility to decide constitutional questions and that its decisions would serve as precedents for later generations. Should, for example, Senate approval be required before the president could dismiss an official whose appointment required Senate confirmation? As we have seen, Madison thought not.[3] Far more contentious would be the fight over treasury secretary Alexander Hamilton's proposal to charter a Bank of the United States. In arguing that the Constitution gave Congress no such authority, Madison attempted to lay down a list of canons of constitutional construction. No interpretation should undermine the basic characteristics of a republican government. The clear language of the Constitution should be respected; doubtful provisions should be interpreted in terms of their consequences. The intent, or "meaning," of the parties should be honored, although he was not clear who those parties might be, and he drew criticism when he noted the Philadelphia convention had explicitly rejected a provision empowering Congress to charter corporations. The convention debates had not yet been made public. And finally, an important power, like chartering a bank, would not have been omitted if the framers had supported it.[4]

Madison lost the battle over the Bank of the United States, but the controversy drew him closer philosophically to Jefferson. Both men, and most Virginians, distrusted banks and considered finance to be a form of speculative profiteering that would corrupt republican politics. Neither man believed the last paragraph of Article I, Section 8, authorizing Congress "to make all Laws which shall be necessary and proper" for executing its enumerated powers, could be stretched to include the creation of a national bank. Jefferson provided President Washington with a legal opinion opposing the national bank bill. The secretary of state, interestingly enough, began by invoking the Tenth Amendment, reserving to the states and to the people all powers not delegated to the federal government. Jefferson rejected the idea that language giving Congress a responsibility to "promote ... the general Welfare," embedded as it was in Article I, Section 8, empowering Congress to levy taxes, could reasonably be read as a grant of an additional substantive power.[5]

Madison did not believe Hamilton's initiatives, which also included refinancing the national debt, the assumption of state war debts, and the use of federal power to promote manufacturing, enjoyed broad popular support. In his mind, the treasury secretary's successes suggested the limits of the system of checks and balances the Philadelphia convention had built into the Constitution. Madison, in response, put a new emphasis on cultivating and mobilizing public opinion against what he now saw as an overbearing Federalist minority.[6] Gone were his laments about the misdeeds of the state governments. Jefferson, meanwhile, grew increasingly fearful of the "consolidation" of political power and suggested another remedy: revising the state constitutions to make state governments stronger and more democratic. "The only barrier [to federal authority] in their power is a wise government," he wrote to Archibald Stuart. "A weak one will lose ground in every contest."[7]

The outbreak of war in February 1793 between Great Britain and France's revolutionary government provoked a new series of constitutional crises as Hamilton's Federalist bloc rallied to the British cause while a Democratic-Republican faction forming around Jefferson and Madison sympathized with the French. Madison and Jefferson, suspicious of a pro-British neutrality, complained that Washington's Neutrality Proclamation of April 1793 usurped Congress's authority over foreign policy. Jefferson encouraged Madison to enter into an exchange of anonymous essays with Hamilton over the merits of the proclamation and then, gauging the political winds, encouraged him to drop the issue. The public favored neutrality, and no one benefited politically by openly challenging Washington. Madison did not seem to mind the change in strategy.[8]

In the course of the war, the Washington administration negotiated the controversial and far-ranging Jay Treaty with Great Britain. Jefferson and Madison opposed the agreement, but they could not prevent its ratification by the Senate. The treaty created three commissions to resolve issues left undecided by the accord; they were to be funded in part by a congressional appropriation, which gave Madison an opportunity to sabotage the treaty in the House of Representatives. Madison's assault raised two constitutional issues. In light of the Senate's express authority to ratify or reject a treaty, could the House refuse to abide by an international agreement approved by the Senate, and could the House compel the president to provide it with documents related to the treaty negotiations? Citing the debates of the Constitutional Convention, Washington answered both questions in the negative. A frustrated Madison, in a change of position from the Bank of the United States debates, responded by turning to another source to determine the Constitution's meaning: "If we were to look . . . for the meaning of the instrument, beyond the face of the instrument, we must look for it not in the general convention, which proposed, but in the state conventions, which accepted and ratified the constitution." Despite Madison's objections, the House voted, by a narrow margin, to fund the Jay Treaty commissions.[9]

The rapprochement with Great Britain was followed by the XYZ Affair and the Quasi-War, or Undeclared Naval War, with France during the presidency of John Adams. Wartime paranoia and Democratic-Republican opposition to Federalist foreign policy led a Federalist Congress to pass the

Alien and Sedition Acts of 1798, which, among other provisions, gave the president broad discretion to deport aliens and outlawed "false, scandalous and malicious" criticism of Congress or the president. Madison had by then left Congress. Jefferson, ironically, was serving as vice president by virtue of the odd provision in the original Constitution that filled the office with the second-place finisher in the presidential race. Jefferson had lost a close contest to Adams in 1796.[10]

Madison's and Jefferson's response to the Alien and Sedition Acts raised constitutional and political questions that dogged them for the rest of their lives. Madison drafted the Virginia Resolutions for the Virginia assembly. Asserting a right "to interpose for arresting the progress of the evil," the assembly declared the Alien and Sedition Acts to be unconstitutional. It was not altogether clear at the time what consequences would flow from such "interposition," but the Kentucky Resolutions, which Jefferson had written and which were adopted by that state's assembly, proved to be even more problematic. Jefferson argued in his original draft that the Constitution was a compact among the states and that a state had a right to judge the validity of a federal law. "Every state," he wrote, "has a natural right in all cases not within the compact . . . to nullify of their own authority all assumptions of power by others within their limits," and Jefferson's draft declared the federal statutes to be "void." To some readers, moreover, the nullification theory led logically to a right to secede from the union. The resolutions' sponsor in the Kentucky legislature deleted the references to nullification, and Madison persuaded Jefferson to take a more conciliatory approach. Nevertheless, Jefferson's commitment to state sovereignty would become well known, and Madison late in life found himself denying the allegation that they had ever endorsed nullification or secession, except as a matter of natural, not constitutional, law and only in the most extraordinary circumstances.[11]

Madison said the Virginia and Kentucky Resolutions had simply been intended to spur opposition to the Alien and Sedition Acts through ordinary political channels, and while the resolutions were not well received by the majority of the other state assemblies, that is essentially what happened. The Democratic-Republicans earned a reputation as the party of limited federal authority and freedom of expression, won control of Congress, and elevated Jefferson to the presidency in 1801. In his inaugural address, Jefferson struck a moderate tone, emphasizing both majority rule and individual rights, in particular freedom of religion and the press, the right to habeas corpus, and the right to trial by jury. He pledged to support the state governments and "the General Government in its whole constitutional vigor."[12]

Jefferson thought the federal government had grown far too much, and he wanted to reduce its domain to foreign affairs and interstate commerce. "If we can prevent the government," he wrote one correspondent, "from wasting the labors of the people, under the pretense of taking care of them, they must become happy." Accordingly, Jefferson cut the army and navy budgets, eliminated all internal taxes, dismissed a number tax collectors, and launched a plan to pay off the national debt, although he did not try to abolish the Bank of the United States. He also appointed James Madison his secretary of state.[13]

The two most memorable events of Jefferson's presidency, the Louisiana Purchase of 1803 and the Embargo Act of 1807, did not fit nicely with his philosophy of strict construction and limited government. Jefferson believed the acquisition of Louisiana from France would require a constitutional amendment. In July 1803, he sent Madison a fairly detailed amendment providing for the incorporation of the territory into the United States. Madison responded with some proposed revisions and a shorter substitute amendment, but he thought the federal government enjoyed an implied power to expand the nation's boundaries. Article II, Section 2, of the Constitution provided that the president "shall have Power, by and with the Advice and Consent of the Senate, to make Treaties, provided two thirds of the Senators present concur," and nations routinely altered borders by treaty.[14]

Jefferson apparently hoped an amendment and the treaty with France could proceed through Congress simultaneously. When reports from Paris indicated that Napoleon might abandon the treaty if ratification were to be delayed, the president decided to seek a subsequent constitutional amendment, to be effective retroactively. Jefferson believed a public official, in cases of national emergency, sometimes had a duty to take extralegal actions and then "throw himself on the justice of his country." Madison, by contrast, thought an amendment sanctioning the purchase after the fact would do more to undermine the Constitution than simply assuming the transaction was constitutional. By mid-September, Jefferson had apparently accepted Madison's strategy. He remained personally convinced of the need for an amendment, but "if . . . our friends shall think differently, certainly I shall acquiesce with satisfaction; confiding, that the good sense of our country will correct the evil of construction when it shall produce ill effects." After the Senate, which did not share Jefferson's constitutional qualms, approved the purchase of Louisiana by a better than three-to-one vote, he let the issue of a constitutional amendment drop.[15]

In December 1807, Jefferson signed the Embargo Act banning exports and prohibiting the departure of American ships for foreign ports. As the

Napoleonic wars raged in Europe, the British and French had each attempted to restrict the other's trade with the United States. The Embargo Act was an extreme measure by any standard, and the administration never made clear whether it was intended to protect American ships and sailors or to pressure the belligerents to lift their restrictions on American commerce. The act also contributed to President Jefferson's mixed record on civil liberties. Jefferson, for example, remained a staunch defender of freedom of religion, even resisting a proposal to declare a national day of prayer, but the administration's attempts to prohibit illegal trade led to searches and seizures that struck many later critics as egregious violations of the Fourth Amendment. In the closing days of Jefferson's presidency, Congress repealed the embargo and replaced it with the Non-Intercourse Act, prohibiting trade with Great Britain and France only.[16]

Jefferson did not, however, waver in his conviction that a president should serve only two terms, and notwithstanding widespread support for a third term, he refused to run for reelection in 1808, thus helping to establish the two-term tradition for American presidents.[17] The decision came easily. The embargo imbroglio had made his last year in office a miserable one, and in Madison he had a handpicked successor. Madison entered the White House pledging "to support the Constitution, which is the cement of the Union; as well in its limitations as in its authorities." He promised to protect the rights of the states and the rights of the people, especially freedom of religion. He extolled the freedom of the press and, in the republican tradition, warned against the danger of large standing armies. Madison also voiced support for internal improvements by "authorized means," which would be a critical qualifier.[18]

The War of 1812 with Great Britain, and the events leading up to it, dominated Madison's presidency. Although the mild-mannered Virginian was not a particularly effective wartime president, he won praise for his defense of civil liberties, tolerating near-treasonous opposition to the war in Federalist-dominated New England. About as close as he came to violating his principles was to issue, most reluctantly, an occasional call for a voluntary day of prayer. At the end of the war Madison seemed ready to embrace a larger role for the federal government in the nation's economy, but the changes in his position were subtle. In December 1815 he sought a constitutional amendment to allow federal funds to be spent on internal improvements. When Congress passed an internal improvements bill, with no amendment on the books, he vetoed it.[19]

The charter of the First Bank of the United States had expired in 1811. Madison had allowed his secretary of the treasury, Albert Gallatin, to support a recharter bill, but Madison, a longtime foe of the bank, did not personally intervene on its behalf, and the bill failed. However, the difficulty the administration experienced financing the War of 1812 apparently convinced Madison of the need for a national bank, and before he left office Madison signed legislation chartering a Second Bank of the United States. Madison explained his change in position not as an evolution in his own thinking or as his acceptance of a "living Constitution" that could change with the times but as his acquiescence to the contrary views of his fellow citizens. The constitutional question, he told Congress, had been resolved by repeated expressions of support for the bank by the legislative, judicial, and executive branches, "accompanied by indications, in different modes, of a concurrence of the general will of the nation." As he explained in a private memorandum, his critics erred in attributing his change of position to a "change of opinion, instead of precedents superseding opinion."[20]

After Jefferson and Madison retired to Virginia, admirers routinely solicited their views on constitutional questions. During the controversy in 1819 and 1820 over Missouri's admission into the union as a slave state, they agreed that Congress had no authority to ban slavery within a state. Both men now embraced "diffusion," the idea that if slaves were dispersed throughout the nation and not concentrated in a single region, individual slave states would be more prone to abolish slavery. It was a new position for Jefferson, who as a member of the Confederation Congress had sought to ban slavery in the West. At the same time, he and Madison continued to support gradual emancipation and colonization, and Jefferson indicated that it was the one area where he would accept a loose construction of the Constitution, if one was necessary to start a colonization movement.[21]

In the years remaining to them—Jefferson lived until 1826 and Madison until 1836—Madison attempted to defend a moderate nationalism and to explain some of his, and Jefferson's, earlier, less temperate or more ambiguous statements. Madison generally sought to avoid direct challenges to majority opinion that could aggravate already explosive political conflicts. As always, their disagreements did no damage to their relationship. Nearing death in February 1826, Jefferson asked Madison to "take care of me when dead," and Madison tried. Or, as Madison put it, "Allowances ought to be made for a habit in Mr. Jefferson as in others of great genius[,] of expressing in strong and round terms, impressions of the moment." At the height of the controversy over the First Bank of the United States, Jefferson had written Madison that any Virginian who worked for the bank should be executed by the state for treason.[22]

They debated in their correspondence one of the thorniest questions of their earlier years: the proper scope of federal judicial review. Jefferson had not openly challenged the doctrine of judicial review when it was articulated by Chief Justice John Marshall in *Marbury v. Madison* (1803), but as we have seen, Jefferson believed each branch of the federal government should be able to decide constitutional issues for itself, and conflicts between the state and federal governments ought to be resolved by a convention of the states. To him, federal judges had become a "corps of sappers and miners, steadily working to undermine the independent rights of the States, & to consolidate all power in the hands of the government in which they hold such an important freehold estate." The Supreme Court's decision in *M'Culloch v. Maryland* (1819), upholding the constitutionality of the Second Bank of the United States, irritated him, and he was outraged by *Cohens v. Virginia* (1821), in which, Jefferson thought, the Supreme Court had wrongly asserted jurisdiction over the Virginia court of appeals and reversed its decision.[23]

Madison believed that "in a government whose vital principle is responsibility," by which he almost certainly meant responsibility to the people, the legislative and executive departments could not be "completely subjected to the Judiciary." He agreed with Jefferson that the Constitution should be interpreted as it was understood when it was ratified, but he rejected Jefferson's presumption that federal jurisdiction should be limited to cases involving foreigners and citizens of different states. Madison cited federal bankruptcy laws as an example of laws, explicitly sanctioned by the Constitution, that could apply in a case involving citizens from a single state. And while he complained about the broad discretion *M'Culloch v. Maryland* had given Congress, he agreed with the court's exercise of jurisdiction in *Cohens v. Virginia*. Unless the Supreme Court was the ultimate constitutional arbiter, Madison reasoned, federal law would vary from state to state. The mutual dependence of the branches of the federal government would force them to compromise their differences, but the federal and state governments had the resources to act independently. If they disagreed, chaos could result. Madison believed the Constitution intended for the Supreme Court to exercise the power of judicial review and had provided adequate safeguards against its abuse. When abuses occurred, the amendment process would be safer than Jefferson's solution: another constitutional convention. The force of public opinion and improvements in the state courts, Madison predicted, would over time tend to harmonize state and federal jurisprudence.[24]

Madison considered the latitude the court had extended to Congress to be a greater threat to the Constitution than was judicial activism, but he generally did not publicize his concerns. In December 1825, Jefferson sent Madison a petition he had drafted for the Virginia assembly protesting federal support for canal construction. Fearful that Virginians were developing a reputation for obstructionism, Madison persuaded him not to submit it to the legislature. Madison, even though as president he had vetoed an internal improvements bill, now considered the question of "canals, etc." decided. The majority of their fellow Americans seemed convinced of their benefits, and the majority, he wrote Jefferson, must rule. Madison did not think the advocates of internal improvements had usurped power but had only abused Congress's enumerated powers, an abuse that could be combated through the normal political process.[25]

In a similar vein, Madison criticized a resolution of the Virginia assembly declaring protective tariffs to be unconstitutional. Governor William B. Giles had supported the resolution and cited a letter from Jefferson condemning legislation that favored manufacturing interests over agriculture. To Madison, the letter typified Jefferson's tendency to use broad language that could easily be misconstrued. More substantively, as had been the case with the national bank and with internal improvements, history and practice—not, it might be noted, a Supreme Court decision—had settled the constitutional issue for Madison.[26]

Nevertheless, tariffs provoked even greater opposition in the South than did the Bank of the United States or federal judicial review. In response to the protective tariff of 1828, South Carolina lawmakers, led by John C. Calhoun, developed the theory that a state convention could declare a federal statute unconstitutional and thereby null and void. If the other states disagreed, the nullifying state could leave the union. In 1792, Madison had questioned the wisdom of a protective tariff but had never doubted its constitutionality, and he saw the nullification theory as a threat to the union. The toughest battle he fought in his last years was to rebut the charge that the Virginia and Kentucky Resolutions had endorsed nullification. He had contributed to his dilemma by not explaining how, in the Virginia Resolutions, a state's "interposition" could be implemented. "It was not necessary for the object & reasoning of the resolution," he wrote during the nullification crisis, "that the mode should be pointed out." After leaving the White House, Madison typically avoided becoming publicly engaged in political controversies, but nullification and the prospect of disunion and civil war troubled him so deeply that he wrote several letters in opposition and published what were for him rare essays in Washington's *National Intelligencer* and in the prestigious *North American Review*.[27]

As always, constitutional law was made in the crucible of political controversy. Both Jefferson and Madison typically favored a strict construction of the Constitution as it was understood when it was adopted. Jefferson never reconciled himself to judicial review as practiced by Federalist judges. Concerned about stability and predictability, Madison, unlike Jefferson, yielded to precedents expanding the authority of the federal government, including the federal courts. In the interest in civic engagement, Jefferson would defer, as much as possible, to local majorities. In the interest of preserving the union, Madison submitted more willingly to national opinion. Jefferson's last letter expressed his optimism that "all eyes are opened, or opening to the rights of man." Madison's final public statement was a call "that the Union of the States be cherished and perpetuated." They were fitting epitaphs.[28]

NOTES

ABBREVIATIONS

AJC Lester J. Cappon, ed., *The Complete Correspondence between Thomas Jefferson and Abigail and John Adams*, 2 vols. (Chapel Hill: University of North Carolina Press, 1959)

JCC Worthington C. Ford, ed., *The Journals of the Continental Congress, 1776–1789*, 34 vols. (Washington, D.C.: Government Printing Office, 1931–44)

JM James Madison

JMW Jack N. Rakove, *James Madison, Writings* (New York: Library of America, 1999)

JPW Joyce Appleby and Terrance Ball, eds., *Jefferson: Political Writings* (New York: Cambridge University Press, 1999)

PGM Robert A. Rutland, ed., *The Papers of George Mason*, 3 vols. (Chapel Hill: University of North Carolina Press, 1970)

PJM William T. Hutchinson and William M. E. Rachel, eds., *The Papers of James Madison*, 17 vols. (Chicago: University of Chicago Press; Charlottesville: University of Virginia Press, 1962–91)

PTJ Julian Boyd et al., eds., *The Papers of Thomas Jefferson*, 43 vols. (Princeton, N.J.: Princeton University Press, 1950–2017)

ROL James Morton Smith, ed., *The Republic of Letters: The Correspondence between Thomas Jefferson and James Madison, 1776–1826*, 3 vols. (New York: W. W. Norton, 1995)

SWJM Ralph Ketcham, ed., *Selected Writings of James Madison* (Indianapolis: Hackett, 2006)

TJ Thomas Jefferson

TJW Merrill D. Peterson, ed., *Thomas Jefferson, Writings* (New York: Library of America, 1984)

WJM Galliard Hunt, ed., *The Writings of James Madison*, 9 vols. (New York: G. P. Putnam's Sons, 1900–1910)

1. The best introduction to the historiographical debate is Gibson, *Interpreting the Founding*. For more detail, see Gibson's *Understanding the Founding*; and Young and Nobles, *Whose American Revolution Was It?*

2. John Quincy Adams quoted in *ROL*, 1:2–3. For recent expressions of a similar view, see Rakove, *Politician Thinking*, 120; and Schwarz, *Thomas Jefferson*, 26–27.

3. Rakove, *Politician Thinking*, 126.

4. See Robertson, *Constitution and America's Destiny*, 3.

5. JM to Noah Webster, 12 October 1804, Brugger, *Papers of James Madison, Secretary of States Series*, 8:160.

6. See generally Bailey, *James Madison*.

CHAPTER 1

1. TJ to John Harvie, 14 January 1760, *TJW*, 733.

2. "Autobiography," *TJW*, 3–4; Cunningham, *In Pursuit of Reason*, 1–4.

3. "Autobiography," *TJW*, 3–4; Wilson, "Jefferson's Library."

4. Malone, *Thomas Jefferson*, 1:44; "Autobiography," *TJW*, 4; TJ to Martha Jefferson, 21 May 1787, *TJW*, 896–97.

5. "Autobiography," *TJW*, 4; TJ to John Page, 25 December, 1762, ibid., 733–36; Malone, *Thomas Jefferson*, 1:53; Cunningham, *In Pursuit of Reason*, 4–9; Richard, *Founders and the Classics*, 22.

6. "Autobiography," *TJW*, 4–5; TJ to John Sauderson, 31 August 1820, in Bergh, *Writings of Thomas Jefferson*, 1:165–66.

7. Peterson, *Thomas Jefferson and the New Nation*, 12–13; Roeber, *Faithful Magistrates*, xix; TJ to Thomas Mann Randolph Jr., 30 May 1790, *PTJ*, 16:449.

8. Friedman, *History of American Law*, 56; Dill, *George Wythe*, 9; Blackburn, *George Wythe*, 12.

9. Dill, *George Wythe*, 15–19, 24; Blackburn, *George Wythe*, 32–44, 50. On "treating" voters, see Sydnor, *American Revolutionaries*, 53–59.

10. Brown, *American Aristides*, 75–79.

11. Ibid., 75–77; Malone, *Thomas Jefferson*, 1:65; Dumbauld, *Thomas Jefferson and the Law*, 10–15.

12. TJ to John Page, 25 December 1762, *TJW*, 733–36; TJ to JM, 17 February 1826, *ROL*, 3:1964–67.

13. Peterson, *Thomas Jefferson and the New Nation*, 17–18; Pocock, *Ancient Constitution*, vii, 38–46; Corwin, *"Higher Law" Background*, 24–25; Yirush, *Settlers, Liberty, and Empire*, 10.

14. Corwin, *"Higher Law" Background*, 41–50. In *Dr. Bonham's Case*, the court refused to allow the London College of Physicians to punish Dr. Bonham, allegedly pursuant to an act of Parliament, for practicing medicine within the city without a license. Bernard Bailyn has argued that Coke simply meant a court would not interpret a statute to give it an unreasonable effect in violation of existing legal doctrine. Bailyn, *Ideological Origins*, 175–84.

15. Corwin, *"Higher Law" Background*, 54, 73–74.

16. Konig, "Thomas Jefferson and the Law," 350–52; Hayes, *Road to Monticello*, 90. Wirt quoted in Brown, *American Aristides*, 79; TJ quoted in Hayes, *Road to Monticello*, 89.

17. Hayes, *Road to Monticello*, 86; "Autobiography," *TJW*, 5; Dewey, *Thomas Jefferson*, 2–3, 121.

18. Randolph, *History of Virginia*, 182–83.

19. Cunningham, *In Pursuit of Reason*, 12; Bernstein, *Thomas Jefferson*, 8; "Autobiography," *TJW*, 53; TJ to Thomas Turpin, 5 February 1769, *PTJ*, 1:23–25; TJ to John Garland Jefferson, 11 June 1790, *TJW*, 966–68; TJ to John Minor, 30 August 1814, in Looney, *Papers of Thomas Jefferson, Retirement Series*, 7:625–31.

Jefferson also advised a future son-in-law who was contemplating college that when it came to the study of history, "it would be a waste of time to attend a professor of this. It is to be acquired from books," by which he meant books by authors from the period in question. "An author who writes of his own times or of times near his own presents in his own ideas & manner the best picture of the moment of which he writes." TJ to Thomas Mann Randolph Jr., 27 August 1786, *TJW*, 860–64.

20. TJ to John Page, 21 February 1770, *PTJ*, 1:34–37; TJ to Thomas Adams, 20 February 1771, ibid., 61; Dumbauld, *Thomas Jefferson and the Law*, 88; "Autobiography," *TJW*, 5.

21. "Autobiography," *TJW*, 5–6.

22. Cunningham, *In Pursuit of Reason*, 16–17; Hayes, *Road to Monticello*, 75; Chinard, *Commonplace Book*, 52–65.

23. Virginia Nonimportation Resolutions, 17 May 1769, *PTJ*, 1:27–31; "Autobiography," *TJW*, 5–6; Selby, *Revolution in Virginia*, 8–9. Primary authorship of the Virginia nonimportation agreement has traditionally been attributed to George Mason, but not without some scholarly debate. See the editorial notes and related documents in *PGM*, 1:93–113; and Broadwater, *George Mason*, 47–53.

24. Bernstein, *Thomas Jefferson*, 19–20; Randolph, *History of Virginia*, 182; "Autobiography," *TJW*, 6–7.

25. "Autobiography," *TJW*, 6–7.

26. For a thorough treatment of the subject, see Carp, *Defiance of the Patriots*.

27. Association of Members of the Late House of Burgesses, 27 May 1774, *PTJ*, 1:107–9; "Autobiography," *TJW*, 7–9; Selby, *Revolution in Virginia*, 8–10; Bernstein, *Thomas Jefferson*, 20–22.

28. Peterson, *Thomas Jefferson and the New Nation*, 45–50; McCoy, "Political Economy," 102. The ambitious reading list Jefferson sent to Robert Skipwith, another young man who requested his advice, in 1771 sheds some light on his preferences and priorities. Fiction and poetry represented by far the largest category on the list, a canon of Western literature ranging from the *Iliad* and the *Odyssey* to Molière and Dryden. Ancient and modern history made up another substantial section. He listed only three volumes under law: Lord Kames's *Principles of Equity*, Blackstone's *Commentaries*, and a legal dictionary. The entry on religion was longer. The section on "Politicks, Trade" was relatively modest; it consisted of Locke's *Two Treatises of Government*, Montesquieu's *The Spirit of the Laws* and his *Rise and Fall of the Roman Government*, Algernon Sidney's *Discourses on Government*, the political writings of Lord Bolingbroke, Marontel's *Belisarius*, Stuart's *Political Economy*, and Petty's *Political Arithmetic*. TJ to Robert Skipwith, 3 August 1771, *TJW*, 740–45.

29. Malone, *Thomas Jefferson*, 1:101–4. See also Gay, *Enlightenment*, 2:558–68.

30. TJ to John Adams, 28 October 1813, *TJW*, 1304–10.

31. Hayes, *Road to Monticello*, 82–85, 112–13; Perkins, Buchanan, and Brown to TJ, *PTJ*, 1:33–34.

32. McCoy, "Political Economy," 103; Chinard, *Commonplace Book*, 202–32.

33. Ryan, *On Politics*, 2:465–89; Buckley, "Political Theology," 89–91.

34. Chinard, *Commonplace Book*, 33–37, 284; Peterson, *Thomas Jefferson and the New Nation*, 61–62; TJ to Francois D'Ivernois, 6 February 1795, *TJW*, 1022–25.

35. Wood, *Creation of the American Republic*, 227–28; Ryan, *On Politics*, 2:499–518.

36. Cottret, *Bolingbroke's Political Writings*, 202–5; Wilson, *Jefferson's Literary Commonplace Book*, 4–5. Jefferson also apparently took from Bolingbroke the idea that "history is philosophy teaching by examples." In *On the Study and Uses of History*, Bolingbroke attributed the thought to Dionysius of Halicarnassus, who had taken a version of it from Thucydides. See Roeber, *Faithful Magistrates*, 252–53.

37. Cottret, *Bolingbroke's Political Writings*, 202–3.

38. Peterson, *Thomas Jefferson and the New Nation*, 55–56; Herman, *How the Scots Invented the Modern World*, 76–84. See generally Hutcheson, *Essay on the Nature and Conduct of the Passions and Affections* and *Inquiry into the Original of Our Ideas*.

39. Hutcheson, *Inquiry into the Original of Our Ideas*, 9; TJ to Peter Carr, 10 August 1787, *TJW*, 900–906.

40. Herman, *How the Scots Invented the Modern World*, 91–107; Wilson, "Jefferson's Library," 161. See generally Kames, *Principles of Equity*.

41. Colbourn, *Lamp of Experience*, 216–19; May, "Enlightenment"; Chinard, *Commonplace Book*, 44, 48–49.

42. Richard, *Founders and the Classics*, 26–30, 187–95; Wood, *Radicalism of the American Revolution*, 203, 354–55, 403n35.

43. TJ to Isaac Tiffany, 26 August 1816, in Looney, *Papers of Thomas Jefferson, Retirement Series*, 10:349; Richard, *Founders and the Classics*, 119, 156–64, 229; Reinhold, "Classical World." See generally the essays collected in Onuf and Cole, *Thomas Jefferson*.

44. See Beitzinger, "Political Theorist"; and Peterson, *Thomas Jefferson and the New Nation*, 28–31.

45. Ketcham, *James Madison*, 59–60; Newman, "James Madison's Journey," 30–31.

46. Burstein and Isenberg, *Madison and Jefferson*, 6; Newman, "James Madison's Journey," 22–24; Ketcham, *James Madison*, 8–14; A. Miller, "Madison, Nelly Conway."

47. Adair, "James Madison's Autobiography," 197; *PJM*, 1:26n26, 35; Cheney, *James Madison*, 21. Madison quoted in Newman, "James Madison's Journey," 24. See generally Swanson, *Education of James Madison*.

48. Adair, "James Madison's Autobiography," 197; Ketcham, *James Madison*, 13.

49. Adair, "James Madison's Autobiography," 197; *PJM*, 1:164; Cheney, *James Madison*, 17–18; Brant, *James Madison*, 1:106–9; Ketcham, *James Madison*, 51–53.

50. Ketcham, *James Madison*, 23–24; Adair, "James Madison's Autobiography," 193n9; Cheney, *James Madison*, 23; T. Miller, *Selected Writings of John Witherspoon*, 20–24.

51. Newman, "James Madison's Journey," 24–25, 27–30; Noll, *Princeton and the Republic*, 32.

52. Elkins and McKitrick, *Age of Federalism*, 85; May, *Enlightenment in America*, 61–63; Noll, *Princeton and the Republic*, 7, 28; Morrison, *John Witherspoon*, 10, 51.

53. Herman, *How the Scots Invented the Modern World*, 194–95; T. Miller, *Selected Writings of John Witherspoon*, 7–11, 214; Newman, "James Madison's Journey," 25; Rankin, "Witherspoon, John"; Mailer, *John Witherspoon's American Revolution*, 29–36.

54. T. Miller, *Selected Writings of John Witherspoon*, 139, 193, 213.

55. Ibid., 11; Ketcham, *James Madison*, 38; Morrison, *John Witherspoon*, 52–60. Witherspoon quoted in Noll, *Princeton and the Republic*, 38–42.

56. JM to James Madison Sr., 30 September 1769, *PJM*, 1:45–48, and 23 July 1770, 1:49–51; Noll, *Princeton and the Republic*, 50. Nine Princeton alumni signed the Constitution, as opposed to four from Yale and three from Harvard. See T. Miller, *Selected Writings of James Witherspoon*, 20–24.

Student activism at Princeton irritated some traditionalists. One critic complained the school was promoting principles "'perhaps injurious to our happy Constitution.'" In October 1772, after Madison had graduated, the Board of Trustees, apparently fearing reprisals from the royal governor, William Franklin, ordered the president to begin censoring student commencement addresses. See Cohen and Gerlach, "Princeton in the Coming of the American Revolution," 78–79.

57. JM to Thomas Martin, 10 August 1769, *PJM*, 1:42–44; Mattern, "Brackenridge, Hugh Henry"; Alley, "Bradford, William"; Egerton, "Freneau, Philip M."

58. T. Miller, *Selected Writings of John Witherspoon*, 34–35; Brant, *James Madison*, 1:97–99; Adair, "James Madison's Autobiography," 197.

59. Brant, *James Madison*, 1:173; Morrison, *John Witherspoon*, 57; Ketcham, "James Madison and Religion."

60. JM to William Bradford, 9 November 1772, *PJM*, 1:74–77, 28 April 1773, 1:83–84, and 1 December 1773, 1:100–102.

61. Ibid., 25 September 1773, 1:95–97.

62. *Ibid.*, 1:97n2; Adair, "James Madison's Autobiography," 198; Sheldon, *Political Philosophy of James Madison*, xvi.

63. JM to William Bradford, 28 April 1773, *PJM*, 1:83–85, and 24 January 1774, 1:104–8; Adair, "James Madison's Autobiography," 198; Signer, *Becoming James Madison*, 74–76. See generally Bilder, "James Madison."

Lynne Cheney suggests Madison discarded his orthodox faith as his epilepsy improved, and he decided he was not demon-possessed. Cheney, *James Madison*, 39–40. It is a novel theory.

64. JM to William Bradford, 1 December 1773, *PJM*, 1:100–102.

65. Adair, "James Madison's Autobiography," 198; JM to William Bradford, 24 January 1774, *PJM*, 1:104–8, and 1 April 1774, 1:111–14. For an argument that Madison's "animating principle was not freedom *from* religion, but freedom *for* religion," see Loconte, "Faith and the Founding."

66. JM to William Bradford, 24 January 1774, *PJM*, 1:104–8, and 1 April 1774, 1:111–14; Adair, "James Madison's Autobiography," 198–9.

67. William Bradford to JM, 25 December 1773, *PJM*, 1:102–4; JM to William Bradford, 24 January 1774, ibid., 1:104–8; JM to William Bradford, 1 July 1774, ibid., 1:114–17; Cheney, *James Madison*, 45.

68. "Autobiography," *TJW*, 9–10; Malone, *Thomas Jefferson*, 1:173–75.

69. "Autobiography," *TJW*, 9–10; appendix I, *PTJ*, 1:669–76; "Instructions by the Virginia Convention to Their Deputies," 6 August 1774, in Van Schreeven, Scribner, and Tarter, *Revolutionary Virginia*, 1:141–44, 236–39; "Convention Association," 6 August 1774, ibid., 1:230–35.

70. Randolph, *History of Virginia*, 204–5; Cunningham, *In Pursuit of Reason*, 26–31; Malone, *Thomas Jefferson*, 1:180–82. Unconfirmed reports of publication also came from New York, Boston, and Norfolk. On the radicalism of *A Summary View*, see Wood, *Friends Divided*, 92–93.

71. *A Summary View of the Rights of British America*, TJW, 105–7. The Americans' basis for asserting "their constitutional rights" is stated concisely in a brief document that was probably written by Jefferson shortly before the August 1774 convention: they claimed the privilege to make laws for themselves "as the common rights of mankind, confirmed by the political constitutions they have respectively assumed, and also by several charters of compact from the crown." Declaration of Rights, circa 26 July 1774, *PTJ*, 1:119–20.

72. *A Summary View of the Rights of British America*, TJW, 107–11, 115.

73. Ibid., 115–18.

74. Ibid., 119–20.

75. Ibid., 121–22.

76. Appendix I, *PTJ*, 1:670. See Malone, *Thomas Jefferson*, 1:181–89; Hayes, *Road to Monticello*, 153–56; Dumbauld, *Thomas Jefferson and the Law*, 18; Cunningham, *In Pursuit of Reason*, 26–31; Sheldon, *Political Philosophy of Thomas Jefferson*, 36–40; Mayer, *Constitutional Thought*, 390; Malone, "Life of Thomas Jefferson," 3; and Beeman, "American Revolution," 31–33. See generally Ray, "Thomas Jefferson and the *Rights of British North America*."

When Jefferson said only Wythe agreed with him, he may have meant only Wythe agreed that the British king had no authority to dispose of land in America, or in other words, Americans did not take their titles from the monarch. See Steele, *Thomas Jefferson and American Nationhood*, 28–29.

77. JM to William Bradford, 1 July 1774, *PJM*, 1:114–17, 117n7. Madison quoted in Greene, *Constitutional Origins*, 188.

78. Corwin, *"Higher Law" Background*, 77n33; Malone, *Thomas Jefferson*, 1:89–95; Bland, *The Colonel Dismounted* (1764), in Bailyn, *Pamphlets of the American Revolution*, 292–354; Bland, *An Inquiry into the Rights of the British Colonies* (1766), in Jensen, *Tracts of the American Revolution*, 108–26. Bland wrote *The Colonel Dismounted* during the controversy over the Two-Penny Act, an attempt by the House of Burgesses to regulate the salaries of the established clergy that was overruled by officials in London. *An Inquiry into the Rights of the British Colonies* protested the Stamp Act. See generally Greene, *Constitutional Origins*, 79–92. For a recent treatment of Bland's thought, see Yirush, *Settlers, Liberty, and Empire*, 175–78, 229–33.

79. Hopkins, *The Rights of the Colonies Examined* (1764), in Bailyn, *Pamphlets of the American Revolution*, 500–522; Randolph, *History of Virginia*, 204–5; Fairfax Resolves, 18 July 1774, *PGM*, 1:201–10; Middlekauff, *Glorious Cause*, 155–56.

80. "The British American, VII," Rind's *Virginia Gazette*, 14 July 1774, in Van Schreeven, Scribner, and Tarter, *Revolutionary Virginia*, 1:182–87; Yirush, *Settlers, Liberty, and Empire*, 237–39. For more of Thomson Mason's revolutionary writings, see Van Schreeven, Scribner, and Tarter, *Revolutionary Virginia*, 1:187–203. See also McGill, "Meteor and a Generous Mind."

81. See Labaree et al., *Papers of Benjamin Franklin*, for the evolution of Franklin's thinking: Benjamin Franklin to Lord Kames, 25 February 1767, 14:68–69; Franklin to William Franklin, 13 March 1768, 15:75–76; "Arguments Pro and Con," circa 18–20 October 1768, 15:234–35; Franklin to Jacques Barbau-Dubourg, 2 October 1770, 17:233–34; Franklin to William Strahan, 29 November 1769, 16:243–44; and "Marginalia in a Pamphlet by Josiah Tucker," circa 1770, 17:348–400. See also Greene, *Constitutional Origins*, 52–53, 120–21.

82. Greene, *Constitutional Origins*, 122, 256–61; Valerius Poplicola to *Boston Gazette*, 28 October 1771, in Cushing, *Writings of Sam Adams*, 2:261; *Novanglus* (1774), in Thompson, *Revolutionary Writings of John Adams*, 171–72, 182, 221–31; "To the Inhabitants of Great Britain," September 1774, in McRee, *Life and Correspondence of James Iredell*, 1:205–20.

Although Adams eventually denied Parliament's authority over the colonies, in *Novanglus* he found, in the words of Joseph Ellis, "a complex web of overlapping precedents and contested jurisdictions," as opposed to Jefferson's straightforward story of a struggle to preserve ancient Saxon liberties. J. Ellis, *American Sphinx*, 33.

83. *Considerations on the Nature and Extent of the Legislative Authority of the British Parliament* (1774), in Hall and Hall, *Collected Works of James Wilson*, 1:2–31; Greene, *Constitutional Origins*, 162–63. Apologists for Parliament invoked the idea of "virtual representation": the concept that Parliament represented everyone in the empire whether or not a particular individual could vote for a member of the House of Commons. Plausible in England, where few men could vote and constituencies were shaped with no regard to the rule of "one person, one vote," virtual representation made no sense to Americans, where the right to vote was more widely distributed and electoral districts did not vary as greatly in population. See Reid, *Constitutional History*, 45.

84. Chinard, *Commonplace Book*, 39; Becker, *Declaration of Independence*, 105–13; Peterson, *Thomas Jefferson and the New Nation*, 37–38.

85. Heineman et al., *Old Dominion*, 113–14; Coleman, *American Revolution*, 33–34.

86. Reid, *Constitutional History*, 74–75; Randolph, *History of Virginia*, 166–67.

87. Becker, *Declaration of Independence*, 80–87; Peterson, *Thomas Jefferson and the New Nation*, 74–77; Greene, *Constitutional Origins*, 115.

88. Reid, *Constitutional History*, 32–34, 79–84. See McIlwain, *American Revolution*.

89. Jack Greene sees three "constitutions" in play in the mid-1700s: the colonial constitutions, an imperial constitution, and a constitution for the British Isles. See Greene, *Constitutional Origins*, xiv–xv, 177–78. See also Reid, *Constitutional History*, 5–24; Greene, "From the Perspective of Law"; and Yirush, *Settlers, Liberty, and Empire*, 21–26.

90. Greene, *Constitutional Origins*, 47–48; Pocock, *Ancient Constitution*, 49–50, 241; Reid, *Constitutional History*, 56.

91. Sheldon, *Political Philosophy of Thomas Jefferson*, 27–29, 34–35. See also Peterson, *Thomas Jefferson and the New Nation*, 56–61. One leading Jefferson biographer has been especially critical, calling *A Summary View* "an elaborate and largely mythical version of English history." J. Ellis, *American Sphinx*, 31.

92. Malone, *Thomas Jefferson*, 1:193; Cunningham, *In Pursuit of Reason*, 24–25.

CHAPTER 2

1. JM to William Bradford, 23 August 1774, *PJM*, 1:120–22, and 26 November 1774, 1:129–31; Brant, *James Madison*, 1:145–46; Ketcham, *James Madison*, 63; JCC, 1:75–80.

2. JM to William Bradford, 20 January 1775, *PJM*, 1:134–38, and 28 July 1775, 1:159–62; Brant, *James Madison*, 1:162–67.

3. JM to William Bradford, 9 May 1775, *PJM*, 1:144–45; Brant, *James Madison*, 1:178–84; Burstein and Isenberg, *Madison and Jefferson*, 19–20; Ketcham, *James Madison*, 64–65.

4. JM to William Bradford, 26 November 1774, *PJM*, 1:129–31, and 19 June 1775, 1:153; Cheney, *James Madison*, 50–51. See Holton, *Forced Founders*, 148–61.

5. JM to William Bradford, 19 June 1775, *PJM*, 1:151–54, and 9 May 1775, 1:144–46; Militia Commission, 2 October 1775, ibid., 1:163; Adair, "James Madison's Autobiography," 199.

6. TJ to William Small, 7 May 1775, *PTJ*, 1:165–67; TJ to Francis Eppes, 26 June 1775, ibid., 1:174–75.

7. Virginia Resolutions on Lord North's Conciliatory Proposal, 10 June 1775, ibid., 1:170–74; Hayes, *Road to Monticello*, 165; "Autobiography," *TJW*, 11.

8. Editorial note, *PTJ*, 1:169; Peterson, *Thomas Jefferson and the New Nation*, 80–81; Meacham, *Thomas Jefferson*, 88–89; John Adams to Timothy Pickering, 22 August 1822, *JPW*, 609–11. The Virginia convention was essentially the House of Burgesses meeting without the sanction of the royal governor.

9. Declaration of the Causes and Necessity of Taking Up Arms, *PTJ*, 1:187–219.

10. Ibid.; Shain, *Declaration of Independence in Historical Context*, 256–76; J. Ellis, *American Sphinx*, 39–42; "Autobiography," *TJW*, 12. The various drafts are reprinted in *JCC*, 2:128–57.

11. Peterson, *Thomas Jefferson and the New Nation*, 82; Hayes, *Road to Monticello*, 171; Shain, *Declaration of Independence in Historical Context*, 319–24; Resolutions of Congress on Lord North's Conciliatory Proposal, *PTJ*, 1:225–33.

12. TJ to John Randolph, 25 August 1775, *PTJ*, 1:240–43, and 29 November 1775, 1:268–70; Meacham, *Thomas Jefferson*, 93–99.

13. Refutation of the Argument That the Colonies Were Established at the Expense of the British Nation, *PTJ*, 1:277–85.

14. TJ to George Gilmer, 5 July 1775, ibid., 1:185–86; Malone, *Thomas Jefferson*, 1:190–91.

15. Annotated Copy of Franklin's Proposed Articles of Confederation, *PTJ*, 1:177–82; Draft of Report on the Powers of a Committee of Congress to Sit during Recess, 15 December 1775, ibid., 1:272–73.

16. *JCC*, 3:403–4; W. P. Adams, *First American Constitutions*, 59, 72–73.

17. *JCC*, 4:342, 357–58; W. P. Adams, *First American Constitutions*, 60–61; Resolution of the Virginia Convention Calling upon Congress for a Declaration of Independence, 15 May 1776, in Mays, *Letters and Papers of Edmund Pendleton*, 1:178–79.

18. TJ to Thomas Nelson, 16 May 1776, *PTJ*, 1:292–93; Beeman, *Our Lives*, 383–86; Wood, *Creation of the American Republic*, 128; Maier, *American Scripture*, 46–47.

19. J. Ellis, *American Sphinx*, 47–48; Peterson, *Thomas Jefferson and the New Nation*, 100–107; Bailyn, *Ideological Origins*, 193; Wood, *Creation of the American Republic*, 265–66, 273–75; W. P. Adams, *First American Constitutions*, 18–19. Another consideration made written constitutions imperative. Americans had to create new regimes immediately. They could not rely on tradition or give new customs time to develop.

20. J. Ellis, *American Sphinx*, 47–48; Mayer, *Constitutional Thought*, 47.

21. Thompson, *Revolutionary Writings of John Adams*, 286–93. Besides the problem of amendments, *Thoughts on Government* left two other vexing issues unresolved. First, what exactly would the reconstituted governments do? Adams suggested they should provide for the militia and "the liberal education of youth, especially of the lower class," and possibly adopt sumptuary laws, but he went no further. Ibid., 292. Second, he failed to include a bill of rights or any specific provisions to safeguard individual liberties.

22. Draft Constitution, June 1776, *TJW*, 336–37.

23. Ibid., 338–40.

24. Selby, *Revolution in Virginia*, 177; Cunningham, *In Pursuit of Reason*, 43–45; TJ to Edmund Pendleton, 26 August 1776, *TJW*, 755. Gordon Wood has recently observed that

Jefferson's proposal for the Senate "expressed an early, uncharacteristic mistrust of the people." Wood, *Friends Divided*, 110.

25. TJ to Edmund Pendleton, 26 August 1776, *TJW*, 755–56. Jefferson would later reconsider his position on property requirements. As Gordon Wood has written, "Both Madison and Jefferson were baffled by the apparent inability of the people to perceive the truly talented and were thus compelled reluctantly to endorse property as the best possible source of distinction in the new republic." Wood, *Creation of the American Republic*, 218.

26. Draft Constitution, June 1776, *TJW*, 340–41. Somewhat oddly perhaps, Jefferson placed Virginia's members of Congress in the executive branch, although they were selected by the lower house of the state legislature. They were to serve one-year terms and then be out of office for at least a year before being eligible for another term.

27. Ibid., 342–43; TJ to Edmund Pendleton, 26 August 1776, *TJW*, 757; R. Ellis, "Constitutionalism," 121.

28. Draft Constitution, June 1776, *TJW*, 338–45. One study of Revolutionary constitution-making has found Jefferson's treatment of individual rights to be "the most strikingly original sections" of his draft constitution, suggesting that "like Locke, Jefferson felt that the proper function of a majority of the people was to guard human rights rather than to formulate political power." Douglass, *Rebels and Democrats*, 298.

29. Peterson, *Thomas Jefferson and the New Nation*, 100–107; Bernstein, "Thomas Jefferson and Constitutionalism," 422–23; TJ to Edmund Pendleton, 26 August 1776, *TJW*, 756; Draft Constitution, June 1776, *TJW*, 341. Jefferson's estimate of the number of eligible voters may have been too low. See W. P. Adams, *First American Constitutions*, 206.

30. *PTJ*, 1:345, 354, 364; Peterson, *Thomas Jefferson and the New Nation*, 100–107; Mayer, *Constitutional Thought*, 58.

31. J. Ellis, *American Sphinx*, 47; McDonnell, *Politics of War*, 231; editorial note, *PTJ*, 1:329–37; Malone, *Thomas Jefferson*, 1:235–40; Beeman, "American Revolution." For more on the self-confidence of Virginia's elite, see Wood, *Friends Divided*, 131.

32. Certificate of Election, 25 April 1776, *PJM*, 1:165; Adair, "James Madison's Autobiography," 199; George Mason to Richard Henry Lee, 18 May 1776, *PGM*, 1:271–72.

33. Edmund Pendleton to TJ, 24 May 1776, in Mays, *Letters and Papers of Edmund Pendleton*, 1:180–81; Ketcham, *James Madison*, 71. On Mason, see Broadwater, *George Mason*.

34. Selby, *Revolution in Virginia*, 100–101; First Draft of the Virginia Declaration of Rights, circa 20–26 May 1776, *PGM*, 1:277. See also annotation, *PGM*, 1:279–82.

35. First Draft of the Virginia Declaration of Rights, circa 20–26 May 1776, *PGM*, 1:277–78.

36. Ibid., 1:278.

37. Ketcham, *James Madison*, 68–73; First Draft of the Virginia Declaration of Rights, circa 20–26 May 1776, *PGM*, 1:278.

38. Broadwater, *George Mason*, 83; Committee Draft of the Virginia Declaration of Rights, 27 May 1776, *PGM*, 1:281–86.

39. Editorial note, *PGM*, 1:274–76; Randolph, *History of Virginia*, 234–35.

40. Annotation, *PGM*, 1:289–90.

41. Randolph, *History of Virginia*, 254–55. Wartime conditions may explain the convention's tolerance of ex post facto laws and bills of attainder, legislative as opposed to judicial findings of guilt, which were not expressly prohibited by the Declaration of Rights.

Raids led by the Tory Josiah Phillips would, by 1778, convince both Henry and Jefferson of the need for extrajudicial criminal penalties in some cases.

42. Editorial note, *PJM*, 1:170–72; Adair, "James Madison's Autobiography," 199; Bailyn, *Ideological Origins*, 246–72. On Mason's views on church-state relations, see Broadwater, *George Mason*, 86, 89–90, 117–20.

43. *PJM*, 1:174; Brant, *James Madison*, 1:242–50.

44. *PJM*, 1:174–75; Final Draft of the Virginia Declaration of Rights, 12 June 1776, *PGM*, 1:287–91.

45. Brant, *James Madison*, 1:243; Selby, *Revolution in Virginia*, 109–10; editorial note, *PJM*, 1:170–72; *PJM*, 1:179n9; W. P. Adams, *First American Constitutions*, 144–45; Randolph, *History of Virginia*, 255; annotation, *PGM*, 1:289–91. See generally Burstein and Isenberg, *Madison and Jefferson*, 49–50.

46. Editorial note, *PGM*, 1:295–97; Mason's Plan for the Virginia Constitution of 1776, 8–10 June 1776, ibid., 1:299–304; Selby, *Revolution in Virginia*, 112–17.

47. See Peterson, *Thomas Jefferson and the New Nation*, 83–84; Kruman, *Between Authority and Liberty*, ix, 36–37, 155–56; W. P. Adams, *First American Constitutions*, 243–45; and Randolph, *History of Virginia*, 252.

48. Mason's Plan for the Virginia Constitution of 1776, 8–10 June 1776, *PGM*, 1:299–302.

49. Final Draft of the Virginia Constitution of 1776, *PGM*, 1:304–9; Selby, *Revolution in Virginia*, 117. The final draft also imposed term limits on senators, in addition to the term limit on the governor, "making it the first to include detailed prohibitions against reelection." W. P. Adams, *First American Constitutions*, 253.

50. Randolph, *History of Virginia*, 256. Randolph thought it noteworthy that delegates from west of the Blue Ridge did not complain that electing members of the lower house by county would leave their region underrepresented in the assembly.

51. George Wythe to TJ, 27 July 1776, *PTJ*, 1:476–77; Draft Constitution for Virginia, June 1776, *TJW*, 336–45; Final Draft of the Virginia Constitution of 1776, *PGM*, 1:304–9. See also Selby, *Revolution in Virginia*, 119–21. The term "grievance" when used in a petition meant, strictly speaking, "the denial of a constitutional right." Wills, *Inventing America*, 59.

52. Annotation, *PGM*, 1:309–10; Selby, *Revolution in Virginia*, 112–17.

53. Selby, *Revolution in Virginia*, 110–11; TJ to Samuel Kercheval, 12 July 1816, *TJW*, 1396. Complicating the question of the constitution's legal status was the convention's failure to provide a procedure for amendments. Edmund Randolph at one point even suggested that an unwritten constitution was superior to a written one because it could be changed "without agitating the people," implying that amending a written constitution would be a virtual act of revolution. The issue would be resolved over the course of the American Revolution. See Randolph, *History of Virginia*, 251–55. See generally W. P. Adams, *First American Constitutions*, 4–8, 139–40.

54. *JCC*, 5:425; Shain, *Declaration of Independence in Historical Context*, 370–71, 410–12, 461.

55. "Autobiography," *TJW*, 12–18; Notes of Proceedings in the Continental Congress, 7 June–1 August 1776, *PTJ*, 1:311; Shain, *Declaration of Independence in Historical Context*, 213, 375, 410, 441; Maier, *American Scripture*, 38.

56. "Autobiography," *TJW*, 13; Notes of Proceedings in the Continental Congress, 7 June–1 August 1776, *PTJ*, 1:313–14. Although apparently unstated in the debates, the movement toward independence had raised the expectations of the less affluent "out of doors." More moderate members of Congress may have worried that a full-scale revolution

might unleash demands for greater popular participation in politics than they were willing to accept. See Rakove, *Beginnings of National Politics*, 88–96; and Shain, *Declaration of Independence in Historical Context*, 375–81.

57. John Adams to Timothy Pickering, 22 August 1822, *JPW*, 609–11; TJ to JM, 30 August 1823, ibid., 145–47. Shortly after the committees were appointed, Richard Henry Lee left Philadelphia to attend the Williamsburg convention. See Malone, *Thomas Jefferson*, 1:219.

58. *JCC*, 5:433; Parkinson, "The Declaration of Independence," 47–49; Shain, *Declaration of Independence in Historical Context*, 460; Beeman, *Our Lives*, 387–93; Maier, *American Scripture*, 101–2.

59. Maier, *American Scripture*, 50–57; Armitage, *Declaration of Independence*, 30–31. The English Bill of Rights began its life as the Declaration of Rights, a document issued by the extralegal Convention Parliament when it offered the throne to William of Orange after the ouster of James II during the Glorious Revolution. After the convention proclaimed itself a regular Parliament, the Declaration was introduced as a bill, hence the term Bill of Rights, and enacted as a statute. Schwartz, *Bill of Rights*, 1:40–41.

60. Maier, *American Scripture*, 117; McIlwain, *American Revolution*, 191–92; Shain, *Declaration of Independence in Historical Context*, 8–15, 102–4; "Autobiography," *TJW*, 19; Greene, *Constitutional Origins*, 185–86; Yirush, *Settlers, Liberty, and Empire*, 260–61.

61. John Adams to Timothy Pickering, 6 August 1822, in Shain, *Declaration of Independence in Historical Context*, 496; JM to TJ, 6 September 1823, *ROL*, 3:1877.

62. TJ to JM, 30 August 1823, *JPW*, 145–47; TJ to Henry Lee, 8 May 1825, ibid., 147–48; Beeman, "American Revolution," 35–36; J. Ellis, *American Sphinx*, 56–59. On Jefferson and the Scottish Enlightenment, see Wills, *Inventing America*. According to one careful student of Jefferson's thought, it should be noted, "Wills's thesis that Jefferson employed this [moral sense] philosophy in the Declaration of Independence was found entirely unpersuasive in the scholarly community. The brilliant flaw in his argument is that the moral sense philosophy appeared not in Jefferson's revolutionary writings, but in his postrevolutionary political philosophy." Sheldon, *Political Philosophy of Thomas Jefferson*, 155.

63. Parkinson, "Declaration of Independence," 46; Beeman, *Our Lives*, 394–99. For the text of the Declaration of the Causes and Necessity of Taking Up Arms, see Shain, *Declaration of Independence in Historical Context*, 277–82. For Mason's draft of the Virginia Declaration of Rights, see *PGM*, 1:276–78.

64. Maier, *American Scripture*, 191–95; Wills, *Inventing America*, 208–10; Douglass, *Rebels and Democrats*, 7. The founders might also be seen as committed to an equality of opportunity made possible by the availability of land on "an expanding frontier." Morris, *Forging of the Union*, 163.

65. TJ to Roger C. Weightman, 24 June 1826, *TJW*, 1516–17. Jefferson was paraphrasing a speech attributed to the old Cromwellian Colonel Richard Rumbold. See Maier, *American Scripture*, 125; and Adair, "Rumbold's Dying Speech." The thought previously appeared in Sidney's *Discourses Concerning Government*. Ryan, *On Politics*, 2:515. See also W. P. Adams, *First American Constitutions*, 164–74.

66. First Draft of the Virginia Declaration of Rights, circa 20–26 June 1776, *PGM*, 1:277; W. P. Adams, *First American Constitutions*, 193; Maier, *American Scripture*, 134; Koch, *Jefferson and Madison*, 78–80; Shain, *Declaration of Independence in Historical Context*, 482–85; Parkinson, "Declaration of Independence," 51–53. Historians may have worried much more about the deletion of a reference to property than did Jefferson's contemporaries. See Malone, *Thomas Jefferson*, 1:227–28. By the "pursuit of happiness,"

Jefferson probably meant to say the happiness of society was the objective of good governments, a common idea at the time. Schlesinger, "Lost Meaning." See also Thompson, *Revolutionary Writings of John Adams*, 287.

67. "Autobiography," *TJW*, 19–23; Beeman, *Our Lives*, 399.

68. "Autobiography," *TJW*, 19–23; Maier, *American Scripture*, 107–12, 115; Parkinson, "Declaration of Independence," 53–56.

69. "Autobiography," *TJW*, 19, 24; Armitage, *Declaration of Independence*, 37–41; Beeman, *Our Lives*, 399. Given Jefferson's emphasis on diplomacy, it is understandable that Peter Onuf would see in the Declaration evidence of Jefferson's commitment to "a federal republican regime." See Onuf, *Mind of Thomas Jefferson*, 86–89.

Kevin Hayes has suggested another intriguing motive for issuing the Declaration of Independence and announcing it to the world: "What makes an announcement necessary is the idea of civility. As Jefferson had learned reading such works as Adam Ferguson's *Essay on the History of Civil Society*, the principles of civility required that the dissolution of political ties be properly communicated to the world." Hayes, *Road to Monticello*, 180.

70. Editorial note, *PTJ*, 1:413–17; "Original Rough Draft of the Declaration of Independence," ibid., 1:423–28; editorial note, in Labaree et al., *Papers of Benjamin Franklin*, 22:485–86; TJ to JM, 30 August 1823, *JPW*, 145–47; Beeman, *Our Lives*, 393–94; Maier, *American Scripture*, 101–2; Parkinson, "Declaration of Independence," 50.

71. Notes of Proceedings in the Continental Congress, 7 June–1 August 1776, *PTJ*, 1:313–14; "Autobiography," *TJW*, 17–18. See Rakove, *Beginnings of National Politics*, 102–7.

72. "Autobiography," *TJW*, 19–24; J. Ellis, *American Sphinx*, 51–53. Conventional wisdom has long held that Congress's editing improved the committee draft. See Malone, *Thomas Jefferson*, 1:222; and Beeman, *Our Lives*, 407–18. There is, however, room for debate. Robert Middlekauff believes that "for many reasons the Jefferson draft is a much more powerful statement." Middlekauff, *Glorious Cause*, 329.

73. Hayes, *Road to Monticello*, 189; "Autobiography," *TJW*, 18. Jefferson wrote later that the Declaration "was signed by every member present, except Mr. Dickinson," on 4 July. The New Yorkers and some of the Pennsylvania delegates supposedly signed later in the month. If Jefferson's memory is correct, that copy has been lost. Most historians believe a general signing occurred later. A 19 July resolution ordered the Declaration to be engrossed, and the records of the Continental Congress refer to a signing ceremony on 2 August. See TJ to Samuel Adams Wells, 12 May 1819, *TJW*, 1421–22; C. Adams, *Works of John Adams*, 2:485–502; and *JCC*, 6:1071–83. Boyd leaves the issue unresolved in his editorial note, *PTJ*, 1:299–308. Wills, *Inventing America*, 339–44, argues for a later signing.

74. TJ to Robert C. Weightman, 24 June 1826, *JPW*, 148–49; JM to TJ, 8 February 1825, *JMW*, 807–8; Maier, *American Scripture*, xix, 191–95; Shain, *Declaration of Independence in Historical Context*, 16; W. P. Adams, *First American Constitutions*, 103. See also Wills, *Inventing America*, 324; and Douglass, *Rebels and Democrats*, 310–16.

75. Meacham, *Thomas Jefferson*, 110; TJ to William Fleming, 1 July 1776, *PTJ*, 1:412; Maier, *American Scripture*, 160–67, 171; Slauter, "Declaration of Independence." It is telling that the most substantial British rebuttal to the Declaration of Independence, John Lind's *An Answer to the Declaration of the American Congress* (1776), devoted 110 of its 129 pages to the grievance section. Wills, *Inventing America*, 65–66.

76. Maier, *American Scripture*, 126–28; Bernstein, "Thomas Jefferson and Constitutionalism," 421; Colbourn, *Lamp of Experience*, 202–3.

77. Parkinson, "Declaration of Independence," 56–57. Pauline Maier argued plausibly that the Declaration was not intended primarily for foreign consumption. A document proclaiming a right of revolution could not have been appealing to Louis XVI, America's most important potential ally, and a copy of the Declaration did not reach Silas Deane, the American minister to France, until mid-November. See Maier, *American Scripture*, 129–31. But the delay seems to have been mainly the result of bureaucratic bungling and the difficulty of transatlantic travel in the 1700s.

78. On the importance Jefferson attached to emotional bonds in maintaining a political community, see generally Onuf, *Mind of Thomas Jefferson*, 65–76; Steele, *Thomas Jefferson and American Nationhood*, 2–22, 52; and Wills, *Inventing America*, 291. Garry Wills and Joseph Ellis argue the Declaration was not intended to create a new nation. Its purpose, Wills argues, was merely to allow Congress to secure a foreign alliance. Wills, *Inventing America*, 325–33. See also J. Ellis, *Quartet*, xi–xiii. It would be more accurate to conclude that while Congress did not intend to create a strong central government, the Declaration of Independence, the Articles of Confederation, and the Model Treaty demonstrate an undeniable intent to create what would be recognized under international law as a nation-state.

For more on the distinction between a sense of American nationalism and a commitment to a robust nation-state, see Gould, *Among the Powers of the Earth*, 10–11; and Hendrickson, *Peace Pact*, 26–27.

CHAPTER 3

1. Wood, *Creation of the American Republic*, 354; Jensen, *Articles of Confederation*, 125. See also Onuf, *Origins of the Federal Republic*, 12–13; and Rakove, *Beginnings of National Politics*, 145–50.

2. Rakove, *Beginnings of National Politics*, 150–51; Onuf, *Origins of the Federal Republic*, 7–8.

3. Proposed Articles of Confederation, 21 July 1775, in Labaree et al., *Papers of Benjamin Franklin*, 22:120–25; Morris, *Forging of the Union*, 80–82.

4. The First Continental Congress had adopted a one-state, one-vote rule for reasons of its own. It lacked reliable population figures, and it assumed decisions would be made by consensus, rendering representation by population irrelevant, if not impossible. See Rakove, *Beginnings of National Politics*, 136–47; and Morris, *Forging of the Union*, 82–83.

5. *JCC*, 5:425; Morris, *Forging of the Union*, 84–85; Rakove, *Beginnings of National Politics*, 154. The Dickinson draft, as amended, is conveniently reproduced in Jensen, *Articles of Confederation*, 254–62. See also Jensen, *New Nation*, 23–26. Dickinson, who began writing before the Declaration of Independence was adopted, referred to the states as "colonies." They became "states" in the final draft of the Articles, which can be found at *JCC*, 9:907–25.

6. Jensen, *Articles of Confederation*, 251; "Autobiography," *TJW*, 24–31.

7. "Autobiography," *TJW*, 24–27. See Jensen, *Articles of Confederation*, 140–60.

8. "Autobiography," *TJW*, 28–30; TJ to John Adams, 16 March 1777, *AJC*, 1:4–5; Jensen, *Articles of Confederation*, 140–45.

9. Brant, *James Madison*, 2:89; Ketcham, *James Madison*, 98–100; Rakove, *Beginnings of National Politics*, 152–58.

10. Jensen, *Articles of Confederation*, 150–60, 249–53.

11. Ibid., 174–75; Morris, *Forging of the Union*, 87–91.

12. Jensen, *Articles of Confederation*, 252–53; Peterson, *Thomas Jefferson and the New Nation*, 98; A Bill to Give the Articles of Confederation the Force of Law, *PTJ*, 2:111–12; editorial note, *PJM*, 2:75. Jefferson feared that the issue of representation might prevent Virginia from ratifying the Articles of Confederation, but concerns that Congress would negotiate a commercial treaty unfavorable to southern planters proved to be a greater, although not an insurmountable, hurdle. TJ to John Adams, 16 May 1777, *AJC*, 1:4–5, and 17 December 1777, 1:8–9.

13. TJ to John Hancock, 11 October 1776, *PTJ*, 1:524; "Autobiography," *TJW*, 32, 45–46; Jefferson, *Notes on the State of Virginia*, 161; Burstein and Isenberg, *Madison and Jefferson*, 50–51; editorial note, *PTJ*, 2:305–7; Malone, *Thomas Jefferson*, 1:xii, 246–49; Peterson, *Thomas Jefferson and the New Nation*, 108.

14. *ROL*, 1:52–56; Brant, *James Madison*, 1:297; "Autobiography," *TJW*, 36–37; JM to Margaret Bayard Smith, September 1830, *WJM*, 9: 404–405; editorial note, *PJM*, 1:186–87.

15. "Autobiography," *TJW*, 36–37; Ketcham, *James Madison*, 76–77; *ROL*, 1:14.

16. JM to Samuel Harrison Smith, 4 November 1826, *WJM*, 9:265–61; Burstein and Isenberg, *Madison and Jefferson*, xvi–xvii, 51–52; Howe, "Republicanism," 65; Steele, *Thomas Jefferson and American Nationhood*, 135–36; Koch, *Jefferson and Madison*, 291–94. On the complementary nature of the Jefferson-Madison relationship, see also Feldman, *Three Lives*, 31.

17. "Autobiography," *TJW*, 44–45.

18. Randolph, *History of Virginia*, 183; Notes on Locke and Shaftesbury, *PTJ*, 1:544–51; Roeber, *Faithful Magistrates*, 224; Dumbauld, *Thomas Jefferson and the Law*, 75–79; Chinard, *Commonplace Book*, 244–45.

19. Ragosta, *Wellspring of Liberty*, 3–11, 16–17, 32. See also J. Nelson, *Blessed Company*.

20. *PGM*, 1:289; Petition of Dissenters in Albemarle and Amherst Counties, *PTJ*, 1:586–89; "Autobiography," *TJW*, 34–35.

21. Ragosta, *Wellspring of Liberty*, 20–24; Brant, *James Madison*, 1:295–96; Buckley, *Establishing Religious Freedom*, 56–61. Recent scholarship has tended to stress the problem of racial and class conflicts in wartime Virginia. See Holton, *Forced Founders*; and McDonnell, *Politics of War*. Such tensions existed, but they should not be overemphasized. Much apparent "class conflict" involved localized, and understandable, disaffection around conscription and military mobilization. For most white Virginians, sectarian divisions seem to have been a more salient point of contention. See Ragosta, *Wellspring of Liberty*, 44–69.

22. Draft of Resolutions, *PTJ*, 1:530–32. See also editorial note, ibid., 1:525–29; and Selby, *Revolution in Virginia*, 145–47.

23. Outline of Argument in Support of Resolutions, *PTJ*, 1:535–39.

24. Draft of Bill for Exempting Religious Dissenters, 30 November 1776, ibid., 1:532–34; Broadwater, *George Mason*, 118–21; "Autobiography," *TJW*, 36.

25. Peterson, *Thomas Jefferson and the New Nation*, 133–45; Bill for Establishing Religious Freedom, *TJW*, 846–48; editorial note, *PTJ*, 1:525–29; Selby, *Revolution in Virginia*, 145–47; Malone, *Thomas Jefferson*, 1:274.

26. Howe, "Republicanism," 72–77; Steele, *Thomas Jefferson and American Nationhood*, 128–30; Peterson, *Thomas Jefferson and the New Nation*, 110; "Autobiography," *TJW*, 32; Burstein and Isenberg, *Madison and Jefferson*, 52.

27. Bill to Enable Tenants in Fee Tail to Convey Lands in Fee Simple, 14 October 1776, *PTJ*, 1:560–62; Hening, *Statutes at Large*, 9:226–27; Malone, *Thomas Jefferson*, 1:251–55.

28. See Peterson, *Thomas Jefferson and the New Nation*, 113–16; and Selby, *Revolution in Virginia*, 140–41. Where did Jefferson's animus toward primogeniture originate? We cannot be certain, but James Harrington called for its abolition in *Oceana*, where he made a case for the independent yeoman, who could provide his own weapons when called upon for militia duty, thus eliminating the need for standing armies and the consequent high taxes that, Harrington argued, caused political instability. See Ryan, *On Politics*, 2:507–11.

29. Bill for the Revision of the Laws, 15 October 1776, *PTJ*, 1:562–64.

30. Editorial note, ibid., 2:313–21; "Autobiography," *TJW*, 37–38.

31. *PTJ*, 2:442–43, 467–68, 480–81; editorial note, ibid, 2:322–25; Malone, *Thomas Jefferson*, 1:263; JM to Samuel Harrison Smith, 4 November 1826, *WJM*, 9:257. On the problem of determining which bills made up the committee's final report and which drafts are authoritative, see editorial note, *PTJ*, 2:307–13. Bills went through multiple drafts, at least two were discarded, and the 1779 report did not literally include committee bills that had already been adopted, although they were apparently assumed to have been incorporated in the committee's report.

32. *PTJ*, 2:526–27; A Bill for the More General Diffusion of Knowledge, *TJW*, 365–73.

33. Malone, *Thomas Jefferson*, 1:280–81; Peterson, *Thomas Jefferson and the New Nation*, 150–52.

34. Samuel Stanhope Smith to TJ, March 1779, *PTJ*, 2: 246–49; Malone, *Thomas Jefferson*, 1: 283–85; Peterson, *Thomas Jefferson and the New Nation*, 150–52.

35. TJ to Edmund Pendleton, 26 August 1776, *PTJ*, 1:505; Peterson, *Thomas Jefferson and the New Nation*, 124–33.

36. TJ to George Wythe, 1 November 1778, *PTJ*, 2:229–31; A Bill for Proportioning Crimes and Punishments in Cases Heretofore Capital, ibid., 2:492–65; A Bill for the Employment, Government, and Support of Malefactors Condemned to Labor for the Commonwealth, ibid., 2:513; "Autobiography," *TJW*, 39; Peterson, *Thomas Jefferson and the New Nation*, 131. Pennsylvania would be the first state to eliminate mutilation from its criminal code. See Wood, *Radicalism of the American Revolution*, 193.

37. Wood, *Radicalism of the American Revolution*, 322–23. The court bills all appear in *PTJ*, 1:607–49.

38. Editorial note, *PTJ*, 1:605–7.

39. Ibid.; Peterson, *Thomas Jefferson and the New Nation*, 154–56; Roeber, *Faithful Magistrates*, 167–71; TJ to George Wythe, 1 March 1779, *PTJ*, 2:235–36.

40. Bill for the Removal of the Seat of Government, 11 November 1776, *PTJ*, 1:598–602; Bill Declaring Who Shall Be Deemed Citizens, *TJW*, 374–54; "Autobiography," *TJW*, 36. Jefferson claimed years later to have prepared legislation providing for gradual emancipation and the colonization of freed slaves but, sensing no prospect for success, did not introduce it. "Autobiography," *TJW*, 43–44. No draft of the bill has been found, although he did include language abolishing slavery in his 1783 draft constitution. See *JPW*, 342.

41. Peterson, *Thomas Jefferson and the New Nation*, 122–24.

42. TJ to Benjamin Franklin, 13 August 1777, *PTJ*, 2:26–27; Selby, *Revolution in Virginia*, 159–62.

43. Editorial note, *PJM*, 1:192–93; Sydnor, *American Revolutionaries*, 53–58.

44. Ketcham, *James Madison*, 78, 82–85; editorial note, *PJM*, 1:214–26; JM to TJ, 16 March 1784, *ROL*, 1:60; Brant, *James Madison*, 1:337–38.

45. JM to Margaret Bayard Smith, September 1830, *WJM*, 9:404–5; Brant, *James Madison*, 1:354.

46. See the following in *ROL*, vol. 1: Executive Council to Conrad Alexandre Gerard, 8 June 1779, 69; Executive Council to John Jay, 19 June 1779, 79–80; Executive Council to Richard Caswell, 22 June 1779, 85; Executive Council to Richard Henry Lee, 17 July 1779, 88–89; Orders for the Defense of the Western Frontier, 23 July 1779, 95–96; Executive Council to Benjamin Harrison, 30 October 1779, 98–103; Executive Council to Benjamin Harrison, 4 November 1779, 103–4; Executive Council to George Washington, 28 November 1779, 117.

Virginia's decision to ratify the French alliance raised a few eyebrows in Congress, but it seems unlikely that either Jefferson or Madison saw the state's ratification as a challenge to Congress's primacy in foreign affairs. William Fleming to TJ, 22 June 1779, *PTJ*, 3:10–11; Brant, *James Madison*, 1:352–53. At the same time, they believed the state retained some degree of diplomatic autonomy. For example, in November 1779, the Jefferson administration sent a military mission to Spanish officials in New Orleans to, among other things, negotiate a loan. Executive Council to Governor Bernardo de Galvez, 8 November 1779, *ROL*, 1:106–8.

47. Executive Council to Samuel Huntington, 16 December 1779, *ROL*, 1:121; JM to James Madison Sr., 8 December 1779, *PJM*, 1:315–18; Malone, *Thomas Jefferson*, 1:319–20.

48. Peterson, *Thomas Jefferson and the New Nation*, 105, 173–74. Wartime exigencies raised numerous questions of executive power, and Jefferson assumed the executive had some inherent authority, including, for example, the right to appoint and remove staff officers, but he conceded line officers could probably be removed only by a court martial. Notes Concerning the Right of Removal from Office, circa 1780, *PTJ*, 4:281–82.

49. Malone, *Thomas Jefferson*, 1:369.

50. Proclamation Appointing a Day of Thanksgiving and Prayer, circa 20 November 1779, *PTJ*, 3:177–79; Proclamation of Embargo, 30 November 1779, ibid., 3:208–9; TJ to Thomas Sim Lee, 30 January 1780, ibid., 3:279–80; Warrant for Impressing Supplies, 26 October 1780, ibid., 4:75–76.

51. TJ to Matthew Pope, 21 May 1781, ibid., 6:5–6; TJ to von Steuben, 10 March 1781, ibid., 5:119–29.

52. TJ to David Rittenhouse, 19 July 1778, ibid., 2:202–4; TJ to Richard Henry Lee, 17 June 1779, ibid., 2:298–99; Marbois' Queries Concerning Va., ibid., 4:166–67; TJ to D'Anmours, 30 November 1780, ibid., 4:167–68; American Philosophical Society to TJ, 7 February 1781, ibid., 4:544–46; TJ to Timothy Matlock, 18 April 1781, ibid., 5:490. See also Malone, *Thomas Jefferson*, 1:368–69.

53. TJ to Samuel Huntington, 27 July 1780, *PTJ*, 3:508–13; TJ to Horatio Gates, 3 September 1780, ibid., 3:588–89; TJ to Abner Nash, 3 September 1780, ibid., 3:592; TJ to Edward Stevens, 3 September 1780, ibid., 3:593; Nathanael Greene to TJ, 6 December 1780, ibid., 4:183–85; TJ to the Speaker of the House, 10 May 1781, ibid., 5:626–29; TJ to JM, 18 January 1781, *ROL*, 1:158–60; TJ to JM, 6 April 1781, *ROL*, 1:183–84. See also Selby, *Revolution in Virginia*, 214–15.

54. TJ to Baron von Steuben, 26 April 1781, *PTJ*, 5:560; George Washington to TJ, 18 October 1780, ibid., 4:45–46; Nathanael Greene to TJ, 20 November 1780, ibid., 4:130–32; TJ to the Speaker of the House, 28 May 1781, ibid., 6:28–29.

55. TJ to Virginia Delegates in Congress, 27 October 1780, ibid., 4:76–77; John Taylor to TJ, 5 December 1780, ibid., 4:180–81; Garret Van Meter to TJ, 11 April 1781, ibid., 5:409–10; Petition of Robert Poage et al., May 1781, ibid., 6:55–60; TJ to JM, 27 October 1780, *ROL*, 1:148. By the spring of 1781, Jefferson's biggest concern may have been the fear of an uprising of Loyalists and "other disaffected elements in the South." Malone, *Thomas Jefferson*, 1:347. In reality, the British army would be the greater threat.

56. JM to TJ, 3 April 1781, *ROL*, 1:180–82.

57. Selby, *Revolution in Virginia*, 221–22; Malone, *Thomas Jefferson*, 1:340–41; Peterson, *Thomas Jefferson and the New Nation*, 235–39.

58. Notes and Documents Relating to the British Invasions in 1781, *PTJ*, 4:256–78; Selby, *Revolution in Virginia*, 283–85; Malone, *Thomas Jefferson*, 1:358.

59. Samuel Huntington to TJ, 10 September 1780, *PTJ*, 3:625–36; and 2 March 1781, 5:41–42; Onuf, *Origins of the Federal Republic*, 17–18; Alden, *History of the American Revolution*, 344–47; Selby, *Revolution in Virginia*, 141–42; Broadwater, *George Mason*, 129–30.

60. TJ to Edmund Pendleton, 13 August 1776, *PTJ*, 1:491–94.

61. Bills for Establishing a Land Office and for Adjusting and Settling Titles, 8–14 January 1778, ibid., 2:133–67; TJ to Samuel Huntington, 9 February 1780, ibid., 3:286–91. Mason's bill could have benefited the Ohio Company, in which he had invested, but the assembly later decided the company's survey had been defective. See Broadwater, *George Mason*, 126–27. Jefferson did not speculate in western land. Drafts of the bills and helpful annotations also appear in *PGM*, 1:399–409 and 414–22.

62. Peterson, *Thomas Jefferson and the New Nation*, 116–21; Hening, *Statutes at Large*, 10:35–50, 50–65.

63. A Resolution Authorizing the Drafting of a Remonstrance, 13 November 1779, *PGM*, 2:549–50; The Remonstrance of the General Assembly, 10 December 1779, ibid., 2:595–98; Brant, *James Madison*, 2:89–96. See generally Selby, *Revolution in Virginia*, 227–44.

64. TJ to William Fleming, 8 June 1779, *PTJ*, 2:288–89; TJ to David Shepard, 30 January 1780, ibid., 3:280; TJ to Samuel Huntington, 9 February 1780, ibid., 3:286–89; Brant, *James Madison*, 2:96; Ketcham, *James Madison*, 134–35.

65. Joseph Jones to TJ, 30 June 1780, *PTJ*, 3:472–75; Broadwater, *George Mason*, 128–29; Ketcham, *James Madison*, 98–100.

66. Motion on Western Lands, 6 September 1780, *PJM*, 2:72–78; JM to TJ, 20 November 1780, *ROL*, 1:150–52; Selby, *Revolution in Virginia*, 256–59.

67. TJ to Samuel Huntington, 17 January 1781, *PTJ*, 4:386–91; JM to TJ, 18 November 1781, *ROL*, 1:202–3; Brant, *James Madison*, 2:97–101. On Madison and the West, see generally Zemler, *James Madison*.

68. Ketcham, *James Madison*, 95–97.

69. Draft letter to John Jay, 17 October 1780, *PJM*, 2:127–36; *JCC*, 28:900–902, 935–47; Brant, *James Madison*, 2:70, 80–82.

70. Draft letter to John Jay, 17 October 1780, *PJM*, 2:127–36; Brant, *James Madison*, 2:80–82.

71. JM to TJ, circa 5 October 1780, *ROL*, 1:146–47; JM to TJ, 13 December 1780, ibid., 1:153–54; Report on Instructions to John Jay, 2 May 1781, *PJM*, 3:101–7; Brant, *James Madison*, 2:85–88.

72. Selby, *Revolution in Virginia*, 184. See also Peterson, *Thomas Jefferson and the New Nation*, 182–83. See generally McCoy, *Elusive Republic*.

73. Peterson, *Thomas Jefferson and the New Nation*, 170–72, 189–91; TJ to Richard Henry Lee, 17 June 1779, *PTJ*, 2:298–99; JM to William Bradford, 30 October–5 November 1779, *PJM*, 1:311–14. While Congress's financial situation was dire, Madison's projection of its financial needs for 1780 actually proved to be overly pessimistic. See *PJM*, 1:313n6.

74. Adair, "James Madison's Autobiography," 200; Ketcham, *James Madison*, 85–87; "Money," *SWJM*, 4–11. While the "Money" essay focused on Congress, Madison and many of his contemporaries would also excoriate the states for reckless emissions of paper money. See Brant, *James Madison*, 2:28.

75. *ROL*, 1:125–26; Brant, *James Madison*, 2:17–18.

76. JM to James Madison Sr., 20 March 1780, *PJM*, 2:3; JM to TJ, 27–28 March 1780, *ROL*, 1:135–37; JM to John Page, 8 May 1780, *PJM*, 1:21–23; David Jameson to JM, 23 August 1780, *PJM*, 2:63–64; JM to TJ, 17 April 1781, *ROL*, 1:188–89; JM to TJ, 8 May 1781, *ROL*, 1:196–97; Samuel Huntington to TJ, 9 November 1780, *PTJ*, 4:105–8; TJ to Benjamin Harrison, 24 November 1780, *PTJ*, 4:150–51.

77. JM to TJ, 2 June 1780, *ROL*, 1:138–40; JM to TJ, 9 January 1781, ibid., 1:156–57; JM to TJ, 30 January 1781, ibid., 1:162–63.

78. Brant, *James Madison*, 2:17–18; Virginia Delegates to TJ, 5 November 1780, *PTJ*, 4:96; JM to TJ, 22 May 1781, *ROL*, 1:200–201.

79. Ketcham, *James Madison*, 92–95, 100–101; Brant, *James Madison*, 2:14–15.

80. JM to TJ, 6 May 1780, *ROL*, 1:137–38; Brant, *James Madison*, 2:21; Ketcham, *James Madison*, 112–14.

81. Brant, *James Madison*, 2:104–20; Ketcham, *James Madison*, 112–14; Motion on the Court of Appeals, 12 April 1781, *PJM*, 3:66–68.

82. Proposed Amendment to the Articles of Confederation, 12 March 1781, *PJM*, 3:17–20; Motion on Impost, 18 April 1781, ibid., 3:77–78; JM to TJ, 16 April 1781, *ROL*, 1:186–87; *JCC*, 29:236.

83. TJ to Richard Henry Lee, 5 June 1778, *PTJ*, 2:194.

CHAPTER 4

1. TJ to James Monroe, 20 May 1782, *TJW*, 777–79.

2. TJ to Chastellux, 26 November 1782, ibid., 780–81; JM to Edmund Pendleton, 8 January 1782, in P. Smith, *Letters of Delegates*, 18:263–64; Cheney, *James Madison*, 97–98.

3. *ROL*, 1:270–73; TJ to JM, 17 June 1783, ibid., 1:251–60; Malone, *Thomas Jefferson*, 1:406; Burstein and Isenberg, *Madison and Jefferson*, 96–99; Ketcham, *James Madison*, 141.

4. TJ to JM, 20 February 1784, *ROL*, 1:292–99; Peterson, *Thomas Jefferson and the New Nation*, 265–66.

5. Introduction, *PJM*, 7:xxiv–xxvi; JM to Edmund Randolph, 17 June 1783, ibid., 7:158–62, and 28 July 1783, 7:256–58; Motion re Jurisdiction of Congress over Permanent Site, 22 September 1783, ibid., 8:357–58.

6. JM to TJ, 17 July 1783, *ROL*, 1:260–62, 11 August 1783, 1:262–63, and 20 September 1783, 1:264–66.

7. *PJM*, 3:xvii; Ketcham, *James Madison*, 139; Brant, *James Madison*, 2:126–27, 176–79; JM to Edmund Pendleton, 8 January 1782, in P. Smith, *Letters of Delegates*, 18:273–74; JM to Edmund Randolph, 3 June 1783, *PJM*, 7:107–8.

8. Feldman, *Three Lives*, 55; Brant, *James Madison*, 2:190–91, 301; *ROL*, 1:273.

9. TJ to Benjamin Harrison, 16 January 1784, in P. Smith, *Letters of Delegates*, 21:289–90; TJ to JM, 20 February 1784, *ROL*, 1:292–99, and 16 March 1784, 1:305–7.

As a practical matter, "all the great questions," Jefferson wrote George Washington, required a unanimous vote of the delegates, not just of the states. TJ to George Washington, 15 March 1784, *TJW*, 786–87. Washington agreed Congress should meet only for a few months a year, rather than try to meet continuously. See Rakove, *Beginnings of National Politics*, 354–59.

10. TJ to Edmund Pendleton, 18 January 1784, in P. Smith, *Letters of Delegates*, 21:290–92; TJ to JM, 20 February 1784, *ROL*, 1:292–99; Brant, *James Madison*, 2:209–10.

11. Coleman, *American Revolution*, 68–69; Van Cleve, *We Have Not a Government*, 52–53, 75–79, 191–92, 211. For a contrary claim that Congress had requisitioned "more money than existed in the United States," see Gutzman, *James Madison*, 167.

12. *ROL*, 1:274; TJ to JM, 1 January 1784, ibid., 1:288–90; TJ to JM, 20 February 1784, ibid., 1:292–97; JM to TJ, 16 March 1784, ibid., 1:299–301.

13. TJ to JM, 20 February 1784, ibid., 1:292–99; JM to TJ, 16 March 1784, ibid., 1:301; TJ to JM, 8 and 11 May 1784, ibid., 1:314–16.

14. "Autobiography," *TJW*, 48–50; JM to TJ, 7 September 1784, *ROL*, 1:343–44; Peterson, *Thomas Jefferson and the New Nation*, 274–75.

15. "Autobiography," *TJW*, 70–71.

16. TJ to JM, 11 December 1783, *ROL*, 1:287–88; TJ to Chastellux, 16 January 1784, *TJW*, 785–86; TJ to JM, 20 February 1784, *ROL*, 1:292–99, 25 and 30 April 1784, 1:309, and 1 July 1784, 1:321.

17. David Howell to Jonathan Arnold, 21 February 1784, in P. Smith, *Letters of Delegates*, 21:380–85; TJ quoted in Meacham, *Thomas Jefferson*, 175.

18. JM to TJ, 3 October 1785, *ROL*, 1:386–89.

19. Ibid., 18 November 1781, 1:202–3, 15 January 1782, 1:209–11, and 18 March 1782, 1:212–13; TJ to JM, 24 March 1782, ibid., 1:213–14; Observations on State Territorial Claims, 1 May 1782, *JMW*, 14–16. See generally Onuf, *Origins of the Federal Republic*, 75–102.

20. JM to Edmund Randolph, 10 June 1783, *PJM*, 7:133–36; TJ to Benjamin Harrison, 11 November 1783, in P. Smith, *Letters of Delegates*, 21:152–54; TJ to JM, 17 June 1783, *ROL*, 1:251–52; Burstein and Isenberg, *Madison and Jefferson*, 93; Jensen, *New Nation*, 352–53; Malone, *Thomas Jefferson*, 1:412–14. See also editorial note, *PTJ*, 6:571–75.

21. See editorial note, *PTJ*, 6:581–600.

22. Burstein and Isenberg, *Madison and Jefferson*, 106; Report on Government for Western Territory, 1 March 1784, *TJW*, 376–78.

23. TJ to JM, 25 and 30 April 1784, *ROL*, 1:308–9; Peterson, *Thomas Jefferson and the New Nation*, 281–84.

24. Report of a Committee to Establish a Land Office, 30 April 1784, *PTJ*, 7:140–48; TJ to William Carmichael, 18 August 1785, ibid., 8:401–2; TJ to David Hartley, 5 September 1785, ibid., 8:481–85.

25. See Morris, *Forging of the Union*, 226–30; and Peterson, *Thomas Jefferson and the New Nation*, 280–81.

26. TJ to JM, 20 February 1784, *ROL*, 1:292–99; Ketcham, *James Madison*, 170–71.

27. JM to TJ, 6 May 1783, *ROL*, 1:243–44; 11 October 1784, 1:345–46; 20 August 1784, 1:337–42. On the fur trade, see Van Cleve, *We Have Not a Government*, 69–72.

28. Rakove, *Beginnings of National Politics*, 349–52; JM to Lafayette, 20 March 1785, *JMW*, 24–29.

29. Rakove, *Beginnings of National Politics*, 349–52; JM to Lafayette, 20 March 1785, *JMW*, 24–29.

30. "Autobiography," *TJW*, 75; Jensen, *New Nation*, 58–59. Jensen argued that the Confederation's finances were far less desperate than commonly believed and that Dutch bankers in particular considered the United States to be a good credit risk. See ibid. at 384. Jefferson and Madison were not so sanguine.

A federal impost would have fallen most heavily on a commercial state like Rhode Island; merchants disliked it, and since it was seen as apt to shift state taxes from duties to land, it also drew opposition from farmers. Dougherty, *Collective Action*, 60–62.

31. Brant, *James Madison*, 2:211–12, 215; JM to Edmund Randolph, 22 January 1783, *PJM*, 6:55–56; JM to Edmund Randolph, 28 January 1783, *PJM*, 6:153–58. Madison seems to have used the terms "general revenue" and "permanent revenue" interchangeably. Editorial note, *PJM*, 6:310.

32. Debates of 28 January 1783, *PJM*, 6:143–47.

33. JM to TJ, 11 February 1783, *ROL*, 1:220–21.

34. Notes on Debates, 19 February 1783, *PJM*, 6:261; 20 February 1783, 6:264–70

35. Speech of 21 February 1783, *JMW*, 17–20; Ketcham, *James Madison*, 117–18.

36. James Madison's Memorandum for Thomas Jefferson on a Revenue Plan, circa 6 March 1783, *ROL*, 1:236–39; James Madison's Annotations for Thomas Jefferson on the Report for Restoring Public Credit, circa 26 March 1783, ibid., 1:239–41. Using population to determine a state's financial obligation to the national treasury raised the question of how to count slaves. Madison negotiated a compromise in which a slave would be counted as three-fifths of a free person. Brant, *James Madison*, 2:240–42.

37. JM to TJ, 22 April 1783, *ROL*, 1:242–43; TJ to JM, 7 May 1783, 1:244–46, 1 June 1783, 1:248–49, and 17 June 1783, 1:252–52.

38. Address to the States by Congress on Finances, 26 April 1783, *SWJM*, 15–21. Madison conceded that counting slaves for purposes of determining a state's financial obligations to Congress presented a "material difficulty" and explained the three-fifths compromise as "the effect of mutual concessions." He also defended, ironically, Congress's decision, in repaying holders of government securities, not to discriminate between original purchasers who had bought at face value and secondary purchasers who had bought their securities at a much lower market value. Hamilton, in 1783, opposed assumption and supported discrimination among creditors. When the issues reemerged in a new government after the Constitution took effective, he and Madison reversed positions.

39. Report on Arrears of Interest on the National Debt, 5 April 1784, *PTJ*, 7:65–80; TJ to JM, 8 and 11 May 1784, *ROL*, 1:314–16; Rakove, *Beginnings of National Politics*, 337–42; Middlekauff, *Glorious Cause*, 585–90. Despite the failure of the impost of 1783, Congress began basing state requisitions on population. See generally Kaminski, "Constitution without a Bill of Rights."

40. Rakove, *Beginnings of National Politics*, 342–45; Van Cleve, *We Have Not A Government*, 104; Schwarz, *Thomas Jefferson*, xiii–2, 96–97. See generally Marks, *Independence on Trial*.

41. Marks, *Independence on Trial*, 52–57.

42. JM to TJ, 13 May 1783, *ROL*, 1:246–47; JM to Edmund Randolph, May 1783, *JMW*, 20–24; Feldman, *Three Lives*, 71. Robertson sees Madison as more of a free trader because free trade would arguably have benefited Virginia's export-oriented economy. Robertson, *Constitution and American Destiny*, 77–78.

43. JM to TJ, 10 June 1783, *ROL*, 1:248–51; Rakove, *Beginnings of National Politics*, 345–49; Marks, *Independence on Trial*, 59–63.

44. JM to TJ, 20 September 1783, *ROL*, 1:264–66; Jensen, *New Nation*, 163–66, 175, 213. Jensen noted U.S. goods could go to the West Indies in British ships, ibid., 175, 197–98

45. Marks, *Independence on Trial*, 76; Peterson, *Thomas Jefferson and the New Nation*, 290–91; TJ to JM, 11 November 1784, *ROL*, 1:349–53, and 18 March 1785, 1:365–67. See also Schwarz, *Thomas Jefferson*, 32–33.

46. JM to TJ, 20 August 1785, *ROL*, 1:373–75.

47. TJ to George Washington, 15 March 1784, *TJW*, 787–88; TJ to John Jay, 23 August 1785, ibid., 818–20; TJ to G. K. van Hogendorp, 13 October 1785, ibid., 834–37; Malone, *Thomas Jefferson*, 2:22–27.

48. Morris, *Forging of the Union*, 206–7; "Autobiography," *TJW*, 54; Report on Letters from the American Ministers in Europe, 20 December 1783, *PTJ*, 6:393–402. Jefferson said the committee had described the United States as a single nation because it did not want Great Britain to adopt different trade regulations for different states. Notes for Consideration of the Commissioners, Fall 1784, *PTJ*, 7:478–79.

49. Brant, *James Madison*, 2:205.

50. JM to TJ, 25 April 1784, *ROL*, 1:307–8; TJ to JM, 8 and 11 May 1784, ibid., 1:314–16.

51. Charles Thomson to TJ, 16 May 1784, *PTJ*, 7:261–71; editorial note, ibid., 7:463–70; Notes for Consideration of the Commissioners, Fall 1784, ibid., 7:478–79.

52. Notes on Commerce of the Northern States, May–July 1784, ibid., 7:323–55; TJ to Elbridge Gerry, 11 November 1784, ibid., 7:501–2; Jensen, *New Nation*, 404–5; *JCC*, 28:201–5; TJ to Richard Price, 1 February 1785, *TJW*, 798–99.

53. TJ to James Monroe, 17 June 1785, *TJW*, 805–9; TJ to John Adams, 7 July 1785, *AJC*, 1:38–39; R. Ellis, "Constitutionalism." See also Peterson, *Thomas Jefferson and the New Nation*, 304–5.

54. JM to James Monroe, 17 June 1785, *TJW*, 805–9.

55. Peterson, *Thomas Jefferson and the New Nation*, 314–20, 328–29; Morris, *Forging of the Union*, 209–10.

56. Marks, *Independence on Trial*, 36–45.

57. Ibid., 36–45.

58. TJ to John Page, 20 August 1785, *PTJ*, 8:417–19; "Autobiography," *TJW*, 59–61; Peterson, *Thomas Jefferson and the New Nation*, 313–14.

59. Reply to the Representation of Affairs in America by British Newspapers, circa November 1784, *TJW*, 571–74; TJ to G. K. van Hogendorp, 13 October 1785, ibid., 834–37; Malone, *Thomas Jefferson*, 2:92–93; Middlekauff, *Glorious Cause*, 591–92; Jensen, *New Nation*, 196–97; Morris, *Forging of the Union*, 132–61.

60. James Monroe to TJ, 16 June 1785, *PTJ*, 8:215–20; JM to James Monroe, 7 August 1785, *JMW*, 36–39; James Monroe to TJ, 15 August 1785, *PTJ*, 8:381–84.

61. TJ to James Monroe, 11 May 1785, *PTJ*, 8:148–50; TJ to G. K. van Hogendorp, 29 July 1785, ibid., 8:324–25; TJ to William Carmichael, 18 August 1785, ibid., 8:401–2; TJ to David Hartley, 5 September 1785, ibid., 8:481–85; TJ to JM, 1 September 1785, *ROL*, 1:380–83; TJ to John Adams, 24 September 1785, *AJC*, 1:68–69; TJ to John Adams, 19 November 1785, *AJC*, 1:94–97.

62. Peterson, *Thomas Jefferson and the New Nation*, 307; Rakove, *Beginnings of National Politics*, 346–49; McCoy, "Political Economy," 109–10; Answers and Observations for

Demeunier's Article on the United States in the *Encyclopédie méthodique*, 24 January 1786, *TJW*, 575–77.

63. JM to TJ, 10 December 1783, *ROL*, 1:286–87; 11 February 1784, 1:290–91; 17 February, 1784, 1:291–92; TJ to JM, 8 and 11 May 1784, ibid., 1:314–16.

64. JM to TJ, 16 March 1784, ibid., 1:299–305; TJ to JM, 8 December 1784, ibid., 1:353–55; JM to TJ, 22 January 1785, ibid., 1:364; JM to TJ, 27 April 1785, ibid., 1:367–71; Malone, *Thomas Jefferson*, 2:86–87; Ketcham, *James Madison*, 145–50; Koch, *Jefferson and Madison*, 19.

65. TJ to Baron von Geismar, 6 September 1785, *PTJ*, 8:499–500; TJ to Nathaniel Tracy, 17 August 1785, ibid., 8:398–99.

66. TJ to Charles Bellini, 30 September 1785, *TJW*, 832–34.

67. TJ to Rev. James Madison, 28 October 1785, *JPW*, 105–7.

68. Ibid.

CHAPTER 5

1. "A Sketch Never Finished nor Applied," circa 1830, *JMW*, 832–33; William Short to TJ, 14 and 15 May 1784, *PTJ*, 7:256–58; Wood, *Creation of the American Republic*, 394–95; Banning, *Sacred Fire of Liberty*, 46–47.

2. Banning, *Sacred Fire of Liberty*, 98. See generally editorial note, *PJM*, 8:122–23. See also Middlekauff, *Glorious Cause*, 593–601.

3. JM to TJ, 10 December 1783, *ROL*, 1:286–87, and 16 March 1784, 1:302; Banning, *Sacred Fire of Liberty*, 49.

4. Morris, *Forging of the Union*, 197; JM to TJ, 3 July 1784, *ROL*, 1:321–24, 9 January 1785, 1:355–64, and 22 January 1786, 1:405. Jefferson, who spent a good bit of his time in Europe trying to put the best face possible on American affairs, told French officials that if British creditors were all allowed to foreclose on their debts at the same time, it would depress land values, bankrupt planters, and leave their debts unpaid. Amplification of Subjects Discussed with Vergennes, circa 20 December 1785, *PTJ*, 9:107–15.

5. JM to TJ, 3 July 1784, *ROL*, 1:321–24; Ketcham, *James Madison*, 158–60.

6. JM to TJ, 3 July 1784, *ROL*, 1:321–24; JM to George Washington, 9 December 1785, *JMW*, 47–50; JM to TJ, 9 January 1785, *ROL*, 1:355–64; Ketcham, *James Madison*, 171–72.

7. *ROL*, 1:280, 394–95; JM to TJ, 22 January 1786, ibid., 1:401–9. Madison sent Jefferson a copy of the draft resolution.

8. JM to George Washington, 9 December 1785, *JMW*, 47–50.

9. Hayes, *Road to Monticello*, 233–46; TJ to JM, 24 March 1782, *ROL*, 1:213–14, and 25 May 1784, 1:318–20; *ROL*, 1:334.

10. TJ to JM, 11 May 1785, *ROL*, 1:372; TJ to Charles Thomson, 21 June 1785, *PTJ*, 8:245–46; TJ to Francis Hopkinson, 6 July 1785, *PTJ*, 8:262–64; TJ to James Monroe, 17 June 1786, *TJW*, 804–5; Jefferson, *Notes on the State of Virginia*, xxii–xxiv, 138–43, 159–61.

11. JM to TJ, 15 November 1785, *ROL*, 1:382; Jefferson, *Notes on the State of Virginia*, 291n7.

12. Jefferson, *Notes on the State of Virginia*, 83–85.

13. Ibid., 164–65. Madison expressed similar thoughts in the 1790s. "The life of the husbandman is pre-eminently suited to the comfort and happiness of the individual. . . . *Virtue*, the health of the soul, is another part of his patrimony, and no less favored by his situation." "Republican Distribution of Citizens," *National Gazette*, 5 March 1792, in Meyers, *Mind of the Founder*, 184.

14. Jefferson, *Notes on the State of Virginia*, 174–75.

15. Peterson, *Thomas Jefferson and the New Nation*, 266–68; JM to TJ, 16 March 1784, *ROL*, 1:299–305.

16. Wood, *Creation of the American Republic*, 275–76, 437–38; R. Ellis, "Constitutionalism," 121–22; Banning, *Sacred Fire of Liberty*, 133–34; Malone, *Thomas Jefferson*, 1:380–81.

17. Editorial note, *PTJ*, 6:278–84; TJ to JM, 7 May 1783, *ROL*, 1:244–46, and 17 June 1783, 1:251–52; Malone, *Thomas Jefferson*, 1:400–401.

18. JM to TJ, 10 December 1783, *ROL*, 1:286–87, 11 December 1783, 1:287–88, and 15 May 1784, 1:318.

19. Jefferson, *Notes on the State of Virginia*, 118. In the 1780s, visitors supposedly rated Virginia's constitution the worst in America and blamed it for the postwar decline in the quality of the state's political leadership. Greene, "Intellectual Reconstruction."

20. Jefferson, *Notes on the State of Virginia*, 118–20.

21. Ibid., 119–20.

22. Ibid., 121–25.

23. Ibid., 125–26.

24. Editorial note, *PTJ*, 6:278–84; Jefferson, *Notes on the State of Virginia*, 209–22. Jefferson's 1776 draft constitution can be found at *TJW*, 336–45. The constitution as adopted can be found at *PGM*, 1:304–10.

25. Jefferson, *Notes on the State of Virginia*, circa 214, 220.

26. Ibid., 214–15; TJ to JM, 20 February 1784, *ROL*, 1:292–99; JM to TJ, 16 March 1784, *ROL*, 1:299–305.

27. Jefferson, *Notes on the States of Virginia*, 216–19. Following the traditional practice, Jefferson's superior courts included a court of admiralty, a general court of common law, and a High Court of Chancery. The superior court judges would constitute the state supreme court, which Jefferson styled the court of appeals. The governor would appoint inferior court judges, but as further evidence that while Jefferson wanted to reform Virginia's state government, he did not want radical change, the assembly would continue to appoint superior court judges.

Jefferson also favored keeping the general court, where judges were supposed to follow the letter of the common law, separate from the chancery court, where judges enjoyed discretion to fashion remedies not available at common law. He feared chancery's flexibility could infect the common law. "Relieve the judges from the rigors of text law, and permit them, with pretorian discretion, to wander into it's [*sic*] equity, and the whole legal system becomes incertain." TJ to Philip Mazzei, 1785, *PTJ*, 9:67–72.

28. Jefferson, *Notes on the State of Virginia*, 219–20; Burstein and Isenberg, *Madison and Jefferson*, 100–101.

29. Notes for June 1784 Speech, *PJM*, 8:77–78. Madison had apparently studied, in addition to Jefferson's draft constitution, the constitutions of Massachusetts, New York, Pennsylvania, Delaware, North Carolina, South Carolina, and Georgia as reproduced in Francis Bailey's *The Constitutions of the Several Independent States of America*, which had been published in Philadelphia in 1781. Madison's other criticisms included a lack of turnover in the membership of the county courts and the council of state and the lack of an express "mode of expounding [the] Constitution." This would prove to be a vexing issue. The idea the courts could be the final arbitrators of a constitution's meaning was novel at best in 1784, and Madison would not readily embrace it. The editors of Jefferson's

papers, it might be noted, interpret Madison's notes to suggest he was more open to the idea of judicial review in 1784 than he would be even a few years later. Editorial note, *PTJ*, 6:282–84.

30. JM to TJ, 3 July 1784, *ROL*, 1:321–24; TJ to JM, 8 December 1784, ibid., 1:353–55; editorial note, *PJM*, 8:75–79; editorial note, *PTJ*, 6:282–84.

31. JM to TJ, 20 August 1784, *ROL*, 1:337; JM to Caleb Wallace, 23 August 1785, *SWJM*, 29, 33.

32. JM to Caleb Wallace, 23 August 1785, *SWJM*, 29–30.

33. Ibid., 31.

34. Ibid., 32.

35. Ibid., 30.

36. Ibid., 30–31, 33.

37. Ibid., 31. Madison's reference to the British courts could be interpreted as an endorsement of judicial review, but such a view must be an anachronism. Madison elsewhere complained about courts exercising superiority over legislatures, and British courts, in any event, did not exercise the power of judicial review. He may have been referring to the common-law rule of interpretation under which a court, where possible, gives an ambiguous or seemingly arbitrary statute a reasonable interpretation. Or he may simply have meant that British judges had escaped the corruption that he thought had infected the monarchy and Parliament.

It was generally agreed that public officials ought to be subject to impeachment, but it was not obvious where impeachment cases should be tried. Madison suggested they be heard before representatives of each of the branches of the state government. Ibid., 31. Jefferson had been more specific and recommended creating a court of impeachment consisting of three members of the council of state, one member from each of Virginia's three superior courts, two members of the lower house, and one senator. A two-thirds majority would be required for a conviction. Draft Constitution, June 1783, *JPW*, 345.

38. JM to Caleb Wallace, 23 August 1785, *SWJM*, 33–34. Madison's commitment to constitutional stability, it might be noted, was hardly absolute. Tradition and veneration on the one hand, and reason and deliberation, on the other, had to be balanced against each other. See generally Bailey, *James Madison*.

39. Jefferson, *Notes on the State of Virginia*, 87, 286n6; Burstein and Isenberg, *Madison and Jefferson*, 124–25; Onuf and Gordon-Reed, *"Most Blessed of the Patriarchs,"* 10.

40. Jefferson, *Notes on the State of Virginia*, 162–63.

41. "Autobiography," *TJW*, 43–44.

42. JM to Joseph Jones, 28 November 1780, *PJM*, 2:209–11; Broadwater, "James Madison and the Dilemma of American Slavery," 306, 313.

43. JM to Edmund Pendleton, 3 September 1782, *PJM*, 5:101–3; Motion on Slaves Taken by the British, 10 September 1782, ibid., 5:111–13; Report on Property Recaptured by Land, 23 December 1782, ibid., 5:432–36; JM to TJ, 13 May 1783, *ROL*, 1:246–47; JM to Edmund Pendleton, 26 July 1785, *PJM*, 8:327–29; JM to James Madison Sr., 8 September 1783, *PJM*, 7:304–5.

44. Memorandum on Colonizing Freed Slaves, circa 20 October 1789, *JMW*, 472–73; Broadwater, "James Madison and the Dilemma of American Slavery," 313–14, 317–22. See also Broadwater, *James Madison*, 187–201. Madison's approach to slavery at Montpelier

ultimately failed. Burdened with debt, his widow, Dolley Madison, was forced to sell the estate and divide slave families. For a highly critical assessment of Jefferson's performance as a slave owner, see Pybus, "Thomas Jefferson and Slavery." A compulsive collector who invested constantly in Monticello, Jefferson also accumulated heavy debts and freed none of his slaves, except for members of the Hemings family, who, in all likelihood, were relatives. In contrast to Pybus, one of the greatest of Jefferson's biographers has claimed that next to promoting public education, Jefferson's first priority for Virginia was the end of slavery. Peterson, *Thomas Jefferson and the New Nation*, 91–92.

45. J. Miller, *Wolf by the Ears*, 4–17; Malone, *Thomas Jefferson*, 1:141, 187; Draft Constitution, June 1776, *TJW*, 344.

46. Bill to Prevent the Importation of Slaves, 16 June 1777, *PTJ*, 2: 22–24; "Autobiography," *TJW*, 33–34; A Memorandum (Services to My Country), circa 1800, ibid., 702; Malone, *Thomas Jefferson*, 1:264–65; Jefferson, *Notes on the State of Virginia*, 87.

47. J. Miller, *Wolf by the Ears*, 22; TJ to JM, 17 June 1783, *ROL*, 1:255.

48. "Autobiography," *TJW*, 43; J. Miller, *Wolf by the Ears*, 21; Ketcham, *James Madison*, 148. Jefferson's papers do contain a bill, dated October 1785, to prohibit the introduction of any new slaves into Virginia. "A Bill Concerning Slaves," *JPW*, 470–72. Madison may have spoken in support of it during the 1785 session.

49. JM to Ambrose Madison, 15 December 1785, *PJM*, 8:442–43; JM to TJ, 22 January 1786, *ROL*, 1:405; J. Miller, *Wolf by the Ears*, 36–37.

50. See generally Davis, *Inhuman Bondage*.

51. Peterson, *Thomas Jefferson and the New Nation*, 283; J. Miller, *Wolf by the Ears*, 28–29; Ketcham, *James Madison*, 148–49; Morris, *Forging of the Union*, 180; TJ to Chastellux, 7 June 1785, *TJW*, 799–800; TJ to Richard Price, 7 August 1785, *JPW*, 469–70; Answers and Observations for Demeunier's Article on the United States in the *Encyclopedia Methodique*, 24 January 1786, *TJW*, 591–92.

52. *PJM*, 6:292, 407–8; Cheney, *James Madison*, 93–94.

53. The Port Bill, *PJM*, 8:64–66; Brant, *James Madison*, 2:315–16; McCoy, "Virginia Port Bill."

54. JM to TJ, 20 August 1784, *ROL*, 1:337–42; TJ to JM, 11 November 1784, ibid., 1:349–53.

55. McCoy, "Virginia Port Bill," 297, 301; JM to George Washington, 9 December 1785, *JMW*, 47–50.

56. Protest by a "Private Citizen" against the Port Bill, circa November–December 1786, *PGM*, 2:859–64; McCoy, "Virginia Port Bill," 302.

57. Amplification of Subjects Discussed with Vergennes, circa 20 December 1785, *PTJ*, 9:107–15; *ROL*, 1:330–31; editorial note, *PJM*, 8:163–65. See also Ketcham, *James Madison*, 161–62.

58. JM to TJ, 11 February 1784, *ROL*, 1:290–91; TJ to JM, 20 February 1784, 1:292–97, and 25 and 30 April 1784, 1:292–310; JM to TJ, 15 November 1785, ibid., 1:392.

59. Editorial note, *PTJ*, 2:322–25; editorial note, *PJM*, 8:389–94; JM to Samuel Harris Smith, 4 November 1826, *WJM*, 9:256–61; TJ to G. K. van Hogendorp, 13 October 1785, *PTJ*, 8:632.

60. "A Bill for Establishing Religious Freedom," *PTJ*, 2:545–53; Burstein and Isenberg, *Madison and Jefferson*, 107; Ketcham, *James Madison*, 165–66; Beeman, "American Revolution," 41.

61. Ragosta, "Virginia Statute," 80. The general assessment was by no means a Virginia phenomenon. No less a figure than John Adams supported a general assessment in Massachusetts. See Buckley, *Establishing Religious Freedom*, 55–81.

62. A version of the Bill for Establishing Religious Freedom showing Jefferson's original draft with amendments made by the General Assembly is reproduced at Ragosta, "Virginia Statute," 87–88. Jefferson expressed similar views in his *Notes on the State of Virginia*. People were answerable to God for their religious opinions, but "reason and free inquiry are the only effectual agents against error." Attempts to impose Christianity had made "one half the world fools, and the other half hypocrites." Pennsylvania and New York had flourished without a religious establishment, and if they harbored a variety of sects, they were "all sufficient to preserve peace and order." Jefferson, *Notes on the State of Virginia*, 159–61.

63. Bill No. 84, *PTJ*, 2:555.

64. "A Bill for Establishing Religious Freedom," *PTJ*, 2:545–53; TJ to Joseph Priestly, 9 April 1803, *TJW*, 1120–22; TJ to Benjamin Rush, 21 April 1803, *TJW*, 1122–26. For an introduction to Jefferson's views on religion and politics, see Neem, "Republican Reformation." For a contrary view of Jefferson's bill, see Pocock, "Religious Freedom." Pocock argues the statute tended toward the establishment of a "religion of free inquiry," which dismissed religion as a matter of opinion about which nothing could be said conclusively, hardly the attitude of an orthodox believer. In other words, Jefferson supported freedom of religion as a way to achieve freedom from it.

65. JM to TJ, 20 August 1785, *ROL*, 1:373–80.

66. Brant, *James Madison*, 2:352; "Memorial and Remonstrance against Religious Assessments," circa 20 June 1785, *JMW*, 29–36.

67. "Memorial and Remonstrance against Religious Assessments," circa 20 June 1785, *JMW*, 29–36; Ragosta, "Virginia Statute," 77.

68. "Memorial and Remonstrance against Religious Assessments," circa 20 June 1785, *JMW*, 29–36.

69. Ibid.; Ragosta, "Virginia Statute," 88.

70. JM to TJ, 22 January 1786, *ROL*, 1:403; "Memorial and Remonstrance against Religious Assessments," circa 20 June 1785, *JMW*, 29–36.

71. See Banning, *Sacred Fire of Liberty*, 85.

72. JM to TJ, 16 March 1784, *ROL*, 1:299–305; TJ to JM, 25 and 30 April 1784, ibid., 1:310.

73. Resolutions Appointing Virginia Members of a Potomac River Commission, 28 June 1784, *PJM*, 8:89–90; Resolutions Authorizing an Interstate Compact on Navigation and Jurisdiction of the Potomac, 28 December 1784, ibid., 8:206–7; Broadwater, *George Mason*, 153–54.

74. Mount Vernon Compact, *PGM*, 2:812–23.

75. JM to TJ, 27 April 1785, *ROL*, 1:367–71; *PJM*, 8:413n3; JM to George Washington, 9 December 1785, *JMW*, 47–50; Act Ratifying the Chesapeake Compact with Maryland, circa 24–26 December 1785, *PJM*, 8:457–61; "A Sketch Never Finished nor Applied," circa 1830, *JMW*, 834–36.

76. "A Sketch Never Finished nor Applied," circa 1830, *JMW*, 833–34; editorial note, *PJM*, 8:406–9; Banning, *Sacred Fire of Liberty*, 65–66.

77. "A Sketch Never Finished nor Applied," circa 1830, *JMW*, 833–36; JM to James Monroe, 22 January 1785, *PJM*, 8:482–84.

CHAPTER 6

1. Peterson, *Thomas Jefferson and the New Nation*, 331; Malone, *Thomas Jefferson*, 2:153–54; TJ to George Wythe, 13 August 1786, *TJW*, 857–60.

2. JM to TJ, 22 January 1786, *ROL*, 1:401–9; TJ to JM, 8 February 1786, ibid., 1:409–12.

3. TJ to Archibald Stuart, 25 January 1786, *TJW*, 843–45.

4. Answers and Observations for Demeunier's Article on the United States in the *Encyclopedia Methodique*, 24 January 1786, *TJW*, 575–79. Congress had approved requisitions based on population, but the Articles of Confederation did not expressly authorize them.

5. TJ to JM, 8 February 1786, *ROL*, 1:409–12; Malone, *Thomas Jefferson*, 2:160–62.

6. Notes on Professor Ebeling's Letter of 30 July 1795, *TJW*, 697–99; TJ to John Cartwright, 5 June 1824, ibid., 1490–96; "Autobiography," ibid., 70–71, 75. Jefferson also indulged in some revisionist history of his own during the partisan battles of the 1790s when he claimed his Federalist opponents, chiefly Alexander Hamilton, and to a lesser extent John Adams, had opposed reasonable reforms in the 1780s because they hoped to provoke a crisis that would produce a monarchy. See "The Anas, 1791–1806," 4 February 1818, ibid., 662–65, 671–72.

7. Meacham, *Thomas Jefferson*, 180–81; TJ to JM, 25 April 1786, *ROL*, 1:417–18; TJ to John Page, 4 May 1786, *TJW*, 852–54; "Autobiography," *TJW*, 57–58. For more on the nation's diplomatic weakness as a motive for constitutional reform, see Perkins, *Creation of an American Empire*, 58–59; and Herring, *From Colony to Superpower*, 46–52.

8. "Of Ancient and Modern Confederacies," in Meyers, *Mind of the Founder*, 47–56. For example, Madison's *Federalist* Nos. 18–20 drew heavily on the memorandum. See also Rakove, *Original Meanings*, 25–31.

We may not fully appreciate the impression the Dutch experience made on the founders. A power struggle between the Patriot Party, which controlled the States General of the United Netherlands, and the stadtholder, the prince of Orange, who was supported by royalists and aristocrats, divided the country and led to foreign intervention. France supported the Patriots. Great Britain and Prussia backed the stadtholder. An alleged insult to the princess of Orange led her brother, the Prussian king, to send 20,000 troops to the Netherlands. During the Constitutional Convention, Benjamin Franklin, in opposing an absolute veto for the president, cited the stadtholder as evidence that executives always sought more power. "The present Stadtholder is ready to wade thro' a bloody civil war to the establishment of a monarchy." Farrand, *Records*, 1:102–3. See also Peterson, *Thomas Jefferson and the New Nation*, 356–57.

9. JM to TJ, 19 June 1786, *ROL*, 1:423–28. Madison, Forrest McDonald has argued, hoped to stop the evolution of American society at "the commercial agricultural stage" in order to avoid the luxury and corruption he associated with more economically advanced stages of development. McDonald, *Novus Ordo Seclorum*, 134–36.

10. JM to TJ, 18 March 1786, *ROL*, 1:413–16, and 19 June 1786, 1:423–28.

11. JM to TJ, 18 March 1786, *ROL*, 1:413–16, and 12 August 1786, 1:428–33; Banning, *Sacred Fire of Liberty*, 71–73; Ketcham, *James Madison*, 176.

12. Burstein and Isenberg, *Madison and Jefferson*, 128–29; JM to TJ, 18 March 1786, *ROL*, 1:413–16; JM to James Monroe, 19 March 1786, *JMW*, 50–51; JM to TJ, 12 May 1786, *ROL*, 1:419–23, and 12 August 1786, 1:248–33.

13. JM to TJ, 18 March 1786, *ROL*, 1:413–16. Jefferson, by contrast, was less worried about adding new states. Growth, he thought, would "drown the little divisions at present" troubling the nation. TJ to Archibald Stuart, 25 January 1786, *TJW*, 843–45.

14. Cheney, *James Madison*, 122–23; Rakove, *Original Meanings*, 44; JM to TJ, 12 August 1786, *ROL*, 1:428–33; JM to James Monroe, 11 September 1786, *JMW*, 59.

15. "A Sketch Never Finished nor Applied," circa 1830, *JMW*, 834–36; Address of the Annapolis Convention, 14 September 1786, in Syrett, *Papers of Alexander Hamilton*, 3:686–90; Ketcham, *James Madison*, 185–86. The poor attendance at Annapolis should not be seen as evidence of widespread opposition to reform. New Hampshire, Massachusetts, Rhode Island, and North Carolina had also appointed delegates, but for different reasons they did not make it to the convention. Hugh Williamson of North Carolina, for example, arrived in Annapolis after the convention had adjourned.

16. TJ to JM, 16 December 1786, *ROL*, 1:457–60. Jefferson's goals for reform might have been relatively modest in part because he took a broader view of the existing powers of Congress than did some of his contemporaries. Jefferson challenged John Adams's statement in his *Defence of the Constitutions of the United States* that Congress was a diplomatic and not a legislative body. Jefferson argued that the states had delegated at least some legislative and executive functions to Congress. TJ to John Adams, 23 February 1787, *AJC*, 1:170.

17. "A Sketch Never Finished nor Applied," circa 1830, *JMW*, 836–39. See generally Condon, *Shays's Rebellion*.

18. "A Sketch Never Finished nor Applied," circa 1830, *JMW*, 836–39; JM to TJ, 19 March 1787, *ROL*, 1:469–74; JM to George Washington, 16 April 1787, *JMW*, 80–85; JM to TJ, 23 April 1787, *ROL*, 1:474–77; Malone, *Thomas Jefferson*, 2:156–59; Gutzman, *James Madison*, 54–65.

19. TJ to Maria Cosway, 12 October 1786, *TJW*, 871; John Adams to TJ, 30 November 1786, *AJC*, 1:156; Abigail Adams to TJ, 29 January 1787, *AJC*, 1:168; Steele, *Thomas Jefferson and American Nationhood*, 112–13.

20. TJ to JM, 30 January and 5 February 1787, *ROL*, 1:460–65; TJ to Edward Carrington, 16 January 1787, *TJW*, 879–81; TJ to Abigail Adams, 22 February 1787, *AJC*, 1:142–73; TJ to William Carmichael, 26 December 1786, *PTJ*, 10:632–35; TJ to David Hartley, 2 July 1787, *PTJ*, 11:525–26; TJ to Thomas Brand Hollis, 2 July 1787, *PTJ*, 11:527.

21. JM to George Washington, 7 December 1786, *JMW*, 59–61; TJ to JM, 16 December 1786, *ROL*, 1:457–60, and 30 January and 5 February 1787, 1:460–65; Gutzman, *James Madison*, 60–61; JM to TJ, 4 December 1786, *ROL*, 1:454–57. Van Cleve minimizes the significance of Shays's Rebellion in persuading the assembly to support a constitutional convention and attributes more importance to lawmakers' desire to create a government that could defend the frontier against Indian attacks. Van Cleve, *We Have Not a Government*, 252–56.

22. JM to TJ, 4 December 1786, *ROL*, 1:454–57, and 15 February 1787, 1:466–68.

23. JM to Edmund Pendleton, 24 February 1787, *JMW*, 61–65; JM to TJ, 19 March 1787, *ROL*, 1:469–74, and 23 April 1787, 1:474–77. Madison accused Henry of favoring a partition of the union and the creation of a southern confederacy. See JM to TJ, 6 June 1787, *ROL*, 1:479. Recent historians have been more charitable. There is not much evidence for Madison's claims. See Gutzman, *James Madison*, 84. Richard Beeman has suggested that Henry probably did not say of the Philadelphia convention that he "smelt a rat," a phrase that has been repeatedly attributed to him. Henry likely declined to serve because he had

just retired as governor and was preoccupied by personal and local affairs. Beeman, *Plain, Honest Men*, 92.

24. JM to TJ, 19 March 1787, *ROL*, 1:469–74; Ketcham, *James Madison*, 180.

25. JM to TJ, 19 March 1787, *ROL*, 1:469–74, 23 April 1787, 1:474–77, and 6 June 1787, 1:479; "A Sketch Never Finished nor Applied," circa 1830, *JMW*, 836; Burstein and Isenberg, *Madison and Jefferson*, 147–48.

26. "A Sketch Never Finished nor Applied," circa 1830, *JMW*, 839–40; JM to TJ, 19 March 1787, *ROL*, 1:469–74.

27. JM to Edmund Randolph, 8 April 1787, *WJM*, 2:336–40; JM to George Washington, 16 April 1787, *JMW*, 80–85. Madison saw the Senate as a mainly deliberative body in which individual states apparently might not have representation. Rakove, *Politician Thinking*, 79–80.

28. JM to Edmund Randolph, 8 April 1787, *WJM*, 2:336–40; JM to George Washington, 16 April 1787, *JMW*, 80–85; Rakove, *Original Meanings*, 51. Forrest McDonald placed Madison between "court-party nationalists and the republican ideologues," which is a fair description of Madison's politics over the length of his career, but Kevin Gutzman has probably better captured Madison's attitude in the spring and summer of 1787: Madison wanted "to reduce the states to mere subdivisions of the centralized structure." F. McDonald, *Novus Ordo Seclorum*, 203; Gutzman, *James Madison*, 67. Madison's ambitions for the new government were largely negative, to be sure, and more modest than those of Hamilton. Madison hoped a stronger central authority could regulate dangerous factions within the states. Beeman, *Plain, Honest Men*, 29. It might be noted that while Madison told Randolph he had borrowed his congressional negative from the British monarch's veto power, he did not mention that fact to Jefferson. Feldman, *Three Lives*, 103.

29. Rakove, *Original Meanings*, 28; Banning, *Sacred Fire of Liberty*, 74–75.

30. Cheney, *James Madison*, 123–24; "Vices of the Political System of the United States," April 1787, *JMW*, 69–80.

31. "Vices of the Political System of the United States," April 1787, *JMW*, 71–72.

32. Ibid., 72–74.

33. Ibid., 74–75.

34. Ibid., 75–76.

35. Ibid., 76–79.

36. Ibid., 80. Madison's theory of factions has often been traced to Hume. See Adair, "'That Politics May Be Reduced to a Science.'" The theory provided a rebuttal to Montesquieu's maxim that representative governments could flourish only in small republics where citizens shared a common interest. See F. McDonald, *Novus Ordo Seclorum*, 162–66.

37. JM to TJ, 15 May 1787, *ROL*, 1:477; Farrand, *Records*, 1:1–2.

38. See the following in *PTJ*: TJ to C. W. F. Dumas, 14 June 1787, 11:471; TJ to David Hartley, 2 July 1787, 11:525–26; TJ to James Currie, 4 August 1787, 11:681–83; TJ to Benjamin Hawkins, 4 August 1787, 11:683–84; TJ to William Hay, 4 August 1787, 11:685–86; TJ to Gaudenzio Clerici, 15 August 1787, 12:38–39.

39. TJ to Edward Carrington, 4 August 1787, ibid., 11:678–80.

40. TJ to Edmund Randolph, 3 August 1787, ibid., 11:672–73; TJ to Joseph Jones, 14 August 1787, ibid., 12:33–35; TJ to George Washington, 14 August 1787, ibid., 12:36–38; TJ to Francis dal Verme, 15 August 1787, ibid., 12:42–43.

41. JM to TJ, 6 June 1787, *ROL*, 1:477–80; Beeman, *Plain, Honest Men*, 55–56, 65, 127–29. Beeman believes the Pennsylvania delegates, and in particular James Wilson, helped Madison clarify his thinking about a national executive. Wilson favored a strong president independent of Congress. Madison's 6 June letter, however, suggests the limits of his support for what his generation called "high toned" government. Commenting on John Adams's recent *Defence of the Constitutions of the United States*, Madison complained it contained comments "unfriendly to republicanism." Madison told Jefferson, "Men of learning find nothing new in it, Men of taste many things to criticize." *ROL*, 1:479. Madison rarely personalized political disagreements, but he never liked Adams.

The delegates also agreed at the start of the convention that issues apparently decided could be reconsidered, which allowed them a needed flexibility, but which gave the debates a rather circular quality and produced a sometimes confusing record.

42. "The Virginia Plan," 29 May 1787, *JMW*, 89–91; "A Sketch Never Finished nor Applied," circa 1830, ibid., 840–41; Farrand, *Records*, 3:559–60; Beeman, *Plain, Honest Men*, 70–71.

43. "The Virginia Plan," 29 May 1787, *JMW*, 89–91.

44. Farrand, *Records*, 1:53–54; Gutzman, *James Madison*, 77.

45. Farrand, *Records*, 1:109–10; Speech of 6 June 1787, *JMW*, 94–95; Beeman, *Plain, Honest Men*, 107, 140, 152–55. In Madison's defense, he was trying to incorporate into a system of checks and balances two novel institutions, a republican executive and a federal judiciary, that later generations could take for granted.

46. See Rakove, *Original Meanings*, 62–77.

47. Farrand, *Records*, 1:37–39, 49, 137–38; Ketcham, *James Madison*, 200; Speech of 6 June 1787, *JMW*, 92–93. For an argument that Madison wanted to "refine" public opinion, not stifle it, see Sheehan, *Mind of James Madison*, 62, 86.

Bilder, *Madison's Hand*, questions whether Madison discussed factions on 6 June and generally challenges the veracity of his notes on the convention. For an effective rebuttal, see Uzzell, "New Investigation."

48. Farrand, *Records*, 1:167–68; Speech of 7 June 1787, *JMW*, 98–99; Speech of 8 June 1787, *JMW*, 99–100; Cheney, *James Madison*, 131.

49. Farrand, *Records*, 1:196–202.

50. Gutzman, *James Madison*, 89; Farrand, *Records*, 1:214–15, 218–19, 232–34. Madison also believed the Senate should appoint federal judges and be allowed to originate money bills, ideas that were approved but later defeated. He thought "the Senate would be generally a more capable sett [*sic*] of men" than House members. Farrand, *Records*, 1:232–34.

51. Farrand, *Records*, 1:224–32; Ketcham, *James Madison*, 204.

52. Farrand, *Records*, 1:242–45. See also Beeman, *Plain, Honest Men*, 161.

53. Farrand, *Records*, 1:325–26; Speech of 19 June 1878, *JMW*, 101–8; Ketcham, *James Madison*, 207.

54. TJ to JM, 20 June 1787, *ROL*, 1:480–83. Jefferson is hardly remembered as an advocate of judicial supremacy, but he reasoned that if Congress exercised a veto on state laws, no power could restrain it, but if the federal courts welded a similar power, Congress would "watch and restrain them." One of Jefferson's greatest biographers has argued that Jefferson generally opposed the abuse of power that seemed most likely at the moment, and in 1787, "the danger of judicial supremacy was exceedingly remote." Malone, *Thomas Jefferson*, 2:163–64.

55. Farrand, *Records*, 1:354–55; Speech of 21 June 1787, *JMW*, 108–9.

56. Farrand, *Records*, 1:360–62, 422; Speech of 26 June 1787, *JMW*, 110–11.

57. Speech of 28 June 1787, *JMW*, 112–15; Speech of 29 June 1787, ibid., 115–17.

58. Farrand, *Records*, 1:468–69; Speech of 30 June 1787, *JMW*, 117–19. Madison's proposed compromise, which no one seems to have taken very seriously, would have done away with the three-fifths ratio for counting slaves.

59. Farrand, *Records*, 1:510–16.

60. Ibid., 1:526; Beeman, *Plain, Honest Men*, 201–2.

61. Speech of 5 July 1787, *JMW*, 120–21.

62. Speech of 14 July 1787, ibid., 123–25. See McCoy, "James Madison," 256.

63. Farrand, *Records*, 2:15–19; Cheney, *James Madison*, 141–42; Ketcham, *James Madison*, 213–14.

64. Farrand, *Records*, 2:27–28.

65. Speech of 23 July 1787, *JMW*, 129. In fact, Madison supported ratification by special conventions not only because they would likely be more sympathetic to the Constitution than state legislatures, which were being asked to give up some power, would be, but also because he wanted to establish the clear superiority of the Constitution over other laws. See Farrand, *Records*, 2:476; and Ketcham, *James Madison*, 218. Madison probably was not influenced at the time by Jefferson's letter of 20 June 1787, which argued judicial review would be a more efficient check on the states than the congressional negative, because he had apparently not received it. In a letter dated 6 September 1787, Madison refers to "the shortness of the interval between the receipt of your letter of June 20. and the date of this." *ROL*, 1:490. On the negative generally, see Hobson, "Negative on State Laws."

66. JM to TJ, 18 July 1787, *ROL*, 1:483–84; TJ to John Adams, 30 August 1787, *AJC*, 1:194–96.

67. Farrand, *Records*, 2:33; Speech of 17 July 1787, *JMW*, 125–27; Cheney, *James Madison*, 142–43; Ketcham, *James Madison*, 216–17. Especially after the Great Compromise was approved, Madison supported a vigorous, but not overweening, executive. He argued strongly that the president should be subject to impeachment. Speech of 20 July 1787, *JMW*, 128. He recommended, however, that an impeached president be tried in the Supreme Court to avoid making the office excessively dependent on Congress; Sherman pointed out the flaw in the proposal: the president appoints the judges. Farrand, *Records*, 2:551. Despite his unhappiness with the composition of the Senate, Madison thought the Senate, by a two-thirds vote, should be able to make a peace treaty without the concurrence of the president. Executives derive so much power from war that a future president, he argued, might be reluctant to make peace. Farrand, *Records*, 2:540–41. Madison also favored a three-fourths majority of both houses of Congress to override a presidential veto, but the convention adopted the two-thirds requirement by a vote of 6–4–1. Farrand, *Records*, 2:586–87.

68. Speech of 19 July 1787, *JMW*, 127–28; Farrand, *Records*, 2:57–58.

69. Farrand, *Records*, 2:99–101.

70. Speech of 25 July 1787, *JMW*, 130–32.

71. Ibid.

72. John Dickinson to George Logan, 16 January 1802, in Hutson, *Supplement to the Records of the Federal Convention*, 300–302; Cheney, *James Madison*, 145–47.

73. John Dickinson to George Logan, 16 January 1802, in Hutson, *Supplement to the Records of the Federal Convention*, 300–302.

74. Speech of 7 August 1787, *JMW*, 132–33. For an argument that Madison believed in majority rule but wanted to create a system of checks and balances to impede rash action and control momentary passions so that the end result of the legislative process would reflect a stable and reasonable majority view, see Weiner, *Madison's Metronome*.

75. Speech of 9 August 1787, *JMW*, 134–35; Farrand, *Records*, 2:249–50, 268–63.

76. Beeman, *Plain, Honest Men*, 273–75.

77. Farrand, *Records*, 1:551–53, 2:177–89, 2:324–25; Ketcham, *James Madison*, 220; Beeman, *Plain, Honest Men*, 288–89.

78. See generally Klarman, *Framer's Coup*, 283–91.

79. Farrand, *Records*, 2:364, 400–401.

80. Ibid., 2:415, 417; Cheney, *James Madison*, 148–49. Shortly after approving the slave trade compromise, the convention adopted with little debate a provision requiring the return of fugitive slaves. Edward Coles, who later served as Madison's secretary, said that Madison told him delegates who were also members of Congress had worked to include a fugitive slave clause in the Constitution and in the Northwest Ordinance of 1787 to make "the constitution more acceptable to slaveholders." Hutson, *Supplement to the Records of the Federal Convention*, 321.

81. Farrand, *Records*, 2:451–52; Ketcham, *James Madison*, 224–25. For Mason's allegation of a Deep South–New England deal, see Thomas Jefferson's Notes, 30 September 1792, *PGM*, 3:1275–56.

82. JM to TJ, 6 September 1787, *ROL*, 1:490–92. Notwithstanding Madison's alarm over Shays's Rebellion, neither he nor Jefferson seemed much concerned about popular protest in Virginia. Van Cleve, *We Have Not a Government*, 235–37.

83. "A Sketch Never Finished nor Applied," circa 1830, *JMW*, 841–42; Burstein and Isenberg, *Madison and Jefferson*, 149–59.

84. Madison's personal financial interests had no significant impact on his performance. See Ketcham, *James Madison*, 229–30. According to one quantitative analysis, Madison voted consistently with his economic interests on nine of sixteen major issues, not a particularly high correlation. McGuire, *To Form a More Perfect Union*, 90–91. Political considerations played a larger role. Madison's support for proportional representation obviously served Virginia's political interests since it was by far the most populous state in 1787. Robertson, *Original Compromise*, 230.

CHAPTER 7

1. Edward Carrington to JM, 23 September 1787, *PJM*, 10:172; Maier, *Ratification*, 53–59; JM to George Washington, 30 September 1787, *JMW*, 137.

2. Gutzman, *James Madison*, 161–62; George Mason, "Objections to This Constitution of Government," circa 16 September 1787, *PGM*, 3:991–94; JM to TJ, 24 October and 1 November 1787, *ROL*, 1:503–4. The lack of a bill of rights immediately became a controversial point. See JM to Edmund Randolph, 21 October 1787, *PJM*, 10:199. Mason complained directly to Jefferson. George Mason to TJ, 26 May 1788, *PGM*, 3:1044–46.

3. JM to George Washington, 30 September 1787, *JMW*, 138; Cheney, *James Madison*, 155–56; Maier, *Ratification*, 53–59; Klarman, *Framers' Coup*, 417.

4. JM to Edmund Pendleton, 20 September 1787, *PJM*, 10:171; Malone, *Thomas Jefferson*, 2:164–71; TJ to John Adams, 28 September 1787, *AJC*, 1:199–200.

5. JM to TJ, 24 October and 1 November 1787, *ROL*, 1:495–96.

6. Ibid., 1:497–98.

7. Ibid., 1:498–501.

8. Ibid., 1:501–2.

9. Ibid., 1:503.

10. Ibid., 1:504–7; JM to George Washington, 18 October 1787, *JMW*, 140–42.

11. "Autobiography," *TJW*, 71–72; Gish and Klinghard, "Republican Constitutionalism"; Glover, *Fate of the Revolution*, 100; Kaplan, "Jefferson and the Constitution"; Mayer, *Constitutional Thought*, 225: Peterson, *Thomas Jefferson and the New Nation*, 360–69.

12. TJ to William S. Smith, 13 November 1787, *TJW*, 910–12; TJ to John Adams, 13 November 1787, *AJC*, 1:211–12.

13. TJ to John Adams, 13 November 1787, *AJC*, 1:211–12; TJ to Alexander Donald, 7 February 1788, *TJW*, 919–20; "Autobiography," *TJW*, 73–73. Edmund Randolph also objected to the absence of presidential term limits. Maier, *Ratification*, 90.

14. TJ to William S. Smith, 2 February 1788, *PTJ*, 12:557–58.

15. TJ to John Adams, 13 November 1787, *AJC*, 1:211–12; TJ to Edward Carrington, 21 December 1787, *PTJ*, 12:445–47; TJ to Alexander Donald, 7 February 1788, *TJW*, 919–20. It is unclear whether Jefferson intended for his nine/four plan to lead to the second constitutional convention that Anti-Federalists wanted. Compare Burstein and Isenberg, *Madison and Jefferson*, 179–80; and "Autobiography," *TJW*, 72.

16. Detached Memorandum, circa 1819, *JMW*, 768–69; JM to George Washington, 18 November 1787, ibid., 158–59; JM to George Washington, 20 November 1787, *PJM*, 10:283; JM to Edmund Randolph, 2 December 1787, *PJM*, 10:290; JM to George Washington, 7 December 1787, *PJM*, 10:295. On questions of authorship, see the introduction in Cooke, *Federalist*.

17. Cheney, *James Madison*, 164–65; JM to George Lee Turberville, 11 December 1787, *PJM*, 10:314; Cooke, *Federalist* No. 38, 247; Cooke, *Federalist* No. 10, 63. Madison's faith in the ability of congressional elections to produce victors superior to state politicians was in part a matter of numbers. In larger districts, the percentage of "fit characters" to available offices was greater, and more voters would participate in their selection.

For an elegant essay stressing the novelty of Madison's arguments, see Agresto, "'System without a Precedent.'" Agresto suggests Madison believed that, in part by taming factions, the Constitution would not only preserve rights but ultimately allow for their expansion.

18. Cooke, *Federalist* No. 14, 83–89.

19. Ibid., No. 51, 347–53.

20. JM to TJ, 9 December 1787, *ROL*, 1:507–11. Madison continued, with virtually no evidence, to accuse Henry of wanting to defeat the Constitution, rupture the union, and create a southern confederacy that he would lead. See, for example, JM to Edmund Randolph, 10 January 1788, *PJM*, 10:355–56. Most historians dismiss the charges as pure fantasy. See Glover, *Fate of the Revolution*, 54; Gutzman, *James Madison*, 151, 158; and Ketcham, *James Madison*, 235. Why did Madison make them? We can only speculate. Once Henry emerged as the voice, literally, of Virginia Anti-Federalism, Madison had a political motive to demonize him. Madison seems to have sincerely believed that defeat of the Constitution would have led to the partition of the United States; he might have assumed that die-hard opponents of ratification favored that result. And of course he never liked Henry and was probably prepared to believe the worst about him. On Henry's role in the ratification debate, see Kukla, *Patrick Henry*, 321–48; and Kidd, *Patrick Henry*, 183–211. For a survey of the range of opinions in Virginia, see Kukla, "Spectrum of Sentiments."

21. JM to TJ, 9 December 1787, *ROL*, 1:510.

22. Ibid., 20 December 1787, 1:515. On ratification in North Carolina, see Howard, "State That Said No."

23. TJ to JM, 20 December 1787, *ROL*, 1:511–12.

24. Ibid., 1:512–13.

25. Ibid., 1:513–14.

26. Ibid., 1:514.

27. JM to Edmund Randolph, 10 January 1788, *JMW*, 190–93.

28. Cheney, *James Madison*, 164–65; Cooke, *Federalist* No. 37, 231–39.

29. Cooke, *Federalist* No. 40, 258–62.

30. Ibid., 263–65.

31. Ibid., No. 41, 268–78. One of Madison's most recent biographers sees in *Federalist* No. 41 Madison's first attempt to offer a method of constitutional interpretation. In discussing the general welfare clause, Madison opined that while all parts of an instrument should be given effect, ambiguous provisions should be read narrowly. Feldman, *Three Lives*, 203–4.

32. Cooke, *Federalist* No. 43, 293.

33. Ibid., No. 48, 332–38.

34. Ibid., No. 49, 338–39; Rakove, *Politician Thinking*, 146–48. Article V of the Constitution provides that a constitutional convention can be called upon the application of the legislatures of two-thirds of the states.

35. Cooke, *Federalist* No. 49, 339–41. Neither did Madison welcome the idea of periodic conventions. If they were too frequent, they would be caught up in the passions of the moment. If they were too infrequent, they would not deter unconstitutional actions. See ibid., No. 50, 338–43. For an alternative reading of *Federalist* No. 49, which puts less emphasis on the value of "veneration," see Bailey, *James Madison*, 21–32.

36. Cooke, *Federalist* No. 55, 374; Report of the Pennsylvania Minority, 18 December 1787, in Ketcham, *Anti-Federalist Papers*, 247–49; Speeches of Melancton Smith, 20–21 June 1787, in Ketcham, *Anti-Federalist Papers*, 340–47.

37. Cooke, *Federalist* No. 56, 378.

38. Ibid., No. 57, 384–90, and No. 58, 391–97. Madison's argument that Congress would expand the House of Representatives as appropriate is another case of subordinating a personal opinion to the cause of ratification. During the Constitutional Convention, he had belittled the origination clause, requiring tax and spending bills to originate in the House. As we have seen, he did not consider it a meaningful concession to the large states. In *Federalist* No. 58, he described it as a "powerful instrument" by which the more populous states could pressure a Senate supposedly dominated by the small states to enlarge the House. Ibid., No. 58, 394.

39. Ibid., No. 55, 378.

40. Ibid., Nos. 18–20, 110–29, and No. 38, 239–49; JM to TJ, 19 February 1788, *ROL*, 1:530–32.

41. Cooke, *Federalist* No. 42, 279, and No. 43, 281–82. Madison implied that all the American states would surely agree to the end of the trade in twenty years, and in fact Congress did pass legislation in 1808 to prohibit the trade beginning in 1809.

42. Ibid., No. 43, 288–98.

43. Ibid., No. 44, 299–305.

44. Ibid., No. 39, 251–53, No. 52, 353–59, No. 53, 359–66, and No. 63, 422–31. For more on the Senate, see also ibid., No. 62, 415–22.

45. Ibid., No. 47, 323–31.

46. Ibid., No. 39, 250–57.

47. Ibid., No. 54, 371, and No. 62, 416. After Hamilton left New York City early in 1788 on legal business, Madison wrote twenty-two essays in forty days. Cheney, *James Madison*, 165. For an argument that Madison's *Federalist* essays reflected changes in his thinking that began at the Constitutional Convention, see Banning, "Practical Sphere."

48. Cooke, *Federalist* No. 45, 308–14, and No. 46, 315–23; Gutzman, *James Madison*, 183.

49. JM to TJ, 6 February 1788, *ROL*, 1:529–30; TJ to C. W. F. Dumas, 12 February 1788, *PTJ*, 12:583–84; Edward Carrington to TJ, 14 May 1788, *PTJ*, 13:156–58; JM to TJ, 10 August 1788, *ROL*, 1:547–49.

50. Archibald Stuart to JM, 14 January 1788, *PJM*, 10:374; Tench Coxe to JM, 16 January 1788, ibid., 10:375.

51. Berstein and Isenberg, *Madison and Jefferson*, 173–75; Maier, *Ratification*, 84–85; Gutzman, *James Madison*, 191; Ketcham, *James Madison*, 240; Glover, *Fate of the Revolution*, 58–59. Madison's argument for an "extended republic," for example, may have been most important in shaping his own thinking. See Gibson, "Inventing the Extended Republic."

52. TJ to JM, 18 November 1788, *ROL*, 1:566–68; TJ to Thomas Mann Randolph, 30 May 1790, *JPW*, 260–63; TJ to Francois D'Ivernois, 6 February 1795, *TJW*, 1022–25; Onuf, *Jefferson's Empire*, 54–55; TJ to JM, 1 February 1825, *ROL*, 3:1923–24.

53. JM to Edmund Pendleton, 30 September 1787, *PJM*, 10:171; JM to Ambrose Madison, 8 November 1787, ibid., 10:244; JM to Eliza House Trist, 25 March 1788, *JMW*, 353; Maier, *Ratification*, 225–26; Ketcham, *James Madison*, 251.

54. JM to George Washington, 15 February 1788, *PJM*, 10:510, and 3 March 1788, 10:555; Glover, *Fate of the Revolution*, 90. Maier, *Ratification*, covers these events in great detail. For a more concise, but still thorough, survey, see Rutland, *Ordeal of the Constitution*. Despite popular agitation over the absence of a federal bill of rights, the Massachusetts amendments did not focus on individual liberties. They included these provisions: (1) powers not "expressly delegated" to the national government remained with the states; (2) there should be one representative for every 30,000 people, but no more than 200; (3) Congress should not exercise its powers to regulate elections unless a state failed to act or adopted "regulations subversive of the rights of the people"; (4) no direct taxes could be imposed unless impost and excise taxes proved insufficient and a state had failed to meet its requisitions; (5) commercial monopolies were banned; (6) grand juries were required in criminal cases; (7) federal courts lacked jurisdiction in diversity cases not involving significant sums of money; (8) either party could request a jury in diversity cases; and (9) no federal official could accept a title or office from a foreign state or ruler. Bailyn, *Debate on the Constitution*, 1:943–45.

55. Glover, *Fate of the Revolution*, 47; Maier, *Ratification*, 237–40; George Lee Turberville to JM, 16 April 1788, *PJM*, 11:24; JM to TJ, 22 April 1788, *ROL*, 1:534–35; JM to John Brown, 27 May 1788, *PJM*, 11:60; JM to Rufus King, 13 June 1788, *PJM*, 11:133.

56. Maier, *Ratification*, 231–32; TJ to George Washington, 2 May 1788, *PTJ*, 13:124–29; TJ to C. W. F. Dumas, 15 May 1788, *PTJ*, 13:159–61; TJ to Moustier, 17 May 1788, *PTJ*, 13:173–76; TJ to Edward Carrington, 27 May 1788, *JPW*, 363–65. See also Boles, *Jefferson*, 191–96.

57. Glover, *Fate of the Revolution*, 9–14; Ketcham, *James Madison*, 254–55.

58. Speech of 6 June 1788, *JMW*, 354–61. See also Speech of 14 June 1788, ibid., 385–87.

59. Speech of 6 June 1788, ibid., 361–65; Speech of 11 June 1788, ibid., 366–79; Speech of 12 June 1788, ibid., 366–79.

60. Maier, *Ratification*, 271; Speech of 11 June 1788, *JMW*, 366–79; JM to Tench Cox, 30 July 1788, *PJM*, 11:210.

61. Speech of 12 June 1788, *JMW*, 380–84. On the Mississippi question and related issues, see R. Smith, "Foreign Affairs."

62. Speech of 17 June 1788, *PGM*, 3:1086; Speech of 17 June 1788, *JMW*, 391–92.

63. Speech of 20 June 1788, *JMW*, 393–95. In *Chisholm v. Georgia* (1793), the Supreme Court held that a state could be sued against its will in a federal court. The decision was overruled by the Eleventh Amendment.

64. Speech of 20 June 1788, *JMW*, 396–400. For an example of an Anti-Federalist critique of federal judicial power, see George Mason's speeches of 19–20 June 1788, *PGM*, 3:1101–11.

65. Cheney, *James Madison*, 170; Maier, *Ratification*, 275–76; Patrick Henry, Speech of 9 June 1788, in Jensen, *Documentary History*, 9:1051–52. See also Jensen, *Documentary History*, 9:1088n7.

66. Edmund Randolph, Speech of 10 June 1788, in Jensen, *Documentary History*, 9:1096–97; Ketcham, *James Madison*, 259; Speech of 12 June 1788, *JMW*, 380–84.

67. Edmund Pendleton, Speech of 12 June 1788, in Jensen, *Documentary History*, 10:1201–02; Patrick Henry, Speech of 12 June 1788, in ibid., 10:1210–11.

68. Speech of 12 June 1780, *JMW*, 380–84; Speech of 24 June 1788, ibid., 401–7. For the Anti-Federalist amendments, which were developed somewhat piecemeal, see *PGM*, 3:1068–72, 1115–18, 1119–20.

69. See Gutzman, *James Madison*, 204–5; Maier, *Ratification*, 268–69, 310; Ketcham, *James Madison*, 267–68; and Glover, *Fate of the Revolution*, 144–45.

70. Maier, *Ratification*, 307–9; JM to Alexander Hamilton, 27 June 1788, *JMW*, 407–8; Glover, *Fate of the Revolution*, 145–46. For the amendments approved by the Virginia convention, see *PGM*, 3:1068–72, 1115–18, 1119–20.

CHAPTER 8

1. TJ to Francis Hopkinson, 13 March 1789, *TJW*, 940–42.

2. TJ to C. W. F. Dumas, 30 July 1788, *PTJ*, 13:436–37; TJ to David Humphreys, 18 March 1789, ibid., 14:676–79; TJ to Richard Price, 8 January 1789, *TJW*, 935.

3. TJ to John Jay, 3 August 1788, *PTJ*, 13:463–69; TJ to Stephen Cathalan Sr., 13 August 1788, ibid., 13:507–8; TJ to George Washington, 4 December 1788, *TJW*, 930. Admittedly, Jefferson did worry about foreign speculators buying an inordinate amount of domestic debt.

4. TJ to John Brown Cutting, 8 July 1788, *PTJ*, 13:315–16; TJ to William Carmichael, 12 August 1788, ibid., 13:502–3; JM to TJ, 8 October 1788, *ROL*, 1:554–55; TJ to George Washington, 4 December 1788, *TJW*, 930; TJ to Baron von Geismer, 20 February 1789, *PTJ*, 14:582–83; TJ to Francis Hopkinson, 13 March 1789, *TJW*, 940–42. In his later years, Jefferson concluded that because four of the first five presidents had retired after two terms—John Adams had lost to Jefferson when he sought a second term—the two-term tradition had acquired "the force of precedent," and if a president sought a third term, "I trust he would be rejected on this demonstration of ambitious views." "Autobiography," *TJW*, 72–73.

5. JM to Alexander Hamilton, 20 July 1788, *JMW*, 408; Crow, *Chronicle of North Carolina*, 58; JM to TJ, 24 and 26 July 1788, *ROL*, 1:541–43, and 10 August 1788, 1:547–49.

6. JM to TJ, 23 August 1788, *ROL*, 1:549–51; TJ to William Short, 20 September 1788, *PTJ*, 13:619–21; JM to TJ, 21 September 1788, *ROL*, 1:551–53; TJ to Thomas Paine, 17 March 1789, *PTJ*, 14:671–73.

7. James Madison's Observations on Thomas Jefferson's Draft of a Constitution for Virginia, circa 15 October 1788, *ROL*, 1:155–56.

8. Ibid., 1:557–58.

9. Ibid., 1:558–59.

10. Ibid., 1:558; TJ to Francis Hopkinson, 13 March 1789, *TJW*, 940–42.

11. James Madison's Observations on Thomas Jefferson's Draft of a Constitution for Virginia, circa 15 October 1788, *ROL*, 1:561–62; TJ to Francis Hopkinson, 13 March 1789, *TJW*, 940–42.

12. TJ to JM, 31 July 1788, *ROL*, 1:543–46.

13. JM to TJ, 17 October 1788, ibid., 1:562–66. Madison's claim he had "always" supported a bill of rights might rightly be described as an "exaggeration." Maier, *Ratification*, 441–46.

14. JM to TJ, 17 October 1788, *ROL*, 1:562–66.

15. Ibid.

16. See generally Gibson, "James Madison"; and R. Ellis, "Constitutionalism," 123.

17. TJ to JM, 15 March 1789, *ROL*, 1:586–89. Jefferson agreed with Madison that, for the foreseeable future, the threat to liberty in America would come from the legislative branch, but he did not expressly embrace Madison's logic, that is, that a self-seeking majority would produce an oppressive legislature. Younger Americans, Jefferson thought, "are all republicans."

18. Ibid.

19. B. Schwartz, *Bill of Rights*, 1:40–46, 214–19. English documents like the Magna Carta and the 1689 Bill of Rights were also aimed at the monarch, not the legislature. Applying a bill of rights to all branches of the government was another intellectual hurdle Madison had to overcome. See Berkin, *Bill of Rights*, 40–41.

20. B. Schwartz, *Bill of Rights*, 1:249.

21. George Mason to Mr. Brent, 2 October 1778, *PGM*, 1:433–39; Rutland, *Birth of the Bill of Rights*, 176, 197–200.

22. Rutland, *Birth of the Bill of Rights*, 104. For early examples of judicial review, see the cases collected at B. Schwartz, *Bill of Rights*, 1:403–31. For an argument challenging the weight of those precedents, see Sosin, *Aristocracy of the Long Robe*, 212–22, 251. For an argument that the emergence of judicial review had less to do with specific precedents than it did with the need to maintain proper boundaries between state and local governments, growing concerns with legislative activism, and the increasing independence of the judiciary, see Rakove, "Origins of Judicial Review."

23. Levy, *Origins of the Bill of Rights*, 33. See also Cooke, *Federalist* No. 39, 256; No. 78, 521; No. 80, 534–41; and No. 81, 541–52.

24. In *Federalist* No. 44, Madison had written that the success of any congressional "usurpation" would depend on the cooperation of both "the executive and judiciary departments," but "in the last resort, a remedy must be obtained from the people." Cooke, *Federalist* No. 44, 305. His language suggests that he assumed that the federal courts might not always prevent enforcement of an unconstitutional law and that relief might ultimately have to come through the electoral process. In general, Madison's references to judicial review in *The Federalist* "are few and fleeting." Rakove, "Judicial Power," 1526.

25. Speech of 19 May 1789, *JMW*, 434–36; Speech of 16 June 1789, ibid., 453–57; Speech of 17 June 1789, ibid., 457–65; JM to Edmund Pendleton, 21 June 1789, ibid., 465–67. According to Gordon S. Wood, "Both Jefferson and Madison thought that judges might act as the guardians of popular rights and might resist encroachments on these rights, but they never believed that judges had any special or unique power to interpret the Constitution." Wood, "Origins of Judicial Review Revisited," 795.

26. Mayer, *Constitutional Thought*, 263, 290–91; R. Ellis, *Jeffersonian Crisis*, 9; Killenbeck, *M'Culloch v. Maryland*, 77; TJ to Abigail Adams, 11 September 1804, *AJC*, 2:279; TJ to John Cartwright, 5 June 1824, *JPW*, 382–88; "Autobiography," *TJW*, 73–75. For Madison's views on the judiciary in his later years, see JM to TJ, 27 June 1823, *ROL*, 3:1867–75; and the documents collected in Meyers, *Mind of the Founder*, 357–93.

27. Wood, *Empire of Liberty*, 407–32. See generally W. Nelson, Marbury v. Madison.

28. JM to Edmund Randolph, 2 November 1788, *JMW*, 423–25; George Nicholas to JM, 2 January 1789, *PJM*, 11:407.

29. JM to Edmund Randolph, 23 November 1788, *JMW*, 425–27; JM to TJ, 8 December 1788, *ROL*, 1:578–81; Rakove, *Politician Thinking*, 94–95.

30. JM to TJ, 8 December 1788, *ROL*, 1:578–81, and 12 December 1788, 1:581–82; JM to George Eve, 2 January 1789, *JMW*, 427–29; JM to Edmund Randolph, 1 March 1789, *JMW*, 429–30.

31. JM to George Eve, 2 January 1789, *JMW*, 427–29.

32. JM to Edmund Randolph, 1 March 1789, ibid., 429–30; JM to TJ, 29 March 1789, *ROL*, 1:605–7. Ames quoted in Burstein and Isenberg, *Madison and Jefferson*, 192. For a detailed account of Madison's first congressional race, see DeRose, *Founding Rivals*.

33. TJ to JM, 12 January 1789, *ROL*, 1:583–86; Malone, *Thomas Jefferson*, 2:223, 228.

34. TJ to John Adams, 10 May 1789, *AJC*, 1:237–38; TJ to Diodati, 3 August 1789, *TJW*, 956–59; TJ to Maria Cosway, 25 July 1789, *PTJ*, 15: 305–6; Meacham, *Thomas Jefferson*, 222–26.

35. Malone, *Thomas Jefferson*, 2:228–31; TJ to Rabout de St. Etienne, 3 June 1789, *TJW*, 954–56; "Autobiography," *TJW*, 85.

36. Malone, *Thomas Jefferson*, 2:218–19; "Autobiography," *TJW*, 85–97. See generally W. H. Adams, *Paris Years of Thomas Jefferson*, 251–98.

37. TJ to William Short, 3 January 1793, *TJW*, 1004; Malone, *Thomas Jefferson*, 2:231–34; W. H. Adams, *Paris Years of Thomas Jefferson*, 278; *PTJ*, 15:138.

38. Peterson, *Thomas Jefferson and the New Nation*, 370–78. Gordon Wood has written that Jefferson "was always optimistic; indeed, he was a virtual Pollyanna about everything." Wood, *Revolutionary Characters*, 115.

39. TJ to Diodati, 3 August 1789, *TJW*, 956–59.

40. Fragments of a Draft of the First Inaugural Address, circa January 1789, in Rhodehamel, *George Washington*, 702–16; First Inaugural Address, 30 April 1789, in ibid., 733; Address of the House of Representatives to the President, 5 May 1789, *PJM*, 12:132; Cheney, *James Madison*, 186–90. See generally Leibiger, *Founding Friendship*.

41. *ROL*, 1:594; Brant, *James Madison*, 3:264–66; Gutzman, *James Madison*, 247–49; Labunski, *James Madison*, 199–200; Levy, *Origins of the Bill of Rights*, 11; Berkin, *Bill of Rights*, 97–98; Speech of 17 August 1789, *JMW*, 470.

42. Cheney, *James Madison*, 193–201; JM to TJ, 27 May 1789, *ROL*, 1:613–14, 13 June 1789, 1:614–15, and 30 June 1789, 1:618–24; TJ to JM, 28 August 1789, *ROL*, 1:627–31.

43. Speech of 8 June 1789, *JMW*, 437–40.

44. Ibid., 441.

45. Ibid., 441–44. Ralph Ketcham has argued that Madison believed Americans had expanded freedom of speech and religion beyond their common-law definitions and that a bill of rights could make those differences clear. Ketcham, *James Madison*, 290. To avoid appeals of trivial matters to federal appellate courts, Madison also proposed the Constitution require a specific minimum dollar amount be at issue, but he did not specify the amount. Speech of 8 June 1789, *JMW*, 443.

46. Speech of 8 June 1789, *JMW*, 444–46.

47. Ibid., 446–50.

48. The first ten amendments would not be consistently described as "the Bill of Rights" until well after the Civil War. On the terminology, see Bordewich, *First Federal Congress*, 86, 117, 140–41; and Veit, Bowling, and Bickford, *Creating the Bill of Rights*, ix.

49. Goldwin, *From Parchment to Power*, 85; B. Schwartz, *Great Rights of Mankind*, 169–70.

50. Goldwin, *From Parchment to Power*, 143–44; George Mason to John Mason, 31 July 1789, *PGM*, 3:1162–68; Speech of 14 August 1789, in Veit, Bowling, and Bickford, *Creating the Bill of Rights*, 70, 175.

51. See the following in Veit, Bowling, and Bickford, *Creating the Bill of Rights*: Thomas Sedgework to Benjamin Lincoln, 19 July 1789, 263–64; Pacificus, 14 August 1789, 275–77; Frederick A. Muhlenberg to Benjamin Rush, 18 August 1789, 280–81; Benjamin Goodhue to Michael Hodge, 20 August 1789, 283; Robert Morris to Richard Peters, 24 August 1789, 288; Richard Peters to JM, 24 August 1789, 288–89.

52. JM to Richard Peters, 19 August 1789, *JMW*, 471–72. Madison probably meant the legislative process was nauseous, not the amendments themselves, but the question has been much debated. See Finkelman, "James Madison and the Bill of Rights"; Bowling, "'Tub to the Whale'"; and Hutson, "Drafting of the Bill of Rights."

53. B. Schwartz, *Bill of Rights*, 2:1050; Virginia Declaration of Rights, 12 June 1776, *PGM*, 1:289; Goldwin, *From Parchment to Power*, 88–89.

54. DePauw, *Documentary History*, 4:27; Veit, Bowling, and Bickford, *Creating the Bill of Rights*, xv–xvi, 17; Thomas Paine, "Candid Remarks on a Letter Signed Ludlow," 1777, in B. Schwartz, *Bill of Rights*, 1:314–18; Goldwin, *From Parchment to Power*, 86–87; Berkin, *Bill of Rights*, 71–72. Adoption of Madison's preamble, Lance Banning has written, "would have meant . . . that it could never have been plausibly denied that the fundamental principles of the Declaration of Independence . . . are part of the American Constitution." Banning, *Jefferson and Madison*, 17.

55. DePauw, *Documentary History*, 1:135–60, 4:35; *Daily Advertiser*, 14 August 1789, in Veit, Bowling, and Bickford, *Creating the Bill of Rights*, 128–29; *Congressional Register*, 14 August 1789, in Veit, Bowling, and Bickford, *Creating the Bill of Rights*, 136–38; B. Schwartz, *Great Rights of Mankind*, 179. The reports of the relevant debates can also be found in B. Schwartz, *Bill of Rights*, 2:1076–77, 1125–26.

56. Labunski, *James Madison*, 216; Goldwin, *From Parchment to Power*, 108–10; B. Schwartz, *Bill of Rights*, 2:1121–23.

57. Speech of 15 August 1789, *JMW*, 467; Brant, *James Madison*, 3:268–71.

58. Brant, *James Madison*, 3:271–73; Conference Committee Report, 24 September 1789, in Veit, Bowling, and Bickford, *Creating the Bill of Rights*, 49–50.

59. Goldwin, *From Parchment to Power*, 159–62; Veit, Bowling, and Bickford, *Creating the Bill of Rights*, 38–39n13.

60. DePauw, *Documentary History*, 4:40–43; Speech of 15 August 1789, *JMW*, 468–69; Brant, *James Madison*, 3:273–75.

61. DePauw, *Documentary History*, 4:47–48; *ROL*, 1:599n29; B. Schwartz, *Bill of Rights*, 2:1008, 1203.

Did the Bill of Rights accomplish Madison's goal of eliminating Anti-Federalism as a viable political force? As late as 1987, one eminent historian could write, "It still remains unclear . . . what happened to the Antifederalists and their opposition to the Constitution after the new government went into effect." R. Ellis, "Persistence of Antifederalism," 296. The Bill of Rights probably helped secure ratification of the Constitution in North Carolina and Rhode Island. On the other hand, after he had seen the amendments passed by the House, George Mason confessed "much Satisfaction," but he still wanted several substantive amendments limiting the power of the federal government. George Mason to Samuel Griffin, 8 September 1789, *PGM*, 3:1170–73. Virginia's senators, Richard Henry Lee and William Grayson, were not appeased. Grayson complained to Patrick Henry that the House amendments "are good for nothing, & I believe as many others do, that they will do more harm than benefit." William Grayson to Patrick Henry, 29 September 1789, in Veit, Bowling, and Bickford, *Creating the Bill of Rights*, 300; Gutzman, *James Madison*, 255. In a sense, history vindicated the skeptics. Before the 1920s, when the Supreme Court, through the post–Civil War Fourteenth Amendment, began applying parts of the Bill of Rights to the states, they had little practical, legal effect. Amar, *Bill of Rights*, 284–90.

Divisions among Anti-Federalists, however, impaired their ability to carry on the fight for additional amendments. Many Anti-Federalist leaders did not want to undermine the legitimacy of the new government or their own credibility by refusing to accept the apparent will of the majority of voters. If Anti-Federalism as a political movement disintegrated, what Saul Cornell has called "the spirit of Anti-Federalism" endured. Many voters remained skeptical of centralized political power. The gaps and ambiguities in the Constitution gave them new opportunities to try to limit the scope of federal authority. By the 1790s, the debate over the meaning of the Constitution superseded the debate over its merits. See Cornell, *Other Founders*, 138–43, 147–67; Siemers, *Antifederalists*, 223–25; and Rutland, *Ordeal of the Constitution*, 289–314.

62. Malone, *Thomas Jefferson*, 2:243; Meacham, *Thomas Jefferson*, 231–32; "Autobiography," *TJW*, 98–99.

63. Burstein and Isenberg, *Madison and Jefferson*, 203–4; George Washington to TJ, 21 January 1790, in Rhodehamel, *George Washington*, 754–56. Jefferson quoted in *ROL*, 1:648.

64. TJ to JM, 6 September 1789, *ROL*, 1:631–36, and 9 January 1790, 1:640; Banning, *Jefferson and Madison*, 27–37; Sloan, "Earth Belongs in Usufruct to the Living." In retirement, however, "Jefferson refused to yield ownership of history" to posterity. "He . . . endeavored to memorialize himself as an enduring symbol of light, liberty, and the timeless rights of mankind." R. McDonald, "Thomas Jefferson and Historical Self-Construction," 290.

65. JM to TJ, 4 February 1790, *ROL*, 1:650–53.

66. Ibid.; Cheney, *James Madison*, 208; TJ to John Cartwright, 5 June 1824, *JPW*, 382–88.

67. JM to Samuel Kercheval, 12 July 1816, *TJW*, 1395; Onuf, *Jefferson's Empire*, 84; Sloan, "Earth Belongs in Usufruct to the Living," 304. One classic study of the Jefferson-Madison relationship described Madison as "the more astute politician," which is debatable. Koch, *Jefferson and Madison*, 63.

68. See Yazawa, *Contested Conventions*, for a recent study emphasizing the fundamental weaknesses of the Articles of Confederation.

69. *ROL*, 1:600. Lance Banning, for example, put Madison's views on the proper scope of federal power somewhere between the localism of Patrick Henry and the vigorous nationalism of Alexander Hamilton. See Banning, "'To Secure These Rights.'" Jefferson also fell between the two extremes, although he was closer to Henry.

AFTERWORD

1. See generally Wood, *Revolutionary Characters*, 144–72; and Broadwater, "James Madison and the Constitution."

2. Gutzman, *Thomas Jefferson*, 9–10; Crawford, *Twilight at Monticello*, 130–33; TJ to Joseph C. Cabell, 2 February 1816, *TJW*, 1377–81. Jefferson's constitutional conservatism did not mean he opposed progress or reform. The major project of his retirement was, with Madison's support, the founding of the University of Virginia. He favored revising the Virginia Constitution to apportion assembly seats more equitably, to expand suffrage, and to provide for the popular election of the governor and local officials. To make judges more accountable to the people, he thought they ought to be elected or be subject to removal by the governor and a simple majority of the legislature. TJ to John Taylor, 28 May 1816, *TJW*, 1391–95; TJ to Samuel Kercheval, 12 July 1816, *TJW*, 1395–1401. After the War of 1812, the great agrarian also acknowledged the need to "place the manufacturer by the side of the agriculturist." TJ to Benjamin Austin, 9 January 1816, *TJW*, 1371.

3. Speech of 19 May 1789, *JMW*, 434–36; Feldman, *Three Lives*, 265. Madison's arguments against the need for Senate approval rested on public policy and the nature of executive power. In another early case, he used one provision of the Constitution to interpret another. Article I, Section 8, authorized Congress to establish "the Seat of the Government of the United States" in a federal district ceded to it by one or more states. But what was "the seat of Government" and how was it to be established? Madison reasoned from Article II, Section 1, which required Electoral College results to be transmitted to the seat of government and read before the House and Senate, and concluded the seat of government must be where Congress met and then assumed the president must sit with it. Because both branches had an interest in the matter, formal legislation would be needed to fix the site of the capital. Jefferson agreed and sent an opinion to that effect to President Washington. JM to TJ, circa 14 July 1790, *ROL*, 1:659.

4. Speech of 2 February 1791, *JMW*, 480–90.

5. Dunn, *Dominion of Memories*, 121; Opinion on the Constitutionality of a National Bank, 15 February 1791, *TJW*, 416–21; TJ to George Washington, 9 September 1792, *TJW*, 992–1001; Feldman, *Three Lives*, 319–23. Jefferson, it might be noted, concluded his opinion by conceding that, where the constitutional issue was unclear, the president ought to defer to Congress.

6. Feldman, *Three Lives*, 338–41; Bailey, *James Madison*, 111. For a detailed analysis of Madison's view of public opinion, see Sheehan, *Mind of James Madison*.

7. TJ to George Washington, 9 September 1792, *TJW*, 992–1001; TJ to Archibald Stuart, 23 December 1791, ibid., 983–84.

8. *ROL*, 2:748–49, 754–56; TJ to JM, 11 August 1793, *ROL*, 2: 802–5. See generally Frisch, *Pacificus-Helvidius Debates*.

Madison and Jefferson differed with Washington over his response to the development of an opposition faction. Madison especially resented Washington's suggestion that the Whiskey Rebellion, a short-lived tax revolt in western Pennsylvania, had been incited by local Democratic-Republican clubs. Madison opposed the rebellion but saw the criticism of a political faction as a threat to the freedoms of speech, press, and assembly, and he helped defeat a House resolution to censure the groups. JM to TJ, 30 November 1794, *ROL*, 2:861.

9. JM to TJ, 13 December 1795, *ROL*, 2:903–4, and 13 March 1796, 2:926; Speech on the Jay Treaty, 6 April 1796, *JMW*, 568–80; Bailey, *James Madison*, 155. On Madison's view of the state conventions as the definitive source in determining the intent of the framers, see McCoy, *Last of the Fathers*, 75–79.

10. On the Alien and Sedition Acts, see Halperin, *Alien and Sedition Acts*. The XYZ Affair illustrated that even a founder could get confused about what the Constitution said. Initially Jefferson took comfort in "that provision which requires two-thirds of the legislature to declare war." A few weeks later, after consulting the Constitution, he corrected himself. A declaration of war required only a simple majority. TJ to JM, 21/22 March 1798, *ROL*, 2:1029, and 19 April 1798, 2:1029.

11. Virginia Resolutions, 21 December 1798, *JMW*, 589–91; Draft of the Kentucky Resolutions, October 1798, *TJW*, 449; *ROL*, 2:1066–71; Meyers, *Mind of the Founder*, 230. What did Jefferson think about secession? He never advocated it publicly, but at one point in the nullification crisis he appeared to have thought the states protesting the tariff of 1828 should have threatened to secede if their grievances were not addressed. He also said once that if a state wanted to leave the union, it should be allowed to go. See Boles, *Jefferson*, 500–503; Gutzman, *Thomas Jefferson*, 63–64; and McCoy, *Last of the Fathers*, 146.

Jefferson was especially alarmed by the Sedition Act's assumption of a federal common, criminal law, which he feared could lead to an unwarranted expansion of the jurisdiction of the federal courts. See TJ to Edmund Randolph, 18 August 1799, *TJW*, 1066–69; and TJ to Gideon Granger, 13 August 1800, *TJW*, 1078–80. Jefferson had been infuriated by a charge Supreme Court justice James Iredell had given to a Richmond grand jury in May 1797. It led to a federal presentment against Virginia congressman Samuel Cabell. Cabell had allegedly made seditious remarks, a common-law crime, in correspondence with his constituents. In a petition to the Virginia House of Delegates, Jefferson proposed his own fanciful legal remedy: the jurors should be impeached and punished for violating a representative's natural right to communicate with the voters. Jefferson admitted there was no relevant statute to apply, and Madison questioned the propriety of involving the state assembly in a federal court proceeding. The House of Delegates approved the petition, minus some of Jefferson's criticism of the jurors, but took no further action. TJ to JM, 3 August 1797, *ROL*, 2:985–90; *ROL*, 2:973–75, 1112; Gutzman, *Thomas Jefferson*, 45.

In another example of Jefferson's concern about the abuse of federal judicial power, Jefferson proposed state jury pools be elected and jurors be assigned to trials by lot. He hoped the federal courts would follow the lead of the state courts, as they sometimes did in such matters. TJ to JM, 26 October 1798, *ROL*, 2:1075–78.

12. First Inaugural Address, 4 March 1801, *TJW*, 492–96. In truth, the Democratic-Republican victory owed much to Aaron Burr's astute political organizing in New York. See Sharp, *Deadlocked Election*, 82–88.

Because Jefferson and Burr, his running mate, received the same number of electoral votes, the 1800 election went to the House of Representatives. When the lame-duck,

Federalist-controlled House hesitated to declare Jefferson the winner, Madison demonstrated his own capacity for extra-constitutional action. He proposed that if Congress did not resolve the deadlock before Adams's term expired, Jefferson and Burr should convene the new Congress, with its Democratic-Republican majority, and let it make the decision. JM to TJ, 10 January 1801, *ROL*, 2:1140–44. Ultimately, the Federalists relented and elected Jefferson.

13. First Annual Message, 8 December 1801, *TJW*, 501–9; TJ to Thomas Cooper, 29 November 1802, ibid., 1109–11. For a recent treatment of Jefferson's presidency, see Boles, *Jefferson*, 323–427.

14. TJ to JM, July 1803, *ROL*, 2:1269–71; JM to TJ, July 1803, ibid., 2:1270; TJ to JM, 24 August 1803, ibid., 2:1270–71.

15. TJ to John C. Breckinridge, 12 August 1803, *TJW*, 1136–39; TJ to Wilson Cary Nicholas, 7 September 1803, ibid., 1139–41; TJ to John B. Colvin, 20 September 1810, ibid., 1233; Feldman, *Three Lives*, 463; *ROL*, 2:1288–90.

Did Madison change his position from the Jay Treaty debate regarding the role of the House of Representatives in the treaty-making process? He advised Jefferson against sending the Louisiana Purchase treaty to the Senate and House at the same time—its implementation would require passage of an appropriations bill—to "avoid, what the Theory of our constitution does not seem to admit, the influence of deliberations and anticipations of the H. of Rep. on a Treaty depending in the Senate." JM to TJ, 1 October 1803, *ROL*, 2:1297–99.

16. *ROL*, 3:1505–7, 1551–53. For a critical assessment of Jefferson's performance, see Levy, *Jefferson and Civil Liberties*.

17. "Autobiography," *TJW*, 73; TJ to John Taylor, 6 January 1805, ibid., 1153–54; *ROL*, 3:1548.

18. First Inaugural Address, 4 March 1809, *JMW*, 680–82.

19. *ROL*, 3:1761; Seventh Annual Message to Congress, 5 December 1815, *JMW*, 710–18; Veto Message, 3 March 1817, *JMW*, 718–20; McCoy, *Last of the Fathers*, 11–16.

20. Veto Message, 30 January 1815, in Richardson, *Messages and Papers*, 2:540; Detached Memorandum, circa 1819, *JMW*, 756. Madison actually vetoed one bank bill on technical grounds before signing the bill creating the Second Bank of the United States. Generally, and in the case of the Bank of the United States specifically, Madison believed that in the interests of certainty and predictability, legislative precedents should be as binding on lawmakers as judicial precedents were on judges. JM to Charles Jared Ingersoll, 25 June 1831, in Meyers, *Mind of the Founder*, 390.

21. JM to Robert Walsh, 27 November 1819, *JMW*, 737–45; TJ to Jared Sparks, 4 February 1824, *TJW*, 1487; Boles, *Jefferson*, 472, 490–92; Crawford, *Twilight at Monticello*, 194–99: Gutzman, *Thomas Jefferson*, 78–81. Jefferson believed a constitutional amendment would be needed to abolish slavery and complete the process of colonization. As a member of the first Congress, Madison had helped pass a series of compromise resolutions, in response to antislavery petitions, strictly construing the federal government's authority over slavery. See Broadwater, "'Those from Whom I Derive My Public Station.'"

22. TJ to JM, 1 October 1792, *ROL*, 2:740; JM to Nicholas P. Trist, May 1832, *JMW*, 860.

23. W. Nelson, Marbury v. Madison, 72; "Autobiography," *TJW*, 74; TJ to William Johnson, 12 June 1823, *TJW*, 1469–77.

24. JM to TJ, 4 June 1810, *ROL*, 3:1634, and 27 June 1823, 3:1867–70; JM to Spencer Roane, 29 June 1821, *JMW*, 777–79; Dunn, *Dominion of Memories*, 145. See also Meyers, *Mind of the Founder*, 368–71.

25. JM to Spencer Roane, 6 May 1821, *JMW*, 772–77; JM to TJ, 17 February 1825, *ROL*, 3:1927–28; TJ to JM, 24 December 1825, *ROL*, 3:1943–46; JM to TJ, 28 December 1825, *ROL*, 3:1947–48. As president, Jefferson had supported internal improvements and had signed the Cumberland Road Act, but as did Madison, he also suggested Congress consider a constitutional amendment to ensure their constitutionality. Dunn, *Dominion of Memories*, 87; Gutzman, *Thomas Jefferson*, 61.

26. TJ to William Branch Giles, 26 December 1825, *TJW*, 1509–12; JM to Joseph Cabell, 18 September 1828, *JMW*, 818–19.

27. Dunn, *Dominion of Memories*, 171–81; McCoy, *Last of the Fathers*, 123; JM to Edward Everett, 28 August 1830, *SWJM*, 340–48; JM to Joseph C. Cabell, 18 September 1828, in Meyers, *Mind of the Founder*, 370–80, and 30 October 1828, 380–89; Notes on Nullification, 1835–36, in Meyers, *Mind of the Founder*, 435.

28. TJ to Roger C. Weightman, 24 June 1826, *TJW*, 1517; "Advice to My Country," 1834, *JMW*, 866.

BIBLIOGRAPHY

PRIMARY SOURCES

Adair, Douglas. "James Madison's Autobiography." *William and Mary Quarterly*, 3rd ser., 2, no. 2 (1945): 191–209.

Adams, Charles Francis, ed. *The Works of John Adams.* 10 vols. Boston: Little Brown, 1856.

Appleby, Joyce, and Terrance Ball, eds. *Jefferson: Political Writings.* New York: Cambridge University Press, 1999.

Bailyn, Bernard, ed. *The Debate on the Constitution: Federalist and Antifederalist Speeches, Articles, and Letters during the Struggle over Ratification.* 2 vols. New York: Library of America, 1993.

———. *Pamphlets of the American Revolution, 1750–1776.* Cambridge, Mass.: Harvard University Press, 1965.

Bergh, Albert, ed. *The Writings of Thomas Jefferson.* 20 vols. Washington, D.C.: Thomas Jefferson Memorial Association, 1907.

Boyd, Julian, et al., eds. *The Papers of Thomas Jefferson.* 43 vols. Princeton, N.J.: Princeton University Press, 1950–2017.

Brugger, Robert J., et al., eds. *The Papers of James Madison, Secretary of State Series.* 11 vols. Charlottesville: University of Virginia Press, 1986–2017.

Cappon, Lester J., ed. *The Complete Correspondence between Thomas Jefferson and Abigail and John Adams.* 2 vols. Chapel Hill: University of North Carolina Press, 1959.

Chinard, Gilbert, ed. *The Commonplace Book of Thomas Jefferson: A Repertory of His Ideas on Government.* Baltimore: Johns Hopkins University Press, 1926.

Cooke, Jacob E., ed. *The Federalist.* Middletown, Conn.: Wesleyan University Press, 1961.

Cottret, Bernard, ed. *Bolingbroke's Political Writings: The Conservative Enlightenment.* New York: St. Martin's Press, 1997.

Cushing, Harry Alonzo, ed. *Writings of Sam Adams.* 3 vols. New York: G. P. Putnam's Sons, 1906.

DePauw, Linda Grant, ed. *Documentary History of the First Federal Congress.* 24 vols. Baltimore: Johns Hopkins University Press, 1972–2017.

Farrand, Max, ed. *The Records of the Federal Constitutional Convention of 1787.* Rev. ed. 4 vols. New Haven, Conn.: Yale University Press, 1937.

Ford, Worthington C., ed. *The Journals of the Continental Congress, 1776–1789.* 34 vols. Washington, D.C.: Government Printing Office, 1931–44.

Frisch, Morton J., ed. *The Pacificus-Helvidius Debates of 1793–1794: Toward the Completion of the American Founding*. Indianapolis: Liberty Fund, 2007.

Hall, Mark David, and Kermit L. Hall, eds. *The Collected Works of James Wilson*. 2 vols. Indianapolis: Liberty Fund, 2007.

Hening, William Waller, ed. *The Statutes at Large: Being a Collection of All the Laws of Virginia*. 13 vols. Richmond: Samuel Pleasants, 1819–23.

Hunt, Galliard, ed. *The Writings of James Madison*. 9 vols. New York: G. P. Putnam's Sons, 1900–1910.

Hutcheson, Francis. *An Essay on the Nature and Conduct of the Passions and Affections, with Illustrations on the Moral Sense*. Edited by Aaron Garret. Indianapolis: Liberty Fund, 2002.

———. *An Inquiry into the Original of Our Ideas of Beauty and Virtue*. Rev. ed. Edited by Wolfgang Leihold. Indianapolis: Liberty Fund, 2008.

Hutchinson, William T., and William M. E. Rachel, eds. *The Papers of James Madison*. 17 vols. Chicago: University of Chicago Press; Charlottesville: University of Virginia Press, 1962–91.

Hutson, James H., ed. *Supplement to the Records of the Federal Convention of 1787*. New Haven, Conn.: Yale University Press, 1987.

Jefferson, Thomas. *Notes on the State of Virginia*. Edited by William Peden. 1954. Reprint, Chapel Hill: University of North Carolina Press, 1982.

Jensen, Merrill, ed. *Tracts of the American Revolution, 1763–1776*. Indianapolis: Hackett, 2003.

Jensen, Merrill, et al., eds. *The Documentary History of the Ratification of the Constitution*. 26 vols. Madison: State Historical Society of Wisconsin, 1976–2008.

Kames, Lord. *Principles of Equity*. Edited by Michael Lobban. Indianapolis: Liberty Fund, 2014.

Ketcham, Ralph, ed. *The Anti-Federalist Papers and the Constitutional Convention Debates*. New York: Signet, 1986.

———, ed. *Selected Writings of James Madison*. Indianapolis: Hackett, 2006.

Labaree, Leonard W., et al., eds. *The Papers of Benjamin Franklin*. 42 vols. New Haven, Conn.: Yale University Press, 1959–92.

Looney, J. Jefferson, et al., eds. *The Papers of Thomas Jefferson, Retirement Series*. 14 vols. Princeton, N.J.: Princeton University Press, 2004–17.

Mays, David J., ed. *The Letters and Papers of Edmund Pendleton, 1743–1803*. 2 vols. Charlottesville: University Press of Virginia, 1967.

McRee, Griffith J., ed. *Life and Correspondence of James Iredell*. 2 vols. New York: Peter Smith, 1949.

Meyers, Marvin, ed. *The Mind of the Founder: Sources of the Political Thought of James Madison*. Rev. ed. Waltham, Mass.: Brandeis University Press, 1981.

Miller, Thomas, ed. *The Selected Writings of John Witherspoon*. Carbondale: Southern Illinois University Press, 1990.

Peterson, Merrill D., ed. *Thomas Jefferson, Writings*. New York: Library of America, 1984.

Rakove, Jack N., ed. *James Madison, Writings*. New York: Library of America, 1999.

Randolph, Edmund. *A History of Virginia*. Edited by Arthur Shaffer. Charlottesville: University Press of Virginia, 1970.

Rhodehamel, John, ed. *George Washington, Writings*. New York: Library of America, 1997.

Richardson, James D., ed. *The Messages and Papers of the Presidents*. 20 vols. New York: National Bureau of Literature, 1897–1927.

Rutland, Robert A., ed. *The Papers of George Mason.* 3 vols. Chapel Hill: University of North Carolina Press, 1970.

Schwartz, Bernard, ed. *The Bill of Rights: A Documentary History.* 2 vols. New York: Chelsea House, 1971.

Shain, Barry Alan, ed. *The Declaration of Independence in Historical Context: American State Papers, Petitions, Proclamations, and Letters of the Delegates to the First National Congresses.* Indianapolis: Liberty Fund, 2014.

Smith, James Morton, ed. *The Republic of Letters: The Correspondence between Thomas Jefferson and James Madison, 1776–1826.* 3 vols. New York: W. W. Norton, 1995.

Smith, Paul H., ed. *Letters of Delegates to Congress, 1774–1789.* 26 vols. Washington, D.C.: U.S. Government Printing Office, 1976–2000.

Syrett, Harold C. *The Papers of Alexander Hamilton.* 27 vols. New York: Columbia University Press, 1961–87.

Thompson, C. Bradley, ed. *The Revolutionary Writings of John Adams.* Indianapolis: Liberty Fund, 2000.

Van Schreeven, William J., Robert L. Scribner, and Brent Tarter, comps. *Revolutionary Virginia: The Road to Independence.* 7 vols. Charlottesville: University Press of Virginia, 1973–83.

Veit, Helen E., Kenneth R. Bowling, and Charlene Bangs Bickford, eds. *Creating the Bill of Rights: The Documentary Record from the First Federal Congress.* Baltimore: Johns Hopkins University Press, 1991.

Wilson, Douglas L., ed. *Jefferson's Literary Commonplace Book.* Princeton, N.J.: Princeton University Press, 1989.

SECONDARY SOURCES

Books

Adams, William Howard. *The Paris Years of Thomas Jefferson.* New Haven, Conn.: Yale University Press, 1997.

Adams, Willi Paul. *The First American Constitutions: Republican Ideology and the Making of State Constitutions in the Revolutionary Era.* Chapel Hill: University of North Carolina Press, 1980.

Alden, John R. *A History of the American Revolution.* New York: Alfred A. Knopf, 1969.

Amar, Akhil Reed. *The Bill of Rights.* New Haven, Conn.: Yale University Press, 1998.

Armitage, David. *The Declaration of Independence: A Global History.* Cambridge, Mass.: Harvard University Press, 2007.

Bailey, Jeremy D. *James Madison and Constitutional Imperfection.* New York: Cambridge University Press, 2015.

Bailyn, Bernard. *The Ideological Origins of the American Revolution.* Cambridge, Mass.: Harvard University Press, 1967.

Banning, Lance. *Jefferson and Madison: Three Conversations from the Founding.* Madison, Wis.: Madison House, 1995.

———. *The Sacred Fire of Liberty: James Madison and the Founding of the Republic.* Ithaca, N.Y.: Cornell University Press, 1995.

Becker, Carl L. *The Declaration of Independence: A Study in the History of Political Ideas.* New York: Vintage, 1958.

Beeman, Richard R. *Our Lives, Our Fortunes, and Our Sacred Honor: The Forging of American Independence, 1774–1776*. New York: Basic Books, 2013.

———. *Plain, Honest Men: The Making of the American Constitution*. New York: Random House, 2009.

Berkin, Carol. *The Bill of Rights: The Fight to Secure America's Liberties*. New York: Simon and Schuster, 2015.

Bernstein, R. B. *Thomas Jefferson*. New York: Oxford University Press, 2003.

Bilder, Mary Sarah. *Madison's Hand: Revising the Constitutional Convention*. Cambridge, Mass.: Harvard University Press, 2015.

Blackburn, Joyce. *George Wythe of Williamsburg*. New York: Harper and Row, 1975.

Boles, John B. *Jefferson: Architect of Liberty*. New York: Basic Books, 2017.

Bordewich, Fergus M. *The First Federal Congress: How James Madison, George Washington, and a Group of Extraordinary Men Invented the Government*. New York: Simon and Schuster, 2016.

Brant, Irving. *James Madison*. 6 vols. Indianapolis: Bobbs-Merrill, 1941–61.

Broadwater, Jeff. *George Mason, Forgotten Founder*. Chapel Hill: University of North Carolina Press, 2006.

———. *James Madison: A Son of Virginia and a Founder of the Nation*. Chapel Hill: University of North Carolina Press, 2012.

Brown, Imogene. *American Aristides: A Biography of George Wythe*. East Brunswick, N.J.: Associated University Presses, 1981.

Buckley, Thomas E. *Establishing Religious Freedom: Jefferson's Statute in Virginia*. Charlottesville: University of Virginia Press, 2013.

Burstein, Andrew, and Nancy Isenberg. *Madison and Jefferson*. New York: Random House, 2010.

Carp, Benjamin L. *Defiance of the Patriots: The Boston Tea Party and the Making of America*. New Haven, Conn.: Yale University Press, 2010.

Cheney, Lynne. *James Madison: A Life Reconsidered*. New York: Viking, 2014.

Colbourn, Trevor. *The Lamp of Experience: Whig History and the Intellectual Origins of the American Revolution*. Chapel Hill: University of North Carolina Press, 1965.

Coleman, Aaron N. *The American Revolution, State Sovereignty, and the American Constitutional Settlement, 1765–1800*. Lanham, Md.: Lexington Books, 2016.

Condon, Sean. *Shays's Rebellion: Authority and Distress in Post-Revolutionary America*. Baltimore: Johns Hopkins University Press, 2015.

Cornell, Saul. *The Other Founders: Anti-Federalism and the Dissenting Tradition in America, 1788–1828*. Chapel Hill: University of North Carolina Press, 1999.

Corwin, Edward S. *The "Higher Law" Background of American Constitutional Law*. 1955. Reprint, Indianapolis: Liberty Fund, 2008.

Crawford, Alan Pell. *Twilight at Monticello: The Final Years of Thomas Jefferson*. New York: Random House, 2008.

Crow, Jeffrey J. *A Chronicle of North Carolina during the American Revolution, 1763–1789*. Raleigh, N.C.: Division of Archives and History, 1975.

Cunningham, Noble E. *In Pursuit of Reason: The Life of Thomas Jefferson*. Baton Rouge: Louisiana State University Press, 1987.

Davis, David Brion. *Inhuman Bondage: The Rise and Fall of Slavery in the New World*. New York: Oxford University Press, 2006.

DeRose, Chris. *Founding Rivals: Madison, Monroe, the Bill of Rights, and the Election That Saved a Nation*. Washington, D.C.: Regnery, 2011.

Dewey, Frank L. *Thomas Jefferson: Lawyer*. Charlottesville: University Press of Virginia, 1986.

Dill, Alonzo Thomas. *George Wythe: Teacher of Liberty*. Williamsburg: Virginia Independence Bicentennial Commission, 1979.

Dougherty, Keith L. *Collective Action under the Articles of Confederation*. New York: Cambridge University Press, 2001.

Douglass, Elisha P. *Rebels and Democrats: The Struggle for Equal Rights and Majority Rule during the Revolution*. Chapel Hill: University of North Carolina Press, 1955.

Dumbauld, Edward. *Thomas Jefferson and the Law*. Norman: University of Oklahoma Press, 1978.

Dunn, Susan. *Dominion of Memories: Jefferson, Madison, and the Decline of Virginia*. New York: Basic Books, 2007.

Elkins, Stanley, and Eric McKitrick. *The Age of Federalism: The Early American Republic, 1788–1800*. New York: Oxford University Press, 1993.

Ellis, Joseph. *American Sphinx: The Character of Thomas Jefferson*. New York: Alfred A. Knopf, 1996.

———. *The Quartet: Orchestrating the Second American Revolution, 1783–1789*. New York: Alfred A. Knopf, 2015.

Ellis, Richard E. *The Jeffersonian Crisis: Courts and Politics in the Young Republic*. New York: Oxford University Press, 1971.

Feldman, Noah. *The Three Lives of James Madison: Genius, Partisan, President*. New York: Random House, 2017.

Friedman, Lawrence M. *A History of American Law*. 3rd ed. New York: Simon and Schuster, 2005.

Gay, Peter. *The Enlightenment: An Interpretation*. 2 vols. New York: Alfred A. Knopf, 1966–69.

Gibson, Alan. *Interpreting the Founding: Guide to the Enduring Debates over the Origins and Foundations of the American Republic*. Lawrence: University Press of Kansas, 2006.

———. *Understanding the Founding: The Crucial Questions*. 2nd ed. Lawrence: University Press of Kansas, 2010.

Glover, Lorri. *The Fate of the Revolution: Virginians Debate the Constitution*. Baltimore: Johns Hopkins University Press, 2016.

Goldwin, Robert A. *From Parchment to Power: How James Madison Used the Bill of Rights to Save the Constitution*. Washington, D.C.: American Enterprise Institute, 1997.

Gould, Eliga A. *Among the Powers of the Earth: The American Revolution and the Making of a New World Empire*. Boston: Harvard University Press, 2012.

Greene, Jack P. *The Constitutional Origins of the American Revolution*. New York: Cambridge University Press, 2011.

Gutzman, Kevin R. C. *James Madison and the Making of America*. New York: St. Martin's Press, 2012.

———. *Thomas Jefferson, Revolutionary*. New York: St. Martin's Press, 2017.

Halperin, Terri Diane. *The Alien and Sedition Acts of 1798: Testing the Constitution*. Baltimore: Johns Hopkins University Press, 2016.

Hayes, Kevin J. *The Road to Monticello: The Life and Mind of Thomas Jefferson*. New York: Oxford University Press, 2008.

Heineman, Ronald L., et al., *Old Dominion, New Commonwealth: A History of Virginia, 1607–2007*. Charlottesville: University of Virginia Press, 2007.

Hendrickson, David C. *Peace Pact: The Lost World of the American Founding*. Lawrence: University Press of Kansas, 2003.

Herman, Arthur. *How the Scots Invented the Modern World: The True Story of How Western Europe's Poorest Nation Created Our Modern World and Everything in It*. New York: Three Rivers Press, 2001.

Herring, George C. *From Colony to Superpower: U.S. Foreign Relations since 1776*. New York: Oxford University Press, 2008.

Holton, Woody. *Forced Founders: Indians, Debtors, Slaves, and the Making of the American Revolution in Virginia*. Chapel Hill: University of North Carolina Press, 1999.

Jensen, Merrill. *The Articles of Confederation: An Interpretation of the Social-Constitutional History of the American Revolution, 1774–1781*. Madison: University of Wisconsin Press, 1970.

———. *The New Nation: A History of the United States during the Articles of Confederation, 1781–1789*. Boston: Northeastern University Press, 1981.

Ketcham, Ralph. *James Madison: A Biography*. Charlottesville: University Press of Virginia, 1990.

Kidd, Thomas S. *Patrick Henry: First among Patriots*. New York: Basic Books, 2017.

Killenbeck, Mark R. *M'Culloch v. Maryland: Securing a Nation*. Lawrence: University Press of Kansas, 2006.

Klarman, Michael L. *The Framers' Coup: The Making of the United States Constitution*. New York: Oxford University Press, 2016.

Koch, Adrienne. *Jefferson and Madison: The Great Collaboration*. New York: Alfred A. Knopf, 1950.

Kruman, Marc W. *Between Authority and Liberty: State Constitution Making in Revolutionary America*. Chapel Hill: University of North Carolina Press, 1986.

Kukla, Jon. *Patrick Henry: Champion of Liberty*. New York: Simon and Schuster, 2017.

Labunski, Richard. *James Madison and the Struggle for the Bill of Rights*. New York: Oxford University Press, 2006.

Leibiger, Stuart. *Founding Friendship: George Washington, James Madison, and the Creation of the American Republic*. Chapel Hill: University of North Carolina Press, 1999.

Levy, Leonard W. *Jefferson and Civil Liberties: The Darker Side*. Chicago: Ivan R. Dee, 1989.

———. *Origins of the Bill of Rights*. New Haven, Conn.: Yale University Press, 1999.

Maier, Pauline. *American Scripture: Making the Declaration of Independence*. New York: Alfred A. Knopf, 1997.

———. *Ratification: The People Debate the Constitution*. New York: Simon and Schuster, 2010.

Mailer, Gideon. *John Witherspoon's American Revolution*. Chapel Hill: University of North Carolina Press, 2017.

Malone, Dumas. *Jefferson and His Time*. 6 vols. Boston: Little, Brown, 1948–74.

Marks, Frederick W., III. *Independence on Trial: Foreign Affairs and the Making of the Constitution*. Wilmington, Del.: Scholarly Resources, 1986.

May, Henry F. *The Enlightenment in America*. New York: Oxford University Press, 1976.

Mayer, David N. *The Constitutional Thought of Thomas Jefferson*. Charlottesville: University Press of Virginia, 1994.

McCoy, Drew. *The Elusive Republic: Political Economy in Jeffersonian America*. New York: W. W. Norton, 1980.

———. *The Last of the Fathers: James Madison and the Republican Legacy*. New York: Cambridge University Press, 1989.

McDonald, Forrest. Novus Ordo Seclorum: *The Intellectual Origins of the Constitution*. Lawrence: University Press of Kansas, 1985.

McDonnell, Michael A. *The Politics of War: Race, Class, and Conflict in Revolutionary Virginia*. Chapel Hill: University of North Carolina Press, 2007.

McGuire, Robert A. *To Form a More Perfect Union: A New Economic Interpretation of the Constitution of the United States*. New York: Oxford University Press, 2003.

McIlwain, Charles H. *The American Revolution: A Constitutional Interpretation*. 1923. Reprint, Ithaca, N.Y.: Cornell University Press, 1961.

Meacham, Jon. *Thomas Jefferson: The Art of Power*. New York: Random House, 2012.

Middlekauff, Robert. *The Glorious Cause: The American Revolution, 1763–1789*. New York: Oxford University Press, 1982.

Miller, John C. *The Wolf by the Ears: Thomas Jefferson and Slavery*. Charlottesville: University Press of Virginia, 1991.

Morris, Richard B. *The Forging of the Union, 1781–1789*. New York: Harper and Row, 1987.

Morrison, Jeffry H. *John Witherspoon and the Founding of the American Republic*. Notre Dame, Ind.: University of Notre Dame Press, 2005.

Nelson, John K. *A Blessed Company: Parishes, Parsons, and Parishioners in Anglican Virginia, 1690–1776*. Chapel Hill: University of North Carolina Press, 2001.

Nelson, William E. Marbury v. Madison: *The Origins and Legacy of Judicial Review*. Lawrence: University Press of Kansas, 2000.

Noll, Mark A. *Princeton and the Republic, 1768–1822: The Search for a Christian Enlightenment in the Era of Samuel Stanhope Smith*. Princeton, N.J.: Princeton University Press, 1989.

Onuf, Peter. *Jefferson's Empire: The Language of American Nationhood*. Charlottesville: University Press of Virginia, 2000.

———. *The Mind of Thomas Jefferson*. Charlottesville: University Press of Virginia, 2007.

———. *The Origins of the Federal Republic: Jurisdictional Conflicts in the United States, 1775–1787*. Philadelphia: University of Pennsylvania Press, 1983.

Onuf, Peter, and Nicholas P. Cole, eds. *Thomas Jefferson, the Classical World, and Early America*. Charlottesville: University of Virginia Press, 2011.

Onuf, Peter, and Annette Gordon-Reed. *"Most Blessed of the Patriarchs": Thomas Jefferson and the Empire of Imagination*. New York: Liveright, 2016.

Perkins, Bradford. *The Creation of an American Empire, 1776–1865*. Vol. 1 of *The Cambridge History of American Foreign Relations*. 4 vols. Edited by Warren Cohen. New York: Cambridge University Press, 1993.

Peterson, Merrill D. *Thomas Jefferson and the New Nation*. New York: Oxford University Press, 1972.

Pocock, J. G. A. *The Ancient Constitution and the Feudal Law: English Historical Thought in the Seventeenth Century*. Cambridge.: Cambridge University Press, 1957.

Ragosta, John A. *Wellspring of Liberty: How Virginia's Religious Dissenters Helped Win the American Revolution and Secured Religious Liberty*. New York: Oxford University Press, 2010.

Rakove, Jack N. *The Beginnings of National Politics: An Interpretive History of the Continental Congress*. New York: Alfred A. Knopf, 1979.

———. *Original Meanings: Politics and Ideas in the Making of the Constitution*. New York: Alfred A. Knopf, 1997.

———. *A Politician Thinking: The Creative Mind of James Madison*. Norman: University of Oklahoma Press, 2017.

Reid, John Phillip. *Constitutional History of the American Revolution*. Abridged ed. Madison: University of Wisconsin Press, 1995.

Richard, Carl J. *The Founders and the Classics: Greece, Rome, and the American Enlightenment*. Cambridge, Mass.: Harvard University Press, 1994.

Robertson, David Brian. *The Constitution and America's Destiny*. New York: Cambridge University Press, 2005.

———. *The Original Compromise: What the Constitution's Framers Were Really Thinking*. New York: Oxford University Press, 2013.

Roeber, A. G. *Faithful Magistrates and Republican Lawyers: Creators of Virginia Legal Culture, 1680–1810*. Chapel Hill: University of North Carolina Press, 1981.

Rutland, Robert A. *The Birth of the Bill of Rights, 1776–1791*. Chapel Hill: University of North Carolina Press, 1962.

———. *The Ordeal of the Constitution: The Antifederalists and the Ratification Struggle of 1787–88*. Boston: Northeastern University Press, 1983.

Ryan, Alan. *On Politics: A History of Political Thought*. 2 vols. New York: Liveright, 2012.

Schwartz, Bernard. *The Great Rights of Mankind: A History of the American Bill of Rights*. Madison, Wis.: Madison House, 1992.

Schwarz, Michael. *Thomas Jefferson, James Madison, and the British Challenge to Republican America, 1783–1795*. Lanham, Md.: Lexington Books, 2017.

Selby, John E. *The Revolution in Virginia, 1775–1783*. Williamsburg, Va.: Colonial Williamsburg Foundation, 1988.

Sharp, James Roger. *The Deadlocked Election of 1800: Jefferson, Burr, and the Union in the Balance*. Lawrence: University of Press of Kansas, 2010.

Sheehan, Colleen A. *The Mind of James Madison: The Legacy of Classical Republicanism*. New York: Cambridge University Press, 2015.

Sheldon, Garrett Ward. *The Political Philosophy of James Madison*. Baltimore: Johns Hopkins University Press, 2001.

———. *The Political Philosophy of Thomas Jefferson*. Baltimore: Johns Hopkins University Press, 1991.

Siemers, David J. *The Antifederalists: Men of Great Faith and Forbearance*. Lanham, Md.: Rowman and Littlefield, 2003.

Signer, Michael. *Becoming James Madison: The Extraordinary Origins of the Least Likely Founding Father*. New York: Public Affairs, 2015.

Sosin, Jack M. *The Aristocracy of the Long Robe: The Origins of Judicial Review in America*. New York: Greenwood, 1989.

Steele, Brian. *Thomas Jefferson and American Nationhood*. New York: Cambridge University Press, 2012.

Swanson, Mary-Elaine. *The Education of James Madison*. Montgomery, Ala.: Hoffman Center, 1992.

Sydnor, Charles S. *American Revolutionaries in the Making: Political Practices in Washington's Virginia*. New York: Free Press, 1952.

Van Cleve, George William. *We Have Not a Government: The Articles of Confederation and the Road to the Constitution*. Chicago: University of Chicago Press, 2017.

Weiner, Greg. *Madison's Metronome: The Constitution, Majority Rule, and the Tempo of American Politics*. Lawrence: University Press of Kansas, 2012.

Wills, Garry. *Inventing America: Jefferson's Declaration of Independence*. Garden City, N.J.: Doubleday, 1978.

Wood, Gordon S. *The Creation of the American Republic, 1776–1787*. New York: W. W. Norton, 1969.

———. *Empire of Liberty: A History of the Early Republic, 1789–1815*. New York: Oxford University Press, 2009.

———. *Friends Divided: John Adams and Thomas Jefferson*. New York: Penguin, 2017.

———. *The Radicalism of the American Revolution*. New York: Vintage, 1991.

———. *Revolutionary Characters: What Made the Founders Different*. New York: Penguin, 2006.

Yazawa, Melvin. *Contested Conventions: The Struggle to Establish the Constitution and Save the Union, 1787–1789*. Baltimore: Johns Hopkins University Press, 2016.

Yirush, Craig. *Settlers, Liberty, and Empire: The Roots of Early American Political Thought, 1676–1775*. New York: Cambridge University Press, 2011.

Young, Alfred F., and Gregory H. Nobles. *Whose American Revolution Was It? Historians Interpret the Founding*. New York: New York University Press, 2011.

Zemler, Jeffrey A. *James Madison, the South, and the Trans-Appalachian West, 1783–1803*. Lanham, Md.: Lexington Books, 2014

Articles and Essays

Adair, Douglass. "Rumbold's Dying Speech, 1685, and Jefferson's Last Words on Democracy, 1826." *William and Mary Quarterly*, 3rd ser., 9, no. 4 (1952): 521–31.

———. "'That Politics May Be Reduced to a Science': David Hume, James Madison, and the Tenth Federalist." In *Fame and the Founding Fathers: Essays by Douglass Adair*, edited by Trevor Colbourn, 132–51. Indianapolis: Liberty Fund, 1998.

Agresto, John. "'A System without a Precedent': James Madison and the Revolution in Republican Liberty." *South Atlantic Quarterly* 82, no. 2 (1983): 129–44.

Alley, Robert S. "Bradford, William." In *James Madison and the American Nation, 1751–1836*, edited by Robert A. Rutland, 46–47. New York: Scribner, 1994.

Banning, Lance. "The Practical Sphere of a Republic: James Madison, the Constitutional Convention, and the Emergence of Revolutionary Federalism." In *Beyond Confederation: Origins of the Constitution and American National Identity*, edited by Richard Beeman, Stephen Botein, and Edward C. Carter II, 162–87. Chapel Hill: University of North Carolina Press, 1987.

———. "'To Secure These Rights': Patrick Henry, James Madison, and the Revolutionary Legitimacy of the Constitution." In *To Secure the Blessings of Liberty: First Principles of the Constitution*, edited by Sarah Baumgartner Thurow, 281–304. Lanham, Md.: University Press of America, 1988.

Beeman, Richard R. "The American Revolution." In *Jefferson: A Reference Biography*, edited by Merrill D. Peterson, 25–46. New York: Scribner, 1986.

Beitzinger, A. J. "Political Theorist." In *Jefferson: A Reference Biography*, edited by Merrill D. Peterson, 81–99. New York: Scribner, 1986.

Bernstein, R. B. "Thomas Jefferson and Constitutionalism." In *A Companion to Thomas Jefferson*, edited by Francis D. Cogliano, 419–38. Malden, Mass.: Wiley-Blackwell, 2012.

Bilder, Mary Sarah. "James Madison, Law Student and Demi-Lawyer." *Law and History Review* 28, no. 2 (2010): 389–449.

Bowling, Kenneth R. "'A Tub to the Whale': The Founding Fathers and the Adoption of the Bill of Rights." *Journal of the Early Republic* 8, no. 3 (1988): 223–51.

Broadwater, Jeff. "James Madison and the Constitution: Reassessing the 'Madison Problem.'" *Virginia Magazine of History and Biography* 123, no. 3 (2015): 202–35.

———. "James Madison and the Dilemma of American Slavery." In *A Companion to James Madison and James Monroe*, edited by Stuart Leibiger, 306–23. Malden, Mass.: Wiley-Blackwell, 2013.

———. "'Those from Whom I Derive My Public Station': James Madison, the Politics of Race, and the Fate of Slavery in the Western Territories." *Journal of East Tennessee History* 87 (2015): 64–83.

Buckley, Thomas E. "The Political Theology of Thomas Jefferson." In *The Virginia Statute for Religious Freedom: Its Evolution and Consequences in American History*, edited by Merrill D. Peterson and Robert C. Vaughn, 75–107. New York: Cambridge University Press, 1988.

Cohen, Sheldon, and Larry Gerlach. "Princeton in the Coming of the American Revolution." *New Jersey History* 92 (1974): 69–92.

Egerton, Douglas R. "Freneau, Philip M." In *James Madison and the American Nation, 1751–1836*, edited by Robert A. Rutland, 154–55. New York: Scribner, 1994.

Ellis, Richard E. "Constitutionalism." In *Jefferson: A Reference Biography*, edited by Merrill D. Peterson, 119–33. New York: Scribner, 1986.

———. "The Persistence of Antifederalism after 1789." In *Beyond Confederation: Origins of the Constitution and American National Identity*, edited by Richard Beeman, Stephen Botein, and Edward Carter II, 295–314. Chapel Hill: University of North Carolina Press, 1987.

Finkelman, Paul. "James Madison and the Bill of Rights: A Reluctant Paternity." *Supreme Court Review* 1990 (1990): 301–47.

Gibson, Alan. "Inventing the Extended Republic: The Debate over the Role of Madison's Theory in the Creation of the Constitution." In *James Madison: Philosopher, Founder, and Statesman*, edited by John R. Vile, William D. Pederson, and Frank J. Williams, 63–87. Athens: Ohio University Press, 2008.

———. "James Madison, Republican Government, and the Formation of the Bill of Rights: 'Bound by Every Motive of Prudence.'" In *A Companion to James Madison and James Monroe*, edited by Stuart Leibiger, 108–26. Malden, Mass.: Wiley-Blackwell, 2013.

Gish, Dustin A., and Daniel P. Klinghard. "Republican Constitutionalism in Thomas Jefferson's *Notes on the State of Virginia*." *Journal of Politics* 74, no. 1 (2012): 35–51.

Greene, Jack P. "From the Perspective of Law: Context and Legitimacy in the Origins of the American Revolution." *South Atlantic Quarterly* 85, no. 1 (1986): 56–77.

———. "The Intellectual Reconstruction of Virginia in the Age of Jefferson." In *Jeffersonian Legacies*, edited by Peter Onuf, 225–53. Charlottesville: University Press of Virginia, 1993.

Hobson, Charles. "The Negative on State Laws: James Madison, the Constitution, and the Crisis of Republican Government." *William and Mary Quarterly* 36, 3rd ser., no. 2 (1979): 215–35.

Howard, Thomas L., III. "The State That Said No: The Fight for the Ratification of the Federal Constitution in North Carolina." *North Carolina Historical Review* 94, no. 1 (2017): 1–58.

Howe, John. "Republicanism." In *Jefferson: A Reference Biography*, edited by Merrill D. Peterson, 59–79. New York: Scribner, 1986.

Hutson, James H. "The Drafting of the Bill of Rights: Madison's 'Nauseous Project' Reconsidered." *Benchmark* 3, no. 6 (1987): 309–20.

Kaminski, John P. "The Constitution without a Bill of Rights." In *The Bill of Rights and the States*, edited by Patrick T. Conley and John P. Kaminski, 16–45. Madison, Wis.: Madison House, 1992.

Kaplan, Lawrence. "Jefferson and the Constitution: The View from Paris, 1786–1789." *Diplomatic History* 11 (1987): 321–36.

Ketcham, Ralph L. "James Madison and Religion: A New Hypothesis." In *James Madison and Religious Liberty*, edited by Robert S. Alley, 175–83. Buffalo, N.Y.: Prometheus, 1985.

Konig, David Thomas. "Thomas Jefferson and the Law." In *A Companion to Thomas Jefferson*, edited by Francis D. Cogliano, 349–63. Malden, Mass.: Wiley-Blackwell, 2012.

Kukla, Jon. "A Spectrum of Sentiments: Virginia's Federalists, Antifederalists, and 'Federalists Who Are for Amendments,' 1787–1788." *Virginia Magazine of History and Biography* 96, no. 3 (1988): 276–96.

Loconte, Joseph. "Faith and the Founding: The Influence of Religion on the Politics of James Madison." *Journal of Church and State* 45, no. 4 (2003): 699–715.

Malone, Dumas. "The Life of Thomas Jefferson." In *Jefferson: A Reference Biography*, edited by Merrill D. Peterson, 1–24. New York: Scribner, 1986.

Mattern, David B. "Brackenridge, Hugh Henry." In *James Madison and the American Nation, 1751–1836*, edited by Robert A. Rutland, 46. New York: Scribner, 1994.

May, Henry F. "The Enlightenment." In *Jefferson: A Reference Biography*, edited by Merrill D. Peterson, 47–58. New York: Scribner, 1986.

McCoy, Drew R. "James Madison and Visions of American Nationality in the Confederation Period." In *Beyond Confederation: Origins of the Constitution and American National Identity*, edited by Richard Beeman, Stephen Botein, and Edward C. Carter II, 226–58. Chapel Hill: University of North Carolina Press, 1987.

———. "Political Economy." In *Jefferson: A Reference Biography*, edited by Merrill D. Peterson, 101–18. New York: Scribner, 1986.

———. "The Virginia Port Bill of 1784." *Virginia Magazine of History and Biography* 83, no. 3 (1975): 288–303.

McDonald, Robert M. S. "Thomas Jefferson and Historical Self-Construction: The Earth Belongs to the Living?" *The Historian* 61, no. 1 (1999): 289–310.

McGill, Kathy O. "A Meteor and a Generous Mind: The Revolutionary Political Thought of Thomson Mason." *Virginia Magazine of History and Biography* 125, no. 1 (2017): 98–131.

Miller, Ann L. "Madison, Nelly Conway." In *James Madison and the American Nation, 1751–1836*, edited by Robert A. Rutland, 289. New York: Scribner, 1994.

Neem, Johann N. "A Republican Reformation: Thomas Jefferson's Civil Religion and the Separation of Church and State." In *A Companion to Thomas Jefferson*, edited by Francis D. Cogliano, 91–109. Malden, Mass.: Wiley-Blackwell, 2012.

Newman, Paul Douglas. "James Madison's Journey to an 'Honorable and Useful Profession,' 1751–1780." In *A Companion to James Madison and James Monroe*, edited by Stuart Leibiger, 21–38. Malden, Mass.: Wiley-Blackwell, 2013.

Parkinson, Robert G. "The Declaration of Independence." In *A Companion to Thomas Jefferson*, edited by Francis D. Cogliano, 44–59. Malden, Mass.: Wiley-Blackwell, 2012.

Pocock, J. G. A. "Religious Freedom and the Desacralization of Politics: From the English Civil Wars to the Virginia Statute." In *The Virginia Statute for Religious Freedom: Its Evolution and Consequences in American History*, edited by Merrill D. Peterson and Robert C. Vaughn, 43–73. New York: Cambridge University Press, 1988.

Pybus, Cassandra. "Thomas Jefferson and Slavery." In *A Companion to Thomas Jefferson*, edited by Francis D. Cogliano, 270–83. Malden, Mass.: Wiley-Blackwell, 2012.

Ragosta, John A. "The Virginia Statute for Establishing Religious Freedom." In *A Companion to Thomas Jefferson*, edited by Francis D. Cogliano, 75–90. Malden, Mass.: Wiley-Blackwell, 2012.

Rakove, Jack N. "Judicial Power in the Constitutional Theory of James Madison." *William and Mary Law Review* 43, no. 4 (2002): 1513–47.

———. "The Origins of Judicial Review: A Plea for New Contexts." *Stanford Law Review* 49, no. 5 (1997): 1031–64.

Rankin, Richard. "Witherspoon, John." In *James Madison and the American Nation, 1751–1836*, edited by Robert A. Rutland, 454–55. New York: Scribner, 1994.

Ray, Kristofer. "Thomas Jefferson and the *Rights of British North America*." In *A Companion to Thomas Jefferson*, edited by Francis D. Cogliano, 31–43. Malden, Mass.: Wiley-Blackwell, 2012.

Reinhold, Meyer. "The Classical World." In *Jefferson: A Reference Biography*, edited by Merrill D. Peterson, 135–56. New York: Scribner, 1986.

Schlesinger, Arthur M. "The Lost Meaning of 'The Pursuit of Happiness.'" *William and Mary Quarterly*, 3rd. ser., 21, no. 3 (1964): 325–27.

Slauter, Eric. "The Declaration of Independence and the New Nation." In *The Cambridge Companion to Thomas Jefferson*, edited by Frank Shuffelton, 12–34. New York: Cambridge University Press, 2009.

Sloan, Herbert. "The Earth Belongs in Usufruct to the Living." In *Jeffersonian Legacies*, edited by Peter Onuf, 281–315. Charlottesville: University Press of Virginia, 1993.

Smith, Robert W. "Foreign Affairs and the Ratification of the Constitution in Virginia." *Virginia Magazine of History and Biography* 122, no. 1 (2014): 40–67.

Uzzell, Lynn. "A New Investigation into Madison's Notes on the Convention: Solving the Mystery of His June 6 Speech." *American Political Thought* 6, no. 4 (2017): 517–49.

Wilson, Douglas L. "Jefferson's Library." In *Jefferson: A Reference Biography*, edited by Merrill D. Peterson, 157–79. New York: Scribner, 1986.

Wood, Gordon S. "The Origins of Judicial Review Revisited, or How the Marshall Court Made More Out of Less." *Washington and Lee Law Review* 56, no. 3 (1999): 787–809.

INDEX

Clark, George Rogers, 69, 74
Clarke, Samuel, 18
Clinton, George, 157, 187
Coercive (Intolerable) Acts, 8–9, 14, 21, 28
Cohens v. Virginia (1821), 208
Coke, Lord, 4–5
College of New Jersey. *See* Princeton
   University (College of New Jersey)
Common Sense (Paine), 33. *See also* Paine,
   Thomas
commonsense philosophy, 16–17
congressional veto (negative), 134, 141, 144,
   146–47, 156–57, 240n54
Connecticut Compromise. *See* Great
   Compromise
Connecticut Plan, 55
Constitution (U.S.): contrasted with
   Declaration of Independence, xiii–xiv,
   200; signers of, 17; drafting of, 138–51;
   supremacy clause in, 143, 152; and
   ratification debate, 154–55, 159–61,
   163–70; necessary and proper clause
   in, 167, 202; and ratification in Virginia,
   170–77. *See also* Bill of Rights (U.S.)
Constitutional Convention. *See*
   Constitution (U.S.)
Continental Congress, 54, 223n4;
   approves Continental Association, 28;
   recommends formation of new state
   governments, 33; passes Declaration of
   Independence, 51–52; debates Articles
   of Confederation, 55–58; fiscal problems
   of, 77–79
Cornwallis, Lord, 72
Cosway, Maria, 131–32, 188
council of revision, 113, 139, 140, 141, 181;
   proposed by TJ, 110

Dane, Nathan, 155
Deane, Silas, 55, 58
Declaration of Independence, 12, 45–53,
   164, 195, 220–21n56, 222n69, 222n73,
   223n77, 223n78; contrasted with U.S.
   Constitution, xiii–xiv, 200
Declaratory Act, 135
Democratic-Republicans, 53, 203, 204

Dickinson, John, 17, 23, 25, 31, 55–56;
   at Constitutional Convention, 141,
   142–43, 149
Douglas, William, 2
Dr. Bonham's Case (1610), 5, 212n14
Dunmore, Lord, 8, 9, 25
Dyer, Eliphalet, 55

economy: American, 78, 84, 94, 98, 129; in
   Virginia, 103, 129
Electoral College: creation of, 147–49, 156
Ellsworth, Oliver, 145, 150, 151
Embargo Act (1807), 205–6
English Declaration of Rights (1688), 39, 47,
   183–84, 221n59
entail, 59, 63
Epicurus, 13
Episcopalians. *See* Anglicans
Estates General, 188, 189
Eve, George, 187

factions: JM on, 137, 141, 152, 156–57, 159–60
Farmers-General, 97
Fauquier, Francis, 3
federal district: creation of, 82, 167
Federalist, The (*The Federalist Papers*), 159,
   169–70, 172
Federalist No. 10, 159
Federalist No. 14, 160
Federalist Nos. 18–20, 166
Federalist No. 37, 163
Federalist No. 38, 159
Federalist No. 39, 168, 184
Federalist No. 40, 163–64
Federalist No. 41, 164
Federalist No. 42, 166–67
Federalist No. 43, 164
Federalist No. 44, 167–68
Federalist No. 45, 169
Federalist No. 46, 169
Federalist No. 48, 164
Federalist No. 49, 164–65
Federalist No. 51, 160
Federalist Nos. 55–58, 165–66
Federalist No. 63, 170
Federalist Party, 53, 203

28–30; as delegate to Virginia convention of May–June 1776, 38–45; advocates separation of church and state, 41–42; on Declaration of Independence, 53; service on governor's council, 68–69; elected to Congress, 69; and western lands, 74–75, 77; defends American access to Mississippi River, 76–77; confronts Congress's fiscal woes, 77–79; supports reform of Articles of Confederation, 79–80

—and the Confederation era: as moderate nationalist, 82–84; supports western cession, 87; defends American access to Mississippi River, 89–90; supports strengthening Congress, 90–92, 98–99, 104–5; and Anglo-American trade, 93–94; on free trade and commercial treaties, 94–95; continues legal studies, 99–100; returns to Virginia assembly, 102–5; views on state constitutional reform, 110–14, 233–34n29; sponsors Port Bill, 118–19; writes "Memorial and Remonstrance against Religious Assessments," 120–22; and Annapolis conference, 125, 129–31; writes "Of Ancient and Modern Confederacies," 128; reacts to Shays's Rebellion, 131–32

—and the Constitutional Convention: elected delegate to, 133; prepares for, 134–36; writes "Vices of the Political System of the United States," 136–38; drafts Virginia Plan, 138–40; reports on convention to TJ, 138–39, 147, 151–52, 155–57; defends proportional representation, 141, 142, 144–45; opposes Great Compromise, 145–46; debates presidential selection process, 147–49; objects to slave trade compromise, 151

—and the new republic: agrees to support bill of rights, 183, 187–88; elected to Congress, 186–88; as Washington's "prime minister," 190; drafts constitutional amendments, 191; introduces amendments, 191–92; defends bill of rights, 192, 194; supports religious

freedom amendment, 195–96; debates value of stable laws with TJ, 198–99; and rules of constitutional interpretation, 201–2, 251n3, 252n9; opposes Hamilton's fiscal policies, 202–3; drafts Virginia Resolutions, 204; opposes Federalist foreign policy, 204; as secretary of state, 205–6, 253n15; as president, 206–7, 253n20

—and the ratification debate: writes *Federalist* essays, 159–60, 163–69, 170; reports to TJ on progress of ratification, 160–61; and the Virginia ratifying convention, 170–77; opposes second constitutional convention, 179–80; on TJ's draft state constitution, 180–81; debates need for bill of rights with TJ, 181–83; on judicial review, 184–86, 247n24

—in retirement: defends TJ's legacy, 207; and federal courts, 208–9, 210; opposes nullification, 209; advocates preservation of Union, 210

Madison, James, Sr., 14, 15, 28

Madison, Nelly, 14

Mandeville, Bernard de, 11–12, 16

Marbury v. Madison (1803), 208

Marshall, John, 120, 172, 184, 208

Martin, Luther, 147, 151

Martin, Thomas, 15

Mason, George, 23, 48, 49, 107, 111, 184, 213n23; drafts Virginia Declaration of Rights, 38–42; drafts Virginia constitution of 1776, 42–45; supports amendment on religious freedom, 61–62; and legal reform in Virginia, 63–64; and western lands, 73–75; attacks Port Bill, 119; negotiates Mount Vernon Compact, 124; at Constitutional Convention, 138, 145, 151; as Anti-Federalist, 154, 161, 172, 174; on JM's proposed constitutional amendments, 193, 250n61

Mason, Thomson, 24, 107

Massachusetts: amendments proposed by ratifying convention in, 171, 245n54

Maury, James, 2

McClurg, James, 138, 147

M'Culloch v. Maryland (1819), 208
"Memorial and Remonstrance against
   Religious Assessments," 122–23, 126
Mennonites, 122
Methodists, 65, 117
Mississippi River: American access to,
   75–77, 173–74
Missouri: controversy over slavery in,
   115, 207
Monroe, James, 96, 98, 172, 186–87
Montesquieu, Baron von, 14, 78, 160, 168,
   170; influence on TJ, 7, 10–11
Morris, Gouverneur, 146–47, 151
Morris, Robert, 80, 83, 91, 97, 193
Mount Vernon Compact, 124–25, 136
Muhlenberg, Frederick, 193

natural law, 10, 21, 23, 76, 167; and the
   Declaration of Independence, 47–48, 49,
   51, 52, 53
Navigation Acts, 21, 31, 150, 151
Nelson, Thomas, 72
Netherlands, The: political turmoil in, 128,
   158, 237n8
Neutrality Proclamation (1793), 203
New Hampshire, 171, 177
New Jersey Plan, 142–43, 144
New York, 86, 171
Nicholas, George, 72, 176, 177
Nicholas, Robert Carter, 9, 41, 61, 62
Non-Intercourse Act (1809), 206
North, Lord, 30
North Carolina, 161, 171, 176, 179, 194,
   250n61; foreign attachment controversy
   in, 50–51
Northwest Ordinance of 1787, 88
Notes on the State of Virginia (Jefferson), 70,
   105–7, 114, 157, 168, 180
nullification theory, 209

Olive Branch Petition, 33
Ordinance of 1784, 87–88, 117
Otis, James, 5

Page, John, 2, 4, 195
Paine, Thomas, 33, 35, 157, 195

paper money, 74, 77, 84, 133, 134, 136, 147,
   228n74; and the ratification debate, 157,
   167. See also economy
Parliament: jurisdiction of, 20–26
Paterson, William, 142–43, 146
Pendleton, Edmund, 38, 39, 41, 61, 161,
   172, 175–76; sponsors amendment on
   freedom of religion, 42; and legal reform
   in Virginia, 63–64, 120
Peters, Richard, 194
Pinckney, Charles, 141, 145, 147
Pinckney, Charles Cotesworth, 146, 151
Pitt, William (the Younger), 92–93
Plato, 12
Port Bill, 118–19
Presbyterians, 60, 65, 120, 122. See also
   Princeton University; Witherspoon,
   John
presidency, 135, 139, 147–49, 156, 241n67,
   246n4; TJ's criticisms of, 158, 162,
   172, 179
primogeniture, 59, 63, 225n28
Princeton University (College of New
   Jersey), 15, 16, 17, 18, 215n56
proportional representation, 134,
   140–41. See also Great (Connecticut)
   Compromise

Quakers, 28, 117, 122
Quasi-War (Undeclared Naval War), 203–4

Randolph, Edmund, 8, 23, 27, 40, 59, 124,
   125, 130; on TJ as lawyer, 6; on the cause
   of the American Revolution, 25; on
   Virginia constitution of 1776, 43, 44, 45,
   220n50, 220n53; JM reads law with, 100;
   at Constitutional Convention, 138, 139,
   146, 150; refuses to sign Constitution,
   154–55; supports bill of rights, 161;
   and Virginia ratifying convention, 172,
   175; supports second constitutional
   convention, 179–80; on Virginia
   Declaration of Rights, 184
Randolph, Jane, 2
Randolph, Peyton, 30, 32
Reid, Thomas, 16–17